THE PSYCHOLOGY OF DEAFNESS

The Psychology of
DEAFNESS

TECHNIQUES OF APPRAISAL
FOR REHABILITATION

by Edna Simon Levine

New York and London
COLUMBIA UNIVERSITY PRESS

The investigation for this volume was supported, in part, by a fellowship from the Federal Office of Vocational Rehabilitation

In tribute to DONALD H. DABELSTEIN
whose selfless dedication to the welfare of the disabled
will influence rehabilitation progress for all time

FOREWORD

THE IMPACT of hearing loss on the individual is one of the great areas in human behavior that science has scarcely more than probed gingerly here and there. The overwhelming proportion of research in hearing has centered in its medical and physiological ramifications with heavy emphasis on cause of impairment, prevention, cure, alleviation, and the nature of hearing. All workers in the field can take justifiable pride in the results, such as the improved surgical and treatment techniques, the exciting progress both in hearing aids and in public acceptance of them, the phenomenal growth of hearing clinics, and sharply increased attention to noise management.

Conversely, consideration about the *psychology* of deafness reveals only a few determined workers struggling to shed some light. The very important matter of how man adjusts to such major sensory deprivation has been investigated by only a handful of earnest searchers. One of the most dedicated is Edna Simon Levine, whose convincing rationale is presented in the chapters that follow. Psychologists, counselors, teachers, audiologists, medical workers, in fact all diagnosticians and planners will find in these pages answers to many behavior problems of the deaf and the hard of hearing that have puzzled them repeatedly.

One can understand why there has been relatively little exploration of the psychology of the deaf. The deaf are so few. They are less than one quarter of a million persons, scarcely more than one tenth of one percent of all our people. In a representative crowd of 700 Americans, we would find no more than one who is deaf. Spread thinly through a fluid population of 175,000,000 souls, the deaf may well pass unnoticed, for they have about the same capacities in mobility, strength, and intelligence as the general public. They have no visible characteristics that set them apart. They generally become known only as communicative demands reveal their severe disability.

The hard of hearing, however, are a much larger group. They are more than two and one quarter million people. Hence they are much more in our consciousness. Accordingly, one would expect to find a rather substantial body of psychological data about them. The relative void of authoritative guidelines for students and workers in the field underscores the timeliness and significance of Dr. Levine's treatise.

This writer is one of the many who deeply appreciate Dr. Levine's mastery of the extraordinarily complex psychology of serious hearing impairment. He has observed at firsthand her great capacity to adjust theory to the hard facts of existence. He has shared with her the thrilling satisfactions of pioneering new concepts and projects in the broad field of hearing loss. Accordingly, it is with much confidence that he recommends this text to all current and future servants of the deaf and the hard of hearing. Out of their application to its precepts will arise a better day in educational, social, and economic welfare services for people with serious hearing loss.

Boyce R. Williams, *Consultant*
Deaf and the Hard of Hearing
Office of Vocational Rehabilitation
Department of Health, Education,
and Welfare

CONTENTS

Foreword, by Boyce R. Williams   vii

Introduction   3

Part One: The Implications of Hearing and Impaired Hearing

1. Implications of Hearing   17
   The Role of Hearing   18
2. Early Severe Deafness   27
   The Basic Problem   28
   Psycholinguistic Implications   30
   Psychosocial Implications   41
   Implications of Variable Factors   47
   Psychological Studies   50
3. Progressive and Sudden Hearing Loss   56
   Progressive Deafness   56
   Sudden Deafness in Adulthood   69

Part Two: Psychological Practice in a Rehabilitation Setting

4. The Rehabilitation Setting   77
   The Rehabilitation Setting: General Features   78
   Special Features and Problems of Psychological Practice
        with the Physically Disabled   80
5. Major Lines of Psychological Inquiry   95
   Factors Influencing Psychological Reaction to Physical
        Disability   96

Psychodynamic Processes   100
The Problem of Accepting Physical Disability   113
Summary   116

Part Three: Psychological Examination and Evaluation of Persons with Impaired Hearing

INTRODUCTION: THE PSYCHOLOGICAL EXAMINATION   121

Purpose of the Examination   121
Methods and Techniques of Examination   122
Problems in the Examination of the Hearing-impaired   123
Purpose of the Guides   124

SECTION A: THE DEAF

6. The Case History   126
   Special Considerations in the Case Histories of the Deaf   127
   Scope of History Inquiry   156
   Reliability of History Data   156
   Recording History Data   159
7. The Diagnostic Interview   161
   Methods of Communicating with Deaf Persons   162
   The Language of Communication   169
   Conduct and Scope of the Interview   171
   Communicating with Deaf Children   175
8. Psychological Testing: Adults   177
   The Basic Testing Problem   179
   Verbal Test Selection   181
   Test Administration   184
   Test Batteries for Deaf Adults   186
   Interpretation of Test Findings   210
9. Psychological Testing: Children   214
   Special Considerations in the Psychological Testing of
       Deaf Children   214
   Tests Suitable for Deaf School-Age Children   220
   Tests Suitable for the Preschool and Nursery Levels   230
   Problems of Differential Diagnosis in Young Children   237

10. Observation   241
    General Observation   241
    Psychological Test Behavior   243
    Observation in Diagnosis   244
    Observation in Vocational Rehabilitation Evaluation   247

SECTION B: THE HARD OF HEARING

11. Special Emphases in the Psychological Examination   248
    The Case History   251
    The Interview   255
    Psychological Testing   265
    Observation   270
    Counsel the Person—Not the Disability   273

SECTION C: THE PSYCHOLOGICAL REPORT

12. Reporting the Results of the Psychological Examination   278

Part Four: Preparation for Progress

13. Research   289
    The Clinical Need   289
    Scope of Research in Impaired Hearing   290
    Organizing for Research   293
    Needed Research in the Psychological Aspects of Im-
       paired Hearing   303

Appendixes

A. Sectional Diagram of the Human Ear   309
   Diagram of How We Hear   310
B. Definitions and Classifications of Hearing Impairment   311
C. Causes of Impaired Hearing   315
D. Techniques in the Assessment of Auditory Acuity   317
E. Methods of Communication and Systems of Instruction
      in Use among the Deaf   321
F. Manual Methods of Communication   323

G. Chronological Listing of Selected Published Psychological Studies of the Deaf and Tests Used   325

H. A Guide to Test Publishers and Distributors   336

I. National Nonmedical Organizations for the Aurally Impaired   341

Glossary   345

Bibliography   351

Index   371

INTRODUCTION

INTRODUCTION

THIS BOOK comes at a time of great events in the rehabilitation of physically disabled persons. Two such events are especially gratifying to the author. First is the unprecedented interest in the psychological aspects of physical disability,[1] particularly auditory disability; second, the rapidly developing affiliation between rehabilitation and psychology.[2] Both these achievements are due largely to the unflagging efforts of the United States Office of Vocational Rehabilitation, whose encouragement and support made this book possible.

The major purpose of the volume is to provide guides for the psychological appraisal of adults and children with impaired hearing. The complex problems associated with this invisible but potentially devastating disability have only recently begun to arouse psychological interest despite the fact that the vast body of sufferers is estimated at upwards of 15,000,000 persons throughout the country.[3] The demand for psychological services among the members of this traditionally neglected group is fast outstripping the small, specialized supply.

[1] James F. Garrett, ed., *Psychological Aspects of Physical Disability* (Rehabilitation Service Series No. 210; Washington, D.C.: Office of Vocational Rehabilitation, Department of Health, Education, and Welfare, 1952).

[2] B. Wright, ed., *Psychology and Rehabilitation* (Washington, D.C.: American Psychological Association, 1959).

[3] Eleanor C. Ronnei, "The Hard of Hearing," in *Special Education for the Exceptional*, edited by M. E. Frampton and E. D. Gall, Vol. II (Boston: Porter Sargent, 1955).

The reader will find that the rationale of the psychological procedures to be discussed owes as much to rehabilitation as to psychology; for the greater part of the story of man's struggles to
adjust to physical defect is to be found in the annals of rehabilitation. In a broad sense, therefore, this book represents a blending
of the skills and experiences of both specialties, and serves to convey
some of the basic concepts involved in psychological practice with
the physically disabled.

For psychologists newly entering a rehabilitation frame, familiarity with the evolution of these basic concepts provides valuable
guidance in adjusting to the new environment; for rehabilitation
counselors and other members of the rehabilitation team, such
knowledge furnishes a helpful orientation to their new associate—
the psychologist. Since the evolution of the mutual goals of
rehabilitation and psychology also represents the background and
setting in which the action of this book takes place, the story of that
evolution forms a natural introduction to the contents.

Rehabilitation and clinical psychology are young professions
that owe their rapid rise to the increasing urgency of man's need
for security, fulfillment, and acceptance. As organized services,
they have much in common. Both trace their modern beginnings
to the exigencies of the First World War, psychology commanding
attention for its feat of large-scale examination and sorting of
inductees, and rehabilitation for its assistance to the war-disabled.
In each case, the origins by present standards were meager. Dynamic
psychology was only beginning to gather momentum in the late
years of World War I, and clinical psychology was in its infancy.[4]
Those were the days when the shift was from "pure psychology"
and the study of sensations to a new kind of applied psychology
that sought to explore and quantify "original nature" by means of

---

[4] A. A. Roback, *History of American Psychology* (New York: Library Publishers, 1952).

psychophysical measures and mental tests. The psychologist of today would be inclined to regard his counterpart of the 1920s as a static technician. As for rehabilitation, its scope was equally limited.[5] Vocational placement was the main objective; rehabilitation operated largely as an employment-retraining program for physically disabled veterans who were vocationally handicapped. Even prostheses were considered ancillary to vocational training and placement.

With the post-World War I shift of psychology and rehabilitation from wartime problems to civilian needs, a wide range of nonservice-connected disabilities clamored for attention, together with their social, psychological, and educational implications. To meet the needs, expanded facilities were essential, together with a broadened philosophy of operations that encompassed more than job-training. But rehabilitation was heavily dependent upon legislative approval, and the necessary appropriations were difficult to come by. There was still a strong inclination to look upon the seriously disabled as objects for philanthropy, public relief, private charity, or custodial care, and upon the less seriously disabled as potential job-trainees. Legislation for rehabilitation was a relatively new concept that was kept before the public eye through the efforts of dedicated groups concerned with the problems of special disabilities.[6] Thus, for two decades following the war, progress in rehabilitation was slow and spasmodic.

The first major advance was made in the years of World War II with the passage by Congress in 1943 of a number of significant amendments to the Vocational Rehabilitation Act. Known as the Barden-LaFollette Act or Public Law Number 113, the enactments redefined vocational rehabilitation services to mean "any services

---

[5] John A. Kratz, "Vocational Rehabilitation, Past, Present, and Future in the United States," *Rehabilitation Review*, Vol. II (1954).

[6] Henry H. Kessler, *Rehabilitation of the Physically Handicapped* (New York: Columbia University Press, 1947).

necessary to render a disabled individual fit to engage in a re-
munerative occupation." [7] Under this broadened interpretation,
such aids as the following became available: prostheses, medical
examination, and guidance for the purpose of obtaining or holding
employment; occupational tools, licenses, and equipment; corrective surgery and hospitalization; and maintenance during the period
of vocational training. Special provisions were also made for the
blind and for persons with mental disabilities.

Nevertheless, despite the expanded services, increasing numbers
of rehabilitation failures made their appearance whose problems
were not ameliorated by the new facilities. Many were just as
incapacitated after "rehabilitation" as before. Others suffered
profound and persistent handicap from relatively mild impairment.
None complied with the rehabilitation theory of the time that
still carried over from former years in which the amount of
handicap was presumed the equivalent of the amount of physical
damage, and rehabilitation was considered complete with physical
restoration and vocational placement. In these cases, there appeared
little predictable relationship among amount of physical impairment, success of physical restoration, amount of residual incapacitation, and employability. Here was a puzzle of increasing concern
to rehabilitation workers.

While rehabilitation was struggling with its problems, American
psychology was experiencing a sweeping shift of interest from the
academic to the clinical, and from theory to practice. Closer
integration of the two was in progress, and the field was hot with
debate concerning systems, methods, rationale, competencies, and
professional responsibilities. Clinical psychology was crystallizing
into a specialty, but it still had far to go. The tenor of the times
is expressed in the following statement by Louttit, one of the great

---

[7] "Regulations Governing the Plans and Program of Vocational Rehabilita-
tion Pursuant to Public Law 113, 78th Congress, 1st Session," p. 12. Issued by the
Federal Security Agency, Office of Vocational Rehabilitation, Washington, D.C.,
October 9, 1943.

names in the development of the profession: "Considering the diagnostic and therapeutic methods available, the clinical psychologist can perhaps most profitably work with children, and with that section of the adult population whose abilities and behavior place them in a childlike group." [8] For those who wonder why rehabilitation did not open the door to psychology long before this, the answer is implied in this statement made as late as 1936. On the one hand, psychology was not sure of what it had to offer; on the other, rehabilitation was not clear as to the services it yet required.

The period of significant advance in clinical psychology began at about the same time as in rehabilitation, during the early 1940s. In rehabilitation, the reason for the behavior of the failures had finally been traced to the distinction between physical disability and handicap. The distinction may not appear important at first glance, but the implications are explained by Garrett as follows:

It is unfortunate that workers in the field become confused in semantics and fail to differentiate between disability and handicap. The word *disability* is a static word, merely indicating that the individual has some defect or impairment, whereas the concept of *handicap* is a dynamic one that carries with it the fact that this defect or impairment interferes with the individual's reaching his maximum.

As a dynamic term, handicap carries with it a demand for individual analysis and evaluation. It also carries with it the implication that, in appraising the individual vocationally, we must at the same time take into consideration the *possibility* of his having handicaps in other areas, such as physical, mental, and social.[9]

In effect, disability defines the physical defect, but handicap encompasses the defect as well as its psychosocial and vocational implications. With the realization that there were psychological as

[8] C. M. Louttit, *Clinical Psychology* (New York and London: Harper & Brothers, 1936), p. 9.

[9] James F. Garrett, "Counsel the Man—Not the Disability," p. 1. Reprinted from *The Crippled Child*, National Society for Crippled Children and Adults, April, 1952.

well as physical problems involved in handicap, it followed that treatment for handicap must include treatment of the person as well as the disability. As this concept gained recognition, "whole man" entered the rehabilitation scene, and with him his complex psychological structure.

Clinical psychology in the meanwhile had also consolidated its objectives about whole man. The consensus was that the total person, regardless of age or setting, represented its professional responsibilities, and preserving the psychological integrity of whole man, its professional function. Comparing Louttit's observations of 1936 with the following statement made by Shaffer in 1954, we now find this attitude:

The characteristic responsibilities of clinical psychologists are similar whether they work in universities, the community, hospitals, schools, prisons, or industries. Their duties cut across the varied kinds of persons and problems with which they deal—whether school child or neurotic adult, psychotic patient or delinquent juvenile, mental defective or unhappy senescent. With all these persons, psychologists first try to achieve an understanding based on the hypothesis of their science and the techniques of their profession. Then they apply their understandings so as to help the people help themselves.[10]

To help the person help himself is the stated goal of rehabilitation today. The means toward this end is "total rehabilitation." In practice, total rehabilitation is the philosophy, approach, and goal of modern service. As a philosophy, it observes the principle of the essential unity of man, his person, and his problems. They are one and inseparable, both in concept and in treatment. As an approach, total rehabilitation represents a combined professional attack upon the multiple implications of disability, recognizing that no single specialty possesses all the competencies required for the total treatment of the whole person. And as a goal, total rehabilitation is attained when a disabled person succeeds in

[10] Eli A. Rubinstein and Maurice Lorr, eds., *Survey of Clinical Practice in Psychology* (New York: International Universities Press, Inc., 1954), p. vii.

establishing himself in the way of life that is as commensurate as possible with his living requirements and human needs.

With increasing convergence of professional philosophies, the demand for psychologists in rehabilitation is currently reaching unprecedented proportions.[11] Major impetus toward hastening the integration of the professions has come through legislative advances, notably the passage by the 83d Congress of the Vocational Rehabilitation Amendments of 1954, known as Public Law 565.[12] Under this act, the Federal Office of Vocational Rehabilitation is empowered to pay public and private nonprofit organizations part of the costs of research in the vocational rehabilitation of the physically disabled, the mentally ill, and the mentally retarded.

Although the general objectives of the enactment still center in vocational considerations, the major purpose of the program is to increase knowledge of the broad areas of psychological adjustment to disability.[13] Toward this end, funds are also authorized for the training of workers "to increase the number and competency of rehabilitation personnel"[14] and for individual fellowships to "enlarge and enrich our research resources through the development of competent research workers in the professional fields which contribute to the vocational rehabilitation of disabled persons."[15] Not only is the program destined to broaden even further at the federal-state level, it is also stimulating heightened research among

[11] Health Resources Advisory Committee, *Mobilization and Health Manpower: A Report of the Subcommittee on Paramedical Personnel in Rehabilitation and Care of the Chronically Ill* (Washington, D.C.: Government Printing Office, January, 1956).

[12] Office of Vocational Rehabilitation, *New Hope for the Disabled: Public Law 565* (Washington, D.C.: Government Printing Office, 1956).

[13] Office of Vocational Rehabilitation, *Announcement: Research and Demonstration Grants in Vocational Rehabilitation* (Washington, D.C., September, 1957, OVR 36–58).

[14] Office of Vocational Rehabilitation, *Training Grant Programs of the Office of Vocational Rehabilitation* (Washington, D.C., March, 1958), p. 2.

[15] Office of Vocational Rehabilitation, *Announcement: Rehabilitation Research Fellowships* (Washington, D.C., June, 1957), p. 1.

private as well as other government agencies and in all related disciplines. Thanks to Public Law 565, areas of disability are coming to scientific attention that were long the stepchildren not only of society but even of rehabilitation itself. Such an area is that of the deaf [16] to be discussed in subsequent chapters.

Psychology for its part is becoming increasingly attracted to the opportunities currently offered by rehabilitation. Formal acknowledgment of this interest was made by the American Psychological Association with the admission of Division 22, the National Council on Psychological Aspects of Disability, in September, 1958, and also through the application for a grant under Public Law 565 to study the role of psychology and psychologists in rehabilitation. The Princeton Conference was held for this latter purpose in February, 1958.[17]

Finally, steady increase in the numbers of physically disabled persons in the population is exerting the pressure of practical need for closer working relationships between psychology and rehabilitation. Advances in medical science, public health practice, and the general economic level are prolonging as well as saving the lives of many thousands of persons who would ordinarily have died, but who survive to find themselves chronically disabled. Additional increase in disability comes by way of the increased accident toll of occupational mechanization, the rising health hazards of growing urbanization, and the mounting casualties of increased frequency of war.

Some idea of the scope of the problem is contained in the following statistics. It has been estimated that there are 28,000,000 Americans suffering some type of chronic illness and that among them are more than 2,000,000 persons of employable age who require vocational rehabilitation services.[18] The latter figure does not in-

[16] Edna S. Levine, *Youth in a Soundless World* (New York: New York University Press, 1956).

[17] Wright, *Psychology and Rehabilitation.*

[18] Health Resources Advisory Committee, *Mobilization and Health Manpower,* p. 1.

clude the millions of children and aged for whom special services are also required. It is further estimated that in every five known disabled persons, there is one so severely handicapped as to require additional services for longer periods of time.[19] Finally, it has been stated that "among every 100 children, there are at least 6 who have to be considered 'exceptional.' " [20] As summarized by the Task Force on the Handicapped of the Office of Defense Mobilization, these events and statistics "have combined to produce a society in which disability will become a major obstacle to national strength and vitality unless a determined and concerted effort is made to cope with it." [21]

This is the conclusion reached by nations throughout the world today. In 1950 the United Nations Educational, Scientific, and Cultural Organization, the United Nations International Children's Emergency Fund, the United Nations International Labour Office, and the World Health Organization adopted an international program for the prevention of disability and the rehabilitation of handicapped persons, based on the following theses:

Firstly, that the handicapped person is an individual with full human rights, which he shares in common with the able-bodied, and that he is entitled to receive from his country every possible measure of protection, assistance, and opportunity for rehabilitation.

Secondly, that by the very nature of his physical handicap he is exposed to the danger of emotional and psychological disturbance, resulting from a deep sense of deprivation and frustration, and that he therefore has a special claim on society for sympathy and constructive help.

Thirdly, that he is capable of developing his residual resources to an unexpected degree if given the right opportunities of so doing, and of becoming in most instances an economic asset to the country in-

[19] Kenneth W. Hamilton, *Counseling the Handicapped in the Rehabilitation Process* (New York: The Ronald Press, 1950), p. 213.

[20] Clemens E. Benda, *Developmental Disorders of Mentation and Cerebral Palsies* (New York: Grune & Stratton, 1952), p. xxii.

[21] *Report of the Task Force on the Handicapped to the Chairman of Manpower Policy, Office of Defense Mobilization* (Washington, D.C., January 25, 1952), p. 13.

stead of being a burden on himself, on his family and on the State.

Fourthly, that handicapped persons have a responsibility to the community to contribute their services to the economic welfare of the nation in any way that becomes possible after rehabilitation and training.

Fifthly, that the chief longing of the physically handicapped person is to achieve independence within a normal community, instead of spending the rest of his life in a segregated institution, or within an environment of disability.

Sixthly, that the rehabilitation of the physically handicapped can only be successfully accomplished by a combination of medical, educational, social and vocational services, working together as a team.

The first task which therefore confronts all international agencies is that of using all possible means to secure general acceptance throughout the world of this new conception of physical disability.[22]

Whole man and the psychological aspects of disability are currently arousing international as well as national concern.

And so it is that from a point of common origin but disparate objectives clinical psychology and rehabilitation have finally come to share mutual goals and philosophies. They are ready for one another, ready to join forces in behalf of the physically disabled. Basic to their alliance is reciprocal understanding. This obtains not only for the professions as organized specialties but more particularly for the professional workers themselves.

In regard to psychologists, the one who is familiar with the principles of rehabilitation and the basic implications of physical impairment is immeasurably better prepared to render service in the respective disability areas than the one who is not. The plan of the present volume was structured in accordance with this concept.

The major emphasis of the text falls upon the physically disabled individual as a person rather than as an anonymous member of a disability group, and upon the implications, rationale, and techniques that form the base for the psychological understanding and

[22] United Nations, *Rehabilitation of the Handicapped*. Social Welfare Information Series, Special Issue (New York, September, 1953), pp. 5–6.

treatment of *persons* with impaired hearing. For this reason, statistical, nosological, and other special information necessary for area-orientation is confined whenever possible to Appendixes, Glossary, and Bibliography. The text deals with people.

Basic to understanding these people is an appreciation of the incalculable debt the human organism owes the sense of hearing. Once this is appreciated, the otherwise vague and invisible handicaps of hearing loss begin to take on form. When they finally stand forth in all their manifold implications, a psychologist is ready to begin thinking about the complex task of investigation and examination, and not before. The most important section of the book, therefore, is its beginning: Part One—The Implications of Hearing and Impaired Hearing.

Further orientation is provided by Part Two—Psychological Practice in a Rehabilitation Setting. To grasp the implications of a particular disability is one thing; to know what is involved in the rehabilitation of a sufferer is another. Contrary to popular misconception, physical disability does not reduce all those who are similarly affected to one common denominator. If anything, individual differences are increased rather than lessened by physical impairment. As a result, psychological practice in rehabilitation requires a broad base of knowledge concerning factors that make for differences in individual reactions to physical disability as well as of factors that make for differences in response to rehabilitation procedures. These special factors necessitate somewhat different emphases in psychological procedures and interpretations than are commonly applied to the nondisabled, and a number are discussed in this section. In addition, the section has purposely been made general in regard to type of disability because it deals with basic concepts, and these obtain for impaired hearing as for other disabilities. It is important that a worker with the acoustically disabled realize this lest he become area-provincialized.

In the next section, Part Three, we come to grips with the

problem of the psychological examination and evaluation of hearing-impaired persons. All that has gone before is essential groundwork for this complex and often experimental task. Far more will have to be known than is known before the procedures used in examining persons with hearing loss can be carried out with the relative assurance that sustains a worker with the hearing.

This brings us logically to the final section of the book, Part Four—Preparation for Progress. Here is where the answers lie, in research that is purposively directed, knowledgeably formulated and conducted, and cohesively integrated. This section is particularly close to the heart of the author for the promise it gives of solving for future workers many of the unknowns that handicap the clinician of today. That this volume may help broaden the scope of research and refine the techniques of psychological practice with hearing-impaired persons is the author's earnest hope.

Part One

THE IMPLICATIONS OF HEARING
AND IMPAIRED HEARING

1. IMPLICATIONS OF HEARING

ORDINARILY, a sound practical guide to the psychological aspects of sensory dysfunction is a reasonable understanding of the values of the unimpaired function. This is the general rule. But in applying it to an understanding of the varied types of deafness,[1] a curious problem arises.

The unimpaired counterpart of deafness is hearing. And it happens that the values of hearing in human experience are generally as little recognized and as difficult to grasp as the implications of deafness. Both are intangible functions that operate through unseen structures. Neither provides visual aids to understanding.

Further, to hear is as natural and effortless an occurrence as it is invisible. Man would as soon ask himself how breathing keeps him physically alive as how hearing keeps him psychologically alive. He simply does not think of it at all. As for the handicaps of auditory defect, they are equally hidden from view. They do not "show, the way a distorted limb or a missing finger or blinded eyes 'show.' "[2] The sufferer " 'limps' only socially, 'fumbles' only psychologically, 'stumbles' only vocationally."[3] Crippling takes place in ways that are not readily observed, and because of this the implications of auditory handicaps are not easy to identify.

To obtain the "feel" of deafness, therefore, is a difficult assign-

[1] See Appendix B: Definitions and Classifications of Hearing Impairment.
[2] William G. Hardy, *Children with Impaired Hearing: An Audiologic Perspective* (Children's Bureau Publication No. 326, 1952), p. 1.
[3] *Ibid.*

ment for one who hears. Some workers resort to self-inflicted auditory isolation and seek the answer by plugging up their ears the better to find out what life lacks under these conditions. The experiment does indeed impart something of the handicaps of sudden, marked deafness in adulthood; but it yields only a fraction of the fundamental import of hearing and even less of the experiences of the other main types of auditory impairment, namely, progressive deafness and early profound deafness.

As a result, workers entering the field often find themselves without a base of inner reference for appreciating the complex psychosocial problems of defective audition. To meet this disadvantage, the present discussion of the psychological implications of impaired hearing is begun with a brief introductory digest of the implications of hearing itself in human experience and development.

The Role of Hearing

Because the ear can perceive sound and the brain interpret it, man is enabled to reach out from his own small world of self into the minds, hearts, and worlds of his fellow man; to enter other eras, cultures, and civilizations; to become one of the company of mankind. He does this through the medium of verbal language, and the "miracle of language" [4] is the epochal outcome of man's ability to hear.

IN THE EVOLUTION OF MAN

It is difficult to believe that there was a period in time when man had no verbal language, when he was completely without this means of self-expression, communication, and deliberation. But scholars are generally agreed that such must have been the case.[5]

[4] Charlton Laird, *The Miracle of Language* (Cleveland and New York: The World Publishing Company, 1953).

[5] Ruth Nanda Anshen, ed., *Language: An Enquiry into Its Meaning and Function* (New York: Harper & Brothers, 1957).

Although the primitive creature that was man in those days lacked a verbal tongue, he nevertheless possessed the ability to hear, a brain to think with, and above all the urge to survive.

Survival in prehistory demanded among other things a particularly high peak of alertness to the dangers of the natural environment. Vision, of course, served an important function in this regard, but its scope was limited only to what the eye could see. It was to hearing that man had to turn to protect himself from the dangers of the unseen.

In so doing, man achieved some of his first experiences in conceptual thinking: he learned to abstract meaning from the sounds of nature. Thunder meant storm; the howling of wolves, danger; the sudden frantic cry of birds, a prowling enemy; the snap of twigs, the stealthy approach of someone or something. To man, these became meaningful sounds because they lent themselves to reliable association with specific phenomena. For example, thunder always sounded like thunder and never like the chirp of a bird; neither could the cry of a bird be mistaken for the roar of a lion; nor the roar of a lion for the splash of rain. The sounds of nature were consistent and therefore easily interpreted. Not so, however, the noises uttered by preverbal man himself. The specificity and consistency of utterance that endows spoken sound with symbolic meaning was still in its earliest rudiments.

The greatest handicap this presented was in the banding together of functional groups. Such groups possess far greater powers of survival than single individuals or small, scattered bands. This man knew. But he was also aware that to be functional, groups had to have a common tongue, easy communications, and a method of contact among group members that did not depend on seeing alone.

To achieve these conditions, man turned again to his ability to hear. He now set himself the task of abstracting meaning from the noises uttered by his companions as he had already done with the sounds of nature. But this presented difficulties in what must presumably have been a primitive Tower of Babel. Far simpler to select a particular utterance and by common consent and usage ascribe a definite meaning to it, thus making it the spoken symbol for an object, a person, or an activity.

Eventually, a code was evolved of systematized sounds and groups of sounds to be voiced for specific purposes. Man had not only abstracted meaning from sound, he now endowed it with meaning. The record of how this was accomplished is lost in time, although there are numbers of interesting theories on the subject.[6] But that it was accomplished is the important thing; for the achievement marks not only the beginning of verbal language but also the end of man's days as a lone wanderer upon the face of the earth. For with the development of verbal language, the advance was begun from coexistence among man-creatures to communion among mankind. Hearing had brought this to pass.

As expressed by Laird, "Man as we know him could not exist without language, and until there was language." [7] "Without language, no humanity. Without written language, no civilization." [8] And since, as Sapir reminds us, "language is primarily an auditory system of symbols," [9] it can be added that without the ability to hear, no language could ever have evolved of sufficient caliber to create man of today out of the nonverbal creature of prehistory.

IN INDIVIDUAL DEVELOPMENT

No less impressive than in the evolution of man is the role of hearing in the development of the individual. And here too its influence begins long before there is awareness of the spoken word, almost in fact from the time of birth. The world of the infant at this time is a diffuse mass of vague sensations. If the babe were

[6] Mario Pei, *The Story of Language* (Philadelphia and New York: J. B. Lippincott, 1949).

[7] Laird, *Miracle of Language*, p. 9.   [8] *Ibid.*, p. 269.

[9] Edward Sapir, *Language, an Introduction to the Study of Speech* (New York: Harcourt, Brace and Company, 1921), p. 17.

capable of perceiving all the new stimuli that impinged on him, the results would be overwhelming. Fortunately, he is spared this shattering experience by reason of his incompletely developed nervous system. It is the plan of nature to have a rhythm of development between the sensori-motor and psychic systems so that each may reinforce the other in the infant's slow and gradual climb to maturity. A major aid in this climb is the sense of hearing.

Gesell and Amatruda state that "the full term neonate assumes nothing less than listening attitudes to the sound of the human voice within the first fortnight after birth." [10] With such precocious perception of sound, it is not surprising to find associations between sound and concept already present in early infancy.[11] Certain sounds tell the baby that someone is hurrying to him; others call to mind his rattle; still others inform him that he is not alone, that someone is hovering nearby. There are sounds that please and sounds that frighten; those that soothe and others that startle.

As maturation proceeds and perceptions sharpen, the great ocean of sound takes on ever-increasing form and meaning. Long before the baby is ready for the spoken word, he is responding to the concepts aroused by gross sounds alone, just as his preverbal ancestor did before him. And even more important, he is stimulated by them, mentally, socially, and emotionally.

In addition, there is another aspect of sound to which the infant comes to respond that is of great if not generally recognized importance in psychic development, namely, the source. Gradually the baby comes to perceive in some indefinable audio-kinesthetic way that in the diffusion of what he hears, certain sounds seem in closer "touch" with him than others. It must be recalled that in the beginning the infant is scarcely aware that he is a separate entity from the mass of stimuli and sensations that constitute his

[10] Arnold Gesell and Catherine S. Amatruda, *Developmental Diagnosis*, 2d ed. (New York: Paul Hoeber, Inc., 1947), p. 270.

[11] M. M. Lewis, *How Children Learn to Speak* (New York: Basic Books, Inc., 1959).

world. But as he continues to mature and to listen to the sounds about him, he eventually senses that he himself is producing some of them, and what is more that he can produce them at will. This startling discovery becomes part of an epochal psychic awareness that is in progress, namely, the infant's ultimate identification of self as distinct from surroundings. Because he was able to hear himself, he was given powerful assistance in finding himself.

In the course of self-discovery, this auditory perception of himself as distinct from others stimulates the development of increasingly advanced relationships between the infant and his environment. He is no longer a passive receptacle. He is a consciously contributing participant. Because he can hear himself, he realizes that he can give the world a self-created product in his own vocal utterances. Consciously produced vocalizations are among the earliest creations the baby can give or withhold at will. They thereby assume high psychic import, as illustrated by the withholding of utterance in certain types of emotional disturbance. Thus, well before the first year of life, experiences conveyed through hearing play a major role in initiating mental, social, and emotional development, and are intimately incorporated into the beginning psychic structure.

The role of hearing in further development becomes increasingly important as time goes on. Maturation is a highly complex process for the human being and extends over a period of some fifteen to twenty years. Intricate preparation is necessary before the helpless baby of today will be capable of dealing effectively and independently with the complex problems of living that await him. The steps and events of preparation are beyond the scope of this discussion, except to emphasize that the course of psychological development is heavily dependent upon the nature and amount of sensory stimulation capable of being received from the environment.

Concerning the relative values of such stimuli, the frequently quoted words of Helen Keller are singularly appropriate here. She designates as the "most vital stimulus" of all "the sound of the voice," because, as she says, "it brings language, sets thoughts astir, and keeps us in the intellectual company of man." [12]

The hearing child lives in a world where a language that has taken countless centuries to evolve awaits his developmental needs and is his just for the hearing. Through the use of verbal language, he is eventually able to master the vast masses of knowledge he will require for independent living. He accumulates information from many sources on countless subjects ranging from things, places, events, and people to social customs, attitudes, prohibitions, and traditions. He learns about the great events of the past, the even greater possibilities of the future, the great names in history, science, the arts, sports. He explores attitudes and acquaints himself with morals, ethics, faiths, opinions, prejudices, superstitions, beliefs. He acquires skills and bodies of knowledge. He exchanges views with his fellows; compares opinions; finds out how and what others think and feel. He learns to interpret behavior, understand motives. He gains insights and forms value-judgments. He comes to appreciate that often it is not what is said that counts but how it is said. This too he learns through hearing. Intonations of voice, stress, modulations, inflection, all of these make language and ideas living things for him and not just a matter of words alone. In the development of the individual as well as of cultures, "language is the great symbolism from which other symbolisms take their cue." [13]

Finally, not only does hearing play a major role in the individual's psychic development, it also supplies the means for maintaining relationships within the society of man. Through

[12] Helen Keller, *Helen Keller in Scotland* (London: Methuen and Company, 1933), p. 68.

[13] Benjamin Lee Whorf, *Language, Thought, and Reality* (Published jointly by The Technology Press of Massachusetts Institute of Technology, John Wiley & Sons, Inc., New York, and Chapman & Hall, Ltd., London, 1956).

hearing, a free flow of communication is possible both within groups and among groups—without regard to spatial restriction—concerning thoughts, information, reactions and feelings, commands, warnings, threats, directions, and all the multitude of messages that are part of the tempo of civilization. And at the same time, the individual still retains auditory contact with the settings from which messages proceed; he is still in contact with the bustle and climate of background activities that form the accompaniment to the major themes of life and extend his perceptions by an added dimension.

Because he hears, man feels himself always a part of the context of living, in the family, in the community, and in society. Even when alone, he is never farther away than the sounds of nature, the sound of man's voice, the hubbub of man's energies in action. Hearing the stir of life about, he is part of it. He belongs. In short, it is well-nigh beyond the powers of narration and imagination to encompass the scope of what we know and what we are that comes to us by way of what we hear. The debt man owes the auditory mechanism is without measure.

IN PSYCHODYNAMIC RESEARCH

Although much has been written on language and communications, especially by psycholinguists, semanticists, and students of cognitive functioning, the role of hearing in psychic development has been singularly neglected. References are few and far between. As Knapp says, "The ear, in psychodynamic investigation, is a silent area." [14]

Of the sparse number of references available outside the field of *impaired* hearing, the most pertinent come from psychiatry. Bleuler, among the first of the dynamically oriented psychiatrists, was also among the first to make particular mention of the critical role of hearing in human experience. He declared that "we perceive

[14] Peter Hobart Knapp, "The Ear, Listening and Hearing," *Journal of the American Psychoanalytic Association*, 1 (1953), 672.

the whole cultural achievement of older generations directly or indirectly through hearing and all our relations to human environment are regulated through language." [15] Freud too was among the pioneers in psychiatry who acknowledged the importance of hearing in the witty metaphor "The ego wears an auditory lobe." [16]

Among the writings of contemporary psychiatrists, the observations of the psychoanalyst Isakower are especially interesting.[17] The Isakower "formula" concerning the position of the auditory sphere in psychic development is that "just as the nucleus of the ego is the body, so the human auditory sphere, as modified in the direction of its capacity for language, is to be regarded as the nucleus of the superego." [18] It is to be hoped that this hypothesis will be further explored through planned research. In this connection, a highly unusual experimental group is available among persons born profoundly deaf in whom the "human auditory sphere" is nonfunctional in its capacity for language.

The sparse total of references to the significance of the ear as a body part as well as a perceptual mechanism is brought together in an interesting contemporary contribution by Knapp [19] which includes some of his own observations together with those of Abraham, Jones, and the forementioned Isakower among others. Knapp summarizes this review with the statement that the "exact part played in the mysterious birth of speech, the relation of auditory perception to identification and character formation, the interaction between sound and symbol in the development of

[15] Eugen Bleuler, *Textbook of Psychiatry* (New York: The Macmillan Company, 1936), p. 55.

[16] Sigmund Freud, *The Ego and the Id* (London: The Hogarth Press, 1947), p. 29.

[17] Otto Isakower, "On the Exceptional Position of the Auditory Sphere," *International Journal of Psychoanalysis*, XX (1939), 340–48.

[18] Otto Isakower, "Spoken Words in Dreams," *Psychoanalytic Quarterly*, XXIII (1954), 1–2.

[19] Knapp, "The Ear, Listening and Hearing," *Journal of the American Psychoanalytic Association*, I (1953), 672.

language are unsolved questions." [20] He also remarks on the fact that "the ear can function as a tentacle, plucking pearls from the sea of words and exploring depths that vision does not reach." [21] Considering all that the ear plucks from the sea of words and sound in addition to the pearls, there is little doubt that much can be learned of human behavior from investigations of the role of hearing in psychic development. Here is virgin territory for research.

[20] *Ibid.*, p. 680.   [21] *Ibid.*, p. 683.

2. EARLY SEVERE DEAFNESS

IN THE LIGHT of the values of hearing, it comes as no surprise to find that impaired hearing can constitute a violent blow to man's psychic structure. Its effects cover the entire range of reaction and disturbance. At one extreme, defective audition raises a barrier to development that can be scaled only through the efforts of a wholly unusual type of special education. At the other, it possesses the power to traumatize personality into serious disorganization. And between these extremes are the countless varied repercussions of hearing loss.

Of them all, early severe deafness—especially when congenital —is the most unique; for here is found the closest modern equivalent to the linguistic state of preverbal man. To be born without the ability to hear is to be born without the natural ability to acquire verbal language; and without verbal language, normal human development is blocked.

This is the situation that characterizes the smallest but most unusual section of the hearing-impaired population, numbering less than one quarter of a million persons throughout the country. Commonly known as "deaf-mutes" or the "deaf and dumb," its members are technically termed "the deaf." They are not mute, for there is no vocal impairment. Neither are they dumb, for many are taught to speak through special instructional techniques. The great handicap of the deaf lies in the fact that permanently impaired hearing occurs during the most vulnerable time of life

—from birth through early childhood—and is so severe that it deadens the most powerful developmental stimulus of all—the sound of the human voice.

For one born deaf, the task ahead is to become a part of life without ever hearing the sound-patterns of living. The problems of the deaf are the products of this distinctive environmental experience. Whether this creates a "unique psychology of the deaf" is the traditional question associated with the group. In answer, it can only be said that the problems of the deaf would be the same for those who hear if they could be subjected to the same environmental circumstances as those who do not. There is no innate psychological difference between the deaf and the hearing.

The deaf baby comes into the world with the same psychological needs and potentials as the one who hears. The inner well-being of deaf individuals is subject to the same psychological principles that govern the well-being of all humankind. It is not the deaf person who is innately different, nor his psychology that is intrinsically "unique." It is his environment that is wanting. It is wanting in the stimulation provided by sound in general and the sound of the voice in particular.

The Basic Problem

Not to hear the voice is not to hear spoken language. Not to hear spoken language means that a preverbal child will remain in complete ignorance of this basic verbal tool for human communication and communion unless extraordinary measures are taken to teach him that there are such things as words, what words are for, how sounds are combined to form spoken words, how words are combined to form connected language, and how verbal language is applied not only to objects, people, activities, and the like but to all aspects of living, feeling, thinking, and reasoning. Without such highly technical instruction the small, profoundly deaf child would be doomed to go through life a completely nonverbal being, unable to enter into any verbal communication with others, any verbal deliberation with himself, nor make any significant contact with the knowledge, customs, culture, and climate of the civilization into which he was born.

Such was the lot of the deaf in ancient and medieval times before special instructional techniques were devised.[1] Not only the public but eminent scientists of the day held the deaf to be uneducable, fools, idiots, doomed souls. Some of the more extreme misconceptions were gradually eliminated when special education opened the door to the verbal world for the deaf; but others still persist. To the general public, the deaf are still odd, different, peculiar.

These attributes, however, are more appropriately applied to the path of development of the deaf.[2] Although their way passes through the same noisy bustle of life-in-action as with the hearing, it is a strangely deadened road for those who cannot hear. For the small deaf child who has not yet learned the basic wherefores of social and interpersonal activity, it is like moving through a silent motion picture—without sound and without meaning.[3]

Such a child does indeed see people about him working lips and faces at one another with intent and purpose and is aware that something important is taking place, but he cannot fathom what it is. He watches silent people responding soundlessly to one another and cannot grasp the magic that conveys messages between them, initiates their actions, and directs their behavior. The members of his own family try to bring him within their circle through these same strange means; but even they cannot break through the

[1] Kenneth W. Hodgson, *The Deaf and Their Problems* (New York: Philosophical Library, 1954).

[2] Edna S. Levine, "The Emotional Problems of Young Deaf Children," *The Illinois Advance*, Illinois School for the Deaf, Jacksonville, LXXXVIII (1955), 1–3, 12–13.

[3] Edna S. Levine, *Youth in a Soundless World* (New York: New York University Press, 1956).

invisible barrier that separates him not only from them but from all others as well. The path of the deaf child leads through the hubbub of life, but not to the meaning.

Psycholinguistic Implications

Meaning comes with language, above all with verbal language, and verbal language for the deaf comes through special education. But to learn language the way a child born deaf must learn it is as taxing an achievement as is known to man.[4] The child must learn to master a completely unfamiliar and highly involved skill— a language he has never heard—in order to become acquainted with an inordinately complex society in which he can take little part until he has acquired reasonable mastery of that skill. In other words, he must master one unknown in order to gain access to the other.

The difficulties involved are far beyond the average person's experiences or imagination. For the general public and for many parents of deaf children, it is usually the speech aspect of the problem that commands the major attention. "The poor little deaf child cannot talk." There is nothing else wrong with him so far as the public can see. Therefore the mistaken conclusion is reached that deafness is a speech problem, and this is followed by the even more mistaken assumption that a hearing aid and speech lessons will soon put everything right.

However, the generic problem of early profound deafness is not speech but verbal language. Speech is an ancillary problem. To explore the implications involved, it is again necessary to turn to the hearing world to see by contrast what the deaf world lacks.

We recall the hearing child's ability to associate gross sounds with their related concepts while still an infant. To continue from

[4] Mildred A. Groht, *Natural Language for Deaf Children* (Washington, D.C.: Alexander Graham Bell Association for the Deaf, Inc., 1958).

this point, as the infant's discriminative abilities sharpen, the same principles of perception and association are applied in relating word-sounds to the objects, activities, and feelings they represent. With the passing of time, the pattern of language evolution becomes a wonderful game for the child. He listens, practices, imitates, experiments. He finds that he no longer has to rely on vague vocal utterances to indicate his wants and feelings. He has discovered a way that possesses far greater accuracy and precision. It is by means of the spoken word.

Sensori-motor investigations of the environment are joined by linguistic explorations; motor experiences, by sharpened mental perceptions. As maturation proceeds, the wish to know strives for verbal as well as motor expression, and with the help of a powerful word the child proceeds to find out. The word is "What?" Countless "Whats?" fill the air. "What that?" "What the name of this?" "What your name?" "What you do?" "What you say?" As the answers come in they become the springboard for further mental activity always directed toward a clearer and broader understanding of the outside world and its inhabitants.

With the child's increasing age, language becomes his accustomed tool for communicating, for thinking, for inner enrichment. The "What?" of his environment being on the way to clarification, the "What for?" level of curiosity makes its appearance. Information about the purpose of objects and not only their names commands attention. "What's that for?" the child wants to know. And before long the "How?" and "Why?" come under consideration. From name to purpose to function to underlying reason, the child advances to steadily higher levels of abstract thinking ability. As language skills take on increasing refinement, so too does he; most important of all, his skills increase in tempo with his maturational requirements.

Through mental exploration and discovery made possible by means of language, the child succeeds in attaining mastery over one unknown after the other in his world. With increased mastery he acquires increased self-confidence, and with increased self-confidence, the push for deeper and broader exploration. The human element comes in for verbal probing too. Will words give him the same magic power over persons as over objects? the child wonders.

The word "No" comes along in time for this exploration. But much to his disappointment, the child finds that "No" alone is not powerful enough to dispel the unwanted. He must also have a supply of things called "reasons." He is expected to give reasons for and he is reasoned with. The world is becoming a "reasonable" place.

Nevertheless, the word "No" still has its uses. The child finds that by uttering an unreasonable "No" and sticking to it, he can create the same havoc and obtain the same pleasing results as by throwing a temper tantrum. He has discovered a verbal means for releasing aggression. Eventually, he will acquire a useful vocabulary of special words and expressions that will stand him in good stead for inflicting punishment on others as well as for reducing his own inner tensions. He will no longer have to depend on acting out alone. Thus fortified, the child pursues his explorations.

Needless to say, the developmental pattern here sketched is by no means so neatly arranged in life. The highly complex and involved dynamics of maturation are not part of the present discussion. The intent here is to trace—and perforce lightly—the stimulus language provides mental growth under "all else being equal" conditions.

To resume: the child's growing familiarity with shades of meaning and variations in ideas conveyed by language fosters increased awareness of the shades of meaning and variations in human behavior. He begins to perceive that life is not a matter of true or false, black or white; that before white becomes black it must pass through many gradations of gray. He learns to weigh and value; think his own way to conclusions; make his own judgments and form his own opinions. In short, he establishes his mental identity as he formerly did his physical identity, and again with the powerful assistance of the "voice that brings language."

With the approach of adolescence a whole new area of exploration unfolds before the youngster. The emotional stirrings and drives he now experiences call for intensive investigation. Hundreds of questions crowd in upon him. The "What?," "What for?," "How?," and "Why?" of his early years return with renewed vigor and urgent demand. Why can't his family leave him alone? Why do they keep prying into his affairs? How can he get them to quit bothering him? How can he break the chains of dependence that tie him to the family as if he were still a little boy? At the same time he finds that girls have taken a turn for the better. How, he wonders, can he make a hit with the girls and how shall he behave if so happen he does? What about this business of love, sex, courtship, and marriage? What shall be the order of precedence and how should each be handled? It then comes to him that vocational choice and preparation really do have an important bearing on his plans for the future. What shall his occupational goal be and how shall he go about preparing himself for it? And every once in a while, as if overcome by the burdens of adolescence, he wants to know what it is all about anyhow.

Only by contrast with the situation of an average deaf adolescent is it possible to appreciate the extent to which verbal language helps the hearing adolescent through this as through previous maturational crises. For the hearing adolescent, language provides information about the dicta of society, its customs, prohibitions, points of view, and attitudes. It transmits knowledge on matters of biological and physiological concern. It facilitates looking ahead, planning for the future, profiting from the experiences of others. The hearing youngster is able to obtain information from a wide range of sources: books, conversations, television, radio, movies, lectures, counselors. In the apprenticeship he serves to man's estate, two of his most vital aids are hearing and language; for where there is verbal language, there is an open door to the world.

By way of contrast, let us now turn to the child born profoundly deaf. We turn to the congenitally deaf child for two reasons. First, he and his peer, the child who became deaf during preverbal babyhood, represent a substantial portion of the deaf population.[5] Second, by using him as target, a number of variable factors are kept in temporary abeyance, and as a result, the sketch presented can be drawn in bolder strokes.

When a child who was born profoundly deaf begins to learn verbal language, even though he begin in early childhood, he is already behind the hearing child so far as the conceptual feel for language is concerned. He has missed all the preliminary auditory practice of associating gross sounds with concepts, of connecting word-sounds with concepts, and finally of fusing word and concept into automatic verbal thinking and expression. He has missed all the mental, social, and emotional stimulation conveyed through sound. He has played no part in the mental explorations leading up to the discovery and application of words and language. When he comes to school, he finds a ready-made body of language waiting to be mastered and facts to be memorized.

This does not mean that the deaf child's mind is blank up to this time. Far from it. All else being equal, his mind also contains concepts, experiences, the urge to know, the wish to explore and discover. But he has gone as far as he can without verbal language. Further maturation requires the establishment of a fluent, two-way system of communication between himself and the world about him. The deaf child must learn the same tongue as the verbal world to speak its idiom and grasp its thinking.

[5] Harry Best, *Deafness and the Deaf in the United States* (New York: The Macmillan Company, 1943), Chapter XI.

However, for the deaf child to acquire verbal language is a vastly different enterprise than for the child who hears. Not until he is afforded highly specialized instruction does the child born deaf learn that there are such things as words. Through vision, touch, and whatever remnants of hearing he has, he learns that things have names, that activities have names, that he himself has a name. He learns that watching lips and faces often gives him the clue to the thoughts, messages, and commands of others. He learns that if he watches very closely, he can see how a particular word looks on the lips and how it differs from other words. Of course, he cannot understand any words or expressions until he is familiar with their meanings. And so he must memorize the meaning and lip-appearance of every word he adds to his lip-reading vocabulary.

To help him in this task, a little picture-dictionary will be made for him so that specific meanings and exact lip reading can be reviewed and reviewed until they are fixed in his mind. At the same time, he is spoken to constantly so that he will know he can get whole thoughts from the lips and not single words alone. And finally, he begins to learn the most exacting feat of all for the congenitally deaf child, and that is how to use voice, breath, lips, teeth, and tongue in creating oral expression.[6]

In the course of time, the deaf pupil is taught that things have qualities as well as names. Things can be big, small, round, red, blue, pretty, and so forth. And already a situation arises that is a common occurrence when language is learned without being heard. From the pupil's point of view, if one can see a ball, or a pencil, or a boat, why not also a big, or a small, or a red? He knows nothing of adjectives and nouns. To him words are names. To get across the relationship of adjective to noun in the absence of heard experience may take weeks of planned project teaching.

When this is finally accomplished, another common problem arises. Having learned nouns first, the pupil has a natural inclina-

[6] C. V. Hudgins, "Some of the Problems Encountered in Teaching Speech to Deaf Children," *American Annals of the Deaf*, XCVIII (1953), 467–71.

tion to use them first in verbal expression. After all, why not say "a dress blue" instead of "a blue dress"? It is done this way in some languages. Only custom dictates that it be done otherwise in English. The hearing child would never question the custom; but the deaf child must remember and memorize, remember and memorize.

To continue, although the young deaf pupil eventually adds to his little picture-dictionary objects that are big, or blue, or small, what kind of visual aid will help him remember such words as "the," "is," "am," and the like? He must take these too on trust and memory. As he advances through the grades, reading and writing help him fix meanings and usage. But the problem of first getting the meanings across to him becomes increasingly difficult as verbal expression becomes more abstract.

Illustration, acting out, and example are used successfully in numbers of instances, thanks to the wit and skill of teachers of the deaf. But hardly does a pupil learn the meaning of a word in one context than he comes across it in another where it has an entirely different meaning. The simple word "cold," for example, may, according to *Roget's International Thesaurus*, be used to signify frigid, lukewarm, cool, indifferent, dull, etc. To one unfamiliar with the vagaries of language and colloquialism, the literal approach to word meanings can lead to some very peculiar linguistic results. Thus, if frigid means cold, then why not say "Are you frigid?" instead of "Are you cold?"; and if "lukewarm" possesses a synonymous relationship to "dull," one should certainly be able to say "a lukewarm knife" or "a lukewarm pupil." And how "cold" could mean "lukewarm" is altogether beyond comprehension.

Many of the oddities of language expression found among the deaf that puzzle the uninitiated are derived from situations such as these. Consider also the difficulties of teaching the meaning of such unknown language elements as: but, because, if, while, as, as if; to say nothing of the complications that arise from such expressions as: to look at, to look like, to look out, to look for, to look out of, to look out for, to look in, to look into.

Learning language naturally is not a matter of reasoning, logic, or instinct. It is a matter of hearing. The pupil who has never heard knows only that which he has been painstakingly taught and which he has remembered. If he has been poorly taught, if he has not fully understood, if he cannot remember, his language will show the consequence.

A common misconception is that language learning for the deaf can proceed almost automatically through lip reading and reading. While it is true that these skills represent the major compensations of deafness, they too must first be learned before they can be applied, and they can be learned only in conjunction with language.

Lip reading is by no means the magic route to language learning or comprehension it is commonly supposed to be. There are numbers of deaf—and hard-of-hearing—people who cannot master this art despite extraordinary language skills, mental endowment, and life achievement. Even where lip-reading ability is above average, the lip reader will still come up against such problems as stiff lips, poker faces, protruding teeth, moustaches, restless heads, mouthing grimaces that make it impossible for him to see anything of the fleeting mouth movements that tell him what the speaker is saying. In addition, there are countless words that require little if any lip movement for utterance and consequently cannot be seen on the lips at all. On the other hand, there are numerous words of completely unrelated meaning that look exactly alike on the lips, as, for example: abuse and amuse; bloom and plume; smell and spell; beach, beech, and peach; clam, clamp, and clap; bump, mum, pump, and pup; meal, peel, and peal. What the special skills are that make a good lip reader is still a matter for research; [7] but the average deaf pupil without these skills who attends a school where

[7] John Tracy Clinic Research Papers, I, II, III. *Studies in Visual Communication* (Los Angeles: John Tracy Clinic, October, November, December, 1957).

lip-reading ability is a prerequisite for education is profoundly handicapped.

As for reading, this can be a particularly frustrating experience for a deaf pupil. Books are based on "hearing" language, and for hearing children they afford information, stimulation, escape, and relaxation. An occasional word of unknown meaning can easily be skipped over, guessed at or looked up without impairing the continuity of the story. But when a deaf child opens a book based upon the interests of his age group, he sees not a story but countless unknown words and expressions, confusing idioms, and unfamiliar grammatical constructions. Teacher-made materials help the younger deaf pupil establish reading techniques and interests. However, as the pupil advances through the grades and as textbooks become part of the course of study, reading is often a matter of deciphering numerous unfamiliar linguistic elements in order to get the point of the contents.

To hold on to the thread of a narrative while decoding the elements is enough to discourage all but the stoutest of hearts, the sharpest of minds, and the most persistent of spirits. Only inspired teaching can maintain motivation. Where this is lacking, the less hardy spirits succumb to reading by intuition, that is, they adapt lip-reading techniques to reading and by putting together a familiar word here, a familiar phrase there, helped out by an illustration or two, they come up with a story. A great deal of mental alertness goes into this kind of reading; but, unfortunately, more goes into it than is derived from it. And because reading is the greatest single source of mental enrichment for the deaf, retardation in reading becomes one of the most serious educational problems.

The foregoing illustrations represent a minute sampling of the handicaps involved in learning verbal language without benefit of hearing. But complex though they are, such difficulties are only the prelude to a greater problem still, namely, learning the *use* of language for mental growth and maturation. Unless verbal language is so used by the deaf, it is nothing more than a mechanical vehicle of elaborate structure and intricate design but with no place to go.

Learning to use language is not a matter of accumulating vocabulary, oral expression, manual expression, grammatical principles, spelling, or even facts. It is a matter of learning how to use all of these to become one of the company of mankind. Language performs this service for a deaf pupil only when he is *trained* to use it toward this end and at every maturational level. For example, the small deaf pupil who wants to know "Name?" of a visitor has caught the spirit of language even though he uses but one word. The one who is satisfied to repeat only what he has been taught, that "My name is Tom. I am six years old," has not.

At the heart of the spirit of language lies flexibility—flexibility in teaching, in usage, and ultimately in thinking. But to enable a young deaf pupil to get his bearings in the world, he is customarily taught the constants for a considerable period of time before being introduced to the elaborations and exceptions. Herein lies one of the most difficult aspects of teaching the use of language to the deaf, and that is to avoid imparting literal mental habits and attitudes to a pupil while at the same time having to employ literal procedures in structuring reality for him.

For example, the young deaf pupil learns that the names of objects are exact; the names of activities are exact; the names of people are exact. As he advances through the grades, word meanings are precise; oral expression follows a designated pattern; so too do sentence structures, grammatical principles, spelling; facts are exact. Eventually, the deaf pupil's mental attitudes and habits of thinking follow the same literal, exact pattern of operation. To free the mind of the average deaf student for wide mental latitudes after years of confinement to the literal and exact is a task that is well-nigh impossible to accomplish to any significant extent. Language for the deaf can be a cage as well as an open door to the world. All else being equal, educational philosophy and curricular goals as well as flexibility of instruction [8] are the major determinants of which it will be.

Thus, at a time when the very young and intelligent hearing child is asking such questions as: "Where does the wind go when it blows away?," "What makes air?," "What was a baby before it was born?," the very young and intelligent deaf child is just beginning to learn the names of objects in his physical environment. Later on, when the hearing pupil is discussing issues of the day as part of his class assignment, his deaf fellow is contributing news in terms of little events and happenings in his own life. Where in class debate the former is tackling such problems as "Should the atomic bomb be outlawed?," the latter contributes: "I saw a picture of an atomic bomb. It explodes with a big cloud. The cloud looks like an umbrella." Such is the handicap of early severe hearing loss.

As a result of the strictures of early deafness, the average young deaf adult on leaving school is apt to be underdeveloped in many areas. To a psychologist newly entering the field, he may even seem backward, odd, lacking. The intrinsic lack is not in the deaf person but rather in his life scope. As a result of its limited area, countless young deaf adults are uninformed and misinformed about many things; their language and communications skills have suffered; their experiences in the ways of the world are impoverished; their understanding lacks depth. The results can be seen in their attitudes and beliefs, in their behavior, and in their approach to new situations. In addition, they are apt to be sensitively aware of their own shortcomings, and even more so of the indifference and misconceptions of the hearing world about the needs and problems of the deaf.

[8] Myrthel S. Nelson, "The Evolutionary Process of Methods of Teaching Language to the Deaf with a Survey of the Methods Now Employed," *American Annals of the Deaf*, XCIV (May, 1949), 230–94; XCIV (September, 1949), 354–96; XCIV (November, 1949), 491–511.

In most instances, however, these young people are still capable of learning and maturing. Often they appreciate the need now as never before. The scholastic and experiential retardations imposed by deafness do not mirror the mental abilities that go into the task of language learning. Apart from the "all else being equal" conditions of the present discussion, the more recent psychological studies show no difference between the potential mental capacities of the deaf and the hearing. The differences that are found lie in the functional aspects of intelligence, particularly in situations requiring thinking and reasoning in terms of abstractions. Here the deaf lag behind the hearing.

It has been the purpose of this discussion to show something of how this lag develops and of how deafness impedes personal development by impairing language development.

Psychosocial Implications

Another important aspect of the problems of the deaf for which psychologists must be prepared concerns social maturity and its related behavior and adjustments. Investigations show that the deaf tend to lag behind the hearing in these areas. This finding is an expected outcome of the preceding discussion.

To be socially mature, a deaf individual would require (a) a prerequisite body of information about social customs, habits, and usage; (b) ample experience in putting such information into practice; (c) sufficient opportunities to enjoy a variety of social and interpersonal relationships; (d) attitudes that impel him to seek such experiences; and (e) a healthy psychic structure that provides wholesome, well-balanced motivation.

Interestingly enough, these very factors affect the social adjustment of the hearing in the same manner as they affect the deaf. The important difference stems from the fact that the deaf are more vulnerable to adverse influences by reason of the situations that auditory disability creates. Information is more difficult to come by for the deaf; experiences and opportunities for social intercourse are more limited; the attitudes needed for gaining a foothold in hearing society require more intensive cultivation; and the developing psychic structure is subject to greater hazards when one is deaf. It follows, therefore, that social maturity is also more difficult for a deaf person to attain than for a hearing one. But as with other personality attributes, the level of social maturity reached by a particular individual is subject to many variables of which the most important are derived from the nature of his early experiences. To gain a surer understanding of how to evaluate such experiences in adulthood, it is again necessary to turn to the beginning years for guidance.

It is by now common knowledge that the most important single influence in determining an individual's attitudes toward others is derived from the character of his original relationships with his parents. Where these relations are satisfying and wholesome, the child will turn a trusting eye to the world, expecting the same happy experiences with others as with his parents. But where parent-child relationships have been lacking in essential satisfactions, the child's attitudes will be infected by the insecurities and unsatisfied needs that characterized his first human experiences—those with his parents.

In applying this concept to the deaf, it is necessary to be mindful of the fact that in the majority of cases, deaf children are born to hearing parents; [9] and further, that the greater number of these parents have had little if any previous experience with deafness. Their ideas about the disability are vague in the extreme, and their feelings are colored by the traditional misconceptions of society.

It is also important to bear in mind that children often have a deep symbolic meaning for parents. They may symbolize strength and virility, an extension of the ego, the means of attaining immortality, the ideal self, an outlet for "the things I couldn't do or

[9] Best, *Deafness and the Deaf in the United States,* Chapter XI, p. 675.

have when I was a child." These values are derived from the parents' own early experiences and are therefore very deeply rooted. When a deaf child is born to such parents, the resultant emotional shock is apt to derive its force not so much from the implications of deafness for the child as from far deeper and more personal sources within the parents' own psychic structures.

Even for a mature, stable adult who is able to accept straightforward facts and answers, it is still difficult to accept child disability. With those who cannot accept even the facts, or who become the willing target of unrealistic influences, the principal sufferer is, of course, the child. To his already heavy burden of auditory disability is added the even heavier burden of disturbed parents. Learning, intellectual growth, inner development, social adaptability, all are endangered, the more so because of the peculiar dependence that deafness creates.

As already mentioned, when a child cannot hear what goes on about him, there is much he sees that he does not understand; and when he is unable to speak the verbal tongue, he cannot very well ask questions of the passing public. He is thus forced to depend upon an "interpreter," so to say, a person who knows about the child's communications problems and who can get information to him in ways he can understand.

Simply by walking down the street and keeping his ears open the hearing child observes a cross-section of life from innumerable sources. He hears what the neighbors have to say to one another; what his playmates are planning in the way of mischief; what the grocer and his customer are arguing about; what the policeman is saying to a careless driver; and so on. He has his finger on the pulse of the public. Everything he hears adds to his social awareness and so to his social assurance.

The deaf child's "public" when he is very young consists of the one or two persons who are closest to him and able to effect some degree of meaningful communication with him. They comprise his life-line to the outside world. They do his hearing for him and try to inform him of what goes on. The amount and accuracy of information thus relayed depends upon the skill, willingness, and patience of the interpreter, and upon the child's own flair for piecing together isolated fragments into meaningful wholes. But no matter how skilled the reporter, the deaf child makes only secondhand contact with society. In contrast to his hearing brother, the deaf child's status is rather that of a hopeful observer waiting to get the point of community happenings and longing to be taken into community activities.

Whether he becomes part of the community or not depends largely upon the "interpreter." All else being equal, it is the wisdom of this person that keeps the child from slipping away into the apathy of indifference or the hostility of frustration, and supplies him with the stimulation and motivation to meet his neighborhood peers halfway. It is the interpreter's manipulations that sway a community to accept or reject a small deaf child.

In the usual course of events, this role of interpreter is first handled by the parents.[10] The child is fortunate indeed whose parents possess understanding, mature acceptance, and an intelligent approach to his problems. Where this is the case, a deaf child can expect every reasonable opportunity for normal development despite his initial need to depend. Under the guidance of experts, his parents learn how to help him help himself along the road to maturity. They learn the importance of keeping him mentally and socially responsive to events outside his own little world. They direct his attention to enriching happenings; provide him with explanations of activities he sees but does not understand; encourage his participation wherever reasonably possible. They learn how to stimulate his curiosity, thinking, and reasoning, what to expect of him in independent enterprise, and how to expand

[10] Harriet Montague, "Parents of Deaf Children," *Proceedings of the Convention of American Instructors of the Deaf* (Vancouver, Washington, June–July, 1952), pp. 358–61.

his scope of participation in social activities in proportion to his increasing abilities and self-assurance. In short, they learn to look upon him as the normal child he is, serving the usual apprenticeship to man's estate.

But when a small deaf child is forced to depend upon parents who lack the ability to understand his problems, who emotionally distort and misunderstand, or who refuse to accept the facts, his situation is precarious in the extreme. Where parents lack the ability for intelligent management, the school is obliged to assume a large measure of the parent role. There are numbers of deaf persons who feel closer to school personnel than to their own families. However, no matter how superior the school, it cannot supplant a parent's interest, nor is it equipped to supply the variety of experiences and opportunities a pupil needs to develop into a socially assured individual.

Where parents distort the implications of deafness, the child may find himself bound to a philosophy of education inappropriate to his human needs. What this means is best told in the words of one who lived through the experience. He relates:

I was the "great experiment," the deaf child "restored" to the hearing world attending public schools. . . . Loneliness.

That's all it ever was, and all it ever will be to me—stark, staring, tearing loneliness. . . . I doubt if I need to explain here what I mean by loneliness. Surely everyone knows how cruel children can be to the child who is "different" in some way or another. They jeer at the child who is wealthy, sneer at the poor boy's clothes and throw mud at the sissies. Then, in time, the rich boy learns democracy, the pauper betters himself, and the coward rears up and fights back. But the deaf child never learns to hear.[11]

Fortunately, this particular story had a happy ending despite the years of tortured childhood and adolescence spent in trying to enter the hearing world through the wrong door at the wrong time. Others do not.

[11] Roger M. Falberg, "Sifting the Sands," *The Silent Worker*, IX (1957), 19.

Where serious parent disturbance is the dominating factor in child management, the victim's lot is a particularly unhappy one. Often the child finds himself bound in dependence to an emotional disorder rather than to a parent. He is seen as a blow to self-esteem, a punishment from above, a trial to be bravely born. He is rejected, concealed, overprotected, or resigned to as the case may be. The major concern is to shield him from the inquisitive eyes of the community, rationalize his condition to family, friends, and neighbors, find a safe blame for his deafness. The major effort is to "make him into a child like other children, no matter what the sacrifice." The fact that he is already a child like other children is lost to view.

The consequence of such attitudes upon deaf children is disastrous; for no matter how self-deceived a parent may be, the child knows. No amount of surface display of affection and concern can fool the unbelievable perceptions of childhood. The child knows when he has been measured and found wanting.

With his main tie to the world thus impaired, there is little for the deaf child to do but remain where he is, in the world where self is the major figure; where the needs of self are the major considerations; and where the gratification of these needs is the immediate concern. Thus are seeds of immaturity sown. They grow and flourish under a variety of unhealthy conditions, under the continuing focus of parent anxiety as well as under the frost of parent indifference. But always they seek from others the kind of nourishment that should have come from the parent source.

Sometimes the influence of a school community provides satisfying substitute sustenance for the child, and a socially adequate pattern of behavior may yet develop. But more often, such children and their parents remain linked in permanent psychic bondage by ties that are hateful to both but which have become part of their way of living. The results upon social adaptability are obvious.

Thus, where serious interpersonal and social inadequacies are found among the deaf, it should not be assumed that the handicapping agent is the organic impairment. It is rather the unwholesome climate of attitudes and influences in which the child was reared. Although nothing can be done to correct the auditory damage, psychological inadequacies can often be helped, providing the psychologist understands their derivation and implications.

Implications of Variable Factors

To facilitate presentation, the foregoing discussion was based upon the early profound deaf as a group, mainly upon those born deaf, and upon "all else being equal" conditions. Actually, age of onset and amount of hearing loss vary considerably among deaf persons. Further, all else is seldom equal. And finally, the deaf "group" is a purely semantic convenience. Just as the deaf individual is composed of a wide variety of personal attributes, so is the deaf group composed of an even wider variety of individuals and individual differences.

At one extreme are the unschooled deaf adults [12] who have never been taught conventional language or methods of language expression and who send and receive messages in homemade gestures and pantomime understood only within the family. At the other extreme are deaf individuals who are masters of language as well as of all methods of communication [13] and who are equally at home in both deaf and hearing society. And between these extremes is the main body of deaf persons representing an unbelievably heterogeneous mixture of language and communications abilities as well as levels of fulfillment, attainment, and adjustment.

There are those who can speak and read lips with amazing skill,

[12] U.S. Office of Vocational Rehabilitation, *Statement of Plan for Providing Services to Unschooled, Educable Deaf Adults* (Washington, D.C., 1949).

[13] Best, *Deafness and the Deaf in the United States*, Chapter XV: "Means of Communication in Use among the Deaf," pp. 201–16. See below, Appendix E: Methods of Communication and Systems of Instruction in Use among the Deaf.

others who can speak but have difficulty in reading lips, still others who can read lips but who cannot speak comprehensibly, and some who can do neither but rely entirely upon writing and/or manual communication. There are deaf persons whose education has been singularly appropriate to their needs in all basic respects and others who have not fared so well. There are those whose oral skills are inferior but whose language skills are unusual; conversely, there are others whose impoverished supply of language is used with exceptional clarity in oral expression.

To continue, there are deaf persons whose school-life contacts with their families have been limited to week-end or holiday visits, and others whose family contacts have been close and intimate, sometimes for better and sometimes for worse. There are some who have no contact whatsoever with other deaf individuals because of family insistence and/or lack of opportunity, and others who cannot communicate with their own families because of a lack of mutually understood methods. Finally there are those of high mental endowment and those of limited mental capacity; the mature and the unbelievably immature; the emotionally healthy and the emotionally disturbed; the sick and the well; the multi-handicapped. There are countless variations and combinations of ability and degrees of adjustment and fulfillment.

It is obvious even from this brief summary that the variety of influences affecting the development of a deaf individual is greater and not less than the number operable among the hearing. The common tendency is to attribute most differences among deaf persons to the I.Q. Intelligence, however, is only one of a number of major determinants; actually it is a far less powerful factor than is generally supposed.

Other variables include such well-known influences toward individual difference as: home and family factors, inherent predispositions, special aptitudes and abilities, socioeconomic-educational opportunities, health status, (other) physical disabilities, community climate. Still others, previously mentioned, are associated with the auditory impairment and include: cause of auditory defect; age of onset of hearing loss; amount of loss sustained at the time of onset; amount of present loss; type of structural involvements and their amenability to medical treatment and/or the use of a hearing aid; and personality organization of the individual at the time of onset of hearing loss. Then there are numerous variables derived from the type and quality of educational experiences. These are critically important factors, both in individual fulfillment and in psychological evaluation of the deaf, and involve such determinants as: age of beginning school; types of schools attended, length of time in each, and methods of instruction used; appropriateness of curriculum to pupil's needs; educational motivations employed; total length of time in school; type and amount of vocational education; type and amount of higher education. And a final variable to be added to the preceding summary is the presence of other deaf members in the family and their relationship to the individual.[14]

Where environmental influences play as important a role in development as they do with the deaf, variations in such influences from person to person acquire more than ordinary significance. And variations there are! In education alone, for example, the physical environments of the schools differ considerably; methods of instruction diverge sharply; and so too does the quality of instruction. Philosophies of education differ; curricular goals vary; and there are exceptionally wide divergencies in the age of beginning school, the age of leaving school, and in what has been learned in between.

When educational influences are unfavorable, even the I.Q. can fail to stem the tide of adversity. When unfavorable family influences are added to adverse educational circumstances, the I.Q. is as nothing before the double onslaught.

[14] The significance of these variables is summarized in Chapter 6.

In short, a deaf individual does not lend himself to surface analysis nor do his problems to ready assessment. Psychological examination and counseling of deaf persons are highly individualized undertakings that require a deep understanding of the manifold factors that influence the nature of the human outcome.

Psychological Studies [15]

Needless to say, the products of such unusual life conditions as the deaf present the psychologist with unique problems in all areas of adjustment and fulfillment: mental, social, emotional; in education, vocation, family and community relations; in courtship, marriage, parenthood. However, the twin factors at the root of most of these problems—language and communications skills—are also responsible for the major difficulties experienced by psychologists seeking to work with the deaf. Not only must such a worker be familiar with the developmental implications of deafness, he must also possess reasonable familiarity with the range of language expression and communications methods used by the deaf in order to make psychologically rewarding contact with his deaf subjects. Because of these unusual requirements, psychological practice and research in the field have suffered severe limitations.

A chronological listing of selected references to studies of the intelligence and personality of the deaf is presented in Appendix G. Attention is also directed to the reviews of research by Barker *et al.*,[16] Berlinsky,[17] and Lavos,[18] in which evaluations of investiga-

---

[15] See Appendix G for a chronological listing of selected references to psychological studies of the deaf.

[16] Roger Barker *et al.*, *Adjustment to Physical Handicap and Illness: A Survey of the Social Psychology of Physique and Disability.* Bulletin No. 55 Revised (New York: Social Science Research Council, 1953).

[17] Stanley Berlinsky, "Measurement of the Intelligence and Personality of the Deaf: A Review of the Literature," *Journal of Speech and Hearing Disorders,* XVII (1952), 39–54.

[18] George Lavos, "Evaluating the Intelligence of the Deaf," in *Special Educa-*

tions are discussed together with some of the problems of research. Most of the investigations thus far conducted deal with comparisons of the intelligence of deaf and hearing groups of pupils on nonlanguage, nonverbal, and performance scale measures. A number deal with personality evaluation by means of rating scale and inventory-questionnaire techniques. A few have experimented with projective techniques and mental tests employing verbal language.

In brief review, the results of the early studies of intelligence are sharply divided between findings that the deaf are about two years retarded mentally as compared with the hearing, and those that find no significant difference in intelligence between the deaf and the hearing. In an effort to resolve this divergence, it was experimentally demonstrated that the type of test used was an important determinant of the type of result obtained; that whereas on certain tests the deaf show significant retardation, on others the same groups perform within the average range. Subsequent studies tend to the conclusion that although the deaf as a group are of average mental endowment, functional lags exist in the areas of conceptual thinking and abstract reasoning.

Personality investigations of the deaf also yield divergent findings. Certain investigations indicate serious personality disturbance of the groups studied, while others show little if any personality and social adjustment difficulties. As with the psychometric studies, here too are instances in which the same experimental group yields different adjustment pictures on different tests.

Studies employing the Rorschach and other projective techniques represent the latest phase of personality investigation of the deaf. Despite the differences among the research groups and the methods of test administration and interpretation in the few Rorschach investigations reported, the following findings were obtained in all: emotional immaturity, personality constriction,

tion for the Exceptional, edited by M. E. Frampton and E. D. Gall, Vol. II (Boston: Porter Sargent, 1955).

and deficient emotional adaptability. The promise shown by the Rorschach test in these studies and in present clinical practice warrants more intensive investigation and validation of its use with the deaf.

The practice of studying the deaf by means of instruments devised for the normally hearing has been severely criticized, particularly in regard to the use of verbal inventory-questionnaire measures in studies of adjustment.[19] Such instruments are designed to sample "hearing" adjustment and maladjustment to an acoustically normal way of life in terms of signs and symptoms known to characterize "hearing" disturbances, stresses, and conflicts. Whether they can be assumed to apply with equal validity to the deaf population is open to serious challenge.

Also questioned is the validity of the results of nonverbal and nonlanguage mental testing—the psychometric methods traditionally used with the deaf of all ages. Lavos observes [20] that the results are subject to a wide variety of hidden influences. He concludes that "from the relatively low order of positive relationship between educational achievement and nonlanguage intelligence, the test measures skills in deaf children which are necessary for their educational growth but insufficient in themselves to control such growth in any major way."[21] Speaking from the medico-psychological viewpoint, Bridgman, in a study of the mental capacity of deaf children by means of nonverbal tests, calls attention to the "considerable proportion of deaf children in the group tested, who showed normal and even at times very superior ability on the nonverbal scales, but whose success in school subjects was no better than that of frankly mentally deficient children."[22]

[19] Fritz Heider and Grace Moore Heider, *Studies in the Psychology of the Deaf*, No. 2, Psychological Monographs, LIII (1941), 59–67.

[20] Lavos, "Evaluating the Intelligence of the Deaf," in *Special Education for the Exceptional*, Vol. II.

[21] *Ibid.*, p. 192.

[22] Olga Bridgman, "The Estimation of Mental Ability in Deaf Children," *Proceedings of the Thirty-first Meeting of the Convention of American Instructors*

The author explores [23] this problem further with a selected group of deaf adolescent girls by means of the Verbal and Performance portions of the Wechsler-Bellevue Scale for Adolescents and Adults, Form I.[24] This investigator concludes that despite the traditional aversion to the use of verbal measures with the deaf, carefully selected, skillfully administered, and cogently interpreted verbal tests of intelligence may well prove to yield far greater clinical returns with deaf subjects in the age range about fifteen years and above than has been previously assumed. With the younger deaf whose vocabulary and language skills are not sufficiently developed for verbal measures of mental capacity, attention is directed to the possibilities of such approaches as the Davis-Eells Test of General Intelligence,[25] with appropriate revision for young deaf subjects, to be used jointly with the various nonlanguage and performance measures presently employed.

Possibly the least contentious findings in the major areas investigated are those that deal with educational achievement, motor skills, and mechanical ability. Regarding educational achievement, the general conclusion is that deaf pupils show a three- or four-year retardation as compared with their hearing peers. The basic cause is attributed to the difficulty of verbal language development in the absence of functional hearing. The consequent retardation in language attainment is carried over to all school subjects that require adequate verbal language comprehension for their mastery. Regarding motor and mechanical ability, the few studies reported indicate that, with the exception of the sense of balance, no significant differences exist between the deaf and the hearing in these areas. In body balance and, interestingly enough, in visual acuity,

───────────────

of the Deaf. Berkeley, California, June, 1939 (Washington, D.C.: Government Printing Office, 1940), p. 333.

[23] Levine, *Youth in a Soundless World.*

[24] David Wechsler, *The Measurement of Adult Intelligence,* 3d ed. (Baltimore: The Williams & Wilkins Company, 1944).

[25] Allison Davis and Kenneth Eells, *Davis-Eells Test of General Intelligence or Problem Solving Ability. Manual* (World Book Company, 1953).

the results with deaf subjects fall below those obtained for the hearing. The reader is cautioned, however, that in these areas of investigation, as in the others reviewed, much more remains to be learned than is yet known.

In short, there is a pressing need for psychological instruments that will enable a worker with the deaf to gain deeper clinical insight than is possible through nonlanguage and performance types of mental tests and the inventory-questionnaire types of personality measures. In this connection it is interesting to note that the psychological tests used in the most recent studies [26] include such instruments as the Rohde-Hildreth Sentence Completion Test,[27] the Monroe Group Rorschach Test,[28] and the Mosaic Test,[29] among others. There is also urgent need for studies of the adult deaf, about whom very little psychological research information is available. Most studies of deaf adults are conducted on subjects belonging to the deaf college population, which represents a minute proportion of the total census. And finally, there is critical need for the application of acceptable research designs and methodologies to investigations of the deaf.

Such, in brief, are some of the problems and questions that are daily fare to psychologists operating in this particular area of auditory disability. As matters now stand, it has not yet been established what pattern of capacities, abilities, attributes, and psychic factors constitutes the norm of deaf adjustment. However,

[26] Richard W. Flint, Francis C. Higgins, and Donald A. Padden, "Doctors' Dissertations and Masters' Theses on the Education of the Deaf, 1897–1955," *American Annals of the Deaf,* Vol. C (September, 1955).

[27] Harold D. Crowley, "A Study of Personality Differences between Hearing and Non-hearing College Students as Determined by the Rohde-Hildreth Sentence Completion Test" (Unpublished Master's Thesis, Catholic University, 1954).

[28] Earl S. Schaefer, "A Comparison of Personality Characteristics of Deaf and Hearing College Students as Revealed by a Group Rorschach Method" (Unpublished Master's Thesis, Catholic University, 1951).

[29] William J. Schanberger, "A Study of the Personality Characteristics of the Deaf and Non-Deaf as Determined by the Mosaic Test" (Unpublished Master's Thesis, Catholic University, 1951).

the spirit of inquiry and research is in the air, and one such study [30] is presently under way, thanks to Public Law 565. Many other opportunities of high challenge await the research-minded psychologist in this unique field of human behavior.

[30] Franz J. Kallman, "Objectives of the Mental Health Project for the Deaf," *Proceedings of the Thirty-seventh Meeting of the Convention of American Instructors of the Deaf*, West Hartford, Conn., June 26–July 1, 1955 (Washington, D.C.: Government Printing Office, 1956), pp. 266–72.

3. PROGRESSIVE AND SUDDEN HEARING LOSS

IN THE preceding chapter, discussion was centered upon the smallest category of acoustically disabled persons—the deaf. The present section deals with the largest, made up of several million individuals who are technically termed "the hard of hearing." [1] Two major subgroups of this vast body will be considered here as further illustration of the multiple implications of hearing loss. They are (*a*) the progressively deafened and (*b*) the suddenly deafened in adulthood.

Progressive Deafness

Whereas the problems of the deaf illustrate the results of severe auditory dysfunction since birth or early childhood, those of the progressively deafened demonstrate the results of slow, gradual loss of hearing that may begin at any time of life. So unobtrusive is the onset and so gradual the loss that in many cases its presence passes unnoticed for years before it is discovered. However, behavioral signs of impaired hearing are manifest long before this time. They are merely attributed to other causes.

[1] See Appendix B: Definitions and Classifications of Hearing Impairment.

In the life of a child the implications of such an unrecognized auditory defect are described by Berry as follows: "The father thinks that Tom is inattentive; the mother calls it preoccupation; the teacher suspects stupidity; his comrades think he does not care; or that he is queer or self-centered." [2] As many different roles are assigned the child as there are subjective misinterpretations of his behavior. He is the dreamy one, the stupid one, flighty, queer, shy. And all the while he is nothing more than the hard-of-hearing one.

Because of these various disguises, the hard-of-hearing child came to psychological attention far later than the deaf child; and because his disability is less dramatic, he provoked considerably less interest and fewer studies. Broadly summarized: in regard to intelligence, the investigations of Waldman, Wade, and Aretz,[3] Sterling and Bell,[4] Madden,[5] and Pintner and Lev [6] tend to the conclusion that the hard-of-hearing school child is somewhat below the normally hearing on verbal intelligence test I.Q.s, with the difference increasing as the amount of hearing loss is greater. However, when testing with a nonlanguage measure, Pintner and Lev found no difference in I.Q. between the hard-of-hearing and normally hearing groups. In regard to educational achievement, the foregoing investigations together with those of Warwick,[7]

[2] Gordon Berry, "The Psychology of Progressive Deafness." Reprint from the *Journal of the American Medical Association*, CI (Nov. 18, 1933), 2–3.

[3] J. L. Waldman, F. A. Wade, and S. W. Aretz, *Hearing and the School Child* (Philadelphia: The Volta Bureau, 1930).

[4] E. B. Sterling and E. Bell, "Hearing of School Children as Measured by the Audiometer and as Related to School Work," *U.S. Public Health Reports*, XLV (1930), 1117–30.

[5] R. Madden, *The School Status of the Hard of Hearing Child* (Contributions to Education No. 499; New York: Teachers College, Columbia University, 1931).

[6] R. Pintner and J. Lev, "The Intelligence of the Hard of Hearing School Child," *Journal of Genetic Psychology*, LV (1939), 31–48.

[7] H. L. Warwick, "Hearing Tests in the Public Schools of Fort Worth," *Volta Review*, XXX (1928), 641–43.

Humphrey,[8] Caplin,[9] Laurer,[10] Prince,[11] and Sprunt and Finger [12] generally concur as to the presence of educational retardation, which is found to increase where the amount of hearing loss is larger. Personality and adjustment studies conducted by Madden,[13] Pintner,[14] and McCormick,[15] while not in complete agreement, nevertheless report tendencies to increased emotional instability in the hard-of-hearing groups as compared with the hearing, with the amount of instability larger where the amount of hearing loss is more severe. Barrett [16] and Pintner and Gates [17] report improvement in adjustment with the use of hearing aids. Fiedler and Stone [18] have investigated the possibility of a "deprivation syndrome" in the Rorschach responses of hearing-im-

[8] J. H. Humphrey, "Hard-of-Hearing Children in the St. Louis Public Schools," *Volta Review*, XXX (1928), 644–46.

[9] D. Caplin, "A Special Report of Retardation of Children with Impaired Hearing in the New York City Schools," *American Annals of the Deaf*, LXXXII (1937), 234–43.

[10] F. A. Laurer, "Hearing Survey among a Group of Pupils of the Syracuse Schools," *American Journal of Public Health*, XVIII (1938), 1353–60.

[11] J. W. Prince, "The Effect of Impaired Hearing at Various Frequencies on Grades and Citizenship," *Journal of Educational Research*, XLII (1948), 234–37.

[12] J. W. Sprunt and F. W. Finger, "Auditory Deficiency and Academic Achievement," *Journal of Speech and Hearing Disorders*, XIV (1949), 26–32.

[13] Madden, *School Status of the Hard of Hearing Child*.

[14] R. Pintner, "An Adjustment Test with Normal and Hard-of-Hearing Children," *Journal of Genetic Psychology*, LVI (1940), 367–81; R. Pintner, "Some Personality Traits of Hard of Hearing Children," *Journal of Genetic Psychology*, LX (1942), 143–51.

[15] H. W. McCormick, "Report of the Subcommittee on Acoustically Handicapped Children," in *Report of the Committee for the Study and Care of Physically Handicapped Children in the Public Schools* (New York: New York City Board of Education, 1941).

[16] K. Barrett, "The Value of Individual Hearing Aids: III. A Comparative Study of the Selective Achievements of Two Groups of School Children," *Volta Review*, XLVI (1944), 681–85.

[17] R. Pintner and A. I. Gates, *The Value of Individual Hearing Aids for Hard-of-Hearing Children* (Washington, D.C.: National Research Council, 1944).

[18] M. F. Fiedler and L. J. Stone, "The Rorschachs of Selected Groups of Children in Comparison with Published Norms, Part I. The Effect of Mild Hearing Defects on Rorschach Performance," *Journal of Projective Techniques*, XX (1956), 273–75.

paired children. Although a number of the foregoing studies leave much to be desired in regard to research design, exercise of controls, and psychological measures used, the cumulative results suggest broad problem-areas beneath the unimpaired façade of the known hard-of-hearing child. It may be assumed that the burdens of the child with unrecognized hearing loss are heavier.

By the time such a child reaches adolescence, the true source of his difficulties may have been discovered. However, this does not lead to automatic adjustment. Adolescence is a particularly trying time in which to accept being different from others. For the youngster to admit the need for adjustment procedures would be to admit being different. The usual reaction, therefore, is to cover up, minimize, deny, overcompensate. Habbe's observation that "the plight of the hard of hearing boy in our public schools probably is less acute than has been suggested by many writers and speakers" [19] may be explained by the fact that the forty-eight experimental subjects of his study were considered hard of hearing if there was a binaural loss greater than nine decibels on the 4-A audiometer and fifteen decibels on the 2-A (both slight losses); that "the large majority, if not all, were aware of their loss . . . had had special, individual otological examinations . . . and had been entered in lip-reading classes"; [20] and that there was an unwillingness on the part of the subjects to report personal problems as well as "a tendency on the part of the hard of hearing boys to *minimize their difficulties*" [21] (italics are the investigator's). There is a strong suggestion that this tendency to minimize was carried over into the subjects' responses to the personality measures used in the study, and hence into the findings of the investigation. By way of contrast, Margaret L. Washington, on the basis of years of intensive rehabilitation experiences with the hard of hearing, is quoted as stating that "the

---

[19] S. Habbe, *Personality Adjustments of Adolescent Boys with Impaired Hearing* (Contributions to Education No. 697; New York: Teachers College, Columbia University, 1936), p. 32.

[20] *Ibid.*   [21] *Ibid.*, p. 74.

most difficult age at which to lose one's hearing is during the period of adolescence." [22]

Often, it is not until adulthood that the problem is finally recognized for what it is. The impact at this time of life can be shattering. Hunt relates his experiences with the adult sufferer as follows:

> Looking at this man, the otologist can readily visualize the boy he used to be. The boy who had the bad case of measles at the age of eight, perhaps. The one who was picked on in school for inattention, jeered at for making mistakes; who had to be forced to take part in group activities; who wasn't interested in girls. Making his painful way through childhood and adolescence, unguided, unaware of why he was always at a disadvantage, the young man chose his career. . . .
>
> Now the man is grown. In spite of his unacknowledged handicap, he has forced from life the things he most wanted—a good job, marriage, family. He has arrived at the otologist's office—why? Because he has everything the normal man wants out of life and he is in mortal fear of losing every bit of it.
>
> The otologist who examines this patient and writes on his record card, "Progressive deafness," has made only superficial diagnosis. The record might more accurately read: "Diagnosis: fear."
>
> Fear of failure, fear of ridicule, fear of people, fear of new situations, chance encounters, sudden noises, imagined sounds; fear of being slighted, avoided, made conspicuous—these are but a handful of the fears that haunt the waking and even the sleeping hours of the sufferer from progressive deafness. Small wonder that, at best, he tends to live in an atmosphere of despondency and suspicion. Small wonder that, at worst, he may not particularly want to live at all.[23]

From the foregoing descriptions it is obvious that the implications of progressive auditory impairment are of an entirely different order from those of early, profound loss. In the latter case, that of the deaf, the natural habitat is a "soundless world"; but the

---

[22] Federal Security Agency, *Rehabilitation of the Deaf and the Hard of Hearing: A Manual for Rehabilitation Case Workers* (Vocational Rehabilitation Series Bulletin No. 26; Washington, D.C.: Office of Education, 1942), p. 29.

[23] Westley M. Hunt, "Progressive Deafness Rehabilitation." Reprint from *The Laryngoscope* (May, 1944), pp. 4, 5.

natural environment of the progressively hard of hearing is the hearing world. The problems of the deaf are derived mainly from having to acquire basic familiarity with a way of life of which they have little if any auditory knowledge and experience. The problems of the progressively deafened arise from having to stand helplessly by, as it were, while the bustle of a familiar environment and way of life fade away into stillness. The problems of the deaf have to do with achieving normal development in a set, abnormal auditory world; those of the progressively deafened, with making constant adjustments and readjustments to each new acoustic environment created by their changing patterns of hearing, and this despite the repeated onslaughts of auditory change upon personal stability and security. The problems of the deaf are essentially developmental; those of the progressively deafened, psychotraumatic. It is a moot question which presents the more trying human experience.

There appears to be little doubt, however, as to which possesses the more disrupting emotional potential. Psychological investigations, observations, and personal accounts all stress the peculiar intensity of the emotional response to decreasing hearing ability. Of the progressively deafened person, Menninger says: "It is as if something vital to one's existence had been torn from him." [24] In his classic study of hard-of-hearing adults, Welles, like succeeding investigators, found his experimental hard-of-hearing group "significantly more emotional, more introverted, and less dominant than the average of their hearing friends," [25] although no differences were found between a group of hearing subjects and a paired group of hard-of-hearing individuals who had successfully surmounted their difficulties. In a Rorschach study of a group of

[24] Karl A. Menninger, "The Mental Effects of Deafness," *Psychoanalytic Review*, XI (1924), 146.

[25] Henry H. Welles, *The Measurement of Certain Aspects of Personality among Hard of Hearing Adults* (Contributions to Education No. 545; New York: Teachers College, Columbia University, 1932).

hard-of-hearing persons, Zucker found a "persistent pattern of submissiveness, resignation, suppressed hostility, and resulting anxiety and depression." [26] Van Horn relates that for the teacher of lip reading, "threats of suicide, rage, depression, isolation, self-hate, shame, and suspicion are part of her daily contacts with her pupils as they go through the period of intense emotional struggle due to sudden loss of hearing or sudden realization that the handicap is permanent and progressive." [27] From personal experience, three outstanding pioneer workers in the field—Peck, Samuelson, and Lehman—state that "everybody who acquires deafness goes through hell." [28]

In contrast to this picture of deep disturbance of the progressively hard of hearing is the following description by Best of the general emotional tone of the deaf group:

The deaf as a lot are not unhappy. They are not morose, sullen, discontented. They remain undismayed. They are good-natured, see the world from an odd angle sometimes, yet are as much philosophers as the average man. . . . When in the company of their deaf associates, they are able to derive fully as large a portion of happiness as any other group of human beings. All things considered, cheerfulness may be said to be an attribute of the larger number of deaf.[29]

Here is further evidence of the pronounced differences between deaf and hard-of-hearing groups. Perhaps one of the reasons for this particular difference is that the respective groups travel along different roads and move in different company. The deaf move

[26] Luise Zucker, "Rorschach Patterns of a Group of Hard of Hearing Patients," *Rorschach Research Exchange and Journal of Projective Techniques,* XI (1947), 71.

[27] Mary Van Horn, in a discussion of "The Mental Effects of Acquired Deafness" by Ruth Brickner, *Volta Review,* XXXI (1929), 413.

[28] Annetta W. Peck, Estelle E. Samuelson, and Ann Lehman, *Ears and the Man: Studies in Social Work for the Deafened* (Philadelphia: F. A. Davis Co., 1926), p. 21.

[29] Harry Best, *Deafness and the Deaf in the United States* (New York: The Macmillan Company, 1943), p. 336.

mainly "in the company of their deaf associates," but the progressively deafened travel the hearing road. Along this latter road are countless young hard-of-hearing people who live in daily terror at the prospect of being caught in the joshing camaraderie of a hearing group; of being singled out in games; of being called on in class; and, worst of all, of missing the "sweet nothings" whispered into their ears on dates. There are young brides filled with guilt and remorse at having burdened another with their deafness and deeply disturbed at the possibility of passing it on to those not yet born; anguished mothers who cannot hear the baby's cry in the night or make anything of the excited prattle of their children; anxious wives who cringe in fear at the thought of every social obligation that must be met; husbands and fathers faced with the prospect of becoming vocational students again in occupations where impaired hearing is no handicap. These are but a few who travel the road of progressive deafness.

Possibly the most difficult part of the way is at the beginning, for here the path is strangely muted. The term "isolation" is commonly used to describe the sensation of being cut off from the world that comes with lessened hearing ability. But the isolation here referred to is not that customarily associated with emotional disorder. In the latter instance, the concept of isolation represents a psychic defense employed as a means of escape from anxiety-provoking stimuli. But where isolation results from impaired hearing, it is not the individual who is seeking escape from the environment. On the contrary, it is the environment that is escaping from the perceptive grasp of the individual. By its very nature, decreased hearing ability simulates the sensation of increased distance between the person and the source of sound. As hearing fades, sound seems to be coming from farther and farther away. Ultimately, some sounds disappear altogether; others are distorted; patterns of sound are no longer recognizable. The resultant sensation of isolation, of detachment from the world, is forced upon all whose hearing no longer serves to keep them in "touch" with life.

Together with the feeling of being detached, a confusing distortion in audio-visual *Gestalt* arises from the sensorially illogical difference between the auditory estimate of the distance of sound and the actual visible evidence of its source. It is as if sound were *heard* as coming from great distances, but *seen* to be quite near at hand. Further disruption in audio-visual balance is caused by the loss of awareness of the direction from which sounds come. And finally, perceptive distortions are compounded in numbers of cases by the additional strains of vertigo [30] and tinnitus.[31] The head noises of tinnitus may vary from mild, occasional buzzings to the wildest of clangings and shrillest screechings. The individual must learn to hear through them and distinguish them from external sounds.

While the sufferer is engulfed in the struggle to bring this incredibly distorted body of sound into some semblance of perceptive order, he is threatened by still another type of auditory problem, namely, decreased ability to gauge and monitor the sounds of his own voice. To a person with obstructive deafness, his voice may sound disproportionately loud, and to avoid what he perceives as shouting, the individual tends to speak lower and lower until he can hardly be heard at all. On the other hand, in cases of severe nerve deafness, the person experiences difficulty in hearing the sound of his own voice, and to overcome this he speaks with unnecessary loudness. As time goes on and hearing lessens, defective enunciation commonly appears together with other poor speech habits that make it difficult for a listener to understand what the hearing-impaired person is saying. As a result, to quote Gifford and Bowler, "many of these hard-of-hearing people live in fear of their

[30] A. J. Wright, "The Deafness of Ménière's Disease," *Journal of Laryngology and Otology*, LVIII (1943), 379.

[31] D. Macfarlan, "Head Noises (Tinnitus Aurium)," Pamphlet No. 120, American Hearing Society, May, 1947.

own voices. They are constantly on the alert to detect the unfavorable reaction of those with whom they talk, trying to regulate by this reaction the volume of their voice." [32] Thus, to the continuing strain of trying not to misunderstand what is said is added the burden of trying not to be misunderstood. From the tensions thus imposed on interpersonal communication, a rift is apt to develop between the hearing-impaired individual and his human environment.

Society itself contributes in no small measure to this rift; for here again the invisible nature of auditory disability redounds to the disadvantage of the sufferer. Nothing of the auditory turmoils he is experiencing "shows" excepting in the changes that take place in his behavior; and since these generally make for strain and tension in interpersonal relations, the usual consensus is "best leave him alone."

To be odd man out is difficult even in casual situations. But where the individual is accustomed to be an integral part of a close relationship, as in the family, on the job, and in the community, to be suddenly left alone is tantamount to ostracism. It is not surprising, therefore, to find many such persons engulfed in torments of despair, panic, rage, and feelings of worthlessness, coming alive in the hope that a medical miracle, such as those performed by Lempert [33] and Rosen, [34] will set them free again, only to return to the depths if it should not. The naive and well-intentioned efforts of family and friends to cheer up such a person may add just enough extra irritation to an already overburdened psyche to cause emotional collapse.

[32] C. G. Bluett, comp., *Handbook of Information for the Hard of Hearing Adult* (Sacramento: California State Department of Education, 1942), p. 23.

[33] Hallowell Davis, *Hearing and Deafness:* Chapter 5, "The Surgical Treatment of Hearing Loss," by T. E. Walsh (New York–Toronto: Rinehart Books, Inc., 1953).

[34] Samuel Rosen, "Mobilization of the Stapes." Reprint No. 679, The Volta Bureau, Washington, D.C.

Where isolation and regression are the individual's established modes of dealing with emotional crises, the feeling of detachment that comes with impaired hearing may, under adverse conditions, easily slip into true psychic detachment. Inability to hear offers such persons a ready-made escape from tensions and responsibilities. They meet these with apathy, withdrawal, or regression to psychic infantilism. In other cases, inability to solve the conflicts activated by hearing loss leads to irritable, hostile hypersensitivity, a "chip on the shoulder" attitude, a suspicious defensive set commonly referred to in the field literature as the paranoid attitude of the hard of hearing. Still other individuals deny the reality of the facts that would otherwise generate deep anxiety. Fowler observes that the "tendency to ignore or deny the first indications of deafness, aversion to consulting an otologist, and even to resent suggestions that hearing is not 'perfectly all right,' persistent objection to using a hearing aid or studying lipreading, until long after these are clearly indicated," [35] are characteristically common signs in otosclerotic progressive deafness.

Other types of personality structures employ still other types of psychic defense. In work with the hearing-impaired, the psychologist will encounter all that exist in the human armamentarium against anxiety. As expressed by Zeckel, the defenses employed by deafened individuals are "not unique. . . . In a great number of cases we have seen that a neurosis existed before the patient lost his hearing. . . . In a great number of cases definite illness becomes manifest because of the additional handicap of deafness. . . . The less neurotic the patient is, the better he will adapt to his deafness." [36]

Where adjustment is ultimately achieved, the types of sat-

[35] Edmund Prince Fowler, "Emotional Factors in Otosclerosis." Reprint from *The Laryngoscope*, LXI (1951), 2.

[36] Adolf Zeckel, "Psychopathological Aspects of Deafness." Reprint from the *Journal of Nervous and Mental Diseases*, CXII (1950), 337, 340.

isfactory compensations as summarized from Menninger [37] are any one or combination of the following: (*a*) perceptual compensation, in which there is a deliberate as well as a more or less unconscious sharpening of sense perception so that latent sensory faculties are developed to fill the gaps left by impaired hearing (lip reading represents a visual perceptual compensation); (*b*) intellectual compensation, in which the philosophical attitude and a purposeful broadening of creative interests and outlets are employed to maintain psychic balance and vigor; (*c*) emotional compensation, through which the individual succeeds in sublimating his disturbance and comes to peace with himself through healthy psychic devices, aided and abetted by the saving grace of a sense of humor; and (*d*) volitional compensation, through which the individual is impelled to achieve not only in spite of but because of his disability.

However, before satisfactory compensations can be achieved, the condition requiring such measures must of course be recognized. In this respect, the hard-of-hearing child fares worse than any other age level or category of auditory disability; worse even than his far more seriously handicapped deaf peer. In the latter case, the presence of disability attracts early attention and once correctly diagnosed commands a wealth of rehabilitation services. But the hard-of-hearing child generally has enough hearing to get by. Maintaining a surface appearance of sensorial intactness, he arouses no feeling of diagnostic urgency.

As a result, the hard-of-hearing child often suffers the weight of his burdens for years before help comes. The better-known part of his problems consists of the unhealthy emotional and social climate in which a child with unrecognized auditory disability is forced to live. The less commonly recognized part of the burden

[37] Menninger, "The Mental Effects of Deafness," *Psychoanalytic Review*, XI (1924), 144–55.

consists of lags and gaps in vocabulary and knowledge that accumulate while the child is getting by.

What the ears do not hear, the young child cannot profit from. It cannot be stressed enough that the hard-of-hearing child is in no less danger of inner deprivation because he appears "normal." In many instances he appears normal because he has consciously or unconsciously narrowed his field of operation and expression to a zone of acoustic security. But outside this zone, in the area of auditory uncertainty where hearing is patchy, distorted, or absent, so too are the vocabulary, language, and concepts that require full hearing for learning and development. The camouflage defense of the hard-of-hearing child proves an excellent disguise. The psychologist must not be deceived by it.

Having thus far noted a number of emotional sequelae of structural auditory impairment, it remains to conclude with the highly provocative evidence put forth by Fowler and Fowler [38] concerning the role of emotional disturbance in *causing* structural damage of the organ of hearing. Fowler states that certain types of neural deafness "frequently do follow emotional or psychic disturbances." [39] He explains that this comes about through the action of the latter on the neurovascular system whereby blood sludges are formed. The sludges eventually find their way to the terminal blood vessels of the cochlea which they succeed in clogging, thus depriving the neural elements involved of necessary oxidation and causing ultimate deterioration and deafness. Fowler calls attention to this concept in the etiology of progressive deafness resulting from otosclerosis as well as of tinnitus, vertigo, and certain types of obstructive, neural, and sudden deafness. Of particular importance for the psychologist is his recommendation that if this thesis is tenable, preventive measures against impaired

[38] Edmund Prince Fowler and Edmund Prince Fowler, Jr., "An Explanation of Certain Types of Tinnitus and Deafness," *The Laryngoscope*, LX (1950), 919–30.

[39] Fowler, "Emotional Factors in Otosclerosis," p. 3.

hearing must include mental hygiene as well as otological precautions.

Sudden Deafness in Adulthood

Although the etiology of sudden deafness is not always clear, its impact is reported as one of life's most terrifying experiences.[40] When severe, there is an abrupt plunge from sound to silence, a situation that represents yet another of the numerous variations in manner of onset of impaired hearing, and the final one to be considered in this section.

Possibly the best-known examples of sudden deafness are the acoustic casualties of World War II on whom the first large-scale studies of the effects of abrupt hearing loss were conducted. A startling finding was the relatively high incidence of psychogenic auditory disorder among the war-deafened.[41] With this unsuspected disclosure, the dramatic phenomenology of psychic dynamisms leapt from the psychiatrist's domain into the field of impaired hearing, where they have commanded major attention ever since. Relegated to a more or less secondary position were investigations of the interrelationship between personality and straight organic hearing loss.

It is, however, upon this interrelationship that present attention is directed. This is so because the primary concern here is with the effects of auditory disturbance upon psychic function, whereas classic psychogenic deafness represents just the reverse phenomenon, namely, the effect of psychic disturbance upon auditory function. As indicated in a simplified manner by Strecker, the psychogenic condition comes about in a manner somewhat as follows:

[40] Richard R. Lehmann, "Bilateral Sudden Deafness," *New York State Journal of Medicine* (May 15, 1954), pp. 1481–88.

[41] See references to psychogenic deafness in George A. Miller, *et al.*, *A Bibliography in Audition* (2 vols.; Cambridge: Harvard University Press, 1950).

1. Unresolved emotional conflicts become converted into clear-cut symptoms, which constitute clinical conversion hysteria and which are readily discoverable upon objective examination.

2. Hysteria represents an escape from a situation no longer tolerable to the personality of the individual. The unconscious mechanism employed is productive of symptoms constituting objective disabilities which, for the time being, render impossible a return to the unbearable situation.

3. The hysterical symptoms are protective; blindness and amnesia blotting out the gruesome sights witnessed on the battlefield and the memory of them; deafness shutting out the cries and groans of the wounded; amnesias erasing the remembrance of seeing a beloved one in the arms of another, etc.

4. Various factors, physical such as concussion, fatigue, or deprivation, trivial illness or an emotionally disturbing situation may act in the role of precipitating factors.[42]

Structural auditory damage is also among the "precipitating factors" that may spark the conversion mechanism. Where this happens, the amount of hearing loss due to structural damage is substantially increased by the action of emotional dynamisms. The amount of increase is termed the "psychogenic overlay." However, the fact that similar neurotic mechanisms may be encountered in otogenic as well as psychogenic hearing loss does not alter the etiological facts. To study the impact of impaired hearing upon the psyche, it is still necessary to start with situations in which impaired hearing is the etiological activator of emotional response rather than the outcome of emotional disturbance.

Pursuing this course leads to a wealth of suggestive information in Knapp's report [43] of a study of war-deafened soldiers, collaboratively conducted by the Psychiatric and Hearing Services of the Deshon General Hospital during World War II. Of particular value is the fact that the study affords an opportunity to examine

[42] Edward A. Strecker, *Fundamentals of Psychiatry* (London: Medical Publications, Ltd.), pp. 137–38.

[43] Peter Hobart Knapp, "Emotional Aspects of Hearing Loss," *Psychosomatic Medicine*, X (1948), 203–22.

the impact of sudden deafness in terms of (1) the general effect of abrupt hearing loss upon the social organism; (2) the varied effects of different amounts of hearing loss; (3) the influences of previous auditory impairment; and (4) the role of the personality in adjustment to sudden deafness.

As reported by the subjects of Knapp's investigation, the most significant single feeling-tone resulting from sudden deafness was loneliness; the most common single fear, that of being thought stupid; and the most keenly felt anxiety, insecurity in social situations. Somatic complaints were also reported, particularly tension headaches. These seemed to be related both to emotional distress and to the strain of having to *listen* in order to hear. Tinnitus was also fairly common and was generally of physiologic etiology. A universally felt lack was the loss of daily background sounds, with associated anxieties felt in regard to traffic, crowds, inability to hear an alarm clock or an order. Also missed were the sounds of nature—the rain, the wind, birds, and the like. The tension of silence—as of holding one's breath until sound breaks through—was a common source of distress.

The relationship between the amount of hearing loss and the effect upon the social organism is summarized by Knapp as follows:

At the threshold of incapacitation, patients were not greatly dependent; frequently their sole complaint was that the world did not talk loudly enough. More often they spoke of how great a strain it was to hear, especially in groups. Still it was possible to "get by" socially. In the 50–70 decibel range, more marked impairment appeared. It often led to a more grossly abnormal facial expression and mannerisms, as well as to more severe emotional reactions, especially of withdrawal. The effort necessary to maintain social bonds sometimes hardly seemed worthwhile. The totally deaf patients felt that these bonds were definitely ruptured. Lipreading, though useful, could not substitute for the quickness and warmth of words that were heard. The men had to adjust as best they could to partial isolation and helplessness.[44]

[44] *Ibid.*, p. 207.

In effect, the greater the amount of sudden hearing loss, the greater the emotional impact.

Differences were also noted between cases of true sudden deafness and those with histories of chronic auditory impairment. This comparison is particularly pertinent to the present discussion. Knapp's study suggests that while patients with true sudden deafness are more apt to be "tinged with depression," they are nevertheless psychologically more flexible than the chronic cases who have in the course of the years "reached equilibrium"; that although the latter experience a less drastic sense of loss, it is a more warping one. The trauma of true sudden loss tends to generate more intense struggles than the gradual pace of progressive impairment, and is thus more accessible to treatment.

Turning from group trends to individual reactions, the study demonstrates that the ultimate determinant of adjustment to sudden deafness lies with the premorbid personality structure. Where the structure is unhealthy, mild loss can cause profound disturbance; where the structure is healthy, the problems of even severe loss can be managed without serious emotional involvement. The compensatory devices employed in the latter instances are essentially the same as those summarized from Menninger for progressive deafness.[45] So also are the neurotic defenses used by the suddenly deafened. These are roughly classified by Knapp as follows: (1) "overcompensated" outgoing striving, an exaggerated display of normal jovial behavior with great emphasis upon talking which presents no handicap to the suddenly deafened and which is used as an escape from listening, which does; (2) denial of hearing loss; (3) retreat from society; (4) neurotic displacement of anxiety into the sphere of somatic preoccupation and complaint; and (5) neurotic exploitation of hearing loss, with the hearing aid used as a "badge of invalidism."

Quite likely the full impact of sudden hearing loss on most of

[45] See above, page 67.

Knapp's subjects was somewhat watered down as a result of the rehabilitation services at their command. It is particularly interesting, therefore, to note the reactions of hearing subjects experimentally deafened for twenty-four hours and to see how they compare with Knapp's group. The former study is reported by Meyerson,[46] whose subjects, a number of children and college students, had the advantage of knowing that their handicap was transient. Even so, the experimenter notes the appearance of "bored, stupid or inappropriate behavior"; evidences of fatigue and irritability; change in quality and intensity of voice; and a tendency to "preoccupation." The college students further reported inner feelings of frustration and aggression resulting from their inability to fully understand oral communication, and a tendency to give up and withdraw from further frustration. Among the children's reactions were observed: increased tension and restlessness; increased alertness to nonverbal clues; decreased initiative in seeking social contacts; and either delayed reaction to oral communication or no reaction. As expressed by Cornell, who subjected himself to a similar experiment for seven days, "They are living in a partial auditory vacuum—a world of silence mixed with distorted and unfamiliar sounds." [47]

To sum up in the words of Bergman, the progressively deafened adult is one "who has suffered the creeping horrors of social isolation, whose life at home and at work has become a nightmare of misunderstandings and frustrations, whose speech and voice have changed so that between the inability to hear accurately and the annoyance with which others react to his own speech his behavior is gradually undergoing unfavorable change." [48] The

[46] L. Meyerson, "Experimental Injury: An Approach to the Dynamics of Physical Disability," *Journal of Social Issues*, IV (1948), 68–71.

[47] C. B. Cornell, "Hard of Hearing for Seven Days," *Hearing News*, XVIII (1950), 3–4, 14.

[48] Moe Bergman, "Special Methods of Audiological Training for Adults," *Acta Oto-Laryngologica*, Vol. XL, Fasc. V–VI (1951–52), p. 336.

abruptly deafened adult experiences in one highly concentrated measure all the pangs and agonies of years of progressive deafness. Again it is a moot question which is the more taxing human experience. There is no doubt, however, that hearing loss of any type bites deep into man's well-being, and that treatment for impaired hearing is as much a concern of psychology as of otology.

Part Two

PSYCHOLOGICAL PRACTICE
IN A REHABILITATION SETTING

4. THE REHABILITATION SETTING

PSYCHOLOGISTS specializing in auditory disabilities usually function in rehabilitation settings guided by the philosophy of total rehabilitation for the whole person. In such settings, the exceptional range and variety of problems, needs, patients, specialists, and general activity are rather new to established habits of psychological practice. It is not uncommon for psychologists entering the busy scene to feel somewhat lost in the beginning,[1] particularly in areas of severe or unusual disabilities such as early profound deafness. In such areas, the combined pressures of a new clinical environment plus the urgent need for modifications and manipulations of techniques and the frustrations of baffling diagnostic problems often prove an overwhelming burden for the new worker. Contrary to popular belief, there is no magic that enables psychologists to plunge into unfamiliar clinical environments and problems with immediate efficiency. Such workers are as much in need of preliminary preparation as are any who specialize in new areas.

In work with the disabled, part of the preparation involves a deep understanding of the intrapersonal implications of a disability. But this is only a part. Equally important is familiarity with the external tensions, the reality problems, and the everyday stresses of a given disability and with the rationale of rehabilita-

[1] Frederick A. Whitehouse, "Teamwork: Philosophy and Principles," The American Association of Medical Social Workers, *Social Work Practice in Medical Care and Rehabilitation Settings*, Monograph II (July, 1955), pp. 1–19.

tion service. It is when the external and the internal aspects of the problem are combined into total understanding on the part of the psychologist that he achieves the necessary frame for effective participation in rehabilitation procedures and for effective interpretation of a physically disabled person's total needs and behavior.

To attain such empathy, the psychologist must be alert to the significance of the information rehabilitation reveals and requires about an individual, and not only to the data derived from the formal psychological examination.[2] In cases of severe and/or unusual disabilities, the latter often tell only half—and sometimes less than half—the story. For a psychologist to complete the story requires familiarity with the basic concepts, problems, and psychodynamics that characterize rehabilitation settings. Since these apply equally to the hearing-impaired as to other disabilities, the orientation offered in this and in the following chapter is discussed in the general context of physical disability rather than that of a single disability group.

The Rehabilitation Setting: General Features

In pattern, rehabilitation settings exist in any one of a wide variety of forms. They may be structured as rehabilitation centers, defined by Redley as facilities "in which there is a concentration of services including at least one each from the medical, psychosocial, and vocational areas, which are furnished according to need, are intensive and substantial in nature, and which are integrated with each other and with other services in the community to provide a unified evaluation and rehabilitation service to disabled people.[3] Or the re-

[2] J. F. Garrett, "Applications of Clinical Psychology to Rehabilitation," in D. Brower and L. Abt, eds., *Progress in Clinical Psychology* (New York: Grune & Stratton, 1952), pp. 443–49.

[3] S. G. DiMichael and J. F. Garrett, "Clinical Psychology in a Rehabilitation Center," in E. A. Rubinstein and M. Lorr, eds., *Survey of Clinical Practice in Psychology* (New York: International Universities Press, Inc., 1954), p. 296.

habilitation setting may take the form of special schools and classes for the congenitally and early-childhood disabled, physicians' offices, patients' homes when homebound services are required, hospitals for the chronically ill, sheltered workshops for those unable to compete in normal work activities, prevocational and vocational training and placement units, mental health and psychiatric installations, out-patient clinics, hospital departments of physical medicine, geriatric centers, veteran installations, and still other types of facilities. In short, wherever the philosophy of rehabilitation is in operation, there will be found a rehabilitation setting no matter how humble its physical structure.

As may be inferred from the types of settings mentioned, the age range of physically disabled persons served by rehabilitation covers the span from birth through senescence. Psychologically, this population constitutes a normative section of society. Therefore, unlike psychologists specializing in behavioral pathologies, those working with the physically disabled deal with a group whose major problems involve learning to live with somatic defect rather than psychopathology. Of course, the latter crops up among the physically disabled as in all groups, but not as a common occurrence. The general psychological problems of the physically impaired are those involving disability-imposed adjustments, readjustments, and acceptances—personal, social, and vocational. A number of these are more fully discussed in the following sections and in the next chapter.

In helping the physically disabled toward total rehabilitation, psychologists must be prepared to work harmoniously and effectively with a wide variety of professional associates. Depending upon the needs of the individual, any combination of the following specialists is commonly involved in rehabilitation programs: physicians, social workers, educators, special educational, occupational, and recreational therapists, physical therapists, vocational rehabilitation counselors, and psychologists. Included on this team, although not specialists in the classic sense, are family and community. The latter represent major influences in the adjustment of physically disabled persons, and as such also fall within the rehabilitation frame. It is obvious that rehabilitation is not a one-man job.

So far as the psychologist's role is concerned, although traditionally associated with the diagnosis and treatment of psychopathological conditions, a competent worker is equally equipped to serve normative groups. This fact is not generally appreciated, and even in rehabilitation there is a strong tendency to pair psychology and psychopathology. It must be emphasized, therefore, that the psychologist is essentially a student of human behavior and that his ability to deal with psychopathology is grounded on training in the normative foundations of behavior.[4] The competent clinician is thus equipped not only to help the everyday person with ordinary problems of living but also to perceive when the seemingly everyday shows signs of deviance; when to apply preventive measures; and when full-dress diagnostic and therapeutic procedures are called for. With such qualifications, the clinical psychologist is in a potentially strong position to render valuable and comprehensive service to rehabilitation.

Special Features and Problems of Psychological Practice with the Physically Disabled

The preceding section having introduced the general aspects, points of special emphasis in psychological practice with the physically disabled are now briefly summarized.

THE PRESSURE OF PRACTICAL NEEDS AND SERVICES

Among the first observations that strike psychologists in rehabilitation centers is the pressure of practical needs that drives

[4] John M. Hadley, *Clinical and Counseling Psychology* (New York: Alfred A. Knopf, 1958).

clients [5] to seek help. The average client seldom comes simply because he feels nervous or maladjusted. He may very well be both of these, but he comes primarily because he has a family to support and needs a job; or a newly acquired disability has turned his world topsy-turvy, and he cannot right it by himself; or he needs to learn to use his prosthesis more effectively, find out about sources of medical attention, vocational training, education, recreation, and the like. There is a practical urgency about his needs that is not found in ordinary psychological practice to anywhere near the extent common in rehabilitation. Often it is in the course of servicing a client's everyday needs that deeper problems are disclosed. This does not remove the urgency of his requirements. They must still be served.

Therefore, one of the first discoveries a psychologist makes is the practical return rehabilitation expects of psychological services. Diagnostic labels and technical ramifications are more suited to the research frame. In rehabilitation practice, the immediate concern is service-centered. This does not mean that the deeper aspects of a client's problems are ignored. One of the unusual advantages of total rehabilitation is that any necessary combinations of treatment approaches can be employed simultaneously. For example, if a client requires vocational evaluation and it is found that he is emotionally disturbed, he does not necessarily have to wait until he has been treated for his disturbance before beginning vocational activities. Through the team approach that characterizes rehabilitation, adjustment and vocational services can be supplied at the

[5] The term "client" is commonly used in rehabilitation to designate any individual being served by a rehabilitation center. Medically oriented facilities often use the term "patient" instead. In a personal communication to the writer, Morton A. Seidenfeld, Director of Psychological Services of The National Foundation, draws the following terminological distinctions: "The term 'client' generally refers to an individual receiving vocational rehabilitation services and counseling; the term 'patient,' to an individual under treatment or diagnosis; the term 'subject,' to an individual who is exposed to an experimental procedure." Because psychological diagnostic procedures with the deaf are still largely experimental, the term "subject" is favored in the present volume.

same time wherever feasible. As a rule, gains in the one stimulate gains in the other. A similar approach obtains for other combinations of services. When psychologists are part of such combinations, the findings of the psychological examination are expected to contribute to the combined-action plans. If they do not, they are of little practical use.

It follows then that the psychologist who is accustomed to submit technical "findings" to psychiatrists will go through the unhappy experience of seeing his findings lost in rehabilitation settings unless they can be integrated into designs for practical solution. The point that Florence Clothier makes in clinical psychiatry applies equally to the service aspects of rehabilitation, namely: "Diagnosis is of value only insofar as it leads to a reasonable and helpful program of therapy." [6] Unless it does, a rehabilitation client's problems have merely been restated in psychological terminology with the need to know what to do about them still pending.

In regard to terminology, Hammond and Allen issue a timely warning in the statement: "Some writers and editors have published remarks accusing psychologists (and others) of using jargon, or writing and speaking an esoteric language, to the confusion and annoyance of everyone else." [7] Psychologists are reminded that if the facts are clear in their own minds, they can be clearly expressed to others. There is no technical expression that cannot be intelligibly interpreted and communicated if its meaning is understood by the user. Intelligible communication is essential in all psychological practice, but particularly in rehabilitation where practical guidance along many avenues is sought by a wide variety of participating specialists who are not familiar with the semantics of psychology.

[6] Quoted in C. E. Benda, *Developmental Disorders of Mentation and Cerebral Palsies* (New York: Grune & Stratton, 1952), p. 506.

[7] Kenneth R. Hammond and Jeremiah M. Allen, *Writing Clinical Reports* (New York: Prentice-Hall, Inc., 1953), p. 133.

THE PROBLEM OF TEST SELECTION AND INTERPRETATION

A question of major concern among psychologists in rehabilitation is the validity of using with physically disabled subjects intelligence and personality tests standardized on the nondisabled. The answer involves two basic considerations: first, the theoretic and statistical bases of test standardization; second, the physical obstacles to testing raised by disability. These are briefly illustrated in the cases of (1) mild physical impairment; (2) severe physical impairment acquired in adulthood; and (3) severe congenital impairment.

MILD PHYSICAL IMPAIRMENT. According to the statistical rationale of test standardization, the closer the conformity between a subject's development and life experiences and those of the standardization population of a given test, the higher the diagnostic authenticity of the test. Applying this rule of thumb to the physically disabled, we find that there are substantial numbers of such persons whose life experiences are in close conformity with those of the population at large. The great majority of mildly disabled individuals fall into this category. In such cases, standard clinical judgment and standardized psychological measures may be used without violating the principles of psychological examination. Whatever modifications in procedure and interpretation may be required in certain instances are presumably minor and pose no threat to test validity.

SEVERE PHYSICAL IMPAIRMENT ACQUIRED IN ADULTHOOD. The same theoretic assumptions apply to the use of standardized tests with numbers of the more incapacitating disabilities when acquired in adulthood. While it is true that physical impairment acquired at this time of life may generate emotional disturbance, it cannot retroactively affect or alter what has gone before in the life of the individual. In so far as a seriously disabled adult's past experiences qualify him for standardized testing, there is no theoretic contraindication to its use.

However, there are several important practical considerations that must be borne in mind that have to do with the selection and interpretation of tests for the seriously disabled. Concerning test selection, the basic aim is to select instruments that provide the fullest clinical picture, psychological time and laborsaving devices notwithstanding. The latter are not for clinical diagnostic appraisal, and especially not for the seriously disabled. Accordingly, the first step in the selection of tests involves a careful search for promising instruments. When a tentative selection has been made, a "matching" process is carried out whereby test is "matched" to disability in such a way that there will be minimum physical interference with (*a*) the comprehension of test directions; (*b*) the expression of response on the part of the subject; and (*c*) adherence to test rationale on the part of the tester. Those tests are ultimately chosen that come closest to satisfying the foregoing criteria. That appropriate instruments cannot always be found is one of rehabilitation's—and psychology's—still unsolved problems.

However, no matter how promising a test may appear from the viewpoint of administration, serious disability poses certain interpretative problems to which the psychologist must be keenly alert. When tests are standardized on representative samplings of a population, valid use of the instruments assumes a representative sampling of problems and experiences on the part of a subject *at the time he is tested* as well as in his past. But when a subject becomes seriously disabled in adulthood, his present experiences are no longer representative of the population at large, nor are they in conformity with those of the test standardization group or, in fact, with those of his own past. The tests still can, of course, indicate points of deviation from normative response; but the examiner must carefully question whether such deviations are derived from the usual psychoenvironmental and developmental determinants or from special disability factors and influences; whether they are to be interpreted as pathological signs or as transient emotional states, such as grief and mourning; whether they represent personal projections or simply a natural response to social devaluation; whether they signify endogenous disturbance or exogenously produced counterreactions. Tests alone cannot make these fine interpretative distinctions. This is the examiner's task. In work with the physically disabled, cogent text interpretation is among a psychologist's paramount responsibilities.

SEVERE CONGENITAL IMPAIRMENT. Clinical judgment assumes even greater importance in the case of serious congenital and early childhood disabilities. Notable examples are the severe congenital sensory deficits. Because such impairment alters the stimulus potentials of perceptive experience, the lives of individuals so affected are spent in unique and unfamiliar places. Some come from the voiceless world of the deaf; others, from the blurred world of blindness [8] or from the strange, tactile world of the deaf-blind.[9] An uninitiated psychologist is lost in these environments. Both he and his psychological instruments take on the character of standardized tools in a world without norms. To complicate matters further, the worker in many of these areas is thrown upon his own resources almost entirely for lack of appropriate testing instruments and technical guides.[10] Finally, there

[8] Wilma Donahue and Donald Dabelstein, *Psychological Diagnosis and Counseling of the Adult Blind* (New York: American Foundation for the Blind, 1950).

[9] Robert J. Smithadas, *Life at My Finger-Tips* (New York: Doubleday & Co., Inc., 1958).

[10] Notable exceptions to the "lack of technical guides" are: Mary K. Bauman and Samuel P. Hayes, *A Manual for the Psychological Examination of the Adult Blind* (New York: The Psychological Corporation, 1951); *Rehabilitation of Deaf-Blind Persons*, Volume I: *A Manual for Professional Workers* (Brooklyn, New York: The Industrial Home for the Blind, 1958); Else Haeussermann, *Developmental Potential of Preschool Children* (New York: Grune & Stratton, 1958); Edith M. Taylor, *Psychological Appraisal of Children with Cerebral Defects* (Cambridge, Mass.: Harvard University Press, 1959).

is the problem of purely operational difficulties resulting from the restrictions imposed by the particular disability, as in the case of the deaf where congenital auditory dysfunction is associated with seriously impaired language abilities and communications skills.

Ideally, areas of severe congenital sensory deficit are supreme fields for research, particularly of the relationship among sensation, perception, cognition, and maturation. But in clinical practice the research challenge of sensory deficit must bow to human need. Where psychological services are required, they must be rendered despite the obstacles.

A competent, adaptable clinician is not deterred by the difficulties. Instead of using tests as measures, he uses them as clinical probes; and instead of rigid adherence to scores and norms, test response is flexibly interpreted in the context of the developmental and environmental restrictions imposed by a particular disability. In certain types of impairments, the physiological involvements may be so severe as to make even this flexible approach difficult if not impossible to employ.[11] This, however, is another problem.

Where the flexible approach can be adopted, standardized intelligence and personality tests are seldom used as measures in the quantitative sense, whereas the achievement types of tests are often used as they stand. The reason is that achievement tests measure static levels of proficiency, while intelligence and personality tests are used to appraise human beings, and as such the test results represent a summation of the past, an appraisal of the present, and a prediction for the future. When tests are calibrated for such assessment in degrees of normative development, they cannot be expected to measure the outcomes of deviate development with valid precision.

Nevertheless, when the quantitative score system of a test is not applicable to a particular subject, there are other test features

[11] Viola Cardwell, *Cerebral Palsy—Advances in Understanding and Care* (New York: Association for the Aid of Crippled Children, 1958).

that can be of great service in clinical appraisal. Responses to test questions represent a remarkably productive source of information, while test administration affords an unusual opportunity for obtaining qualitative data through controlled observation and interview. A resourceful psychologist can use a test for all or for any single one of its multiple attributes as the situation requires. In "unstandardized" areas of human behavior, the qualitative clinical values of standardized tests are often their strongest feature. It is to be regretted that they are not used to greater advantage in everyday test situations.

Operating under such unstandardized conditions impairs the validity of scores and norms in appraising test responses. However, the worker can employ other criteria to check his results. For one, there is the practical criterion of common sense that indicates whether a test item is physiologically suited for a physically disabled subject. "Seeing" items would not do for the blind, nor "hearing" items for the deaf. For another, there is the criterion of clinical insight that tells whether a test item is psychologically appropriate for a particular subject. For example, the appraisal of interpersonal relations based on questions involving social participation would not do for the homebound subject, nor would it be sensible to examine for psychological handicap while a newly disabled subject is mourning his loss. Finally, there is the guidance of disability field authorities that can be counted on to help an examiner distinguish common disability responses from individual deviations as well as to differentiate between suitable and unsuitable test items. In time, the psychologist acquires an inner standardization-sense of his own that enables him to move with relative ease and assurance through complicated disability areas despite his less than adequate instruments. In the process, he gains both in clinical stature and in knowledge of human behavior.

To sum up, the question of using standardized psychological measures as they stand in unstandardized areas of human behavior does not lend itself to an all-or-none response. There are those who claim that because the physically disabled live in the same world as the nondisabled, they should be measured by the same tests and norms. But where deep disparity exists between the groups, "same" tests can prove to be quite different instruments in actual practice unless carefully screened and adapted to insure equivalent returns. On the other hand, there are those who claim that standardized tests have no place in unstandardized areas of disability. The proponents of this view overlook the fact that where tests cannot be used as measures, they can still be used as clinical probes; and where quantitative norms are inapplicable, there are other sources of authoritative guidance. In effect, the final answer rests with the clinical experience and judgment of the examiner and the problems presented by a particular case. However, until more appropriate instruments are devised, there are numbers of available standardized tests as well as projective techniques that can render notable clinical service with seriously disabled persons.

DYNAMIC EVALUATION

To keep pace with the changing situations and problems of individuals undergoing rehabilitation demands unusual flexibility on the part of a psychologist. Examination is not a once-and-for-all procedure but rather a follow-up process of evaluation and re-evaluation. As a client's needs change, it is necessary to know the amount and direction of the change; to appraise the value of present procedures; to establish whether the time is ripe for the next phase of the rehabilitation program, and what it should include.

In addition, improvement in a client's condition may mean that various tests and techniques of examination can now be used that were previously unfeasible. At the same time, a shift in the interpretation of test findings may be required in the light of the changed conditions. This in turn requires a shift in clinical orientation concerning normative behavior as well as deviant signs in the new situation.

In short, dynamic evaluation of the physically disabled requires an understanding of what constitutes significant behavior in the varied settings and changing situations of rehabilitation; how to find and identify such behavior; and what it means in the total picture particularly in regard to a client's ability to attain the rehabilitation goal, the conditions under which he is most likely to succeed, the precautions that need to be observed, and the nature of the residual handicaps if any.

THE PSYCHOLOGIST'S PERSONAL REACTIONS TO PHYSICAL IMPAIRMENT

Psychologists have no special immunity to the general misconceptions and reactions of society toward physical defect. Some experience deep disturbance in the presence of all types of impairment; others are affected only by certain ones. Reaction may be conscious or unconscious and take the form of strong positive identification with a subject, or hostility and rejection. However expressed, in so far as personal response to disability causes a psychologist to function as less than the objective though human tool he should be, diagnosis and treatment will suffer. Rehabilitation is not an advisable area of service for those with persistent affective overresponsiveness to physical impairment.

THE EXPANDED SCOPE OF PSYCHOTHERAPY

It is a common misconception that psychotherapy refers only to the narrow range of analytic depth therapies. Actually, psychotherapy includes, to quote Diethelm, "all kinds and ways of utilizing psychologic means to achieve beneficial psychobiologic changes." [12] Those most commonly used in rehabilitation are re-

[12] Oskar Diethelm, *Treatment in Psychiatry*, 3d ed. (Springfield, Illinois: Charles C. Thomas, 1955), p. 59.

assurance, suggestion and direction, explanation and persuasion, reeducation, ventilation, and environmental manipulation. The reader is referred to Diethelm and Tyson [13] for a review of these and other therapeutic approaches.

Rehabilitation problems requiring intensive treatment are summarized by Kutash as follows:

1) patients who are resistive to the rehabilitation process refusing to make use of needed appliances or prosthetics such as hearing aids, artificial legs, or failing to take medications or recommended surgery, and the like
2) patients who are having inordinate emotional reactions and depressive reactions, or showing personality symptoms not proportionate in degree to the extent of the disability
3) patients who develop an extreme passive-dependency reaction, using their disability for the secondary gains that it brings in order to further their dependency needs
4) patients whose degree of personality, social, or vocational adjustment is out of line with the extent of the handicap or disability
5) frankly neurotic or early psychotic patients who seem motivated for therapy [14]

However, a far broader therapeutic problem in rehabilitation than intensive therapy involves the undoing effects of adverse public attitudes upon individual adjustment to physical impairment. A therapist may apply any of the foregoing therapeutic techniques to help a client accept disability, and may apply them brilliantly; but the results can just as easily as not be outweighed by the sting of social rebuff awaiting the individual in the world outside the therapist's office.

Therefore, in work with the physically disabled, the scope of treatment must be broad enough to include not only the patient but also the figures in his life whose attitudes are sufficiently power-

[13] Robert Tyson, "Current Mental Hygiene Practice: An Inventory of Basic Teachings," Monograph Supplement No. 8, *Journal of Clinical Psychology*, January, 1951.

[14] Samuel B. Kutash, "The Application of Therapeutic Procedures to the Disabled," *Clinical Aspects of Counseling with the Disabled* (Washington, D.C., Rehabilitation Service Series No. 343, 1956), pp. 11–12.

ful to impede successful adjustment. Immediate family members are figures of major importance,[15] but there are many more. Not infrequently, the need for psychotherapy on the part of these persons is greater than the client's. But whatever the situation, they must be won over to the rehabilitation team, for without their cooperation, rehabilitation can become a matter of trying to adjust a disabled individual to social inequity and to the psychopathology of others. Although this too must be done to a certain extent as part of treatment, it is not the major goal. Disability is a family, community, and social responsibility. In so far as each is involved in a disabled person's adjustment difficulties, so does each also belong within the therapeutic frame. The problem is how to reach out and get them there.

PUBLIC EDUCATION AND PREVENTIVE MENTAL HEALTH

An increasingly successful method of gaining public understanding of disability is through programs of public education. Every rehabilitation center recognizes the critical value of social acceptance in individual rehabilitation and holds community education an integral part of its service responsibilities. Provision for community education varies with the financial means of the respective facilities. Programs range from comprehensive coverage including such technical assistance as literature, lectures, and motion pictures to informal consultation among community agencies [16] and leaders. A highly important objective of such programs is preventive mental health, for it is recognized that ignorance of the facts of disability is one of the prime causes of community, family, and individual disturbance.

Although not usually thought of as a therapeutic adjunct, public education is an unusual means for strengthening a psychologist's

[15] Alexander Gralnick, "The Family in Psychotherapy." Reprinted from *Individual and Familial Dynamics,* edited by Jules H. Masserman, M.D. (New York: Grune & Stratton, 1959).

[16] Office of Vocational Rehabilitation, "Rehabilitation Centers Today" (Washington, D.C.: Rehabilitation Service Series No. 490, 1959).

treatment program. By creating a more enlightened community environment, public education directly complements individual therapy, for where a community is better prepared to accept disability, so are the families of disabled persons, and so too the persons themselves.

THE REHABILITATION TEAM

To serve the multiple problems raised by disability requires a wide array of professional specialties. As previously mentioned, these include general and specialized medical practitioners; nursing; occupational therapy; physical therapy; special therapies for sensory impairments; social service; psychology; and vocational and rehabilitation experts. Without the cooperation of these professional associates, it would be impossible for a psychologist to operate successfully in the vast area of rehabilitation. In turn, the other disciplines are increasingly interested in the gains to be derived from psychological services. Together, they form the unit of diagnosis and treatment known in rehabilitation as the "team."

Whitehouse deplores the erroneous idea that "teamwork is a matter of collecting a number of specialists and passing the client thru the various phases of rehabilitation as each professional person performs his services in turn till the client is prepared for the final stage, vocational training and/or placement." [17] The author continues:

This approach might be used to serve the less seriously disabled client. In a rehabilitation center with a seriously disabled client, it is more a process of all professions playing their parts cooperatively from the very beginning with the relative strength of each aspect timed and emphasized according to the complete picture. This rehabilitation timing is most effective when the plans and intentions of all services are known and *each major move by any one service is taken only by prior consultation with the team.* [18]

[17] Frederick A. Whitehouse, "Teamwork, an Approach to a Higher Professional Level." Reprinted from *Exceptional Children,* XVIII (December, 1951), 1.
[18] *Ibid.,* p. 2.

Where a rehabilitation team operates in this ideal way, the psychologist is afforded a unique opportunity of interpreting his specialty to a wide professional audience; of profiting from the knowledge and experience of others; and of gaining thereby in depth of understanding concerning the multiple ramifications and implications of physical disability.

RESEARCH

Research problems in rehabilitation represent the sum of the unknowns of all the participating disciplines and add up to an awesome total. A recent poll of rehabilitation personnel exploring the role of psychology in rehabilitation disclosed the following rank order of problem categories calling for investigation: [19]

1. Psychodynamic and psychosocial: theoretic and clinical
2. Special disability problems
3. Psychological evaluation, tests, and techniques
4. Psychotherapeutic techniques
5. Motivation and resistance
5. Rehabilitation team and team relationships
5. Professional competencies, qualifications, training
6. General rehabilitation issues
6. Rehabilitation and the family
7. Education and learning
8. Attitudes toward the physically disabled
9. Vocational training and placement
10. Professional terminology and communication
11. Vocational evaluation
12. Occupations and job analysis
13. General disability problems
14. Community needs
14. Economic problems, recruitment of workers, retrospective evaluation of rehabilitation

It is assumed that other specialties have equally long lists of problem categories pressing for solution.

[19] B. Wright, ed., *Psychology and Rehabilitation* (Washington, D.C.: American Psychological Association, 1959), pp. 130–38.

There is no doubt that outstanding contributions to behavioral science and human welfare are best achieved through interdisciplinary research [20] and that rehabilitation offers an ideal setting for such studies. But as matters now stand, so great is the number of problems yet to be solved that psychologists in rehabilitation are often obliged to assume the double role of investigator and clinician in the daily course of routine activity. How this works out in the case of auditory disability forms the content of Part Three of this volume.

In conclusion, rehabilitation is jarring psychology out of its rut of clinical complacency into a new spurt of inquisitiveness. Already, belated breaks with tradition are in evidence, as are renewed clinical initiative and a push for scientific advance through research. To be sure, far more remains to be accomplished than has yet been realized; but all the signs are favorable for a productive union between rehabilitation and psychology.

[20] Margaret Barron Luszki, *Interdisciplinary Team Research: Methods and Problems* (New York: New York University Press, 1958).

5. MAJOR LINES OF PSYCHOLOGICAL INQUIRY

IN SERVING the physically disabled, there comes a time when every psychologist finds himself caught up in the key rehabilitation question: What causes an impairment to generate psychological handicap in certain cases and not in others? In mulling over the answer, a number of possibilities come to mind. Perhaps it is the type of impairment that is the deciding factor. But, on second thought, this could not be; for rehabilitation successes and failures appear among persons with damage to similar structures. Is it then the degree of impairment that is the determinant? Again a negative answer, for there are numbers of individuals with relatively negligible damage who suffer greater incapacitation than their far more seriously disabled peers. What of the premorbid personality? Is this where the answer lies? Not entirely. Although a critical determinant, premorbid personality does not account for the variations in outcome found among the congenitally disabled, where there is no premorbid personality so to speak; nor does it explain rehabilitation failures among healthy personalities and successes among the less healthy.

To continue in this vein leads to one conclusion. Short of such catastrophic damage as progressive pathology of the central nervous system, there is no single factor that in and of itself can predict or control adjustment to physical disability. The answer varies from person to person and involves multiple influences and combinations of influences. In rehabilitation, the major lines of psychological inquiry are frequently directed toward establishing what these influences may be in a particular case, their relative importance, and how they can best be manipulated to attain maximum possible adjustment.

From among the areas of inquiry included in full psychological examinations of the physically disabled, a number are of particular importance in the appraisal of handicap. Because the factors involved cut across the physical boundaries separating the various disability groups, they are here too considered in the broad frame of rehabilitation rather than the narrower one of a particular disability. Basically they apply to all groups and are briefly illustrated here in terms of (1) factors influencing psychological reaction to physical disability; (2) psychodynamic processes; and (3) the problem of accepting physical disability.

Factors Influencing Psychological Reaction to Physical Disability

THE NATURE AND EXTENT OF PHYSICAL DAMAGE. By reason of the physiological functions of the structures involved, certain impairments impose greater restrictions and stresses than others, as do more severe degrees of similar physical damage. All else being equal, the less physically or mentally incapacitating the physiological restrictions, the less the likelihood of psychological handicap; or more specifically stated, a physical impairment is intrinsically incapacitating in proportion to its physiological ability to retard or distort normal development and the normal or near-normal perception and/or pursuit of life activities. Among the most potentially handicapping disabilities are those involving severe congenital sensory deficits and, of course, central nervous system damage.

AGE AND MANNER OF ONSET. As a rule, the psychological implications of a serious impairment vary with the time of life it appeared and whether the onset was sudden or gradual. In a case of absolute blindness, for example, the psychosocial implications differ considerably according to whether an individual was born blind, lost his vision while at the height of childhood enjoyment of the visible wonders of the world, suddenly became blind during the exciting time of adolescence or the peak years of adulthood, or gradually lost his vision as he approached the quiet evening of senescence. Even without deep knowledge of blindness, the importance of these differentials can be readily perceived. Where serious disability is congenital, it represents a basic influence on the developing personality. As the child grows up, he suffers no sudden shock as a result of disability because it has always been part of him, and adjustments are made in the course of maturation. However, although he escapes the traumatic impact of abrupt onset, there are other handicapping influences to which a congenitally impaired child is exposed. Among the most common are rejection, overprotection and dependence, inadequate maturational experiences both psychosocial and educational, and character defects. On the other hand, if the same serious disability were to strike in adulthood, it would threaten not only an established way of life but also established habit patterns that may now no longer suffice, hopes and aspirations, an economic and occupational position, family attitudes as well as dependents, and a wide range of interpersonal and social relationships. As a rule, the broad handicaps of congenital and early acquired severe disability are found in developmental and maturational lags; the immediate handicaps of later acquired severe disability, in emotional disturbances and psychosocial-vocational disorganization. Whether such immediate handicaps become chronic depends upon the multiple determinants involved in successful rehabilitation in a given case.

THE PHYSICAL CONDITION OF AN INDIVIDUAL. A basically healthy physical structure is better able to cope with the physical stresses of disability and better able to protect the individual from psychological tensions arising from inadequate constitutional resources. Where disability is added to a sick or already disabled body, restrictions are multiplied and the danger of psychological handicaps thereby increased.

PSYCHOLOGICAL CHARACTERISTICS AND REACTIONS OF THE INDIVIDUAL. It is generally recognized that a given impairment can provoke similar as well as widely differing reactions among persons disabled at the same time of life. That there will be a number of similar consequences of like damage is intrinsic in the physical structure of the human organism. That there will also be varying psychological responses is implicit in the principle of individual differences. The one does not rule out the other. In the past, however, characteristic derivatives of particular disabilities were taken as evidence of the unique psychologies of the disabled. The dramatic façade of impairment obscured underlying personal variations in reaction, and the defects themselves were held to create specific personality types.

In the light of present knowledge, it is recognized that there is no unique psychology of the physically disabled, just as there is no unique psychology of the nondisabled. Structural damage represents a problem to be solved, in many cases by persons who had formerly been physically intact; and in the case of the congenitally and early-childhood disabled, by persons other than the sufferers themselves, usually by the parents. The psychological significance of physical impairment varies with the individual and the situation. Thus, to a well-integrated, emotionally healthy musician, the loss of hearing will represent a severe professional and personal blow but not necessarily a psychically catastrophic experience; to a psychologically sturdy laborer, the loss may entail no more than passing inconvenience; but to a severe neurotic —whether musician, laborer, or whatever—the loss of hearing may be psychically disintegrating because of the symbolic meaning to him of the lost sensory function or the body part involved. All will experience certain common problems of audition, but this does not constitute a unique psychology. On the contrary, each will approach the problem in accordance with its particular significance to him, and will deal with it according to his established pattern of psychological response to such problems. The major determinants of response are derived from one fundamental source, and that is the complex of influences and experiences that went into the making of the particular individual. It is from this source that "psychological characteristics and reactions" are derived. Highly important modifiers of reaction are society's attitudes and environmental resources and liabilities.

ENVIRONMENTAL RESOURCES AND ATTITUDES. The greater the disparity between an individual's actual or potential predisability way of life and the opportunities, attitudes, and relationships that await him after disability, the greater the psychological threat. The threat becomes a psychological handicap when an individual experiences severe social and vocational devaluation as a result of disability, when unhealthy psychic mechanisms are activated, and when community resources are unable to provide needed adjustment services and rehabilitation facilities.

TIME BETWEEN ONSET OF DISABILITY AND COMMENCEMENT OF REHABILITATION. The longer the time that elapses between the onset of disability and the beginning of needed rehabilitation, the less promising the outlook and the greater the prospects of psychological handicap. As time goes by, patterns of inadequate adaptation become fixed, and the individual is less responsive to new procedures and motivations. Optimally, a proper psychological climate for recovery should be instituted from the time of onset of disability.

Although itemized as separate factors for the sake of convenience, in actual operation the foregoing influences function as a unit system, so that in evaluation each must be additionally assessed in terms of the others. In connection with these factors, a pertinent study is reported by Masterman of the kinds of psychological interference with rehabilitation found in a sampling "of 250 handicapped people who were judged by a rehabilitation team to have the potentiality for profiting from rehabilitation services." [1] The study is described as "representative of the kinds of handicapped people with whom rehabilitation workers must be prepared to work." [2] The study group consisted of 135 males and 115 females from one to ninety-one years of age with a mean I.Q. of 88.73 and included welfare and nonwelfare cases, cardiac, obese, arthritic, and blind patients, and speech-handicapped children. In the concluding summary it is stated that "eighty-three percent of the study patients were thus handicapped beyond the actual limitations resulting from physical disability" and that "48 percent, almost half, did have psychological problems serious enough that some kind of special treatment or service was indicated if the rehabilitation goals were to be attained." [3] If representative, these findings are indeed ominous and call for serious consideration of expanded facilities for the intensive study and treatment of factors influencing psychological reaction to dissability.

Psychodynamic Processes

Turning again to Masterman's study, we find that the specific psychological factors which the investigators selected as possible deterrents to rehabilitation were:

[1] Louis E. Masterman, *Psychological Aspects of Rehabilitation* (Initial Status Studies, Kansas City, Missouri: Community Studies, Inc., July, 1958), p. 13.
[2] *Ibid.*, p. 14.   [3] *Ibid.*, pp. 73, 74.

Academic underachievement
Anxiety
Dependency
Depression
Fantasy
Guilt
Hostility
Hypochondriasis
Inadequate emotional control
Interpersonal difficulties
Lack of parental understanding
Lack of self-confidence

Need for tender emotions
Overprotection
Projection of blame
Psychosexual problems
Psychosomatic complaints
Reaction to standards
Rejection
Resentment of authority
Social withdrawal
Thinking inefficiency
Unrealistically high goals [4]

The kinds of outward behavior implied by these terms are familiar to all experienced workers who have ever struggled to achieve total rehabilitation for a client with "psychological problems." However, externally observed problem-behavior is only the tip of the iceberg. It is the vast subsurface mass that constitutes a worker's major obstacle. Some of the implications contained in this hidden mass are briefly illustrated here in terms of (*a*) psychodynamic aspects of sudden, severe disability and (*b*) psychodynamic aspects of motivation.

PSYCHODYNAMIC ASPECTS OF SUDDEN, SEVERE DISABILITY

The initial impact of sudden, severe physical impairment leaves in its wake not only an injured body but often a shaken psychic structure as well. That the body requires immediate attention is usually obvious on inspection. What is not so apparent is that a state of disorientation to self may be present that also requires expert attention. With the suddenly severely disabled in particular, the psychological aspects of rehabilitation begin with self-reorientation.

Orientation to self is a fundamental derivative of human development. It serves to acclimatize an individual to his own characteristic

[4] *Ibid.*, p. 18.

patterns of thinking, perceiving, and reacting; it functions as a base of reference and response to the behavior and attitudes of others, and to the stimulation, values, and influences of a social setting. Self-orientation evolves from the interaction of the three basic developmental forces: body, psychic potentials, and environment. Its maintenance depends upon a balanced interplay of these forces and of their developmental equivalents.

In the course of maturation, the original nuclei of self-orientation (body, psychic potentials, and environment) acquire identities which are perceived by the individual as corporal identity, psychic identity, and social identity. Each of these is bound to the others by strong operational as well as developmental ties. Psychic identity would not be possible without a body; corporal identity could not be achieved without psychic awareness; nor could either be attained without an activating environment.

Furthermore, so closely interrelated are the systems that each has its counterpart within the other. The psychic counterpart of the body is the body-image.[5] This includes not only the physical structure but also the symbolic meaning of the body parts to the individual as well as a mental image of the body in countless actions, roles, and experiences. Not being able to see the body throughout the day as in a mirror, we see it performing in our mind's eye instead. The body in turn is represented within the psychic structure as the nucleus of the self. Self is born with the infant's epochal discovery that his body is something distinct from the external world. Finally, environment is represented within the psychic structure as character, values, and ideals. Together, these confluent systems form the concept known to the individual as "I" as apart from the "you" of the rest of the world. In the external world, "I" and "you" are represented as the units of a social structure.

[5] Paul Schilder, *The Image and Appearance of the Human Body* (New York: International Universities Press, Inc., 1950).

When any one of these interlocking systems comes to harm, the others are endangered. This is implicit in the nature of their relationship. Psychic distress can cause physical symptoms; physical illness, emotional symptoms; and environmental deprivation, both psychic and physical disturbance. These are generally recognized facts.

What is not generally appreciated is that when sudden, severe physical impairment strikes, the impact is felt not only upon the body but in the other systems as well. At the stroke of somatic assault, there is an impaired life environment and a shaken psychic structure. Corporal identity, psychic identity, and social identity are all imperiled, for they are bound to each other in illness as in health.

The initial environmental counterpart of severe physical disability is severe environmental deprivation; the initial psychic counterpart, disorientation to self. Thus, because the newly blinded adult is unable to use his eyes as sensory organs, he is cut off from all visible evidence of and visual contact with his own being. When he automatically turns to the mirror to see how he looks, he sees nothing. Similarly, his world undergoes drastic dissolution from a place of familiar sights, figures, and activities to a visually barren wasteland shrouded in heavy, impenetrable mist. Blindness has swept away all visible points of reference to self as well as to surroundings. The profoundly deafened adult suddenly finds himself a soundless creature whose tread has no audible counterpart in his ears, whose body no longer keeps him acoustically informed of its physical activities, who is separated as by a wall of silence from the sounds of his own voice. His world is now a deadened vacuum in which silent people move busily about their muted ways. The newly crippled adult sees in his remembered place a strange deformed being in a world that is shrunk and imbalanced by the distortions of his impaired bodily movement. Time and compensatory adjustments ease the changes; but in the beginning the impact of sudden physical disability can be a shattering experience.

Something of the effects of such experiences comes to us by way of the growing body of research in environmental deprivation. The studies cover a wide range of situations, some contrived in the laboratory, others occurring in life. In one of the laboratory experiments,[6] the subject's environment is shrunk to a bed in a small, closed cubicle. A state of blindness is simulated by having him wear frosted goggles that admit light but do not allow pattern vision; a state of deafness by having his ears covered with a sponge-rubber pillow; and tactual and motor restraint by covering his hands with gloves and cardboard cuffs that reach from upper forearm to below the fingertips. The result, to quote Hebb, are "dramatic." [7]

Cut off from normal environmental stimulation for as little as a day or so, the subjects developed a wide variety of temporarily impaired functions, including personality changes; disturbed motor control; extensive loss in simple problem solving; peculiar disturbances in visual perception; and extraordinary visual hallucinations and dream states. Of particular interest were reported feelings of bodily otherness and strangeness, of psychophysical disorientation.

The latter findings were confirmed in life by the results of an investigation [8] of the reactions of poliomyelitis patients to confinement in tank-type respirators. Here too it was found that "disorientation was the common substrate" [9] lasting from ten to fifteen days following confinement. Still further confirmation of the disorganizing potentials of drastic environmental change is derived from life studies [10] of factors used to weaken personality in forced

[6] D. O. Hebb, "The Mammal and His Environment," *American Journal of Psychiatry*, III (1955), 826–31.

[7] *Ibid.*, p. 829.

[8] I. Solomon, H. Leiderman, J. Mendelson, and D. Wexler, "Sensory Deprivation: A Review," *American Journal of Psychiatry*, CXIV (1957), 357–63.

[9] *Ibid.*, p. 362.

[10] Group for the Advancement of Psychiatry, Symposium No. 3, *Factors Used to Increase the Susceptibility of Individuals to Forceful Indoctrination*, December, 1956.

indoctrination. Final confirmation comes from the emotionally disrupting potentials of progressive and sudden deafness, as previously reviewed. To sum up in the words of Hebb: "Even at maturity then the organism is still essentially dependent on a normal sensory environment for the maintenance of its psychological integrity." [11]

Sudden, severe physical disability impairs accustomed stimulations from the external world; upsets the balance among somatic, psychic, and environmental derivatives; and by so doing threatens psychological integrity. A strange unreality about self, as about surroundings, engulfs the newly disabled individual. The self with which he had lived all the years of his life, the world in which he grew up, the body image in his mind's eye, the values he attaches to his role in life are still those of the physically intact person he was. As yet, this is the only self he knows; this is the "I." But here before him is the actuality of, let us say, a maimed body and a shrunken world. How to reconcile memory and actuality when neither has a counterpart within the other? In the ensuing struggle, there occur sharp moments of panic and depersonalization during which the self is momentarily lost.

Unlike the experimental subject, the newly disabled person cannot get up and leave his cubicle when anxiety becomes intolerable. His body *is* the cubicle; his changed environment, the outer manifestation of his body's damaged state. He cannot walk out and leave them behind; not unless he walks out through the doors of neurotic or psychotic escape, the traditional exits of the unhealthy psyche.

To help the newly disabled person regain orientation to self, therefore, is the first and crucial step of rehabilitation; for rehabilitation cannot be achieved without active *self*-participation. Mending the damaged body is essential toward this end, but it is not enough. There are ties to reality that must be mended too, and this

[11] Hebb, "The Mammal and His Environment," *American Journal of Psychiatry*, III (1955), 829.

is often more difficult to accomplish. Ties to reality present no tangible substance such as a physical structure with which to work. Knowledge of how to manipulate psychic intangibles to bring about a desired result—as well as awareness of when a desired result has been effected—is no less demanding of technical competence than is the ability to effect physical restoration. The delicate assignment is best supervised or handled by specialists whose knowledge of human behavior qualifies them for the task.

Equally important in helping an individual regain self-orientation are the influences of family and close associates. We see ourselves largely through the eyes of others, and a great part of self-concept is a reflection of how others see us. When a newly disabled person meets the old familiar acceptance in the eyes, bearing, and behavior of his family and friends, he will be moved to adopt the same attitudes toward himself. But if he is not accepted, then he feels all the more another person.

It must be emphasized, however, that regained orientation following severe disability does not imply automatic acceptance of the changes incurred. Orientation to self is the first step; orientation to a *disabled* self, the next. As preparation for the latter, the regained self must now consciously part with its old image in order to make way for the new. In parting, the loss is mourned as for a dearly beloved friend who takes with him the heritage of the past and leaves behind a cold, uncertain future. This is a time of grief, of depression, of bitter denunciation of life and fate, of aggression against the world. It is a time of emotional unburdening that signifies the individual is beginning to take in the reality of his new situation. Whether he will put up the good fight or go under is an aspect of the complex problem of motivation.

PSYCHODYNAMIC ASPECTS OF MOTIVATION

The wish to master reality is inherent in the nature of man. But when reality takes the traumatic form of severe somatic assault, the organism recoils. As a result, the individual's inner drive toward positive adaptation is brought into sharp conflict with the automatic tendency to avoid pain and danger. The outcome of the conflict depends upon the strength of the opposing forces and upon environmental resources. Decisive factors in the struggle are the psychological maturity of the individual; the nature of his past experiences; his present environmental assets and liabilities; and constitutional and genetic determinants. Again the old triad of interlocking systems of soma, psyche, and environment.

THE MATURE PERSONALITY. The mature personality is one that possesses not only a strong inner urge for psychological wholeness but also sufficient free psychic energy and intellectual awareness to master whatever painful facts must be faced in the service of reality. Strong inner motivation for positive adaptation is the crucial asset of the healthy structure. Thus, after the initial disorientation, unburdening, and recoil the mature organism mobilizes it forces and prepares to give battle.

The beginning advance into disability-held territory is hesitant and tentative; for this is unfamiliar ground. The critical need is for outer reinforcements to guide and steady the advance. Such support is derived from rehabilitation services and influences and includes an explanation of what lies ahead; guidance in planning maneuvers and instruction in the use of compensatory aids; the help, confidence, and respect of the rehabilitation team guides; the faith of loved ones; rationale goals; and, above all, knowledge that a role in life is the reward of victory.

With inner motivation supported by such external forces, it becomes possible for the individual to endure the rigors of battle. He may pause for reassurance and even retreat at times. But on the whole, progress is steady providing external rehabilitation motivation is maintained as required. That this is not always possible is one of the great frustrations of rehabilitation workers. A powerful disrupting agent is society. Often, there is a repeated undoing by social devaluation of gains won only through extraordinary feats of personal endurance. Even the healthy personality can go down in defeat before such negative actions and attitudes.

Where outer resources are optimally maintained, the individual's growing inner assurance gradually supplants the need for as much assistance as was originally required. In rehabilitation terms, the person is learning how to help himself. In so doing, he ultimately acquires positive mastery over disability in the service of psychological integrity.

THE NEUROTIC PERSONALITY. With certain individuals, particular events experienced under special conditions arouse strong affective associations with painful conflicts of childhood that were never adequately resolved. Physical impairment can represent such an event. Where this is the case, the automatic reaction to the tensions activated by impairment is to stabilize them through attempting to gain belated mastery over the old conflicts. Toward this end, the individual's habitual psychic mechanisms for dealing with anxiety go into action.

However, the operation of these mechanisms consumes vital psychic energy, and this does not come in unlimited quantities. Thus, the amount available for the purposeful solution of the problems of disability will depend upon how much energy is bound up in the inner struggles. If enough free energy remains for the adaptive demands of rehabilitation, even a neurotic personality can achieve a measure of success in rational adjustment to disability. In many instances, it may be necessary to reinforce the usual rehabilitative measures by such psychotherapeutic services [12] as reassurance; removal of external pressures; modification of attitudes in the environment; opportunity for healthy identifica-

[12] Gustav Bychowski and J. Louise Despert, eds., *Specialized Techniques in Psychotherapy* (New York: Basic Books, Inc., 1952).

tions; provision for the development of acceptable compensations for fear, hostility, and feelings of inadequacy; and opportunities for ventilation. If the individual qualifies for the deeper therapies and is in a sound position to undertake such treatment, there is of course no contraindication.

On the other hand, where a severe neurotic reaction is precipitated by physical impairment, too little free psychic energy is available for effecting healthy adaptations. Whereas the forces of the mature personality are mobilized to deal with disability on a reality level, the energies of the severe neurotic are consumed by internal struggles and the problems of disability become an extension of the more basic neurotic conflicts.

In effecting this latter move, the operation, while psychically economical, is made from weakness. However, there is titanic strength in the weakness of severely neurotic mechanisms. There is strength to resist the demands of objective reality; strength to withstand the ordinary inducements offered by rehabilitation; and strength to oppose the appeals of logic and reason. In the seriously neurotic personality, objective reality is less compelling than the pull of the internal world in which the center of the stage is held by trauma and unsatisfied needs rooted in childhood but more forcefully dominant still than events in the world about. The usual attempts of rehabilitation counselors to motivate individuals trapped in severe neurosis are as nothing before the power of these inner dictates whose basic aim is to reduce anxiety and avoid pain. Appeals to reason and logic fall on deaf ears when screened by such internal masters, for to them the language of rational logic is an unknown idiom.

In some cases, the discomforts of neurosis are alleviated by using disability to gain advantages from the external world or to satisfy inner demands. Such secondary gains phenomena are familiar to most rehabilitation workers. The kind of gain acquired varies with the type of neurosis. As summarized by Fenichel:

In different types of neuroses secondary gains are predominant: in anxiety hysteria, the regression to childhood times, when one was still protected; in hysteria, gaining attention through "acting" and sometimes the gain of material advantages; in compulsion neurosis, narcissistic gains through pride in illness; in organ neurosis, the denial of psychic conflicts by their projection onto the physical sphere.[13]

In short, to pit the inducements to recovery offered by the rehabilitation worker against the powerful inner motivations of the severe neurotic is a discouraging assignment. The worker's appeals are directed largely to the client's rational processes, whereas the thwarting mechanisms are generally well beyond the client's rational control. The individual is not intentionally resisting rehabilitation. He is rather the pawn of his neurosis. Such a person may *know* he is a rehabilitation failure, but it is hard for him to *feel* particularly dismayed about it. He *is* adjusting, albeit on a pathological level. To penetrate his defenses, which in fact may not be at all advisable in a given case, requires highly specialized techniques. In rehabilitating the severe neurotic, therefore, heed should be given the statement by Menninger that "it is in this area that the psychiatrist, with his particular insight into the deep-lying, irrational and unconscious forces that determine the direction and intensity of motivation can make a specific contribution to the rehabilitation team." [14]

CHARACTER AND BEHAVIOR DISORDERS. In the behavioral range between the mild neurotic and the frank psychotic are numbers of psychopathological personality types that belong to neither category. Classified as "character and behavior disorders," such personality types are distinguished by their ingrained constancy of

[13] Otto Fenichel, *The Psychoanalytic Theory of Neurosis* (New York: W. W. Norton & Company, Inc., 1945), p. 462.

[14] James F. Garrett, ed., *Psychological Aspects of Physical Disability* (Rehabilitation Service Series No. 120; Washington, D.C.: Office of Vocational Rehabilitation, 1952), p. 9.

response to widely differing stimuli and experiences. Some consistently react with hostility; others, with passive compliance, resentment, distrust, suspicion of authority figures, or other kinds of set patterns. The motivational difficulties presented are obvious.

The Veterans Administration Technical Bulletin describes these disorders as "characterized by developmental defects or pathological trends in the personality structure, with minimal subjective anxiety, and little or no sense of distress. In most instances, the disorder is manifested by a life-long pattern of action or behavior ('Acting out'), rather than by mental or emotional symptoms." [15] Fenichel states that in a majority of cases "the special attitude has been forced on the individual by the external world." [16]

The treatment of character and behavior disorders is one of psychiatry's traditional problems. This being so, how much greater the difficulties for the conscientious rehabilitation worker who all unaware of the nature of the pathology seeks to motivate such clients to overcome their psychological handicaps. Clinical psychology can be of assistance in identifying such personality types, but psychiatry has yet to point the way to treatment. The pragmatic approaches used in rehabilitation provide an ideal laboratory-in-life for the investigation of treatment devices.

SOCIOCULTURAL INFLUENCES. To bring total rehabilitation to the large mass of disabled people who live in close contact with everyday problems of survival is still another problem in motivation. Rehabilitation is one of the few professions that has attempted to cope with this problem in actual field operations. Social work is another. Both have had ample opportunity to work with the whole of whole man, which must always include his sociocultural environment; both have had close professional experiences

---

[15] Veterans Administration Technical Bulletin TB 10A–78, *Nomenclature of Psychiatric Disorders and Reactions* (Washington, D.C., 1947), pp. 5–6.
[16] Fenichel, *Psychoanalytic Theory of Neurosis*, p. 468.

with the "functional linkages between sociocultural variables and the development of 'disturbed' behavior in the individual." [17]

In their community study of social class and mental illness, Hollingshead and Redlich describe one such linkage as follows:

> The struggle for existence is a meaningful reality to these people. Their level of skill is low, and their jobs poorly paid, and they have no savings to carry them over a crisis. Adults are resentful of the way they have been treated by employers, clergymen, teachers, doctors, police, and other representatives of organized society. They express their resentments freely in the home and in other primary groups. Children hear them, believe them, and react to the targets of the parent's hostility in ways that are generally approved by the parents. . . . As a consequence, hostility breeds more hostility.[18]

There are, of course, many other types of linkages between the varied sociocultural groups and their respective members. The questions that worry the rehabilitation worker are: To what extent can motivation penetrate such ties? through what means? and guided by what theoretic principles?

Answers to these questions should logically be found in the domains of social science and psychiatry. But Hollingshead and Redlich accuse psychiatry of giving "only passing attention to the sociocultural environment that envelops the human being" [19] and both social scientists and psychiatrists of carrying on their researches and developing their theories "in splendid isolation," [20] particularly in the years before World War II. It is therefore not surprising to find divergence between theory and practice in the rehabilitation of man as a sociocultural as well as a psychobiologic organism. Theory has not yet caught up with practice; and the questions of the rehabilitation worker will so remain until the gap is bridged between the theoretic postulates of sociology and those of psychiatry.

[17] August B. Hollingshead and Frederick C. Redlich, *Social Class and Mental Illness* (New York: John Wiley & Sons, Inc., 1958), pp. 9–10.
[18] *Ibid.*, p. 135.   [19] *Ibid.*, p. 9.   [20] *Ibid.*, p. 10.

Rehabilitation can make a significant contribution toward bridging the gap in the form of data gathered through years of varied efforts to "motivate" individuals who represent an extraordinary range of psychobiologic and sociocultural variables. The frames of present studies in rehabilitation therapies [21] are narrowed by established theoretic dogma of one kind or another. A broader and more fundamental line of inquiry would be to subject the results of the various pragmatic measures employed by rehabilitation workers to intensive, systematic analysis in order to check the adequacy of present theory and point the way to necessary reformulation. It is this writer's strong conviction that the wide experiences of the foot soldiers of the service professions—the field and case workers—who minister to human need wherever it is housed, represent a unique source of information for the expansion of therapeutic theory and practice in behalf of that long-neglected body known as the population-at-large.

The Problem of Accepting Physical Disability

In the adjustment to physical defect, the complexities of motivation represent one side of the coin. On the other are inscribed the trying problems the individual faces in accepting reality. Of these, two shall be briefly considered to illustrate something of what is involved when a psychic structure derived from one environment and way of life must bend to the demands of another. The two are (1) self-acceptance and (2) social acceptance.

SELF-ACCEPTANCE. To accept a disabled self is difficult at all times, but especially so when disability attacks during the peak years of adulthood. The individual, having himself been a physically intact member of the community not too long ago, is painfully aware of

---

[21] Leonard Diller, "Rehabilitation Therapies." Reprinted from D. Brower and L. Abt, eds., *Progress in Clinical Psychology*, Vol. III (New York: Grune & Stratton, 1958).

how he formerly regarded the physically disabled. Now that he is disabled, he is faced with the problem of preventing his own past attitudes from contaminating his present problems and self-concept. Among the questions that crowd in upon him are: Where will he now fit in the domestic scene? How will he measure up to his former role of father, husband, sweetheart? How will friends, neighbors, and community regard him? Where will he now belong in the occupational world? Buffeted by doubts, insecurity, and feelings of inadequacy, the individual must nevertheless accept his disabled self if he is ever to achieve mastery over disability.

There is, of course, no universal procedure as to how self-acceptance can be attained. Individual, environment, and type of disability are all involved. However, the basic rehabilitation approach to individual need is through a plan of compensatory enrichment by which an individual's personal resources are maximally developed to foster increased self-esteem and facilitate self-acceptance. Thus, interests and outlets are broadened to make up for the gaps left by disability; physical modalities are raised to their greatest proficiency to narrow the area of physical limitation; distress is sublimated through the redirection of interests and energies toward satisfying and accessible goals; and self-devaluation is diminished by building up the ego. That society may tear it down again is the persistent danger that lurks outside the rehabilitation center.

SOCIAL ACCEPTANCE. As yet, society takes neither kindly nor intelligently to physical disability. Devaluating attitudes appear in many forms and crop up in many places. They appear in forms ranging from maudlin pity to frank rejection. They crop up in family as well as community; in education, vocation, and recreation; in courtship, marriage, and parenthood. When society's attitudes penetrate the disabled person's painfully acquired self-acceptance, the spark of motivation that has kept him going grows dim.

To prevent the spark from going out altogether, to rekindle it, in fact, is among the most pressing of rehabilitation's objectives. It is also one of its outstanding problems; for there are numbers of "outside" persons involved in an individual's rehabilitation, and workers cannot reach them all to modify uncompromising attitudes and misconceptions.

For one, there is the employer. To a disabled individual, a job symbolizes independence, self-esteem, heightened regard in the eyes of others. A job makes it easier for an individual to accept his physical dependencies when he knows that there are others dependent on him for support. Nevertheless, the President's Committee on Employment of the Physically Handicapped reports [22] that employer resistance to hiring the disabled is still one of the most critical of rehabilitation problems. Vocational placement is more difficult to accomplish by far than vocational retraining.[23]

There are other devaluating figures besides employers. Not infrequently, they are members of the individual's immediate family. They may also include friends, co-workers, supervisors, classmates, neighbors, and the like. Traditional misconceptions and superstitions concerning disability are still very much alive in the public mind, and many persons, including those themselves disabled, experience deep inner discomfort in the presence of bodily impairment, even when it is one of the invisible disabilities such as tuberculosis, cardiac damage, epilepsy. In some instances, uncontrollable fears, anxiety, and revulsion are aroused. Where such reactions are experienced by family members, particularly husband or wife, the results can be catastrophic for all concerned.

In short, it requires more than a healthy predisability personality to weather the stresses of social prejudice and ignorance. A healthy

[22] President's Committee on Employment of the Physically Handicapped, *Employer Resistance to Hiring the Handicapped: A Survey Summary* (Washington, D.C., 1956).

[23] Federation Employment and Guidance Service Research Staff, *Survey of Employers' Practices and Policies in the Hiring of Physically Impaired Workers*, May, 1959.

structure is a basic asset; a strong rehabilitation team, a life-line; but the ultimate outcome more often than not lies with the family, the community, and society. Where these are lacking in understanding, even a healthy personality may have trouble in survival.

Summary

Evaluation, treatment, and prevention of psychological handicap are key problems in rehabilitation and major functions of psychologists operating in rehabilitation settings. Of the current psychological approaches to such handicaps, two popular trends stand forth. The first is personality oriented; in this, the major cause of handicap is generally laid at the door of premorbid personality inadequacies stemming from unresolved conflicts and trauma of early childhoood. The healthy premorbid personality is presumably immune from psychological harm. The second approach is disability oriented and bears a striking resemblance to the old "unique psychologies" belief. Here research is centered upon demonstrating a direct relationship between disability and personality characteristics.[24]

While there are certain elements of validity in each of the foregoing viewpoints, their major weakness lies in the fact that they generally fail to take into account other handicap determinants than those contained in their own narrow frames. The range of determinants of psychological reaction to disability reviewed in this chapter include: (*a*) the nature and extent of physical damage; (*b*) age and manner of onset; (*c*) the physical condition of the individual; (*d*) the psychological characteristics of the individual at the time of onset of disability, the impact of disability upon his way of life, and the symbolic meaning of the particular impairment to the individual; (*e*) social attitudes and environmental re-

---

[24] Daniel N. Wiener, "Personality Characteristics of Selected Disability Groups," *Journal of Clinical Psychology*, IV (1948), 285–90; Diller, "Rehabilitation Therapies."

sources; and (*f*) time between the onset of disability and the commencement of rehabilitation.

Turning to the first view, it is agreed that the unhealthy premorbid personality is more apt to acquire additional psychological handicaps as a result of physical disability. But we must bear in mind that the "unhealthy personality" classification includes as heterogeneous an assortment of individuals as the "healthy personality" category, and possibly more so. Examples were given of (*a*) neurotic personalities; (*b*) character and behavior disorders; and (*c*) representatives of various sociocultural influences. There are others. To reduce them all to a common denominator based on some vague "emotional-conflicts" hypothesis is becoming an increasingly common habit among rehabilitation workers. There is great danger that the habit may lead to a corresponding narrowing and uniformity in rehabilitation approach, based on a dichotomy of healthy vs. unhealthy premorbid personality. As to the second view—the "unique psychologies" trend—it requires only brief deliberation to realize that although the various physical disabilities can create common problems and provoke correspondingly common reactions, they cannot create common personalities.

In conclusion, it cannot be emphasized strongly enough that where rehabilitation resources are ample, where rehabilitation is begun soon enough, where family and community attitudes are receptive, and where the type of disability and the circumstances under which it was incurred do not arouse too deep disorganization, even the less healthy personality has a good chance for success. But where rehabilitation resources are inadequate, where there is constant social and vocational devaluation, and where family attitudes are rejective, it is doubtful whether the healthy structure can withstand the impact of serious physical impairment.

The theoretic rationale underlying these and other pragmatic outcomes of rehabilitation may not yet be clearly formulated; but one generalization at least can safely be made at this time, and that is: just as the psychological identity of the human organism is derived from the interaction of body, psychic potentials, and environment, so are the psychological implications of physical disability and the outcomes of rehabilitation determined by the dynamic interdependence of somatic, environmental, and psychic forces. No one of these factors can be considered of less importance than the others in the total rehabilitation of the whole person.

Part Three

PSYCHOLOGICAL EXAMINATION AND EVALUATION OF PERSONS WITH IMPAIRED HEARING

Introduction
THE PSYCHOLOGICAL EXAMINATION

Purpose of the Examination

EFFECTIVE rehabilitation presupposes some broad knowledge on the part of a worker of accepted methods for dealing with given adjustment problems. The matter would be simply solved if every problem had its own routine solution. But this Utopian ideal does not obtain in life. In actual practice, similar needs and problems acquire highly distinctive characteristics by way of the individuals experiencing them. For example, of two hearing-impaired adults with a similar need for speech therapy, the one who is deaf and has never heard the sound of the voice requires an entirely different approach from the one who is hard of hearing and can hear all but certain consonant sounds; or if both are deaf, the one who has never been exposed to speech-development training requires different rehabilitation planning from the one with well-developed speech patterns. The rationale underlying these simple illustrations holds for more complex needs and deeper problems. In effect, appropriate management of a problem requires an understanding not only of the nature of the difficulty but even more of the nature of the individual. To clarify both is the function of the psychological examination. More specifically, the purpose of a psychological examination is to obtain as clear an understanding of an individual and his needs as is necessary to help him effect life adjustments with maximum possible benefit to himself and to society.

Methods and Techniques of Examination

There are four major methods for obtaining the information on which psychological appraisal is based. They are the case history; the interview; observation; and psychological testing. It is a common misconception that these represent techniques of evaluation. They do not. They are merely the means for gathering the necessary facts about a person. Appraisal, on the other hand, lies not in collecting facts but in the identification and interpretation of significant details. The only instrument designed for this latter function is the examiner himself. There is no psychological technique that can replace clinical competence and experience.

The amount of information needed to understand a particular individual and his problems varies from case to case. Intensive psychological examination is neither required nor conducted in all instances. For example, a well-adjusted young high-school graduate who seeks educational or vocational guidance would not need the same scope of examination as a young adult with a history of chronic vocational failure, a child with bizarre behavior, or a senescent in a state of depression. In some cases complete work-up is called for; in others, selected lines of inquiry suffice. Again, clinical judgment determines the design of examination and the amount of information needed for diagnostic appraisal in a given case.

Where problems are serious and difficult to analyze, all four examination approaches are generally used. The special advantage of using all four approaches is that each taps information from a different source, thus providing an examiner with broader coverage than would be possible through a single method. The case history provides information about an individual's past as obtained from a variety of informants representing different points of view. The interview supplies facts given directly by the individual himself.

Observation yields findings that are expressed in a subject's appearance and behavior. Psychological testing provides objective information about an individual's basic endowments and actual levels of function in various significant areas. Through this battery of approaches, a balanced proportion of subjective, objective, and reported information is obtained covering both past and present. It is from the pool of data thus assembled that psychological appraisals are made and predictive inferences drawn.

Problems in the Examination of the Hearing-impaired

In applying these examination techniques to persons with impaired hearing, special problems arise. They range from relatively minor modifications of procedure sometimes required by mildly hearing-impaired adults to highly unique difficulties encountered among individuals severely deaf since birth or early childhood. The major problems of examination are found among this latter group—the deaf—and are derived from difficulties in language and concept communication between examiner and subject as well as from the scarcity of psychological tests that may profitably be used with the deaf. The major difficulties of diagnosis are encountered at the preschool and young childhood levels where impaired hearing may exist with or simulate such conditions as mental defect, congenital auditory imperception, psychiatric disorder, emotional disturbance, and behavioral and learning deviations due to neurological involvements. The problem of differential diagnosis in such instances is extremely difficult.[1] So also is the problem of psychological diagnosis among individuals whose auditory response patterns show persistent and substantial differences between the amount of hearing loss claimed and the amount obtained on

[1] Helmer R. Myklebust, *Auditory Disorders in Children* (New York: Grune & Stratton, 1954).

audiometric testing. Into this category fall the so-called psychogenic cases and malingerers.[2] Even among the straight hard of hearing, who as a group present the least impediments to psychological examination, difficulties appear as the group members approach the borderline between the deaf and the hard of hearing. And a final problem in work with hearing-impaired persons is the time required for a psychological examination. Where communications difficulties arise, three or four times the amount of time ordinarily required may be necessary.

Purpose of the Guides

To cover the total range of problems likely to arise in the psychological evaluation of hearing-impaired individuals is beyond the scope of this volume. In fact, no such herculean objective was contemplated. The principal aim of the guides that follow is to provide psychologists with suggestions and cautions where difficulties in examination are most apt to occur, and to clarify the rationale of special procedures and lines of inquiry.

For the convenience of the reader, the deaf and the hard of hearing are treated in separate sections, with suggestions that apply equally to both noted as they occur. In each group, examination procedures are considered in terms of the four basic approaches, namely: the case history, the interview, observation, and psychological testing. In addition, breakdown into chronological levels is carried out where pertinent. However, it cannot be stressed strongly enough that the basic prerequisite for successful examination is an understanding of the implications of auditory disability. Without this fundamental guide, psychological examination is a static procedure with little if any interpretative significance.

It must finally be noted that the psychological aspects of impaired

[2] N. Rh. Blegvad, "Psychogenic Deafness (Emotional Deafness)," *Acta Oto-Laryngologica*, XL (1951–52), 283–96.

hearing, especially of early severe deafness, have only recently begun to attract clinical interest. The guides are offered at this time in response to practical need and not as standard procedures. On the contrary, it is the writer's aim and hope that this publication will stimulate broader clinical and research studies of auditory dysfunction so that the psychological problems of persons with hearing and language disorders can be more fully explored and more effective procedures of examination developed.

Section A: The Deaf

6. THE CASE HISTORY

THE DATA contained in a case history [1] represent factors and influences that go into the making of a human being. They relate the genetic, somatic, and psychological facts of development; the socioeconomic, cultural, and emotional climate of environment; and the major and minor motivations of behavior. At any time of life, an individual is the product of his past experiences. To a trained psychologist, a full history provides most of the leads needed for understanding the nature and problems of a subject.

Where serious disability was a nuclear influence in development, the case history takes on exceptional value. This is the situation with the deaf. Here, severe auditory restriction and the developing personality are bound together by close historico-genetic ties. But the nature of the ties varies from person to person, and the course of events leading to a given outcome is not easily analyzed. Psychological tests are of limited assistance because they stress present status rather than developmental precedents, and deal with the past mainly by implication. Further, as already noted, the armamentarium of psychological tests for the deaf is exceptionally limited even for the evaluation of present status. Interview also has its drawbacks because of the communications obstacles encountered in the deaf group. As a result, it is to the case history

[1] B. Thompson and A. M. Barrett, eds., *Casework Performance in Vocational Rehabilitation.* Compiled from Proceedings of Guidance, Training, and Placement Workshops. U.S. Department of Health, Education, and Welfare: Office of Vocational Rehabilitation. G.T.P. Bulletin No. 1. Rehabilitation Service Series No. 505, May, 1959.

that psychologists are obliged to turn for major assistance in the diagnostic appraisal of deaf persons.

To understand what a case history has to tell about the deaf requires a reevaluation of ordinary developmental experiences and influences in terms of their vulnerability to deafness. How vulnerable, for example, are mental, scholastic, social, and emotional development to lack of hearing ability; how vulnerable the normal environment, parent-child relations, community acceptance, personal fulfillment? What factors constitute psychological assets and liabilities in the life of one who cannot hear? What attainments represent the average, the unusual, the failing? What personality traits characterize the normative, the exceptional, the deviate? To what extent may the deaf be assessed by hearing standards?

Definitive answers to most of these questions are still matters for research. But there is a goodly amount of sound empiric knowledge from which diagnostic inferences can be drawn. However, in drawing inferences from case history data, the examiner is strongly cautioned that individual items of information have little meaning in themselves. As discrete data, they may be likened to the unassembled pieces of a jigsaw puzzle. It is only when the relationship of the pieces to one another and to the whole is perceived that they fall into logical place and the diagnostic picture emerges.

Special Considerations in the Case Histories of the Deaf

A case history form especially devised by the writer for deaf children and adults is included in this section. Since the general format is familiar to trained clinical psychologists, the rationale of most of the major headings requires no explanation. However, there are a number of special lines of inquiry that warrant particular consideration in the psychological examination of the deaf. The rationale of these is briefly summarized in the following outline. The main headings of the outline correspond to those with similar letters and numbers in the history form.

A PSYCHODIAGNOSTIC AND RESEARCH DATA FORM FOR DEAF* CHILDREN AND ADULTS

Case No.   Research No.

Name   Age   Sex   Date

Home address   Phone

School address   Phone

Business address   Phone

Birth date   Birthplace   Race   Religion

Marital status: never married   married   separated   widowed.   divorced

Major communications methods: oral   manual   writing   pantomime

Parents: name   address

        birthplace   in this country since

        consanguinity

Deafness in family (specify):

II. THE PRESENTING PROBLEM

Referred by   Date

Reason for referral

Brought by   Date

Examined by   Date

Previous psychological consultations   Dates

III. DIAGNOSTIC SUMMARY

Chief difficulties

Diagnostic impression

Recommendations

---

*Deaf: onset of severe hearing loss before establishment of speech and language; or other types of hearing loss with education acquired mainly in schools for the deaf.

IV. HISTORY OF THE PRESENTING PROBLEM

Informant
Interviewed by
Date

·V. CURRENT PSYCHOSOCIAL STATUS

A. INTELLIGENCE

1. As indicated by:
   Learning ability: above average   average   below average
   Occupational status: above average   average   below average
   Family reports: above average   average   below average
   Social activities: above average   average   below average
   Play activities: above average   average   below average
   Interview, observation: above average   average   below average

2. As indicated by mental tests (list mental test history under the headings: *Date Tested; Test Used; C.A., M.A., I.Q.; Tested by; Method of Administration*)

B. SCHOLASTIC ACHIEVEMENT AND SPECIAL APTITUDES

1. Age/grade achievement ratio: retarded   average   accelerated

2. Highest grade completed:
   Graduate of·

3. Achievement and aptitude tests (list most recent test results under the headings: *Date Tested; Test Used; C.A.; Grade Score; Age Score; Special Aptitude Test Results; Tested by*)

C. PERSONALITY AND ADJUSTMENTS

1. As indicated by:
   School reports
   Family
   Employer
   Social role
   Marital adjustment
   Antisocial behavior
   Psychiatric history
   Interview, observation

2. As indicated by personality tests (list personality test history under the headings: *Date Tested; Test Used; C.A.; Test Results—Diagnostic Impression; Tested by; Method of Administration*)

3. As indicated by examiner's observations:
Acceptance of authority: defiant   rational   compliant
Flexibility: stubborn   reasonable   easily swayed
Self-assertion: obstinate   reasonable   passive
Reaction to frustration: explosive   rational control   indifferent
Interpersonal adaptability: irritable   reasonable   unconcerned   other

D. SOCIAL INTERESTS AND PARTICIPATION

1. Activities
Social clubs: member   active worker   officeholder   Club names:
Athletic clubs: member   active worker   officeholder   Club names:
Civic clubs: member   active worker   officeholder   Club names:
Churchgoer
Visiting and entertaining friends
Preference for family activities
Movies
Cards
Hobbies
Play activities (if child)
Other

2. Social preferences for: deaf   hard of hearing   hearing   no special preferences

E. MARITAL PREFERENCES AND ROLE

1. If never married:
a. Reason

b. Mate preferred: hearing   hard of hearing   deaf   no special preferences
Children preferred: hearing   hard of hearing   deaf   no special preferences

2. If married:
a. Reason for choice

b. Reasons if separated, divorced

c. Marital and sexual adjustments

d. Parent role

e. Economic and family management role

f. Intrafamily attitudes

F. SELF-EVALUATION AND ATTITUDES

    1. Attitudes toward:
    Deafness
    The deaf
    The hearing

    2. Concept of self in relation to:
    Others (deaf and hearing)
    Ambitions, frustrations
    Assets, liabilities
    Present problems

    3. Insight and judgment

G. CHECK LIST OF CHILDHOOD BEHAVIOR AND CONDUCT DISORDERS
Nail biting
Thumb sucking
Food faddisms
Vomiting
Eneuresis
Pronounced disobedience
Persistent night terrors
Habitual temper tantrums
Stealing
Abnormal aggressiveness
Truancy
Setting fires
Other

H. CHECK LIST OF PSYCHIATRIC SIGNS

    1. Signs
    Bizarre behavior
    Thinking and judgment disorders
    Mood swings and disturbances
    Disorientation: time   place   person
    Phobias, compulsions, obsessions
    Ideas of: reference   persecution   unreality   sin   guilt   other
    Hallucinations: auditory   visual   olfactory   somatic
    Memory impairments
    Other

    2. Previous psychiatric referrals and reports

I. ANTISOCIAL BEHAVIOR
Begging
Assaultive behavior
Sex misdemeanors
Arrest, probations, served sentences for:
Drinking
Other

VI. HISTORY OF BACKGROUND AND DEVELOPMENT

A. FAMILY HISTORY

1. Direct family line (list information concerning father, mother, full siblings, half siblings, maternal grandparents, paternal grandparents, and children under the headings: *Name; Age or Birth Date; If Deceased, Cause and Age; Household Member; Education; Occupation; Hearing, Deaf, or Hard of Hearing with Age of Onset; Other Disability*)

2. Collateral family line (list foregoing information concerning uncles, aunts, and cousins with close personal relationship to patient and/or with physical and mental disabilities)

3. Parents' marital record
   Date married   Ages at birth of patient
   Present marital status
   Compatability

4. Patient's marital record

   a. Date married   Place
      Previous marriages (dates)
      Reason for termination.
      Compatability with present spouse

   b. Direct and collateral line family history of spouse

5. Family home and neighborhood
   Patient living with
   Language spoken in the home
   Socioeconomic, physical, cultural surroundings

Informants
Social-Service Exchange reports

B. PERSONAL DEVELOPMENTAL HISTORY

1. Prenatal

   a. Parent attitudes toward pregnancy

   b. Maternal condition during pregnancy: physical   emotional
      rH factor   injuries, accidents
      virus infection (month of pregnancy)
      attempts at abortion
      other

   c. Attending physician

   d. Informant

2. Natal
   a. Birthplace   term   birth weight   labor   delivery   mother's condition

   b. Condition of child: normal   resuscitation   jaundice   cyanosis
   hemorrhage   convulsions   injuries   prematurity   incubator   malformations
   congenital anomalies

   c. Attending physician, midwife, other

   d. Informant

3. Schedule of infant development (months)

   a. Nutritional   Remarks

Breast-fed	4	6	8	10	12
Weaned	4	6	8	10	12
Fed self	16	18	20	22	24

   b. Motor

Sat alone	6	7	8	9	10
Walked alone	10	12	14	16	18

   c. Elimination

Bowel control	4	8	12	18	24
Bladder control, day	12	15	18	21	24
Bladder control, night	12	18	24	30	36

   d. Communication
   Response to sounds (fill in)
   Response to voice   " "
   Vocalization   " "

"Syllable" talk	4	6	8	10	12
Verbal talk	8	10	12	14	16

   e. Physical growth

First tooth	5	6	7	8	9

   Height (note abnormalities)
   Weight   "   "

Attending physician

Informant

4. Childhood psychosocial adjustments (preschool to puberty)

   a. Chronological list of child's reactions to new and unusual occurrences (noting child's age) such as onset of deafness, beginning school, change of schools, changes in residence, change in guardianship of child, broken home, death in family, etc.

   b. Parent-child-sibling relations and attitudes pre- and post-disability

   c. Sex instruction: by whom: age of child:
   Child's reaction:

   d. Recreational interests and activities

   e. Religious training and observances

[133]

f. Summary of habit patterns and problems at preadolescence

	Pattern	*If Problem, Since When*	*Management*
Disposition Eating Motor Sensory Elimination Sleep Socialization Adaptability Learning ability Communication Independent activity General health Physical development Sex interests Other			

Informants

C. MEDICAL AND HEALTH HISTORY

1. General health
   Date and findings of last physical examination

   Physician

2. Chronological list of important and/or persistent illnesses, major injuries and accidents, operations, etc., noting especially convulsive disorders, hyperpyrexia, allergies, otological conditions, and infectious and contagious diseases, under the headings: *Condition; Age of Patient; Patient's Reactions: Treatment; Outcome; Attending Physician*

3. List physical, mental, and sensory disabilities not previously mentioned, under the headings: *Disability; Severity; Age of Onset; Treatment; Outcome; Attending Physician*

4. List present physical complaints and treatment

5. Vocational and educational implications of medical history

6. Suggested further medical referrals

D. AUDITORY HISTORY

1. Discovery of impaired hearing

   a. Age "something wrong" was observed
      Signs involved
      By whom observed

[134]

b. Age when authentic diagnosis was established   accepted
    Diagnostician

.c. Record of diagnostic and/or treatment experiences (chronological listing under the headings: *Stated Diagnosis; Diagnostician; Age of Patient; Recommendations Made; Treatments Undergone*)

d. Reactions of family during the auditory diagnostic **period**

e. Reactions of patient during the auditory diagnostic **period**

2. Nature of the auditory impairment

   a. Otological findings: type of impairment
      cause   prognosis   recommendations, treatment

   b. Audiometric findings (chronological listing under the headings: *Date Tested; Average Left and Right db Loss in Speech Range; Test Used; Tested by*)

   c. Accompanying involvements: recruitment   tinnitus   vertigo
      balance impairment   brain damage   psychogenic factors   other
      Reported by

3. Communications compensations and abilities
    Hearing aid: worn since   fitted by
      acceptance   acoustic benefits
    Auditory training: since   by
      acoustic and other benefits
    Lipreading: proficiency
    Speech: comprehensibility
    Main communications methods: oral   manual   writing   pantomime

4. Intrafamily attitudes

5. Implications of auditory history (psychological, educational, vocational)

E. EDUCATIONAL HISTORY

1. Preschool (chronological listing of preschool record under the headings: *Name, Address of Instructional Facility*, i.e., School, Clinic, Tutor, Correspondence Course; *Day or Resident Placement; How Often Home, Visited; Type of Instruction; Adjustments and Problems; Dates Attended; Why Left*)

2. School (chronological listing of school record including tutoring, high school, college, or university under the headings used in the preceding section)

3. Scholastic preferences and rating

    a. Best liked subjects: Least liked subjects:

    b. Highest grades in: Lowest grades in:

    c. School rating: superior   average   dull   failure
       Qualifying remarks:

4. Scholastic goals
Of pupil:

Of parents:

5. Favored extracurricular activities

F. VOCATIONAL AND OCCUPATIONAL HISTORY

    1. Vocational training (chronological listing of vocational training schools, courses, apprenticeships, workshops, etc., under the headings: *Training Center and Address; Dates Attended; Courses Taken; Why Left*)

        a. Training center reports

        b. Vocational aptitude test results

    2. Work history

        a. Jobs held while in school (full, part-time, summer vacation)

        b. Jobs held since leaving school (chronological listing under the headings: *Company Name and Address; Dates Employed; Type of Job; How Obtained; Salary; Why Left*)

        c. Occupational preferences and goals
          Of patient:

          Of parents and family:

        d. Occupational adjustment problems: inadequate vocational training   lack of required aptitudes   insufficient knowledge of occupational world   scholastic retardations   unrealistic goals   lack of adaptability   low frustration tolerance   immature attitudes   poor interpersonal relations   other

e. Employer reports

3. Economic status

Source of Support	Occasional	Usual	Present	Weekly Amount
Salary Parents Relatives Spouse Public relief Insurance Other				

VII. SUMMARY OF FINDINGS

VIII. DIAGNOSTIC INTERPRETATION

IX. RECOMMENDATIONS

X. FOLLOW-UP RECORD

II. *The Presenting Problem.* With the deaf as with the hearing, a psychologist's introduction to his patient is made by way of the presenting problem. If taken at face value, the introduction is apt to be misleading because the presenting problem is generally described by the referring agent in terms of observed behavior rather than basic difficulty. The classic example of the child without speech has already been mentioned. "My child does not talk and she is going on three" is a familiar plaint to speech therapists because on the surface this appears to be a speech problem. But basically, it may involve deafness, mental defect, emotional disturbance or disorder, neurological impairment, or any combination of these. What the referent usually describes are the outer signs of the problem, not the essential difficulties. This is the case with other common presenting problems of deaf patients, such as: "This pupil is supposed to have a high I.Q. but he is one of our slowest learners"; "This pupil has a lot of hearing and he seems bright, but he cannot learn to speak"; "He is moody and hostile around the house. He expects me (the mother) to do everything for him"; "The schools say they have no provision for a child like mine. What's wrong with him?"; "He cannot hold a job." In addition to these are, of course, the usual referrals for behavioral disturbances and disorders. In this connection, it must be noted that the foregoing do not represent common problems of the deaf but rather common reasons for the referral of deaf individuals for psychological examination. In all such cases, it is up to the psychologist to get to the root of the manifest difficulty. To treat signs and symptoms alone without attempting to ascertain cause does not make for optimal therapeutic results,[2] although in some cases cause becomes clarified in the course of experimental treatment. In general, however, the presenting problem serves as a springboard for deeper study rather than as the treatment objective.

V. *Current Psychosocial Status.* The first goal of inquiry in a

[2] Frederick C. Thorne, *Principles of Psychological Examining* (Brandon, Vermont: Journal of Clinical Psychology, 1955).

psychological examination is an appraisal of the individual as he is at present. This sets the stage for the deeper study of how he came to be so, and indicates what subsequent lines of inquiry need to be explored.

A. *Intelligence*. A common beginning in examinations of deaf individuals is with a methodical evaluation of intelligence. This is so because clinical judgments of the intelligence of the deaf can be difficult to make, particularly when a subject's behavior is immature, his scholastic attainment retarded, and communications methods non-oral. Methodical testing serves to clarify the picture, throws light on the mental aspects of the problem under consideration, and suggests rehabilitation services and goals in accordance with the subject's capacity to learn, to think and reason, and to apply knowledge appropriately. Because presently available intelligence tests do not have as great a range of diagnostic usefulness with the deaf as with the hearing, it is necessary to complement their findings with information obtained from other sources, as indicated in the history form (page 129). In addition, the following empirical guides can also be used in screening intelligence. Unless otherwise indicated, they apply to adults with congenital or early profound deafness.

(1) A reading achievement level of fourth to fifth grade suggests at least average mental capacity.

(2) An arithmetic achievement level of fourth to fifth grade suggests above-average mental capacity.

(3) Fluent oral communications ability suggests above-average mental capacity.

(4) The ability to perform complex vocational tasks even without the foregoing attainments suggests above-average mental capacity.

(5) Active, productive participation in social and community activities and independent household management suggest above-average mental capacity.

(6) A pupil with severe congenital or early deafness who is

able to *compete successfully* with hearing peers in a regular school demonstrates at least above-average and more likely superior mental capacity.

(7) Exceptional alertness on the part of such a child or adult in grasping thoughts, ideas, and directions despite serious communications obstacles suggests at least average mental capacity.

Psychologists are strongly cautioned that the converse of the foregoing estimates cannot be taken to indicate mental incapacity. There are numbers of deaf adults with average to superior mental endowment who do not measure up to these levels of proficiency. Again it is the function of the psychologist to ascertain cause.

B. *Scholastic Achievement.* As a rule, the most practical beginning for the psychological examination of the deaf is with an evaluation of language achievement by means of reading and language achievement tests. (See Chapter 8.) It is estimated that the usual retardation imposed by deafness is from four to five years, but there is considerable variation. For the psychologist, knowledge of a subject's level of language achievement is essential in order to communicate with him within his range of comprehension and to select tests that are appropriate to this range. For the vocational counselor, the level of a deaf client's language skills is a highly important consideration in vocational adjustment through eliminating from present consideration those jobs that require a significantly higher level of language comprehension than the client possesses. Where mental endowment is average or above, as it often is despite language retardation, further education is strongly indicated in rehabilitation planning, beginning with language development and leading to broader mental development, personal maturity, and vocational attainments.

C. *Personality.* Whether an individual fulfills or falls short of his mental promise depends on many factors. Important among them is personality. Just as mental capacity provides an index of potential level of intellectual attainment, so does personality disclose the driving forces at an individual's disposal to reach this level. In the case of the deaf, personality examination is particularly difficult for reasons to be discussed subsequently. As a result, a deaf person's real-life performance, behavior, and attitudes are used to complement relatively successful personality test results or replace unsuccessful ones entirely. Personality assets of the deaf are appraised in terms of (1) acceptance of deafness; (2) liberation from the bonds of childhood dependence; (3) inner drive to broaden ego boundaries; (4) participation in the stream of every-day activity; (5) social awareness, conscience, and conformity; (6) perseverance in attaining rational goals; (7) personal initiative and enterprise; (8) success in interpersonal relations; and (9) healthy motivation. Personality liabilities are assessed in terms of maturational, experiential, and educational retardation and in terms of the deep-rootedness of whatever thwarting psychic mechanisms may be in operation. The latter are often particularly difficult to observe clinically in the deaf because side by side with deeply rooted psychic problems are other problems that are largely the result of limited knowledge and life experience and which respond well to educative treatment. If we turn back to the history form, particularly significant leads as to present personality status are to be found under the following headings: Personality, Social Interests and Participation, Self-Evaluation and Attitudes, sometimes Marital Preferences and Role, and the Check Lists of pathological signs.

VI. *History of Background and Development.* From the present status the examination turns to past history in order to ascertain the nature and origin of whatever deviations have been found, as the necessary preliminary to diagnosis and treatment planning.

A. *Family History.* At whatever the time of life, a person's deepest motivations are derived from forces operative during the formative years. Among the most potent are family influences, in both their genetic and their environmental aspects. They represent the major determinants of personality. When deafness enters the picture, family reactions lay the groundwork for the deaf individual's own attitudes, aspirations, and reactions toward himself, his disability, and the hearing world. Rejective family attitudes are a common cause of some of the most deeply rooted emotional and learning problems of the deaf. However, it is not always possible to tell when rejection lies at the root of a deaf person's difficulties. The individual may not know or will not say. As for the family, acceptance and rejection cannot always be distinguished, as when concern, "self-sacrifice," overprotection, and the like actually conceal deep hostility. Therefore, more objective leads to family attitudes are sought in the following lines of inquiry:

Auditory Status of Family. Where parents are deaf and deafness is a common family circumstance, the individual is generally more fully accepted and, as a child, subjected to less emotional tensions than in families where deafness is an unprecedented occurrence. However, these early advantages do not imply that a deaf family environment is uniformly more favorable. This depends on the family. In some, there are distinct disadvantages for a growing child because of the deaf parents' limited range of knowledge and experiences. In this connection, therefore, it is important to know the status and closeness of relationship of the hearing family members to their deaf relatives in order to appraise the quality and amount of guidance they may have given. The rehabilitation worker will also want to know whether such influences can be counted on in service planning.

Hereditary Factors. Another useful index of family attitudes is disclosed by hereditary information. Feelings of taint often associated with hereditary conditions are a common cause of rejection of congenitally deaf persons in families where deafness is an unprecedented or sporadic occurrence. The most acute fears of an hereditary cause of deafness are to be found among the hearing parents and siblings of the congenitally deaf. Here are met grave parent anxieties about having more children; torments of guilt over the suspicion of being the hereditary carrier; casting of blame from parent to parent; mating problems of hearing siblings and children of the congenitally deaf; sometimes family disruption. The effects of such attitudes and tensions upon a deaf child's adjustive environment are obvious. The unfortunate aspect of such attitudes is that a congenitally deaf individual need not necessarily be hereditarily deaf at all. The term "congenital" merely states that the condition was present since birth without any implication as to cause. There are numbers of causes of deafness before birth and at birth that are not related to hereditary factors, such as maternal illnesses in early pregnancy (German measles, mumps, influenza); Rh blood factor; the effects of certain drugs taken by the mother in early pregnancy, as, for example, quinine; maternal syphilis; injuries to the infant at birth. (See Appendix C.) Nevertheless, most families and many workers labor under the misconception that the term "congenital" signifies the operation of hereditary factors. Obtaining the histories of direct and collateral family members helps clarify the hereditary possibility of congenital (and other) deafness of unknown cause, and may also reveal the possibility of other hereditary conditions to which the rehabilitation worker should be alerted.

Family Aspiration Level. Still another index of a deaf person's adjustive environment is derived from the educational, occupational, and socioeconomic status of his family. Under ordinary circumstances, these represent the family level of aspiration. When an individual is impeded by deafness, it is essential to know whether his acceptance by his family is contingent upon his attaining this level; whether he can attain it; and the extent to which a family will accept modified goals without rejecting the deaf member.

B. *Personal Developmental History*

1. *Prenatal.* The life of an individual, as well as the hazards of

living, begins not at birth but at conception. Therefore, in appraising life influences, those must also be considered that were active in the prenatal period.

a. *Parent Attitudes toward Pregnancy.* A psychological environment awaits a child even before he is born, and is determined by the attitudes of the parents in wanting or not wanting the new arrival. Where parent attitudes are unfavorable, a child is handicapped from the start. It may be assumed that the presence of deafness will not alter the picture except to worsen it. In view of the need for early acceptance as a critical factor in a deaf child's adjustment, initial parent attitudes represent important determinants of the child's eventual success or failure.

b. *Maternal Condition during Pregnancy.* Where there is a maternal history involving such illnesses and incidents during pregnancy as those noted in the history form (page 132), there is a grave possibility of permanent damage to the brain of the developing fetus. This possibility must be borne in mind at whatever age there are encountered persistent behavioral deviations, retardations, and unusual learning difficulties (especially in language) that prove unresponsive to the usual psychoeducational and rehabilitative measures. Where brain damage coexists with deafness, the worker is faced with a problem of multi-disability. Here, as in all instances of multi-disability, treatment plans are directed toward (and often limited by) the most disabling of the conditions present. Where the consequences of brain damage are severe, this is the more disabling condition than deafness, and treatment plans should be worked out with specialists in both areas.

2. *Natal.* Permanent damage to brain tissue may also be caused by the physical trauma and events of birth, with results similar to those noted in the preceding section. Listed in the history form are a number of conditions commonly associated with brain damage at birth (page 133).

3. *Schedule of Infant Development.* In diagnosis, it is often

necessary to establish when and how a particular behavioral deviation first made its appearance. An important base of reference is the chronological schedule of infant development. The norms of development for hearing infants serve as well for the deaf except in regard to language and communications. Therefore, when significant lags from the other normative criteria are reported for a deaf infant, they represent important clinical signs of deviant function. The arrangement of normative data in the history form (page 133) facilitates quick comparison with accepted standards, which are the numbers underlined in the form. Naturally, it is not expected that a mother of grown children will remember the chronological details of their development, but even rough recall of outstanding discrepancies by comparison of the subject's development with that of the other children in the family is clinically valuable, particularly in cases presenting diagnostic difficulty.

4. *Childhood Psychosocial Adjustments.* A highly fertile area of origin of adjustment problems is found in the childhood psychosocial experiences of the deaf. It is during these early years when the mind of the deaf child reaches out for broader knowledge and fuller understanding of the world that deafness shows the full force of its powerful restrictions. Of all periods in the lives of the deaf, it is with the events of the developmental and childhood periods a psychologist should be most familiar; for from the restrictions and frustrations imposed at this time spring the majority of subsequent problems.

a. *Adaptation to New Experiences.* With the deaf as with the hearing, the pattern of adult adaptability is based to a considerable extent upon the manner in which a child was prepared to meet new experiences. When a child is deaf, explanations of the meaning of unfamiliar events are seriously hampered by the problem of communication. As a result, many deaf children feel themselves thrown into, rather than prepared for, new experiences. The deaf child who is secure has enough self-confidence and trust in others to maintain his emotional equilibrium. But to an insecure child who cannot hear, even everyday occurrences may loom as threats to which he reacts with anxiety, resistance, apathy, and the like. Such a child would rather do without and remain safely protected by a known environment than risk the dangers of the unknown. Many of the rigid, inflexible deaf adults of today are nothing more than these frightened children of the past.

b. *Parent-Child Relations, Pre- and Post-Disability.* When deafness is acquired in childhood, a more severe and lasting psychological trauma can be caused by the change in parent attitudes and management than by deafness itself. In such cases, there is a break in the usual pattern of parent-child relations. The child, not capable of fully understanding what has happened to his hearing, tends to feel his parents are somehow responsible for not having prevented it from happening. The parents, on the other hand, in their anxiety to apply full-scale rehabilitative measures, are apt to overlook the critical necessity of reestablishing themselves as symbols of security in the child's new and frightening world. It has been the writer's observation in such instances that frequently a child's general hostility at having become deaf centers itself upon the parents because to him they appear more concerned with the problems that have arisen than with his immediate emotional needs. As a result, the child feels himself rejected. Often this is not the case at all. Unless special pains are taken to correct the child's impression, his feelings of hostility may become a fixed attitude toward the hearing world.

c. *Sex Instruction.* As with other facts, so with sex knowledge; barriers of language and communication make it unusually difficult to impart sex information to the deaf in pace with their maturational needs. If this fact is considered in conjunction with the general restrictions and overprotection of their preadult years, it must be assumed that the deaf are thereby rendered more vulnerable to sex maladjustments. It is therefore an essential aspect of the psychological examination to ascertain a deaf individual's sex attitudes in order that preventive and treatment measures may be instituted where required.

d. *Recreational Interests and Activities.* The nature of a deaf child's recreational experiences is an important determinant of his later social initiative and fraternization with the hearing world. Many deaf children suffer bitter treatment at the hands of their hearing neighborhood peers, and find recreational satisfactions only with the deaf. Others are not permitted by their parents to associate with the deaf but are forced into nonaccepting hearing circles. There are also those who are wisely encouraged to develop a wide range of recreational interests, abilities, and activities with both the deaf and the hearing; and still others who are recreationally immobilized by strenuous parental overprotection. Such are some of the common experiences from which the deaf adult's social adaptability, attitudes, and preferences are derived.

e. *Religious Training and Observances.* Most schools for the deaf provide religious instruction for their pupils. As a rule, such training contributes to a deaf child's security and broadens social conscience. In some cases, however, a disturbed child will seize upon religion as an escape from reality or as punishment for wrongdoing. Such situations are not generally found among the deaf; but when they are, the pastoral guidance services of religious leaders of various denominations trained for work with the deaf are of invaluable assistance.

f. *Summary of Childhood Psychosocial Development.* The summation in this section of the history form (page 134) supplies a rough sketch of the foundations from which the adult personality structure develops. Maladjustments, behavioral deviations, and learning disabilities that were present in the developmental period and are still present in adulthood cannot be dislodged by ordinary rehabilitation measures. Highly specialized treatment is required; even then, success is measured in terms of amelioration rather than cure. In effect, the more deeply rooted and malignant the problems, the more difficult their management. On the other hand, the summation also includes resources and personal assets. In rehabilitation, helping a client develop his resources to their maximum possible extent has the effect of minimizing his liabilities. This is a highly important consideration in work with the deaf, since, as is obvious, there are a greater number of deeply rooted difficulties here than among the hearing simply because of the far greater number of severe childhood problems and fewer treatment facilities. The paramount rehabilitation objectives with the deaf, therefore, are (*a*) the prevention of problems during the formative years or (*b*) if the time for prevention is past, the maximum development of individual resources not only to foster self-fulfillment but also to compensate for problems that are too deeply rooted to respond significantly to direct treatment.

C. *Medical and Health History.* Any condition in the life of a deaf child that adds to the restrictions already imposed by deafness [3] increases the obstacles to personal development. Thus far, the emphasis has been on psychological conditions, but additional physical disabilities can prove equally important hindrances to adjustment. Visual disability impairs the major compensatory sense of the deaf; chronic illness means the loss of valuable schooltime that can seldom be made up; physical debility robs a deaf child of the energies he needs to master the countless unknowns in his world and so broaden his ego boundaries; and not infrequently, chronic physical invalidism induces an attitude of psychological invalidism as well. Despite the current shift of rehabilitation interest toward psychological dynamisms, physical factors still play a major role in individual well-being and adjustment.

In the case of adults, health information and the general medical history serve to alert the rehabilitation worker to such specific

[3] Helmer R. Myklebust, "The Deaf Child with Other Handicaps," *American Annals of the Deaf*, CIII (1958), 496–509.

considerations as (1) the need for selective vocational placement due to health incapacities; (2) the amount of time and money required by a client's medical treatment needs; and (3) whether a client's medical needs and vocational requirements can be serviced simultaneously or whether one assumes priority over the other. Additional considerations supplied by a full medical record include (1) the possibility of other disabilities, particularly of vision; (2) the possibility of brain damage as suggested by a medical history of severe cerebral trauma, repeated convulsions, or diseases characterized by high fever and somnolence; and (3) the possibility of psychological disturbances arising from frequent, prolonged, or serious illnesses or alarming medical experiences. Also included in the medical history may be conditions that aggravate deafness, such as allergies, tendency to respiratory infections, adenoid tissue, anemia, chronic fatigue, and hypertension. The worker should be familiar with the implications of such conditions and use the knowledge in vocational planning as well as for referral to a physician when health problems are reported by a client or suspected by the worker. Finally, an account of a client's subjective physical complaints should also be included in the health history as an index of possible hypochondriacal tendencies or other emotional disturbance. All such complaints should of course be screened medically before psychological assumptions are made.

D. *Auditory History* [4]

Discovery of Impaired Hearing. The nature of a family's diagnostic experiences preceding the discovery of deafness provides another index of a deaf child's adjustive environment. Not uncommonly, such experiences are apt to be highly traumatic to parents and child since the identification of deafness in the very young is not easily accomplished. For one, the damaged nerve structures lie inside the skull and hence cannot be seen on otological examination. For another, most young deaf children respond to a

[4] See Appendix B.

number of sounds, often giving the impression they are hearing children. The main signs that something is wrong are seen in behavior and in the absence of speech and language. But as previously noted, somewhat similar signs characterize other deviant conditions. It takes the trained eye of the experienced diagnostician to differentiate among them. By the time such a specialist is reached, both child and family may have weathered many confusing experiences and conflicting diagnoses and be at the point of emotional exhaustion. Not infrequently, the seeds of rejection are sown during this trying time.

Auditory Rehabilitation. In brief review, the auditory impairment of the deaf is characterized by (*a*) early age of onset; (*b*) severe irreversible hearing loss from about the time of onset; (*c*) insufficient hearing ability to understand spoken conversation no matter how loudly shouted; and (*d*) permanent damage to nerve structures of the auditory mechanism. This unfavorable picture suggests that little can be done for the group in the way of auditory rehabilitation; and it is indeed true that no treatment or hearing aid has yet been devised that will restore conversational hearing ability to sufferers of early profound deafness. However, advances in audiology, medical knowledge, and educational practice have introduced several other rehabilitative measures that are of great benefit to those able to profit from them. Important guides in the use of these measures are (*a*) the present age of the individual; (*b*) his background of previous auditory experiences; and (*c*) individual variations in the auditory history.

Auditory Rehabilitation at the Childhood Level. The greatest benefits of auditory rehabilitation among the deaf are achieved when the necessary procedures are begun in early childhood; or if deafness is acquired later, then as soon after onset as is medically and audiologically advisable. The procedures include the hearing aid, auditory training, and special instruction in speech and lip reading. The hearing aid is used to amplify sound and stimulate auditory perception, which is then subjected to auditory training in sound discrimination and recognition. The aim is to cultivate the keenest possible acuity of whatever remaining hearing there is so that it can be used in the development or preservation of speech and lip reading. The longer the time that elapses between the onset of deafness and the use of these procedures, the less promising the outlook. As time goes by, habits of auditory disuse become fixed; there is less possibility of synchronizing auditory training with the learning of speech and lip reading; and often the individual finds auditory stimulation altogether distasteful.

Auditory Rehabilitation at the Adult Level. Where deafness is of long-standing duration and auditory perceptions have been permitted to atrophy through disuse, the advantages of initiating hearing rehabilitation must be carefully weighed. If the aim is to improve oral skills that are already established, gains are likely. But if the purpose is to *begin* the development of speech and lip reading with a deaf adult who lacks these skills, the results will be highly disappointing. The period of readiness for the procedures involved is long past both physiologically and psychologically. The time could be more profitably devoted to improving needed skills that are less difficult to acquire. This is not to say that a deaf adult should not be supplied with a hearing aid if he finds other advantages in its use. Some deaf persons use an aid to hear certain signals associated with particular occupations. Others find psychological satisfaction in hearing whatever sounds an aid transmits even though they are unable to identify them. And finally, there are numbers of deaf adults who wear an aid to inform the public they are deaf and not peculiar, thus sparing themselves many unpleasant experiences.

Individual Variations in the Auditory History. The unusual number of individual differences among the deaf has been previously noted (page 47). Many are derived from differences in auditory experiences. Some common guides are as follows:

(1) The greater the amount of normal hearing experiences before the onset of deafness, the higher the level of expectation in language attainment and oral communication.

(2) The greater the amount of residual hearing, the higher the level of expectation in language attainment and oral communication.

(3) The more effective the use made of residual hearing, even in cases of severe deafness, the higher the level of expectation in oral communication.

(4) Where deviations from the foregoing guides are encountered, it is diagnostically essential to find the reasons. Some common causes of deviation are: emotional disturbance leading to learning problems; mental incapacity; inadequate instructional experiences; special learning disabilities, as in lip reading; and language learning disorders associated with brain damage.

(5) In addition, there are a number of associated otological conditions that require consideration, particularly in vocational planning. Not infrequently, the balance mechanism of deaf persons is impaired, and this should alert the vocational counselor to the dangers of occupations involving climbing, heights, or working near moving, exposed machinery. Occasionally deaf persons are found who have abnormal sensitivity to noise and pressure sensations, or who are troubled by head noises. In all such cases, vocational planning requires close consultation with otologist and audiologist.

E. *Educational History*. General guides to the educational placement needs of hearing-impaired children are outlined in Appendix B, section 5 (page 313). In view of the individual variations among deaf children as well as among educational facilities for the deaf, the following additional guides are offered:

Scholastic Attainment of the Deaf. Because deafness retards the development of verbal language, it slows the pace of all learnings based on verbal language comprehension. To make up for this lag, the deaf pupil requires an appreciably longer period of schooling than his hearing peer. Even so, the average congenitally deaf pupil is about four years behind the hearing in scholastic attainment. Where other adverse circumstances enter the picture, the four-year retardation may expand to five, six, or more years, and this despite average or even superior mental endowment.

Length of Time in School. The age limits of attendance at schools for the deaf vary from school to school. Where preschool facilities are available, the age of admission may be three years or younger. This is the growing trend. Where no preschool facilities are available, the usual age of beginning school is about six years. Such children may or may not make up for the advantage the preschool beginners have had. Children who begin school at the age of eight years or older seldom make up the lost educational time. The age at completion of the school period is about twenty years. Numbers of deaf pupils throughout the country leave school well before this time. The less formal education a deaf individual has had, the more serious his handicaps.

Age-Grade Achievement Levels. Grade levels in schools for the deaf do not conform to those in hearing schools in regard to level of achievement or age of pupil because of the differences in pace of learning and variations in age of admission. There are also variations in grade level among the special schools themselves, and sometimes in the same school from year to year. Therefore, the best guide to the scholastic achievement of a deaf pupil is the achievement test rather than the school grade.

School Philosophies and Educational Experiences. Deaf pupils attend different kinds of schools [5] ranging from the regular hearing schools to residential special schools. The large majority of deaf pupils attend the latter type. The various kinds of schools each have their own particular philosophy of what constitutes a desirable educational approach to the deaf child. In most instances, the philosophies have elements of sound appeal. The problem arises

[5] See Appendix B, section 5, and Appendix E, section 2.

in assembling a school population for whom the respective philosophies are uniformly applicable. Actually, there is no such thing as *the* deaf child. There are thousands of deaf children, every one different from the next. The fundamental need is for individualized service; and this most schools are not prepared to render on a sufficiently broad scale, especially when the needed service is counter to school philosophy. The pupils involved suffer the consequences, both scholastically and personally. Naturally, the schools are not entirely to blame. Other responsible factors have been noted previously, not the least of which are parent attitudes. All must be weighed together in evaluating a subject's educational potentials as compared with his actual attainments. The following represent additional sources of scholastic retardation among deaf persons of average or better intelligence:

(1) *Preschool Level.* Permanent negative attitudes to learning may originate as early as the nursery and preschool levels due to such factors as (1) prematurely applied instructional pressures either at home or in the school; (2) the forcing of formal instruction before physiological or psychological readiness is attained; and (3) emotional trauma resulting from a small child's being sent away from home to board with a tutor or at a residential school.

(2) *School-Age Level.* Scholastic retardation during the school years commonly results from (1) too late a school beginning and too few years in school; (2) methods of instruction inappropriate to a pupil's auditory status, learning abilities, mental capacity, and special learning disabilities; (3) type of school inadequate for a pupil's psychosocial needs and adjustments; and (4) lack of provision for special instructional and psychosocial problems.

(3) *Adult Level.* Scholastic retardations of the past are continued in adulthood mainly because of the lack of facilities for adult education and personal adjustment counseling. Both of these are critical rehabilitation needs of the deaf.

F. *Vocational and Occupational History.* The lines of vocational inquiry in the history form (page 136) may be applied to clients with work experience as well as to those without. In the former case, adjustment is assessed in terms of the following criteria: (1) initiative in getting a job; (2) ability to hold a job; (3) progress made in an occupation; (4) degree of economic independence achieved; and (5) relationship between type of employment and the individual's vocational training, aptitudes and abilities, and vocational goals.

In the case of young deaf adults fresh from school, these are still unknown factors. Vocational planning is therefore based largely on information obtained from the case history, psychological testing, and interview in regard to the following: (1) the individual's present vocational skills and aptitudes; (2) his personal assets and resources; (3) his vocational goals and viewpoints; and (4) the special problems he presents. The client's present qualifications identify his immediate training needs and placement possibilities; his undeveloped resources and other assets provide a guide for future planning; and the special problems he presents indicate the nature of the possible obstacles to vocational adjustment as well as the treatment required.

Common problems of young deaf adults are those related to scholastic attainment, personal maturity, and vocational knowledge and orientation. As a rule, the basic need is for an habilitative rather than a rehabilitative approach: for continued education rather than reeducation; for adjustment to unfamiliar experiences rather than readjustment to familiar ones. Factors of special importance in the vocational adjustment of the deaf are those involving language skills, numerical operations, psychosocial attitudes, and employer understanding. So far as speech, residual hearing, and lip reading are concerned, by the time a deaf individual reaches the vocational age, his patterns are pretty well set, and significant gains are not likely. But a deaf worker must possess a sufficient command of *language* in order to understand printed directions and exchange written communication with his employer and co-workers if he cannot communicate orally. He must be familiar with the terminologies of his trade and apply the numerical operations required by the job. Above all, he must understand the facts and customs of job-holding, its attendant responsibilities and benefits, the need for flexibility in the daily routine, and the meaning of cooperation. To meet him halfway, the employer must be willing to give some thought to the handicaps of deafness and how he can help minimize them in the work environment. All these factors are essential considerations in the vocational adjustment of the deaf, and as such they represent fundamental service-considerations in the vocational rehabilitation of deaf clients.

Scope of History Inquiry

Because the acoustic disability of the deaf is present since birth or early childhood, continues through life, and ramifies through all major life areas, the scope of history inquiry for thorough diagnostic study includes the full life span of the subject. In actual practice, however, this is not always feasible nor even clinically necessary for the experienced psychologist. Such a worker can judge for himself in how great detail the various lines of inquiry need to be followed. However, for the psychologist newly entering the field of the deaf, the development of full histories and the study of the implications and interrelation of history data provide an excellent means of acquiring clinical insight and judgment, and should be done as much for the worker's benefit as for the subject's.

Reliability of History Data

It is obvious by now that assembling the full history of a deaf individual involves an extraordinary number and variety of informants. Commonly included are parents, relatives, friends, otologists and other medical specialists, audiologists, speech therapists, educators, psychologists, social workers, vocational counselors, employers, and various agencies and organizations. Duplication and even triplication of information are not unusual; divergent reports and findings are common. How to appraise the reliability of the masses of assembled data is a customary problem of conscientious workers.

A sound procedure is to build the history on data obtained from primary sources. Primary sources are those with authentic, firsthand knowledge of the individual and of the particular line of inquiry being pursued. For example, specialists who have actually examined the deaf subject are primary sources for their respective findings. So are schools, agencies, and organizations that have had direct and active contacts with him. Parents, relatives, and friends are generally reliable sources of information concerning the socio-economic, cultural, and emotional climate of development, everyday behavior and problems, and sometimes of hereditary factors if they are willing to disclose the facts and ignore the stigma so frequently connected with hereditary conditions.

However, parents are not primary sources for such matters as medical diagnoses, audiometric findings, psychological test results, scholastic attainments. As a rule, technical reports are not given to laymen; and what the examiner is apt to receive from such sources are personal interpretations, or more likely misinterpretations, of the actual facts. Similarly, the opinions of specialists in one field about the findings of specialists in other areas cannot be considered of primary-source validity. Where multidisciplinary appraisal is as necessary as with the deaf, extraprofessional judgments are bound to be made. Many show high perceptive acuity and should be followed through. Others merely demonstrate lack of experience with the deaf as well as with the techniques and rationale of the other specialties. In either event, where personal conjectures are made, they should so be noted when recorded in the history in order that authentic information may be distinguished from the speculative.

Reliable information can sometimes be surprisingly difficult to obtain from parents. Even in the brief histories of young children, uncertainty concerning the course and chronology of events and reactions is not uncommon. With older subjects, it is the usual occurrence. The past is clouded by present problems, lapse of time, and emotional rather than factual recall. Where this is the case, a more objective account of events should be sought from knowledgeable but less deeply involved informants.

Reliable information can also be difficult to obtain from deaf subjects. The deaf child has insufficient communications skills and understanding of the significance of events for reporting. As for the adult, for a substantial part of his life he too has been barred from meaningful insight into many occurrences for lack of the language necessary to understand their full import. Over the course of the years, he is brought here and taken there; things are done to him; all kinds of people observe and test him; events happen about him; plans are made for him; but in the absence of sufficient verbal comprehension and previous experience, there is no explicit way of explaining to him the full purpose of such happenings. The gaps thus created in his life may or may not be filled in later on. In any case, it is an unusual deaf person who can be counted on for a comprehensive account of his life, experiences, and reactions. Nonetheless, every case history should contain wherever possible an autobiographic account of the deaf subject written in his own language. Scant and sketchy though the factual information may be, unusual psychological insights are afforded the perceptive clinician.

In this connection, it should also be noted that when information about a deaf subject is being obtained through interview with others, he should not be present. Otherwise he is exposed to the unpleasant experience of having to sit by knowing his life, habits, and problems are being discussed but unable to follow the course of conversation. For the adult, this is an extremely irritating situation that threatens the establishment of rapport for future procedures of examination and treatment. As for children, interview about a child should not be conducted in the presence of the child. If this is unavoidable, plenty of distracting toys and picture books should be on hand, and the speakers as well as the listeners should maintain strict control over their facial expressions. In the cases of very young children and babies, the interviewees should be requested to come accompanied by someone to care for the infants.

Recording History Data

In assembling a history, it cannot be stressed strongly enough that the purpose is not to accumulate a mass of facts, dates, and names but to reconstruct a life story that has a beginning and a chronological sequence of events, reactions, and consequences leading up to the present. In the process of reconstruction, there will be gaps in the story to fill; facts to check; areas of inquiry to be brought up to date; and follow-up plans to be made. History does not end with the present. It is part of a continuing story that will be referred to by future workers.

Therefore, recording must take cognizance of future as well as present usability. Significant information should be annotated in regard to (*a*) the name and address of the informant; (*b*) the date information was received; (*c*) the period in the subject's life to which it refers; and (*d*) the reliability of the informant and his relationship to the subject. Areas of inquiry should be chronologically complete and brought up to date where necessary, with significant events and reactions noted by date, year, or age of the subject. Annotated digests of written reports and records should be included in their appropriate sections of the history to preserve chronological continuity and to safeguard the information against the loss of the original documents. Above all, recording should not be so abbreviated and cryptic as to be meaningless to all others. In effect, a good history is a concise, sequential record of pertinent facts in a life story, chronologically complete and assessed for reliability.[6]

[6] Nolan D. C. Lewis, *Outlines for Psychiatric Examinations*, 3d ed. (Albany, New York: The New York State Department of Mental Hygiene, 1943).

7. THE DIAGNOSTIC INTERVIEW

IN CONTRAST to reported history, the diagnostic interview gives the individual a chance to tell his own story in his own way, thereby affording the psychologist an exceptional opportunity to see life, people, and events through the eyes of the subject himself. The singular advantages of this technique have scarcely been probed with the deaf. On the one hand, there is a natural reluctance on the part of workers unfamiliar with the group to brave the communications obstacles that interview implies. On the other, there is an equal reluctance on the part of the deaf to tell their stories to uneasy listeners.

In many cases, the impasse yields before the willingness of the interviewer to familiarize himself with the total range of communications abilities of the deaf.[1] These are not limited to manual methods, as is commonly supposed, and a worker need not assume that he must master manual skills for successful interview in all cases. For psychologists who habitually serve deaf subjects, knowledge of all communications methods is essential for clinical practice. But this is too much to expect of a worker who sees only an occasional deaf subject. Nonetheless, the "occasional" client must also be given a chance to be heard. Suggestions are therefore offered in the sections that follow to facilitate the use of interview in the psychological examination of the deaf. The major application of the technique is with the adolescent and adult deaf, since they

[1] See Appendix E.

generally possess sufficient language for interview purposes. Some brief comments are also included concerning the problems of communicating with the preadolescent school population.

Methods of Communicating with Deaf Persons

The communications methods [2] that are used in interviews with deaf adolescents and adults are speech, lip reading, writing, the manual alphabet,[3] and the sign language.[4] Speech and lip reading are used in oral communication; the manual alphabet and the sign language in manual communication; and writing is used either alone or in combination with any of the other methods. Most deaf persons are able to use each of these with greater or lesser skill, employing certain ones with the deaf and others with the hearing. Special considerations in their use are summarized as follows.

ORAL COMMUNICATION

Obviously, the happiest situation for an interviewer unskilled in manual methods is that in which an interview can be successfully conducted in speech and lip reading. Deaf adults who are expert in oral communication usually have good to superior verbal attainments and a broad range of experiences with hearing persons. Sometimes their lip-reading and language skills are so exceptional that the interviewer is apt to forget his remarks are not heard but are received visually. To ease the pressures on persons who are under the strain of having to see rather than hear conversation, and to employ artificially rather than naturally acquired speech, the following procedures are recommended for speaking to, and for understanding the speech of, deaf persons.

[2] G. D. Coats, "Characteristics of Communications Methods," *American Annals of the Deaf*, XCV (1950), 486–91. See also Appendix E.
[3] See Appendix F. [4] See Appendix F.

SPEAKING TO A DEAF ADULT. The following suggestions are offered as guides:

(1) The interviewer and the deaf individual should be seated facing one another and not more than four feet apart.

(2) Light should come from behind the subject and be directed onto the interviewer's face. In this way light glare into the eyes of the lip reader is avoided and he is free to concentrate in comfort upon the speaker's face.

(3) The interviewer's speech should be natural, simple, and clearly enunciated, using whatever modifications in speed and volume are necessary for clearest comprehension. This can be established through brief experimentation. As a rule, the interviewer will find that his natural manner of speaking will not require much, if any, alteration.

(4) To be avoided: grimacing, mouthing, shouting, speaking without voice, and marked slowdown in the delivery of speech. All of these distort mouth movements.

(5) Also to be avoided: talking and smoking or chewing at the same time; resting cheek on hand; bending head, turning face away, and moving about while talking. All of these conceal or impair mouth movements.

(6) Guard against fatigue on the part of the lip reader. A tired lip reader is not a successful one. When fatigue sets in, either pause for a rest or suspend the interview for the time being unless the subject expressly wishes to continue, possibly in written or manual communication.

(7) Watch the face of the lip reader for signs of difficulty in comprehension. Puzzled expressions should be attended to immediately. Either the subject has not grasped a particular thought the interviewer is trying to convey or the vocabulary used has not been lip read successfully.

(8) When difficulties in comprehension arise, clarification is

made by rephrasing the concept or rewording the language into simpler and/or more visible forms BUT NEVER BY CONTINUED REPETITION. Sometimes key words, expressions, and proper names that are particularly difficult to see on the lips may have to be written out.

(9) When the interviewer is not sure a particularly important line of thought has been clearly understood, it should be expressed in several different ways and then discussed with the subject, and clarified further if necessary. Interviewers of the deaf are cautioned that understanding the single words of the vocabulary used does not always guarantee that the whole idea has been grasped by the interviewee.

(10) Pads and pencils should always be available, one set for the subject and a set for the interviewer, with spare pencils in easy reach.

SUGGESTIONS FOR UNDERSTANDING THE SPEECH OF DEAF ADULTS. In successful oral communication with deaf individuals, one side of the coin represents the lip reader's ability to understand the interviewer; but the other involves the interviewer's ability to understand deaf speech. The tones and inflection of deaf voices and the manner and rhythm of enunciation differ from normal utterance. In addition, there are individual variations in patterns of deaf speech just as there are among the hearing. Some patterns are readily understood; others present difficulty.

(1) When difficulties are encountered, a helpful procedure is to permit the deaf subject to talk uninterruptedly for a while to give the interviewer's ear a chance to become attuned to the particular tones and rhythm of the subject's speech. If the interviewer experiences embarrassment listening to uncomprehended speech, or if the subject has little to say, it is often helpful to request him to read aloud on one pretext or another. Having a known verbal context to which to refer helps the listener synchronize the sounds he hears with the words they stand for. During this auditory adjust-

ment period, the interviewer should not strain for precise comprehension but should rather open his ears to the general speech pattern until it finally sets into recognized verbal forms.

(2) If auditory comprehension is still not achieved, the interviewer himself will have to resort to lip reading and watch the subject's mouth movements as skillfully as his own are being watched, combining what he sees with what he hears for comprehension. Whether aware of it or not, most hearing persons use a certain amount of lip reading among themselves. Those who work with the deaf find their natural abilities along these lines of great assistance in understanding difficult deaf speech.

(3) When a deaf subject's speech cannot be understood through hearing and lip reading, written and/or manual communication will have to be used, depending upon the wishes of the subject and the abilities of the interviewer.

(4) Occasional difficulties in comprehension arise even in the course of otherwise successful oral interviews. The interview should not be permitted to bog down on that account. A casual request to write out key words or expressions, or to repeat them, is not taken amiss by deaf persons. Or the interviewer can ask the subject to "tell me more about that." If understanding is still not achieved, the interview should continue nevertheless on the chance that clarification will come about in the course of further discussion. It usually does.

MANUAL COMMUNICATION

Manual communication is used by deaf persons who do not communicate readily through speech and lip reading, as well as by many who do. In the latter case, manual conversation eases the strain of lip reading and talking in prolonged interview and enables the subject to relax somewhat while still continuing to converse. This is a particularly important consideration in cases of emotional disturbance, in which the writer has noted a preference for manual communication even on the part of habitual oralists. Writing, of course, can be used if the interviewer is not familiar with manual methods, but manual communication is swifter. The interviewer who is able to communicate manually is, however, strongly cautioned against introducing these methods into oral interviews without the subject's express wish. Certain deaf persons, called pure oralists, have a profound aversion to manual communication. Some do not even understand it. Even written communication can be distressing to a pure oralist who takes pride in his speech and lip-reading skills. When written communication must be used in such cases, it should be introduced as casually as possible. Other special considerations in the use of manual methods are summarized as follows.

FINGER SPELLING. Of deaf adults who do not habitually communicate through speech and lip reading, those who employ the manual alphabet [5] as their major communications medium present the least interview problems. The words and sentences that are spelled out on the fingers in straight verbal language can just as easily be written out. In addition, the language usage of the habitual finger speller is generally good to superior. Interviews thus conducted in writing have the advantage of providing unusual written records of verbatim conversation.

THE SIGN LANGUAGE.[6] The most serious communications obstacles arise between deaf and hearing persons where the sign language is the subject's major expressive and receptive communications medium. Since the sign language is largely graphic rather than verbal, it is with those who rely heavily on this form of communication that verbal language usage and comprehension are weakest, and concept formation, expression, and understanding require specialized insight. Even written communication with a person whose

[5] See Appendix F. [6] See Appendix F.

communication skills are mainly limited to the sign language may leave the uninitiated baffled. In such cases, it is best to call upon an interpreter.

THE INTERPRETER.[7] To conduct an interview through a third person while at the same time striving for rapport with a deaf subject is not easily done. It is particularly difficult when, as often happens, the third person is a parent or other close relative. If the family member is a hearing person, he may also be unfamiliar with manual methods and may carry out the role of interpreter by talking *about* rather than *for* the subject. In the end, more history data are obtained than interview information.

In addition, most persons, whether hearing or deaf, find it extremely difficult to express themselves freely before family members. Relatives should therefore be discouraged from participating in diagnostic interviews even in the role of interpreter. The major exception arises in the case of illiterate, uneducated deaf adults. Such persons have no conventional method of communication and rely upon homemade signs and pantomime which are best understood within the family.

It is, of course, entirely possible that a young deaf adult may prefer to have a parent or relative by his side, or there may be no other person available to act as interpreter. The interviewer will have to manage as best he can, and count on the testing sessions for more personal contact with the subject.

Where choice of interpreters is possible, the subject's preference should be consulted. Often deaf subjects are as loath to unburden themselves before deaf interpreters as before members of their own families. The deaf community in itself resembles a kind of family. It is best, therefore, to ascertain whether the subject prefers a deaf or hearing person to act as interpreter. Finally, the

[7] The services of interpreters for the deaf can be obtained through schools and special agencies for the deaf, organizations of the deaf, and religious organizations with special facilities for the deaf.

subject should be doubly assured of the confidential nature of all aspects of the psychological examination, especially the interview.

Some further suggestions concerning the conduct of an interpreted interview are as follows:

(1) The interviewer should make every reasonable effort to maintain the focus of interest on the subject, and not on the interpreter. In interpreted interviews, there is always the danger of the interview becoming a conversation between the interviewer and the interpreter, with the subject left to play a subordinate background role. This must be guarded against, both to preserve the subject's integrity as an individual and to arouse his personal interest for future examination procedures.

(2) Subject, interpreter, and interviewer should be seated within comfortable visual range of each other, but the subject should be seated nearer the interviewer to indicate to him that his interests are the major concern.

(3) The interviewer should address himself directly to the subject even though it is the interpreter who is doing the understanding.

(4) The interpreter should be instructed to wait until the interviewer completes his statements before attracting the interviewee's attention. When the interviewer completes his remarks, he turns to the interpreter as the signal to begin.

(5) While his remarks are being transposed into the sign language, the interviewer should observe the facial expression and behavior of the subject to see how his remarks are being received and the manner in which response is made.

(6) If the interviewee's attention remains fixed on the interpreter for longer than necessary, he should be recalled by a light tap on the arm.

(7) Both interviewer and interpreter must maintain control over their facial expressions at all times to avoid conveying false or undesirable impressions to the subject.

(8) There must be no side conversations about the interviewee between the interpreter and the interviewer. The subject should be kept informed of whatever passes between them. If it is wiser that he not be informed, the discussion had best take place in his absence.

(9) The interviewer must maintain friendly control over the proceedings at all times lest closer rapport be established between the subject and the interpreter than between the subject and the interviewer.

The Language of Communication

In interviewing the deaf, it is a common error to consider the problems solved with the selection of appropriate methods of communication. It cannot be stressed strongly enough that the basic aim of an interviewer is to get to the thinking and attitudes of his deaf subject. Methods of communication merely represent the bridge that will get him there. In order to understand what he finds when he finally arrives, familiarity with the *language-usage* habits of the deaf is essential.[8]

VERBAL EXPRESSION OF THE DEAF

Not infrequently, the thinking of deaf persons is formulated in unusual verbal constructions. Some of the reasons therefor have been previously noted (page 30). It is, however, a serious error to assume that defective language usage by a deaf individual denotes defective mental ability or bizarre thinking. Occasionally it does; but more often it does not. A major responsibility of psychologists working with the deaf is to extract the basic thought a subject is trying to express no matter how unusual the language he uses.

[8] Irving S. Fusfeld, "Suggestions on Causes and Cures for Failure in Written Language," *Proceedings of the Thirty-seventh Meeting of the Convention of American Instructors of the Deaf*, West Hartford, Connecticut, June–July, 1955 (Washington, D.C.: Government Printing Office, 1956), pp. 71–79.

LANGUAGE USAGE OF THE INTERVIEWER

VERBAL LANGUAGE. A complementary consideration to the language expression of a deaf subject is the language used by the interviewer himself. A common error is to assume that once a mutually agreeable method of communication has been selected, the interviewer can proceed to express himself in his usual semantic manner. Written communication in particular lends itself to this misconception. As a result, written communications are often addressed to deaf subjects on a plane far above their levels of comprehension. Rather than confess their inability to understand, many hazard guesses usually based on some familiar words in the written context. The dubious validity of information so obtained is obvious. Some practical safeguards against communicating over the heads of deaf persons are as follows:

(1) Whenever possible, secure preliminary information about the deaf subject's level of language achievement. A good index is the reading achievement test score. As previously noted, a most profitable procedure is to initiate the whole psychological examination with a reading achievement test in order to acquire orientation as to the language level at which subsequent proceedings should be conducted.

(2) Another useful procedure is to request samples of written statements from the subject, as, for example, an autobiographic sketch or a statement concerning the kind of help he expects from the worker.

(3) The safest general procedure is to use simple vocabulary and short sentences; omit colloquial expressions, analogies, and complex abstractions; and aim for uncluttered statements, unambiguously expressed.

THE LANGUAGE OF BEHAVIOR. A final note on communicating with deaf persons concerns the interviewer's behavior. As expressed by

Betty C. Wright, "The deaf and the hard of hearing are very observant. (They have to be.) The way you stand or sit, the way you shrug your shoulders (perhaps in impatience), the way you walk from your desk to the door tell a great deal to the keen observer. Your manner, your poise, your smile, the expression in your eyes and on your face, the way you use your hands, all tell a story of indifference or understanding." [9] In interviewing the deaf, the interviewer must be alert to the fact that he is generally more closely observed than observing; and because his *behavior* conveys information, it is essential that he guard against conveying false impressions or revealing through act or facial expression what had best remain concealed.

Conduct and Scope of the Interview

INITIAL MEETING WITH A DEAF INTERVIEWEE

Under ideal conditions, an interviewer prepares himself for a first meeting with a deaf person by studying beforehand all available records and reports, especially those that will provide orientation concerning the subject's auditory status, communications abilities, educational attainments, vocational experiences, and adjustment problems. In actual practice, however, it is not always possible to obtain the necessary records before the first meeting nor to digest the pertinent facts. This need not handicap the proceedings to any significant extent, as indicated in the following summaries.

GREETING THE SUBJECT. When a deaf person arrives for an interview, he is welcomed naturally with a warm handshake, a sincere smile, and a spoken greeting. With people who do not hear,

[9] Betty C. Wright, *Orientation Training for Vocational Rehabilitation Counselors: A Syllabus on Special Problems of the Deaf and the Hard of Hearing for Orientation Institutes* (Washington, D.C.: American Hearing Society, December, 1956), p. 19.

physical contact and facial expression serve to convey the friend-liness that the warmth of the voice conveys to the hearing. In a similar vein, the deaf person should be seated comfortably near the interviewer not only to facilitate communication but also to impart a feeling of friendly interest.

As for the spoken greeting, this serves an important orientation function for the interviewer in that it calls for a spoken response from the subject. From this response it is often possible to arrive at a rough estimate of the amount and duration of hearing loss (from the sound of the subject's voice and the quality of his speech), the general comprehensibility of the speech pattern, and the subject's ability to lip-read common expressions at least. The type of greeting should be a simple "How are you?" This expression is generally familiar to the deaf; it is not difficult to lip-read; and it evokes a spoken response. An added note of friendliness is to include the subject's name in the greeting.

Following this, the interviewer introduces himself by name (also in speech), a simple courtesy that is often omitted with the deaf. There is an underlying purpose here too. Names are not common expressions and are usually difficult to lip-read. How the subject manages the situation supplies significant clues as to his initiative, interest, and favored communications habits. In effect, the manifest purpose of greeting and introduction is to put the subject at ease, create an atmosphere of relaxed, friendly interest, and establish rapport; the underlying purpose, to obtain some rough guides as to the type of interview approach best suited to the particular individual and the communications methods that will likely be needed. Thus, even in the absence of records, the interviewer can still obtain significant points of orientation directly from the subject himself.

CONDUCT OF THE INTERVIEW. In the event that the deaf individual and the interviewer are unable to communicate satisfactorily and no interpreter is available for the first meeting, the time can be used to excellent purpose by administering reading and arithmetic achievement tests. Arrangements can be made to have an interpreter present at the next meeting.

Where subject and interviewer are able to communicate satisfactorily, the interviewer continues with the question "How can I be of help to you?," asked in a sincerely interested manner. It is best to begin thus directly with deaf subjects instead of embarking on explanations about psychological services and purposes, for these are apt to be more confusing than enlightening at this point of procedure. In addition, the subject's response to the direct lead question provides clinically valuable information concerning his insight into his own needs and problems. For example, if the presenting problem is one of chronic vocational failure, it may be stated as: "I need a job"; "I can't hold a job"; or "I am not happy with my work." Each of these statements tells something about the individual and his perception of his problem.

Whatever the answer, however, it creates a natural opportunity for the psychologist to give some preliminary explanation of the procedures to come. Thus: "In order to give you the best help, I want to find out what kind of a job you will be happiest and most successful with. To do this, I must know more about you. So we will talk together and do some tests. We call this guidance. It is done all the time with hearing people as well as with deaf people. This is the way we fit the right person to the right job. Do you understand?"

Such explanation can of course be modified or amplified to suit the subject's language attainments, his experiences, and any answer he may have made to the lead question, even an "I don't know how you can help me." In the latter case, the need to "know more about you" is all the more necessary. It makes sense; and this is an important consideration in work with the deaf. Where explanations and procedures have common-sense appeal, confidence is inspired. Therefore, practical explanations should be given deaf subjects in regard to every phase of the diagnostic procedure.

From this point, the interviewer presents the subject with the next lead opportunity, and that is to tell his story in his own way. Where an individual wants to talk voluntarily, he should of course be encouraged to do so. But not too many deaf persons will take advantage of the offer. To those who live as highly structured an existence as the deaf, the free field of an unstructured interview presents too wide an expanse and too few guides for comfort, especially at a first meeting. At this early stage, the subject is uneasy and shy; the interviewer is still a stranger to him. He does not know what to say or how to begin. For an interviewer to fall back on interrogation has its dangers. Personally directed questions before the subject is ready for them may arouse more embarrassment and anxiety than no interview structure at all.

Again, the most practical course to pursue is to use some of the less complex psychological tests to break the ice. The deaf are used to such tests from their school days on and accept them quite matter-of-factly. Achievement tests and figure and design drawings are eminently suited for the purpose. As the subject gains in self-confidence in the course of succeeding meetings, the conduct of interview proceeds along the same general principles as with the hearing.[10]

SCOPE OF THE DIAGNOSTIC INTERVIEW. The scope of a diagnostic interview encompasses all the information required by an examiner to clarify the needs and problems of a subject. In the case of the deaf, this would include (*a*) acceptance of deafness; (*b*) attitudes toward self, family, and the hearing world; (*c*) liberation from the bonds of childhood dependence; (*d*) social maturity, activities, and interpersonal relations; (*e*) appropriateness of

[10] Frederick C. Thorne, *Principles of Psychological Examining* (Brandon, Vermont: Journal of Clinical Psychology, 1955), pp. 129–41.

goals and aspirations; (*f*) initiative and enterprise; and (*g*) motivations.

Such information is not limited to what the interviewee states. It also includes the parts of the story he is reluctant to discuss as well as his manner of narration; behavior and appearance; mood; major themes and preoccupations; insight; and expressed judgments. The interviewer for his part must not only perceive how best to draw out a particular individual; he must also know where he is drawing him and why; how to direct a rambling discourse into diagnostically meaningful channels without arousing anxiety; how to take notes without irritating the interviewee; and, above all, how to interpret the narrative he receives in terms of its underlying implications.

Of deaf interviewees it can be said that as they acquire increasing confidence in the interviewer, they prove highly cooperative participants who tell their stories and answer questions openly and fully, with unusual frankness singularly unhampered by inner misgivings or false modesty.

Communicating with Deaf Children

Direct communication with elementary-school-level deaf children is unusually difficult for the uninitiated because the children are still in the process of developing language and communications skills, and as yet their attainments are not substantial enough for sustained conversation of the interview type. As a rule, the younger the pupil and the earlier the onset of deafness, the less developed are verbal communications abilities. A common error is to assume that pupils who cannot converse verbally to any significant extent can do so in the sign language. This may be the case with children of deaf parents who communicate manually. It does not obtain for the majority of pupils to the extent commonly supposed.

The sign language is not formally taught in most schools for the deaf on the theory that it will interfere with the learning of verbal language. Nevertheless, many children attending such schools do communicate manually with one another. Some of the signs they use are conventional and recognizable; but many others are corruptions or innovations that the pupils devise themselves, pick up from one another, and pass on to future generations of schoolmates. Such signs are difficult for outsiders to understand. Therefore, when a psychologist has reason to believe that a deaf pupil can impart significant information through the sign language, the interpreter had best be a member of the pupil's school staff.

When a deaf child's conventional communications skills are too scant for sustained use, they are supplemented by such resources as are used by teachers of the deaf, namely, spoken conversation graphically illustrated by pantomime, acting, picture illustration of ideas, drawing, facial expression, or any other reasonable means that crosses the mind of the interviewer. And finally, when the expressive and receptive skills of both interviewer and deaf child are exhausted, there still remain the case history, observation and the language of behavior to tell the child's story for him.

8. PSYCHOLOGICAL TESTING: ADULTS

IN CONTRAST to reported history and subjective interview, psychological testing represents a controlled, objective approach to diagnostic study. Although no substitute for a full clinical examination, testing can provide valuable information concerning mental capacity, personality traits, emotional disturbances and behavioral deviations, achievements and aptitudes, differential diagnosis, educational and vocational potentials, treatment needs, and predictive appraisal. There are tests specifically designed to probe these various areas.

Tests are also designed to serve the special requirements of different kinds of subjects, as, for example, the illiterate, the foreign-language speaking, and the deaf. Classified on the basis of method of administration and response are the following types of tests in common use at the present time.

NONLANGUAGE TESTS. Nonlanguage tests are those that require no verbal language for administration and none for response. Instructions are given in pantomime, and response is made by using pencil markings to perform such non-language test tasks as picture completion, series completion, indicating incongruent elements in a series, indicating similarities in a series, digit-symbol, matching, mazes, and the like.

NONVERBAL TESTS. In nonverbal tests, the instructions are given in verbal language, either spoken or read, but none is required for response. Test items and manner of response are generally similar to those of the nonlanguage tests. In some nonverbal tests, the instructions lend themselves to pantomime adaptation.

PERFORMANCE TESTS. Performance tests are those that call for a manipulative type of response such as form-board fitting, picture-puzzle completion, block designs, and block constructions. Often, paper-and-pencil test items are included in performance scales. The instructions for performance tests are formulated in verbal language but can be adapted to pantomime in many instances. Response requires no verbal language.

VERBAL TESTS. Verbal tests require the use and comprehension of verbal language both in administration and in response.

Of the foregoing kinds of tests, some can be administered to a group of persons at a time, and others only to individual subjects. For clinical evaluation, the individual test is a substantially finer instrument than the group test because it is designed for more detailed and intensive analysis and affords opportunity for a wider range of observed behavior. Group tests may also be individually administered for certain purposes.

In all instances, however, before a psychological test can yield valid and reliable information, it must be standardized; and to maintain its diagnostic authenticity, it should be used with subjects whose general background and experiences are in conformity with those of the standardization population from which the test norms were originally derived. Thus, verbal tests, whether group or individual, assume normal language development and comprehension; and all tests, nonlanguage as well as verbal, that are standardized on representative samplings of a population assume representative background and experiences on the part of a subject.

These are fundamental principles in psychological testing. In the field of the deaf, they constitute basic problems.

The Basic Testing Problem

So far as the writer is aware, there are no psychological tests of any kind, neither nonlanguage, nonverbal, performance, nor verbal, that are standardized exclusively on deaf adults. Therefore, in the diagnostic evaluation of such subjects, psychologists are obliged to turn to measures standardized on the hearing. This is no serious breach in the case of nonlanguage and performance types of mental measures, since many were devised with the deaf in mind. However, using only such measures places severe limitations on the scope of diagnostic inquiry. As a result, verbal tests are also used with deaf adults, both in clinical situations and for vocational, educational, and occupational appraisal. This has aroused considerable debate in the field as well as feelings of professional guilt among psychologists.

In defense of the practice is Brunschwig's statement that "in view of the fact that the deaf dwell for the most part in a hearing world, this procedure seems justifiable." [1] To this, the Heiders counter with the argument that

before such quantitative measures, designed . . . for an average hearing population can be offered for use with the deaf it will be necessary to make broader analyses of the whole life situation of the deaf person to find out what his psychological environment is, to define his life in terms of what he can and cannot do, to find out at what points the restrictions imposed by his deafness become psychologically important and what the "normal" and expedient ways of adjusting to his situation are. [2]

[1] Lily Brunschwig, *A Study of Some Personality Aspects of Deaf Children* (Contributions to Education No. 687; New York: Teachers College, Columbia University, 1936), p. 29.

[2] Fritz Heider and Grace Moore Heider, *Studies in the Psychology of the Deaf*, No. 2, Psychological Monographs, LIII (1941), 66.

The latter view is of course the sounder one, both clinically and theoretically. While this view recognizes that the deaf live in the same physical surroundings as the hearing, it also recognizes that the circumstance can scarcely be considered an intrinsic criterion of test validity. In fact, when the "same" world of the deaf and the hearing is reduced to its psychological equivalents, it becomes two different places: a deaf world and a hearing one. In the deaf world, tests devised for the hearing often acquire unexpected implications; and the test scores, different psychological attributes.

Timely confirmation comes by way of the current study of the United States Civil Service Commission in ways of testing deaf civil service applicants. The attention of the Commission was directed to the fact that "the language used in our tests and in the directions and procedures for these tests could not be readily translated into the limited concepts common to deaf people, and that therefore such tests were not a true measure of the applicant's ability." [3] It should be added that the deaf applicants under consideration were "a college group—people who have demonstrated their ability in the intellectual sphere to the extent that they have been able to pursue college careers successfully." [4]

The kind of situation apt to develop when verbal tests are used indiscriminately with less exceptional deaf job applicants is illustrated by the following anecdote:

The personnel director of a large business concern employing deaf persons became greatly alarmed at the number of personal data forms in which the answer "Yes" had been given by a number of young deaf applicants to the questions "Have you ever been in a mental hospital?" and "Have you ever had fits?"

She unburdened her anxieties to an experienced teacher of the deaf and was promptly reassured. The young people were all right. None had ever been committed to a mental hospital. None had ever had fits. The problem lay in the language of the data forms.

[3] Meyer Shultz and Eva Russell Stunkel, "The Civil Service Commission Studies Ways of Testing the Deaf," *The Silent Worker*, IX (1956), 7.
   [4] *Ibid.*

In the first instance, the words "mental" and "hospital" had never been taught to the deaf applicants as the unit expression "mental hospital." Consequently, they had little opportunity to become familiar with the meaning on their own. But, they were completely familiar with the word "hospital." Most of them had been in a hospital at one time or other and the word stood out like an old friend. Accordingly, they geared their response to this key word, and in so doing obligingly answered "Yes" to the whole question, "Have you ever been in a mental hospital?"

As to the second question, "Have you ever had fits?," all the young women had just completed a course in dressmaking. Great stress had been placed upon the need for accuracy in the cut and fit of the garments they had made. What more reasonable than to assume that the word "fits" in the question was the plural of the term "fit" as in dressmaking. So here too the answer "Yes" seemed entirely suitable to the question.[5]

This then depicts something of the dilemma facing the conscientious psychologist in the field of the deaf: whether to limit testing activities until adequate measures are devised, or whether to select tests that offer clinical promise and adapt them to the needs of the situation. There is but one obvious answer. In order to avoid further curtailment of the already limited psychological services available to the deaf, the latter is unquestionably the more pressing (although interim) solution.

Verbal Test Selection

In selecting verbal tests for the adult deaf, the first consideration is the purpose for which the test is to be used. In general, the only *verbal* tests that can safely be used as they stand (*when properly administered*) are language and reading achievement tests, since the aim here is solely to measure proficiency in these skills. In using verbal tests for any other purpose, there is always an element of risk involved, namely, that a subject's language disabilities, differently derived concepts, and limited life experiences will distort the results.

[5] Edna Simon Levine, *Youth in a Soundless World* (New York: New York University Press, 1956), p. 165.

It is often assumed that any verbal test can be used with deaf subjects if appropriate methods of communication are employed. The fallacy of this assumption can be seen in the "mental hospital" anecdote. The word "mental" is easily communicated, and the word "hospital" also. But method of communication does not impart meaning to an unfamiliar expression or experience. Explanation and/or example are also required. Therefore, in selecting verbal intelligence and personality tests for the deaf, not only must the test language be carefully scrutinized, but even closer scrutiny must be given the test concepts and situations that a deaf subject may never have experienced nor learned about, or to which he is obliged to respond differently from hearing persons by reason of auditory disability and its associated implications. Examples of test items that bear different connotations for deaf and hearing are the following taken from three well-known personality inventories.

From the Minnesota Multiphasic Personality Inventory: [6]
>A-35. My hearing is apparently as good as that of most people.
>A-37. My speech is the same as always (not faster or slower, or slurring; no hoarseness).
>A-42. I have no difficulty in keeping my balance in walking.
>C-31. I have at times stood in the way of people who were trying to do something, not because it amounted to much but because of the principle of the thing.
>D-38. My conduct is largely controlled by the customs of those about me.
>E-16. When I take a new job, I like to be tipped off on who should be gotten next to.
>E-23. I am likely not to speak to people until they speak to me.
>E-55. While in trains, busses, etc., I often talk to strangers.

[6] Starke R. Hathaway and J. Charnley McKinley, *The Minnestota Multiphasic Inventory*, rev. ed. (New York: The Psychological Corporation, 1943).

G-30. At times my thoughts have raced ahead faster than I could speak them.

From the Bernreuter Personality Inventory: [7]

   1. Does it make you uncomfortable to be "different" or unconventional?

 32. Do you prefer traveling with someone who will make all the necessary arrangements to the adventure of traveling alone?

 66. Do you find it difficult to get rid of a salesman?

 82. Are you willing to take a chance alone in a situation of doubtful outcome?

From the Bell Adjustment Inventory: [8]

Do you sometimes feel that your parents are disappointed in you?

Is (was) your mother the dominant member of the family?

Have you often felt that either of your parents did not understand you?

Since deviations from normative "hearing" response to such items of standardized personality inventories generally suggest maladjustment, when a deaf subject takes this kind of structured test he runs the risk of being considered a psychological deviate simply because his answers to certain questions cannot coincide with those of hearing persons. The exhaustive task of rewording, concept-screening, and discarding inapplicable items from the full series of such tests to adapt them to the deaf is of questionable value; for in the end it is still doubtful if adjustment and maladjustment among the deaf can be validly measured in terms of the test norms established for the hearing. At the present stage of psychological ignorance of the deaf, nothing can be taken for

[7] Robert G. Bernreuter, "The Personality Inventory" (Stanford University Press, Stanford University, California).

[8] Hugh M. Bell, "The Adjustment Inventory" (Stanford University Press, Stanford University, California).

granted. Therefore, when verbal measures are used, the minimum compensation that can be offered a deaf subject is to exercise the greatest possible care in the selection, administration, and interpretation of such instruments.

Test Administration

In view of the many uncertainties involved in testing the deaf, when an opportunity arises for carrying out a positive procedure, it should be rigorously followed. Test administration offers such an opportunity. The first prerequisite for testing the deaf, and one that can be achieved readily enough with care and patience, is to make certain the subject understands what he is expected to do with each test task. Unless this is done, an examiner cannot be sure whether test failure was due to inability to perform a task or to inability to understand the instructions. This obtains for nonlanguage as well as verbal tests. The following suggestions are offered to facilitate test administration.

NONLANGUAGE TESTS. The pantomime instructions used in nonlanguage testing are not as easy to carry out as is commonly supposed. The directions that come with a test should be memorized thoroughly, and the examiner should have sufficient preliminary practice in test administration to insure that a smooth message is relayed to the subject. The same must be done when an examiner makes up his own pantomime instructions for nonverbal and performance tests.

VERBAL AND NONVERBAL GROUP TESTS. Not all nonverbal tests can be administered in pantomime. With those that cannot, the language of the test instructions is dealt with as in verbal group tests.

Since most groups of deaf individuals represent a heterogeneous assortment of communications skills and language abilities, the basic aim in verbal group-test administration is to provide for all methods and levels of language comprehension. Where group tests are used routinely with deaf subjects, a most convenient procedure is to construct a permanent oak-tag chart of test directions that can be used over and over again. First, the language of the test instructions should be carefully screened and reduced to short sentences and simple expressions. Then, the simplified instructions are printed on large sheets of oak-tag, using one sheet for each set of instructions plus the corresponding sample tasks. The chart is so constructed that it can be hung in a position clearly visible to all members of the group to be tested; when the test is administered, examiner and group read the instructions and perform the sample tasks together. The chart is a timesaving substitute for a blackboard.

If a group is heavily weighted with nonreaders, the test instructions should be signed and read aloud simultaneously, either by the examiner or an interpreter. The group should not be held up by individual problems of comprehension. These are dealt with separately. It is a good idea to have extra sample tasks on hand for special contingencies. In preparing the samples, the examiner should keep them on a simpler level than the least difficult task of the associated test series to avoid too detailed preliminary practice.

INDIVIDUAL TESTS. The methods of communication through which individual tests are administered include all those discussed in the section on interview plus the pantomime directions mentioned in connection with nonlanguage testing. The methods ultimately chosen depend upon the particular test task and the subject's language and communications abilities. Examiners must always bear in mind that the function of test administration is to impart instruction, and that the manner of administration is dictated by a subject's communications needs rather than by an examiner's limitations.

When comprehension of test instructions is not achieved through the simplification of language and extra sample tasks, an interpreter should be called in. In administering tests through an interpreter, the examiner must be particularly careful to see that test instructions are strictly followed and not modified by the interpreter in such a way as to suggest response. Interpreters must be strongly cautioned against making suggestions to a subject or indicating approval or disapproval of response by facial expression.

Test Batteries for Deaf Adults

Diagnostic information sought through psychological testing generally requires the use of a variety or battery of tests rather than a single instrument. References to the greater number of tests and test scales that have been used with the deaf are presented in Appendix H. The following presents various batteries of tests in current use with deaf adults.

A CLINICAL DIAGNOSTIC BATTERY

A battery of tests compiled from among those listed under the following areas of examination is used by the present writer in the clinical examination of deaf adults. Test selection is based upon the needs of the particular subject and situation, and individual tests are always preferred. Where group tests are used, as in achievement testing, they are individually administered. The information obtained through testing is pooled with the data derived from the case history, interview, and observation for full psychological appraisal.

READING AND LANGUAGE ACHIEVEMENT

As a rule, the clinical battery is begun by establishing the deaf person's level of language attainment. Knowing this provides the psychologist with guides for (*a*) the selection of additional tests;

(*b*) the level of language and concept expression that will have to be used in test administration and in communicating with the subject; and (*c*) the interpretation of test results.

If a subject's level of language comprehension is low, so too will his levels of attainment be in all school subjects that depend on adequate language achievement for mastery. Where this is the case, there is no need to give a full battery of achievement tests. The skill subjects alone suffice.

Although any good achievement test may be used with the deaf, the following are reported to render particularly good service:

American School Achievement Tests, Young and Pratt. Public School Publishing Company. These tests are designed to measure achievement in the skill subjects: reading, arithmetic, and language. Levels: Primary Battery I, Grade 1; Primary Battery II, Grades 2–3; Intermediate Battery, Grades 4–6.

Metropolitan Achievement Tests, Allen, Bixler, Connor, Graham, and Hildreth. World Book Company. Levels: Primary I, Grade 1; Primary II, Grades 2–3.5; Elementary Battery, Grades 3–4.5; Intermediate Battery, Grades 5–6.5; Advanced Battery, Grades 7–9.

Municipal Battery: National Achievement Tests, Speer and Smith. Acorn Publishing Company. Levels: Grades 3–6; Grades 6–8.

Progressive Achievement Tests, Tiegs and Clark. California Test Bureau. The tests in reading, arithmetic, and language are available in separate editions. Levels: Primary Battery, Grades 1–3; Elementary Battery, Grades 4–6; Intermediate Battery, Grades 7–9; Advanced Battery, Grades 9–13.

Stanford Achievement Tests, Kelley, Ruch, and Terman. World Book Company. Levels: Primary, Grades 2–3; Elementary, Grades 3–4; Intermediate, Grades 5–6; Advanced, Grades 7–9.

When applied as measures of language proficiency, achievement tests are used with the deaf as they stand in regard to both content and scoring. The only modification made is in simplifying the instructions when necessary. If the tests are employed as clinical probes rather than as measures, they may be used in any way an examiner considers helpful in broadening his understanding of a deaf individual.

Unless there is strong contraindication, achievement testing is generally begun at about the fourth-grade level and then proceeds in the direction dictated by test performance. If a subject performs more rapidly or at a higher level than seems warranted by his scholastic history and observed language skills, it is wise to check by interrogation to see if the answers are not arrived at through clever guesswork and juxtaposition of key words in the text rather than through actual comprehension. The former is a far more frequent occurrence among the deaf than is suspected and the examiner is cautioned to check achievement test items carefully.

Next in importance to language in achievement testing is arithmetic computation. The deaf are generally poor performers in this area, but occasionally an individual will demonstrate unusual computational ability even though his other achievements are low. This alerts the psychologist to the likelihood of undeveloped mental resources. It must also be remembered that in certain occupations, the ability to handle the numerical concepts of the trade is as important as language comprehension.

MENTAL CAPACITY

1. VERBAL AND PERFORMANCE SCALES: *Wechsler-Bellevue Intelligence Scale, Form I.*[9] In the present writer's experience, this is the most valuable single instrument available for the mental evaluation of most deaf adults as well as a large proportion of older adoles-

[9] David Wechsler, *The Measurement of Adult Intelligence*, 2d ed. (Baltimore: The Williams & Wilkins Company, 1941).

cents. The Scale is composed of two subscales, one verbal and the other performance. Each yields its own I.Q., and both together a combined I.Q. The test is so constructed that direct comparison can be made between Verbal and Performance I.Q.s. Further, the language of the Verbal Scale is relatively simple and direct, and the tasks are of the common-sense type. Finally, the Scale has been standardized on adults and besides yielding I.Q.s alerts the examiner to a number of clinical possibilities. The minor modifications employed by the writer in using the Scale with the deaf are summarized as follows:

a. Modification of the Verbal Scale

(1) Contents. Four tests of this Scale are customarily used. They are: General Information; General Comprehension; Arithmetical Reasoning; and Similarities. Digits Forward and Backward and Vocabulary are usually omitted. The former appears more strongly influenced by lip reading than by intelligence and does not lend itself to satisfactory written presentation. The latter stresses disability rather than capacity.

(2) Administration. The test questions of the Verbal Scale are presented to the subject in somewhat simplified language and on mimeographed form sheets with sufficient space after each question for a written response. Some subjects prefer to read the test questions without interference from the examiner except for the instructions required for each test series. With most subjects, however, the printed forms serve as a basic communications aid which the examiner further clarifies through direct oral and/or manual communication. The written (verbatim) responses are of great assistance in scoring, for at times considerable thought must be given the concept a subject tried to convey before it is possible to apply the appropriate scoring criterion.

The following minor modifications in the language of instruction and test questions are used by the writer:

Information: "I am going to ask you some questions about different things. Some of the questions are easy and some are hard. Do not worry if you cannot answer them all. Only few people can. Just answer as many as you are able." The only language revisions were made in the following questions:

3. How many pints are in one quart?

9. How tall are most American women?

10. Who made the first airplane?

11. How many miles is it from Paris to New York?

14. Who was the first person to find the North Pole?

Comprehension:

1. Pretend you are walking in the street. You find an envelope. There is a letter in it. The envelope is closed and a name and address are written on it. It also has a new stamp. What is the best thing to do with it?

2. Pretend you are in the movies. You smell smoke and then you see a fire nearby (not on the screen). What is the best thing to do?

3. Why isn't it a good idea to be friends with people who do bad things?

4. Why must people pay taxes (money to the government)?

5. Shoes are made of leather. Why?

6. Why does land in the city cost more money than land in the country?

7. Pretend you are lost in a forest. It is daytime. How will you get out? What will you do?

8. Why must we have laws?

9. People must get a license before they can get married. Why?

10. Small children who are born deaf do not know how to talk before they go to school. Why?

Arithmetical Reasoning:

1. How much is $4 and $5?

2. A man spends 6¢ for stamps. He gives the clerk 10¢. How much money will he get back?

3. A man spends 8¢ for stamps. He gives the clerk 25¢. How much money will he get back?

4. One orange costs 4¢. How many oranges can you buy for 36¢?

5. A man walks 3 miles in 1 hour. How many hours will he need to walk 24 miles?

6. A man buys seven 2¢ stamps. He gives the clerk 50¢. How much money will he get back?

7. Seven pounds of sugar cost 25¢. How many pounds can you buy for $1?

8. A man spent $400 for an old car. This was ⅔ of what it cost when it was new. How many dollars did it cost new?

9. Eight men can finish a job in 6 days. How many men can finish it in ½ a day?

10. A train moves 150 yards in 10 seconds. How many feet will it move in ⅕ of a second?

Similarities: "I am going to name two different things. But in some ways they are the same. I want you to tell me in what important way they are the same." Examiner proceeds with the pairs according to the test directions.

b. Modification of the Performance Scale

(1) Contents. All the test items of the Wechsler Performance Scale are used with deaf subjects.

(2) Administration. The following modifications have proved successful *when appropriate methods of communication are used:*

Picture Arrangement: "Look at these pictures. They are supposed to tell a story, but they are in the wrong order. They are mixed up. Put them in the right order. Which should be first; which second; which last? Good. Now I am going to show you other picture stories. But I will show them to you mixed up. You must fix them in the right order, the same as you did this. Do you understand? Let's do this one (the sample) over again to make sure."

Picture Completion: The pictures of this series are consecutively arranged and mimeographed on two sheets of 8½" by 11" paper, pictures 1 through 8 on one sheet, and 9 through 15 on the other. The purpose is to have the subject *draw in* the "most important" missing part. It often happens that deaf subjects do not know the words for certain missing parts, and placing a large finger on a small picture without any accompanying statement does not always tell what part is specified. When a subject does not know what the word "missing" means nor the sign for "missing," the incompleted chair of the Hiskey series is used for purposes of illustration, or the examiner can use a drawing of his own. The Wechsler test items are begun after the subject understands the meaning of this key word.

Block Design: The Wechsler instructions are easily carried out in pantomime.
Object Assembly: The Wechsler instructions are easily carried out in pantomime.
Digit Symbol: The Wechsler instructions are easily carried out in pantomime.

c. Scoring. In the large majority of cases, the quantitative as well as the clinical-diagnostic features of the Scale are applied to deaf subjects, and scoring is carried out in accordance with the Wechsler criteria and norms. In the case of the Verbal I.Q., the four-test scale used is prorated to five. Empiric observation over years of use of the test with deaf adults indicates that, all else being equal, the Verbal I.Q. range from about 85 to 95 represents good average performance; that Performance Scale I.Q.s of the deaf compare very favorably with the Wechsler norms for the hearing; and that the most clinically revealing test items with the deaf are Comprehension, Similarities, and Picture Arrangement. If a deaf subject performs well in these items, mental ability is good to exceptional even though he may perform less well on other tasks. However, the examiner is cautioned that the converse does not follow. A deaf individual may perform poorly on these items and still be of average intelligence. In short, the final appraisal of intelligence depends upon a careful study of each item of response and of whatever unevenness of performance there may be before the Wechsler normative criteria can be intelligently applied. It must also be noted that there are deaf adults with whom the Wechsler Scale cannot be used, excepting as an experimental probing device, because of insufficient language comprehension, scholastic attainment, and background of experience. Tests used with such individuals are discussed in the following section. Finally, although the writer's major experiences in the use of the Wechsler Scale with the deaf have been with Form I, its revision, the Wechsler Adult Intelligence Scale, commonly termed WAIS, appears equally promising.

2. PERFORMANCE SCALES. Where the Wechsler Scale cannot be used with deaf adults or where supplementary information is desired, performance scales are commonly employed. In selecting performance scales for the deaf, the general aim is to choose those in which a sizable variety of items is included in order to probe the broadest possible range of mental ability. Unfortunately, many of these scales have an important structural weakness when used with adults, and that is the mental-age method of evaluating intelligence. Scores are obtainable up to the mental ages from about 14 to 16 years, depending on the test; but beyond this level, test scores as well as many of the test items lose their discriminative significance as mental measures, and the examiner is obliged to fall back on qualitative appraisal and clinical judgment. The following tests are listed in this section on adult testing because they include some special provision for scoring at the adult level. Subsequent reference is made to other scales that can be used with deaf adults. Unless otherwise indicated, no special modification is required in the use of performance and nonlanguage tests with the deaf.

The Arthur Point Scale of Performance Tests.[10] Form I and Revised Form II. Provision for adult scoring is made through extrapolation. Form I consists of: Knox Cube Imitation Test; Seguin-Goddard Form Board; Pintner-Paterson Two-Figure Form Board; Casuist Form Board; Pintner Manikin Test; Knox-Kempf Feature Profile Test; Mare-Foal Form Board; Healy Pictorial Completion Test I; Kohs Block Design Test; Porteus Mazes. Revised Form II contains: Knox Cube Test (Arthur revision); Seguin Form Board (Arthur revision); Arthur Stencil Design Test; Porteus Maze Tests (Arthur printing); Healy Picture Completion Test II.

Leiter-Partington Adult Performance Scale.[11] This short test designed for adult levels consists of: pathways test; stencil design test; painted cube assembly test.

3. NONLANGUAGE TESTS. The following nonlanguage group tests when individually administered contribute useful supplementary data to the findings of the individual tests. All are paper-and-pencil tests.

Army Beta Test (original form). This is one of the original non-language paper-and-pencil tests and consists of: mazes; digit-symbol; substitution; pictorial absurdities; paper form board; picture completion; perceptual speed.

Army Beta Revised. The content is the same as that of the original Army Beta Test, but there is significant modification in the general procedure for computing the I.Q.

[10] Grace Arthur, *A Point Scale of Performance Tests,* Vol. I: *Clinical Manual* (New York: The Commonwealth Fund, 1930).

[11] R. G. Leiter, "The Leiter Adult Intelligence Scale," *Psychological Service Center Journal,* III (1951), 155–239.

McCall Multi-Mental Scale: Nonlanguage. This is a test of pictorial relationships in regard to relations of opposites, of similar pairs, of part to whole, of whole to parts, and of sequences. Although it cannot be used as it stands as a sole measure of the intelligence of deaf adults, the test is nevertheless an interesting screening and supplementary device.

Pintner General Ability Tests (Levels: Elementary, Intermediate, Advanced). These are tests involving graphic relationships and consisting of: figure dividing; reverse drawings; pattern synthesis; movement sequence; manikin; and paper folding.

PERSONALITY

I. VERBAL TESTS

The Rorschach Technique.[12] For reasons previously mentioned in connection with structured verbal adjustment inventories, the present writer favors the use of projective techniques in the personality study of the deaf. Of these, the Rorschach technique has proved highly rewarding at the adult level. (The writer seldom uses this test with preadolescent deaf subjects.) However, since not all deaf persons are equally responsive to this test, it is customarily used in conjunction with other projective devices listed below.

(1) Modifications in administration. The average deaf subject is usually not at his best in unstructured examination procedures. It is therefore wise to delay the use of projective techniques until the individual is completely at ease and relaxed with the psychologist. When the time is ripe for administering the Rorschach Test, the writer introduces it as a test of imagination, having found that this objectifies the procedure sufficiently to allay self-consciousness

[12] Hermann Rorschach, *Psychodiagnostics* (Berne, Switzerland: Hans Huber, 1942).

and anxiety. The methods of communication used are those habitually employed by the subject. The test is begun with the statement: "Now we are going to have a test of imagination. This is a very interesting test because there is no wrong answer! Whatever you say is right; and the more you say, the better. This is how we do it. I am going to show you these cards. You will look at each one for as long as you like and then tell me what it makes you think of, or what it looks like to you. Tell me everything that comes to your mind." During the course of testing, the subject is encouraged to respond as fully as possible and to turn the plates if he has not already done so; he is quietly reassured with a nod and smile when he appears anxious about his responses. The stop watch is handled as inconspicuously as possible. Inquiry is conducted at the conclusion of each set of responses, and every effort is made to deal with the inquiry not as interrogation but rather as an expression of the examiner's interest in knowing how the subject arrived at his answers.

Where a deaf individual has not enough language for either verbal or manual response, Grassi's "graphic Rorschach" approach [13] is tried. The subject is given sheets of blank white paper of similar size to the Rorschach plates and a supply of pencils and crayons of like color to those found in the blots. He is directed in pantomime to draw whatever he sees or likes in the test cards and to indicate or draw the parts he does not like. The single plates are placed before him as he draws and the series presented in proper sequence. The Grassi approach appears a highly promising technique with such deaf subjects. In most instances, it is at least possible to approximate the individual's conformity to popular thinking as well as the nature and amount of deviance from popular response.

(2) Procedures and comments. The noncommittal role of the

13 J. R. Grassi and K. N. Levine, "The Graphic Rorschach Manual," *Psychiatric Quarterly*, Vol. XVII (1943).

examiner is maintained with the deaf as with the hearing; but short of this, sufficient flexibility is permitted to suit the needs of the individual subjects. If, for example, the duration of time required for testing outstrips a subject's interest or patience, testing is discontinued and resumed at a future session. If a subject prefers to write out his responses without interruption for inquiry, this is done and inquiry is dealt with at a subsequent meeting or omitted altogether if the individual shows reluctance. If, as seldom happens, a subject refuses to take the test altogether, he is not forced to do so. The opportunity is offered again some other time, or other tests are used.

It has been the writer's experience that the deaf have a tendency to be somewhat underproductive or constrained in Rorschach response. Hence the need for continual encouragement. In most cases, however, sufficient responses are produced for scoreable analysis, and the rationale of Rorschach scoring and evaluation has been empirically observed to obtain for deaf adults as for hearing. Interpretation of the results is, of course, made in the context of the deaf subject's development and life experiences. But even in this context, the Rorschach Test has proved remarkably effective in identifying psychopathology among the deaf, both in known clinical cases and in numbers of cases in which the clinical evidences of pathology appeared only after considerable lapse of time.

Sentence Completion Tests. When appropriately administered, sentence completion tests often provide quick and striking leads to feelings and attitudes of deaf subjects. The leads so obtained are then used as the basis for further clinical exploration through interview. The writer has found the sentence-completion approach generally more rewarding than the Thematic Apperception Test with the deaf, again because of the more structured nature of the sentence task and the less taxing demands on language and imagination than are required by the Thematic tasks of having to tell stories about pictures. Of the sentence-completion tests available, the Forer Test [14] has the advantage of separate forms for men, boys, women, and girls.

2. NONVERBAL PERSONALITY TESTS

Figure Drawings.[15] The subject is asked to draw a picture of a person. When he is finished, he is asked to draw a person of the opposite sex to that already drawn. Where there are no barriers of communication between examiner and subject, discussion of the drawings based on the Machover questionnaire can be conducted. However, in evaluating personality on the basis of figure drawings whether with or without discussion, special experience in the use of the technique is required by the examiner.

House-Tree-Person Projective Technique (H-T-P).[16] Here, not only a person but also a house (environment) and a tree (development) are drawn by the subject. Provision in scoring is made for verbal and nonverbal response as well as for qualitative and quantitative interpretation.

Kinget Drawing-Completion Test.[17] The subject is presented with a test blank on which are eight squares each containing small geometric stimulus drawings which he is directed to complete in any way he wishes. Scoring and interpretation of personality are based on the subject's graphic productions and not necessarily on verbal associations.

[14] B. R. Forer, *Forer Structured Sentence Completion Test: Men, Boys, Women, Girls* (Los Angeles: Western Psychological Services, 1958).

[15] K. Machover, *Personality Projection in the Drawing of the Human Figure* (Springfield, Illinois: Charles C. Thomas, 1949).

[16] J. N. Buck, "The H-T-P Technique: A Qualitative and Quantitative Scoring Manual," *Journal of Clinical Psychology*, Vol. IV (1948) and Vol. V (1949).

[17] M. G. Kinget, *The Drawing-Completion Test* (New York: Grune & Stratton, 1952).

Make a Picture Story (MAPS).[18] The material of this test consists of 67 die-cut figures of various kinds (male, female, adults, children, indeterminates, animals, etc.) plus various background pictures; personality evaluation is based upon the selection and arrangement a subject uses to tell a story or to act one out dramatically.

Picture Story Completion task of the IES Test.[19] Attention is directed to the Picture Story Completion task of the recently published IES Test as presenting a nonverbal test format of remarkable applicability to the deaf. The test item consists of 13 sets of cartoons in each of which two or three cartoons begin a story which the subject completes by selecting one picture from three choices of story-ending provided for each set. The three aspects of scoring yield an I score which "measures the degree to which the subject sees the outside world as expressing impulses freely; the E score which measures the degree of objective reality with which the subject perceives the external world; and the S score which is intended to reflect the degree to which an individual sees the outside world as moralistic, condemning, and abiding by superego ideals." [20] Inspection of this test item suggests that considerable revision would be required for use with deaf subjects; but the rationale and format are worthy of intensive investigation as a means of personality evaluation of the deaf.

SPECIAL CLINICAL TESTS

Bender Visual Motor Gestalt Test.[21] This is a simple geometric design copying test in which various inadequate, distorted, or

[18] E. S. Shneidman, MAPS Test Manual, Journal of Projective Techniques Monograph, No. 2, 1952.

[19] Lawrence A. Dombrose and Morton S. Slobin, "The IES Test," Perceptual and Motor Skills Monograph Supplement 3, 1958.

[20] *Ibid.*, p. 353.

[21] L. Bender, *A Visual Motor Gestalt Test and Its Clinical Use* (New York: The American Orthopsychiatric Association, 1938).

bizarre reproductions provide leads to certain clinical conditions and pathologies.

Benton Revised Visual Retention Test.[22] This is a test of memory for geometric designs in which various kinds of incorrectly reproduced designs alert the examiner to the possibility of clinical pathology.

Dvorine Pseudo-Isochromatic Plates. This is a color vision test used by the present writer preceding the administration of the Rorschach Test. Its use was dictated by the unusual paucity of color remarks, comments, or manifest color reactions encountered among her deaf subjects. Empiric observation suggests that the infrequency of color reactions among these subjects is not related to color blindness.

Harris Tests of Lateral Dominance.[23] The Harris battery consists of special tests for laterality including manual, ocular, and foot dominance.

Oseretsky Tests of Motor Proficiency.[24] These tests are organized by age levels from 4 to 16 years, but can be used clinically with young adults when the need arises for more detailed observation of motor proficiency. The tests measure general static coordination, dynamic coordination of hands, general dynamic coordination, motor speed, simultaneous voluntary movements, and associated involuntary movements.

[22] A. L. Benton, *A Visual Retention Test for Clinical Use* (Revised) (New York: The Psychological Corporation, 1946).

[23] A. J. Harris, *Harris Tests of Lateral Dominance* (New York: The Psychological Corporation, 1947).

[24] N. Oseretsky, *Oseretsky Tests of Motor Proficiency: A Translation from the Portuguese Adaptation* (Educational Test Bureau, 1946).

OTHER TESTS

There are numbers of additional tests that can be used in a diagnostic battery with deaf adults in addition to those mentioned here. The reader is referred to the listing of psychological tests used with the deaf in Appendix G. Other tests not included in the listing will appear in the batteries that follow and can also be found in the various test catalogues. Some tests particularly suited for the deaf may have escaped notice altogether. The writer would deeply appreciate information about these. However, it must be emphasized that the aim in testing is *not to use as many tests as possible* but rather to use *selected tests judiciously and with skill as well as technical competence.*

A clinical battery may or may not include aptitude and special ability tests. This depends upon the circumstances. As a rule, such tests are part of vocationally oriented batteries, examples of which are presented in the following section.

VOCATIONAL EVALUATION BATTERIES

BATTERY 1: NEW YORK DISTRICT VOCATIONAL
REHABILITATION BATTERY FOR THE DEAF [25]

The following personal communication summarizes the basic procedures and psychological tests used in the evaluation of deaf clients at the New York State Division of Vocational Rehabilitation, New York District Office. Of particular interest is the clinical approach employed in a vocational rehabilitation setting. In keeping with the philosophy of total rehabilitation for the whole person

[25] The description of Battery I: New York District Vocational Rehabilitation Battery for the Deaf was written especially for this publication. Grateful acknowledgment is made by the author to Nelson A. Voorhees, New York District Supervisor, and to Murray Z. Safian, Psychological Consultant to the New York District Office.

is the psychological philosophy of comprehensive examination for the whole person.

Psychological Evaluation of Deaf and Hard-of-Hearing Clients

Individuals with hearing impairments are accepted for vocational rehabilitation services upwards of age 14 (in New York State). In the younger age group they are generally referred to this Office by schools for the deaf, or if they are attending regular schools by the guidance counselors in the schools. Adults with hearing problems are either self-referred or referred by various hospitals, social agencies, or mental hygiene centers throughout the city.

In the course of their counseling relationship, questions about their over-all work potential frequently arise and individuals are referred to a psychologist for an evaluation of intelligence, personality, and vocational potential, or a combination of the three. In the adolescent group where students are still in a school setting, the emphasis in evaluation will initially be on intelligence, achievement, and personality, and, to a lesser degree, on aptitude. Among the adult population, the emphasis will more naturally be on their immediate vocational potential.

For purposes of obtaining information about the optimal functioning of a deaf or hard-of-hearing individual, individual psychological examination seems to be the most desirable technique. It happens, of course, at this agency—primarily with adults where economic pressures are great —that they sometimes cannot expend the time required in individual evaluation and the counselor for purposes of expediency will refer them for group intelligence and aptitude testing. In the case of group testing, it is most desirable to have individuals who are deaf tested in a group of similarly disabled persons. On the other hand, individuals who are hard of hearing can be evaluated in a group composed of individuals with normal hearing, depending, of course, upon their lip-reading ability.

Typical Test Batteries for Psychological Evaluation of the Deaf

Intelligence:
  Wechsler-Bellevue
  Wechsler-Intelligence Scale for Children
  Wechsler Adult Intelligence Scale
    (Where an individual reveals good lip-reading ability and some
    verbal facility or adequate communication skill, either the entire

Scale or parts of the Verbal Scale are given, in addition to the Performance Scale.)

Otis Self-administering Test of Mental Ability, Intermediate or Higher Form

Revised Beta Examination

Personality:

Rorschach

Thematic Apperception Test

(Depending on the client's verbal facility, either given orally or else the particular themes are written out.)

Sentence Completion Test

Figure Drawings

Bender-Gestalt

Aptitude and Achievement:

(The administration of most of the verbal aptitude tests is contingent upon an individual's ability to read at the sixth-grade level. In the event that he does not read at this level, only tests of a manual-manipulative nature and other nonverbal tests are administered. However, depending on the psychologist's perception of the situation, where it is felt that a client, despite certain reading limitations, will be able to handle some of the verbal tests, these will be given.)

Psychological Corporation General Clerical Test

Minnesota Clerical Test

SRA Test of Clerical Aptitudes

Bennett Test of Mechanical Comprehension

Revised Minnesota Paper Form Board Test

SRA Test of Mechanical Aptitudes

Graves Design Judgment Test

Meier Art Judgment Test

Crawford Small Parts Dexterity Test

Purdue Pegboard

Gates Basic Reading Test

Woody-McCall Mixed Fundamentals in Arithmetic

Columbia Vocabulary Test

ACE Psychological Examination for College Freshmen

Interest:

Kuder Preference Record

Lee and Thorpe Occupational Interest Inventory. Intermediate, Advanced

The following summary of the Alpha-Beta-Gregg Battery was contributed as a personal communication by C. G. Bluett, Assistant District Supervisor of the California Vocational Rehabilitation Service. The battery is of particular interest since it was devised by Bluett himself and was statistically treated for normative data.[27] It demonstrates what can be accomplished with a small number of tests when they are combined with extensive experience, insight, and research-mindedness on the part of the tester.

The Alpha-Beta-Gregg Battery

Evaluation of the Deaf

From among many psychological tests used in early experiments, the Revised Alpha Examination Form 5, the Revised Beta, and a number-writing test called the Gregg Test have developed into a desirable and economical screening battery for the deaf. To this battery, the Purdue Pegboard and the Lee and Thorpe Occupational Interest Inventory are generally added; but only the Alpha-Beta-Gregg (A-B-G) part of the complete Battery will be discussed here.

Composition of the A-B-G Battery

Included in the Battery are fifteen short, timed subtests. The Revised Alpha contributes five verbal tests and three numerical tests. The verbal tests are: Common Sense Questions, Vocabulary, Disarranged Sentences, Association, and Reading Comprehension. The numerical tests are: Addition, Arithmetic, and Number Relations. The Revised Beta contributes six nonlanguage tests: the Maze Test, Symbols-Digits, What's

[26] The summary of the A-B-G Battery was prepared especially for this publication by C. G. Bluett. Grateful acknowledgment is made by the author.

[27] C. G. Bluett, "Vocational Survey of the Graduating Class of the California School for the Deaf," *Volta Review*, Vol. XLI (October, November, 1939); C. G. Bluett, "Test and Follow-up of Deaf Graduates," *Volta Review*, Vol. XLVI (November, 1944, through February, 1945); C. G. Bluett, "Normative Data for the Alpha-Beta-Gregg Battery," *Journal of Clinical Psychology*, VIII (July, 1952), 237–45.

Wrong (with this picture?), Spatial Relations, Picture Completion, and a Matching Test of pictures and numbers. The remaining test, the Gregg Test, is a motor test. It is treated as a subtest, but the score is not included in either the Alpha or Beta total scores. It consists of writing 1 2 3 4 5 6 7 8 9 0 as many times as possible in one minute.

Three total scores are obtained from the foregoing battery: a Revised Beta total score, a Revised Alpha total score, and a combined Alpha-Beta total score. Each of the former scores and that of the combined Alpha-Beta are independently scaled and do not represent averages.

Advantages of the A-B-G Battery

The practical advantages of the A-B-G Battery are many. It is economical, since a number of persons may be examined at one time, and appeals to all levels of ability. It is easily administered and scored in over-all time of about one hour, yet provides a comprehensive survey of general mental abilities, verbal and numerical reasoning, and spatial perception, as well as a sampling of academic achievements including arithmetic, vocabulary, and reading skill. It is important that the verbal Alpha Test be included in testing the deaf so that the client may demonstrate his varying abilities. Usually it will be found that a deaf client can understand the directions and can read and answer at least the first few questions of each subtest. When deaf clients are afforded the opportunity of taking verbal tests, the measured difference between the verbal and nonverbal scores provides a valuable index of the level of verbal skill in relation to the potential for further development.

The Composite Work Sheet

A normative Work Sheet on which the above data are summarized in convenient form is used with the A-B-G Battery. (See illustration.)

The standards for the interpretation of the raw test scores appear at the top of the Work Sheet in terms of approximations for Mental Age, Grade, and I.Q. All raw scores appearing in the body of the Work Sheet may thus be directly interpolated in terms of the applicable standard. The titles for Total Scores as well as for the subtest items appear at the left of the Work Sheet.

For purposes of illustration, the Standard Scores and test profiles for two groups are presented. Profile 1 represents the average scores for 40 out-of-school deaf clients with an average age of 25.4 years and an average grade of 10.4, while Profile 2 represents the average scores

① DEAF
CLIENT ② NON DEAF

COMPOSITE WORK SHEET
M& 25.4   10.4
SEX F AGE 25.8 LAST GRADE 10.5 DATE 1959

APPROX. M.A. (Years)............................ 11	12	13	14	16	17	18	19	20	
APPROX. GRADE............................ 5	6	8	9	10	12	13	15	16	
APPROX. IQ (Adult Score)............................ 66	72	84	90	100	107	114	125	130	

PERCENT EXCEEDED............................ 2	7	16	31	50	69	84	93	98	
STANDARD SCORE................ DEAF 30	35	40	45	50	55	60	65	70 NON DEAF	

COMB. ALPHA-BETA TOTAL............(47①)....60...89...119--155--187--217--242..265..287   49②
REV. ALPHA NO.5 TOTAL................(45)....18...29...43--76--100--124--146..165..182   49
  1. Addition.......................(53).....0....3....5----7----8-->9---10...11...12   54
  2. Arithmetic.....................(42).....1....4....6----7----9---10---12...13...15   49
  3. Common Sense..............(44).....0....2....4--6----7---9--11...13...15   51
  4. Vocabulary...................(41).....0....1....6<--11--18--22---28..34...37   48
  5. Dis. Sentences.............(47).....0....2....7--10--13--16---19...22...24   49
  6. Number Relations.........(49).....0....1....4----7-9--9---10--12...14...16   47
  7. Association...................(49).....0....1....4----9--15--23---29...33...36   51
  8. Reading Comprehension.......(42).....0....2...10--6--22---27--31...34...37   49

REVISED BETA TOTAL.............(58)....34...45...60--73--84--93--100..106..113   50
  1. Maze..........................(57).....4....5.... x ----6----7--8--9...x...10   52
  2. Symbols-Digits............(57).....6...10...14--17--20-23--26...29...30   52
  3. What's Wrong..............(54).....4....6....9--10--13--15--17..18...19   49
  4. Spatial Relations..........(57).....1....3....6--8--10--12--14..16...17   50
  5. Picture Completion,......(56).....5....9...11--13--15--17--18...19...20   49
  6. Matching...................(57).....7...10...13--16--18--20--22..23...24   51

MANUAL
  Gregg Numbers.....................(50)....6....7....9--11--12---13--14..16...17   47

for 40 clients selected without regard to disability other than that they were *not* deaf nor severely hard of hearing. The average age of the latter group is 25.8 years, and the average grade 10.5.

The profile for the hearing group is in accord with the expectation for such a heterogeneous group, since none of the subtest scores deviate above the total score of 49 by more than five Standard Score points nor below the total score by more than two Standard Score points. On the other hand, the subtest scores for the deaf group deviate as much as ten Standard Score points above and six points below its own total score level, and the pattern of subtest scores is significantly different from that of the hearing group.

The characteristics of the deaf group causing the significant deviations are known to all who are familiar with the deaf. Arithmetic, Vocabulary, and Reading scores are all significantly low, at about 8th- to 9th-grade level. Also, the Common Sense questions test, which involves rapid reading, is low. In contrast, the Association test, Number Relations, and Disarranged Sentences tests show no significant deviation from the hearing group scores but hover closely about the median for the general population. The last tests are measures of abstract reasoning, and in comparison with the low achievement test scores emphasize Levine's findings [28] that

[28] Levine, *Youth in a Soundless World.*

the deaf have ability to abstract in excess of that represented by their ability to comprehend and to express themselves in writing.

The simple Addition test score is high on the profile and high average in relation to the general population norms, as are the nonverbal tests of the Beta examination. The latter scores are all high on the profile and high average on the norms. Also, they exceed the scores for the hearing group to a significant degree. Only the Gregg test among the nonverbal tasks does not exceed the median, nor is it significantly above the scores of the hearing group.

Conclusion

The deaf group averages considerable potential for further development. The ability to reason abstractly has not been developed to the level of its potential. The fact that the Alpha-Beta-Gregg Battery differentiates between the hearing and deaf groups so clearly and in keeping with the known characteristics of the deaf is excellent recommendation for its use with deaf individuals.

BATTERY III: A REHABILITATION COUNSELOR'S TESTING

KIT FOR THE DEAF

The following recommendations and test battery for the use of rehabilitation counselors were suggested by the Committee on Psychological Services to the Deaf and the Severely Hard of Hearing of the First Institute for Special Workers for the Aural Disabled.[29]

Recommendations to Rehabilitation Counselors

1. The rehabilitation counselor specializing in work with the deaf and the severely hard of hearing should contact one or more qualified psychologists in different sections of the state.

2. The counselor should seek to interest the psychologist in the need for his services, and the need for the latter to learn how to adapt his techniques to the problems of the deaf and the severely hard of hearing.

3. The counselor should be responsible for sending information to the psychologist on important data in the case history which would be

[29] U.S. Office of Vocational Rehabilitation, *Reports of Workshop Committees— First Institute for Special Workers for the Aural Disabled* (Rehabilitation Service Series No. 120; Washington, D.C.: Federal Security Agency, Office of Vocational Rehabilitation, June, 1950).

valuable as background material for a psychological evaluation. This information should be sent before the individual meets with the psychologist.

4. The counselor should deem it his responsibility to inform the psychologist in the special problems of rehabilitating the deaf and the severely hard of hearing. This would entail such things as forwarding bibliographies to the psychologist, discussing special case histories with him, and placing him in contact with schools for the deaf.

5. The counselor should discuss the test results and the case data with the psychologist as a means of mutual benefit, and for the greatest welfare of the client. In the initial stages, these contacts with the psychologist should be frequent. Later they will become less necessary as the psychologist becomes experienced in serving the deaf and the severely hard of hearing, and as the counselor becomes more proficient in interpreting the psychological reports.

Rehabilitation Counselor's Testing Kit

In considering the Counselor's Testing Kit, the Committee felt that a useful although arbitrary division of the deaf clients could be made in terms of a nonreading and a reading group. A discussion on both groups disclosed the fact that the nonreading group could be tested by the counselor with a very limited number of psychological tests. The reading group could be tested with many more of the available psychological instruments.

The Nonreading Group of Deaf or Severely Hard-of-Hearing Adults

The Committee proposes that the following tests be used with nonreaders among the deaf or the severely hard of hearing: Revised Beta Examination (intelligence), Pennsylvania Bi-Manual Worksample (manual), Minnesota Paper Form Board (mechanical), Bennett Mechanical Comprehension Test (mechanical).

In giving instructions for these tests, the counselor would do well to use the sign language or pantomime with the deaf, and an amplifier with the severely hard of hearing whenever possible. In all cases, the counselor should make certain that the client fully understands the directions before proceeding with the test proper.

The Committee also recommends that if the test results show the client's problems to be deeper and more complex than the counselor has anticipated, the client should be sent to expert resources for further evaluation and study.

The Reading Group of Deaf and Severely Hard-of-Hearing Adults
The following tests are recommended (by the Committee) for readers among the deaf and the severely hard of hearing:
Intelligence:
1. Revised Beta Examination (Lindner-Gurvitz Norms)
2. Shipley-Institute of Living Scale. This test yields a vocabulary age, abstract-ability age, mental age, and conceptual quotient.
Clerical:
3. Psychological Corporation General Clerical Test
Manual:
4. Pennsylvania Bi-Manual Worksample
Mechanical:
5. Minnesota Paper Form Board (Form AA)
6. Bennett Mechanical Comprehension Test (Form AA)
Achievement:
7. Stanford Achievement Test, Advanced Form H

COLLEGE-LEVEL TESTING

GALLAUDET COLLEGE TESTS AND TEST BATTERIES [30]

The following personal communication summarizes the educational testing program of Gallaudet College, Washington, D.C., the only college for the deaf in the world. All applicants for admission and all students are routinely exposed to the following tests and batteries:

Entrance Battery:
Stanford or California Achievement Tests, Complete Battery, Advanced Level. (A 9th- to 10th-grade achievement level generally qualifies for admission.)
Algebra: Different standardized tests are used from year to year covering first-year algebra through quadratics.
Language Usage and Principles: These tests are formulated from year to year by the Gallaudet Department of English.

[30] This description of the Gallaudet College Tests and Test Batteries was written especially for this publication. Grateful acknowledgment is made by the author to Leonard M. Elstad, President of Gallaudet College, and to Richard M. Phillips, Dean of Students of Gallaudet College.

At Time of Admission:
> Cooperative School and College Ability Tests: College Ability. This test is used for determining placement whether in the freshman or preparatory class. The cutoff point is based upon the mean of the previous year's freshman class on the same or a similar type of test.

Preparatory Student Battery:
> Students who require preparatory class placement are given the following battery:

> Essential High School Content Battery. This is used as a means of comparing the students with themselves and as a group at the beginning and end of the year. Another form of the same test is given at the end of the year.

> A Lower Extension of the Inglis Tests of English Vocabulary. Grades 6–10.

> Science Research Associates (SRA) Verbal and Nonverbal Tests

> Revised Beta Examination

> Edwards Personal Preference Schedule. This has been given for the past two or three years on an experimental basis.

Freshman Year:
> Repeat of the School and College Ability Tests as a class study and as a basis for next year's placement examination cutoff point.

Sophomore Year:
> Kuder Preference Inventory

> Sequential Tests of Educational Progress (National Sophomore Examinations) in Reading, Mathematics, Social Science, Science, Writing.

Senior Year:
> Graduate Record Examinations (Educational Testing Service). These serve as a measuring device for our own program as well as to provide information for the student in vocational and educational planning.

Interpretation of Test Findings

In the psychological appraisal of physically disabled persons, the expression "test interpretation" is often taken too literally. It is again emphasized that the purpose of psychological testing is to interpret not a test but rather individual behavior and reactions. The test and its scope of possible findings have already been interpreted, as it were, by the test constructor in terms of standardization, rationale, and scoring. But individual responses are clinically meaningful only in the light of a subject's background of experiences. If the background is in conformity with that of the standardization population of a given test, interpretation is facilitated. But if it is not, the examiner must acquire the necessary familiarity with the life context from which such "unstandardized" responses are derived if he is to employ valid procedures of assessment. Since the greater part of this context is supplied by the case history, this technique assumes critical importance in providing a base for the interpretation of the psychological test results of physically impaired subjects from unstandardized areas of disability.

In the case of the deaf and the severely hard of hearing, the following Workshop report,[31] which the writer helped formulate, recapitulates points of special emphasis in psychological test interpretation:

1. The test results based upon tasks involving verbal concepts and language should be interpreted with special care. Individuals who have lost their hearing early in life, or for a considerable time before testing may have acquired language habits enough different from the non-handicapped to depress test scores where language tasks are involved.

2. The older the age of the individual when his deafness occurred, the more it can be assumed that his life experiences are common to hearing persons. Therefore, loss of hearing in later life may not be expected to affect test results involving language tasks as much as loss of hearing in childhood.

3. The test results of deaf people on tests involving language or reading are more safely considered as minimal levels of abilities rather than as the upper limits of abilities.

4. When deafness is an accompanying result of a more basic condi-

[31] *Reports of Workshop Committees—First Institute for Special Workers for the Aural Disabled,* pp. 14–15.

tion, e.g., birth injury involving the nervous system in general, the psychological test results are to be considered primarily in terms of the more basic condition and secondarily in terms of the deafness and other accompanying conditions.

5. The I.Q. as a single score is to be regarded with great caution as an index of mental ability. The sub-test scores of the different mental abilities should be examined most carefully and given emphasis in the total case study.

6. The total test scores and the separate items should both be studied for clues to abilities, achievements, and personality traits. A study of responses on separate items at times may give clues to a richer and more accurate interpretation of test data with other case data. For example, misses on easy items and successes with a considerable number of difficult items may give clues to such conditions as habits of carelessness or inconsistency, inattentiveness, or to neuroticism, or even to gaps in early or later education.

7. The totally deaf and seriously hard of hearing should be tested individually and preferably with individualized tests such as the Wechsler-Bellevue.

8. Special precautions should be taken to make certain that good rapport prevails between the examiner and the deaf client. The use of the manual alphabet and sign language is encouraged as a means of giving test instructions. Otherwise, a natural, somewhat restrained form of pantomime is desirable. The counselors have a special responsibility to prepare the client for the testing experience. If the psychologist does not know the manual alphabet or sign language, the client should be told beforehand by the counselor about the nature of the tests, the need for full cooperation, the need to make certain that the client fully understands instructions before each test, and that the test results will be discussed later with the counselor. Lack of rapport definitely influences the test results. Moreover, the psychologist has more difficulty in evaluating the effects of poor rapport in the deaf because of difficulties in free and uninhibited communication.

9. When the background of the deaf person shows gaps in formal education, the causes for such a fact should be ascertained and be used in interpreting test scores.

10. Conditions of excessive depression, anxiety, idleness, or seclusiveness over long periods of time may be expected to influence test scores.

The test scores will indicate the present level of ability-functioning, but interpretations and prognoses must include an evaluation of the underlying conditions and their interaction upon the psychological test scores.

11. The disability of deafness may be overemphasized in the total case study. Other factors may be much more important and it is always well to be on guard lest such overemphasis obscure other major factors. For example, lack of formal school achievements may be due not to hearing loss but to physical or mental illness, or to neurotic parental concern over the deaf person, or even to poor attitudes of the deaf person himself.

12. Personality traits such as the will to work, adaptability to the hearing world, persistence in solving problems, method of attacking new problems, self-confidence, etc., may be seen in actual operation before, during, and after a testing session. Qualitative observation of the behavior of the deaf client may yield information of considerable significance in the fuller and deeper interpretation of test performance.

9. PSYCHOLOGICAL TESTING: CHILDREN

THE AGE span of the deaf population considered here under the heading "children" is from infancy to puberty, with special attention centered on the preschool level. In the adolescent range, many of the procedures, techniques, and tests may be applied that were discussed in connection with adult testing, with appropriate modification and test selection as required. But with the younger population, and particularly with preschool children, psychological testing requires procedural techniques and clinical qualifications that are different from those employed with older children and adults. A number of the more important ones are briefly reviewed in the section that follows.

Special Considerations in the Psychological Testing of Deaf Children

PURPOSE OF TESTING

With deaf children as with hearing, as we go down the chronological scale, the value of psychological testing as a method of controlled observation increases significantly. With older children and adults, test response is more or less limited to the performance of the task in hand. But at the preschool level, test items represent stimuli for less restrained response not only to tasks in hand but also to the examiner, the environment, and to the total testing situation. For the psychologist, the purpose of testing at this level is largely to obtain a concentrated, firsthand view of a child's development, maturation, and patterns of behavior in significant areas of function. These include motor and sensory function, expressive and receptive communications, mental alertness and ability, social responsiveness, and patterns of emotional reaction. However, since psychological test findings are in the final analysis derived from a relatively circumscribed situation, they do not necessarily tell the full story of behavior but must complement and be compared with the information assembled in the case history (see page 128) before comprehensive interpretation and appropriate recommendations can be made.

QUALIFICATIONS OF THE EXAMINER

In child testing as in all situations involving the psychological examination of the deaf, the basic prerequisites are an examiner's familiarity with the implications of early, severe hearing loss and skill in communicating with deaf subjects. Ideally, preparation for psychological work with the deaf should include a period of internship in special schools for the deaf, for the special schools represent a major developmental and maturational environment in the lives of most deaf persons. Such internships should not be limited to observation but should include actual teaching assignments, lesson planning, psychological testing, case history taking, and the rendering of psychological service to parents and teachers. The scope of experiences and insights afforded the trained psychologist by special schools for the deaf is unparalleled as a short cut to an understanding of the unusual complexities of early deafness and of the technical skills required for psychological appraisal in this area. The psychologist without such training should prepare himself for testing deaf children by observations in classes for the deaf, noting particularly the manner in which teachers communicate with their pupils, and by ample preliminary practice in testing deaf children in order to familiarize himself with the types of test materials used, acquire skill in conveying test directions as well as in the dexterous manipulation of the test materials, perceive the interpretative significance of the various test tasks, and in general achieve a feeling of ease and composure in the company of deaf children.

In addition to this technical preparation, there are important personal qualifications required of the trained clinical psychologist who works with children. Commonly mentioned as foremost qualifications are a genuine fondness and respect for children and a knowledge of the dynamics of child behavior. While there is no doubt that these are basic essentials for child practice, it is nevertheless true that mere possession of these attributes does not necessarily make a successful child practitioner. There are numbers of psychologists who are fond of children and who are unusually well informed concerning the dynamics of child behavior but who admit to being unsuccessful practitioners with young children. In these cases, it would appear that the link is weak between the possession of necessary qualifications and their application in clinical practice.

The successful child psychologist is one who is able to *use* his fondness for children and knowledge of child behavior to establish a deep empathetic relationship with his small patients; who possesses the perceptive sensitivity and acuity that keeps him aware of the feelings, thoughts, and impulses that ebb, flow, and surge through them. The successful worker with children must be able to see through the eyes of a child, and feel what it is the child is experiencing. He must be able to anticipate and predict on the basis of minute behavioral clues. He must be able to subdue his own personality to the needs of the child when this is called for, and adapt his own behavior and examination procedures to whatever exigencies may arise without loss of composure. Essential in all child practice is the psychologist's capacity to achieve this kind of psychic unity with small children. In the case of deaf children who are handicapped in normal expressive and receptive communication, this capacity is a critical qualification for psychological practice.

TECHNICAL SUGGESTIONS AND CAUTIONS

Apart from technical modifications of procedure, the same basic principles of testing obtain for deaf as for hearing children, as summarized in the following suggestions:

(1) Nothing in the testing environment should suggest a doctor's office. The room should be inviting and comfortably furnished for child testing, but no materials other than the test should be exposed to tempt distractibility. The psychologist should avoid wearing a lab coat or other type of uniform that might arouse unhappy associations in the child's mind.

(2) Closed cupboards should contain supplies of nontest materials that can be used as ice-breakers when required, and formal testing should not be begun until the ice is broken.

(3) Testing should begin with a task that is especially interesting and within the range of the child's abilities, yet not so simple as to be dull. Testing should also end on a note of success even if a nontest item must be used to achieve this.

(4) Test tasks should be presented in accordance with the subject's interests and abilities. Items that have less appeal should be carefully interspersed among the more appealing; simpler items should be used to break up a continuity of tasks presenting difficulty. In child testing, it is more judicious to try to maintain test validity in this way than to rigidly adhere to a prescribed sequence in the face of a child's resistance or distress.

(5) The psychologist should guard against taking advantage of a child's wish to please by urging him on when it is apparent that interest and energies are exhausted for the time. Testing should be discontinued when the child can no longer put forth optimal effort.

(6) If a child shows signs of panic and anxiety unless his mother is present, then the mother should be permitted to remain (or any other adult the child wants to stand by). Preferably, only one adult

and no children should be allowed to accompany the subject into the testing room. This third person, usually the mother, should be seated behind the child and off to one side so that the child can see her out of the corner of his eye without having to get up and leave the test-table to assure himself that she is still there. It is a good idea to have a supply of magazines on hand for such contingencies. A relaxed mother is one worry less for the examiner.

(7) The psychologist's behavior and facial expression should be under wise control while testing deaf children of both preschool and school-age levels. Such children commonly look to an examiner's face for signs of approval, disapproval, and clues to test response. The examiner's expression should be pleasantly encouraging but noncommittal. Extravagant praise for good response should be avoided, for when no praise is forthcoming for a poor response the child feels let down and discouraged. The psychologist should rather aim to convey calm confidence that the child is as pleased to be doing a task as the examiner is to be sharing in the proceedings. Further, the child should be made to feel that the effort he is putting forth is as important as success and more important than failure. Failure is acknowledged by: "That was difficult—but you *tried!* Now let's try another one." Success is quietly enjoyed by both. As a deaf child comes to perceive this attitude, he will cease to look for clues in the examiner's facial expression and will concentrate more on the tasks before him and on his own critical faculties.

(8) Because a young deaf child does not understand conversational language, this does not mean that the psychologist remains mute throughout the testing procedure. On the contrary. Most young deaf children would consider this very odd behavior. They are accustomed to being talked to. The examiner should talk to the deaf child as if he were a hearing subject, always remembering to reinforce his important remarks by gesture, facial expression, and pantomime.

(9) In testing young children, the psychologist should not be so eager to get to the test items that he ignores equally important aspects of observation such as watching the child remove his hat and coat when he arrives and put them on again at the conclusion of the test session. In a similar vein, something to eat and drink (cookies and milk) can be served before the child is ready to leave. Apart from the satisfactions derived by the child from such a treat, it affords the psychologist an opportunity to observe a sampling of his eating and drinking habits. To observe a sampling of bathroom habits, the psychologist should not be averse to escorting the child to the bathroom if agreeable to the child.

(10) In testing timid, disturbed, or deviate children, unusual flexibility and alertness is demanded of the psychologist in order that he adapt himself to the child's rhythm of operations, motivational needs, motor drive, energies, and distractibility and at the same time guard test rationale and validity as well as his own noncommittal role of tester. Orthodox procedures are replaced by those that call forth the child's best efforts. If the child insists on sitting on the examiner's or mother's lap, testing is conducted in this manner; if the child is satisfied to perform a task only between excursions about the room, then this is the way it is done; if the child prefers the floor or a chair rather than the testing table, then the floor or the chair takes the place of the table. Such permissiveness is, however, not a blind procedure on the part of the psychologist. A calm, consistent effort is continually made throughout to see the extent to which a disturbed child can be won back to conformity through trust and confidence in the examiner.

(11) Turning to the tests presented in this chapter, the examiner is reminded that a test scale is weakest at its chronological extremes. The age range of the scales used, therefore, should be such as to permit ample sampling both above and below the subject's chronological age.

(12) It is finally emphasized that verbal tests are not suitable

for deaf children in the age range here considered, with the exception of reading and language achievement tests used at the appropriate age-grade levels. Other verbal tests may of course be used experimentally by specialists experienced with deaf children and with the means of communicating with them. In this connection, all examiners of deaf children have to develop facility in the use of pantomime for imparting test instructions. But as previously mentioned, in using pantomime the worker should speak at the same time. Even though the deaf child may not understand all that is said, speaking preserves the naturalness of the procedure and helps the examiner employ appropriate facial expression and a smoother use of gesture.

Tests Suitable for Deaf School-Age Children

Most deaf children enjoy psychological tests. For the school-age child, the test session breaks up the daily routine and supplies interesting activity and individual attention. With younger children, the introduction "We're going to play some games together" provides powerful inducement, particularly when the examiner shows the child a brightly colored box containing a sample game. The older pupil generally knows about psychological testing from previous experience. Still, he should be given some introductory explanation to help him adapt to the present situation and more particularly to the psychologist. Even with older children, a major incentive to do well is derived from a wish to please. If the psychologist is unsure of his ability to communicate the necessary introduction, the help of a member of the school staff can be enlisted, preferably one favored by the pupil. When such explanation is made, the psychologist should be introduced as a "friend" of the staff member. In this role he quickly establishes himself in the child's good graces.

Unlike procedure recommended at the adult level, the psychological examination of deaf children is preferably begun with the manipulative items of performance scales rather than with achievement tests. The former are more like games, hence more appealing to children. The latter are too reminiscent of the classroom and the daily routine. Further, the verbal communication skill of most school-age deaf children is still too elementary for the kind of conversation that can be conducted with adults. Consequently, there is no pressing need for preliminary orientation as to the level of verbal language comprehension that can be used in conversational communication. Achievement testing can be conducted later in the proceedings.

Tests suitable for the deaf school-age population follow. Where group tests are mentioned, they should be administered individually whenever possible. In the diagnostic examination of deaf children, the present writer follows this procedure even with achievement tests, and with remarkably enlightening results concerning the tricks used by deaf children in reading and in arithmetic computation. Finally, it is again emphasized that test instructions must be clearly conveyed and unmistakably understood, or else it is difficult to tell whether failure is due to inability or to lack of understanding of the test directions.

MENTAL CAPACITY

I. PERFORMANCE SCALES

Arthur Point Scales. (See preceding chapter.) Ages about 6 years and over.

Cornell-Coxe Performance Ability Scale.[1] Ages 4½–16 years. Test items are: Pintner Manikin Test; Decroly Matching Game; Knox-Kempf Feature Profile; Kohs Block Design Test; Army

[1] Ethel L. Cornell and Warren W. Coxe, *A Performance Ability Scale: Examination Manual* (Yonkers-on-Hudson, New York: World Book Company, 1934).

Substitution Test; Cornell-Coxe Memory for Designs; Cube Construction Test; Healy Pictorial Completion Test 2.

Drever-Collins Performance Scale.[2] Constructed in Great Britain
and standardized on English school-age deaf children, the scale
consists of: Kohs Block Design Test; Knox-Pintner Cube Test;
Drever-Collins Domino Test; Size and Weight Test; Pintner-
Paterson Manikin and Profile Tests; Pintner's Two-Figure Form-
board and Healy's Puzzle A; Cube Construction; and Drever-
Collins Picture Completion and Healy's Pictorial Completion
Test 1.

Leiter International Performance Scale.[3] Test consists of 68 nonlanguage tasks, and testing materials are arranged in three "age
trays": Tray 1, ages 2–7; Tray 2, ages 8–12; and Tray 3, ages
14–18.

Nebraska Test of Learning Aptitude, Marshall S. Hiskey.[4] Standardized on deaf children from 4 to 10 years of age, the test items
include: memory for colored objects; bead stringing; pictorial associations; block building; memory for digits; completion of
drawings; pictorial identification; paper folding; visual attention
span; puzzle blocks; pictorial analogies.

Ontario School Ability Examination, Harry Amoss.[5] Standardized
on deaf pupils of the Ontario School for the Deaf, Canada, from 5
through 17 years of age, the test consists of six areas of examina-

[2] J. Drever and M. Collins, *Performance Tests of Intelligence,* 2d ed. (Edinburgh: Oliver and Boyd, 1936).

[3] R. G. Leiter, *The Leiter International Performance Scale,* Vol. I: *Directions
for the Application and Scoring of Individual Tests* (Santa Barbara, California:
Santa Barbara State College Press, 1940).

[4] M. S. Hiskey, *Nebraska Test of Learning Aptitude for Young Deaf Children*
(Lincoln, Nebraska: University of Nebraska, 1941).

[5] H. Amoss, *Ontario School Ability Examination* (Toronto, Canada: The Ryerson Press, 1936).

tion: Examination I includes manipulative activities (locomotion, paper folding, block building, forms, knots, Healy Fernald Puzzle, weight arrangement); Examination II, color patterns; III, Knox blocks; IV, dominoes; V, drawings (imitative, copying, design pair, ring design); VI, tapping.

Pintner-Paterson Performance Scale.[6] Ages 4–16 years. This is the famous ancestor of performance scales, specifically designed with the deaf in mind. It is still among the most widely used. The Short Scale consists of: Mare-Foal Form Board; Seguin-Goddard Form Board; Pintner-Paterson Two-Figure Form Board; Pintner-Paterson Five-Figure Form Board; Casuist Form Board; Pintner Manikin Test; Knox-Kempf Feature Profile; Ship Picture Form Board; Healy Pictorial Completion I; and Knox Cube Imitation Test. The Long Scale consists of the foregoing items plus the following: Gwyn Triangle Test; Kempf Diagonal Form Board; Healy-Fernald Puzzle A; Pintner-Paterson Substitution Test; and the Vineland Adaptation Board.

Wechsler Intelligence Scale for Children: Performance Scale.[7] Ages 5 through 15 years. The Performance Scale includes: Picture Completion; Picture Arrangement; Block Design; Object Assembly; and Coding or Mazes. Although this test is used by a number of psychologists in examining deaf children, there is some doubt as to whether it can be considered altogether suitable, particularly at the elementary level. It is the writer's impression that restandardization on deaf children is essential, together with some revision in test content and method of administration.

[6] R. Pintner and D. G. Paterson, *A Scale of Performance Tests* (New York: Appleton, 1917); G. H. Hildreth and R. Pintner, *Manual of Directions for Pintner-Paterson Performance Tests, Short Scale* (New York: Bureau of Publications, Teachers College, Columbia University, 1937).

[7] David Wechsler, *Wechsler Intelligence Scale for Children: Manual* (New York: The Psychological Corporation, 1949).

2. NONLANGUAGE TESTS

The following are most generally used with the deaf school-population as group or supplementary mental tests. They can, of course, be individually administered and are so used by the writer.

Pintner General Ability Tests: Nonlanguage Series. Mentioned in the preceding chapter in connection with adult testing, this non-language group test series was specifically designed with the deaf in mind and is widely known in the field. The complete series ranges from preschool to high-school and college levels.

Chicago Nonverbal Examination, Andrew W. Brown.[8] This is another group test designed with the deaf in mind and was standardized for both verbal and pantomime directions for ages about 8 to 14 years. The subtests included are: digit-symbol (easy); incongruent element in a series; cube-construction counting; relation of parts to whole; similarities; picture reconstruction; picture sequences; pictorial absurdities; association of parts; digit-symbol (difficult).

Goodenough Draw-a-Man Test.[9] The simple task involved in this test—the drawing of a man—is a popular supplement to a more comprehensive examination of deaf children in the age range about 3½ to 12 years. The directions are easily given in pantomime.

[8] A. W. Brown, *Manual of Directions for the Chicago Non-Verbal Examination* (New York: The Psychological Corporation); A. W. Brown, "The Development and Standardization of the Chicago Non-Verbal Examination," *Journal of Applied Psychology,* XXIV (1940), 36–47, 122–29.
[9] F. L. Goodenough, *Measurement of Intelligence by Drawings* (Yonkers-on-Hudson, New York: World Book Company, 1926).

SCHOLASTIC ACHIEVEMENT

The main emphasis in school-age achievement testing is upon the skill subjects: reading, arithmetic, and language. Any good standard achievement test can be used with deaf pupils including those previously listed in connection with adult testing. Achievement testing is best begun slightly below the subject's level of attainment (this can be ascertained from the school), and special pains must be taken to insure the comprehension of test instructions. If the examiner has reason to suspect that a child's answers are derived through guesswork, actual test items should be checked by having the child explain how he arrived at his answers.

In the matter of test selection, the psychologist is advised to consult the catalogues of the various test publishing companies, send away for samples of promising materials, and read over the test contents carefully before making a choice. Consultation with schools for the deaf can be of great help in the selection of appropriate tests. The schools in turn are urged to begin their achievement test programs at the earliest possible grade level so that individual difficulties can be identified and corrected before they become cumulative. Reading achievement tests are available from Grade 1 and up. In addition to the tests already listed, a series that has rendered notable service with deaf school children is the Gates Reading Test Series, ranging from preschool to the tenth grade and published by the Bureau of Publications, Teachers College, Columbia University.

PERSONALITY

In the writer's experience, the personality evaluation of deaf school-age children is better accomplished through clinical observation and the case history than through formal testing; and a more informative procedure than testing is comprehensive observation of a child's behavior in as wide a variety of real-life and interpersonal situations as possible. The weaknesses of verbal personality measures obtain even more acutely for the school-age population than for deaf adults. As for projective play techniques, the results with deaf children are more often than not strongly influenced by the child's previous experiences with the play materials, the locale in which the test is administered, the personality of the examiner, and the mood the child happens to be in at the time. In the case of other projective techniques, such as the Rorschach and thematic tests, test response is always influenced by a deaf child's limited ability to verbalize, or to provide verbal elaborations for such nonlanguage responses as drawings, dramatic acting of stories, and the like. To perceive where the sensory restriction ends and personality begins, so to say, is a most complex task for the uninitiated in interpreting a deaf child's responses to personality tests.

Psychologists in the best position to use personality tests with deaf children are those who specialize in work with this population, particularly psychologists situated in schools for the deaf. And even here, personality as well as certain intelligence tests are employed as clinical-experimental probes rather than as measures of accepted validity, their use being dictated by the pressing need to broaden the scope of tests used with the deaf in order to acquire deeper clinical insight. The point is well illustrated by the following personal communication from The Clarke School for the Deaf, Research Department, concerning the general rationale of the psychological testing program: [10]

The psychological testing program of The Clarke School for the Deaf can be divided into four parts:
1. Tests for prospective applicants
2. Tests for children in the school presenting learning problems

[10] The summary of The Clarke School testing program was prepared especially for this publication. Grateful acknowledgment is made to George T. Pratt, Principal, and to Solis L. Kates, Research Psychologist, of The Clarke School.

3. Tests for children presenting problems which go beyond those involving simple learning
4. Research

The test that is used for prospective applicants is the Leiter International Scale. An attempt here is made to determine the level of intelligence of the child rather than a specific I.Q. While this level is very important, quite a strong emphasis is placed upon the qualitative analysis of the child's problem-solving activities. The children tested are the age group from 3 to 5.

Children who present learning difficulties are ordinarily tested with the WISC when they are 15 or below in age. Other children are tested with the WAIS when they are 16 or older. In each case all the subtests are given with the exception of digit span. The analysis of each of the test results is based upon subtest and subscale scatter. In addition, qualitative analyses of the subject's responses are resorted to very frequently.

With children who present more complicated difficulties than the above group the appropriate Wechsler is administered, and in addition, the Rorschach and appropriate thematic apperception tests are also made use of. Special attention in the interpretation of these tests is paid to factors closely related to conceptual and emotional development.

Finally, the research program involves the use of the suitable Wechsler for control purposes since what we are investigating and will investigate in these children refers to their conceptual capacities. At present we are devising techniques which will attempt to determine the difference between the good learners and the poor learners at the Clarke School.

Personality tests that are currently used as clinical-research devices with school-age deaf children by psychologists specializing in work with the deaf include all those mentioned in connection with adult-level testing, with the verbal tests (Rorschach and Sentence-Completion) usually reserved for the oldest school-age levels. By reason of the procedures used in validation, the Kinget Drawing-Completion Test is also reserved for this adolescent and young adult level. For the names of other apperceptive, thematic, and dramatic-play personality tests, the psychologist is referred to the catalogues of test publishers and distributors. Granted basic experience with deaf children, he is advised to familiarize himself with the test contents and standardization before making a purchase.

Brunschwig Personality Inventory for Deaf Children.[11] Special recognition is accorded this test as the only personality inventory standardized on a deaf school population, or in fact on any deaf population. The Inventory is so constructed that subscores are obtainable for school, home, and social adjustment with a total score for general adjustment. The various scores are derived from a subject's responses to 67 simply worded test items. Of the test, Brunschwig states: "Practically applied, it may be of value in making surveys of pupil adjustment in the intermediate and advanced grades of schools for the deaf and in supplementing information about individual pupils for purposes of guidance, etc." [12] Reference is given to the publication that serves as the manual for this test.[13] In addition to its function as a standardized measure, the test can be used to advantage in clinical interview.

Vineland Social Maturity Scale, Revised, Edgar A. Doll.[14] Designed as a measure of progressive development in social competence, the Vineland Scale is a valuable supplement in the examination of the deaf, providing the items are assessed and interpreted in the light of the restrictions imposed by deafness. The categories of inquiry include: self-help, general; self-help, eating; self-help, dressing; self-direction; occupation; communication; locomotion; socialization.

[11] Lily Brunschwig, *A Study of Some Personality Aspects of Deaf Children* (Contributions to Education No. 687; New York: Teachers College, Columbia University, 1936).

[12] *Ibid.*, pp. 137–38.

[13] R. Pintner and L. Brunschwig, "An Adjustment Inventory for Use in Schools for the Deaf," *American Annals of the Deaf,* LXXXII (1937), 152–67.

[14] E. A. Doll, *Vineland Social Maturity Scale: Manual of Directions* (Educational Test Bureau, 1947).

SPECIAL CLINICAL TESTS

All the special clinical tests mentioned in connection with adult-level testing may be used with the school population at the appropriate age levels. Attention is directed to a revision of the Oseretsky Test, the *Lincoln-Oseretsky Motor Development Scale*,[15] designed to evaluate the motor ability of children between the ages of six to fourteen years.

Occasionally it is necessary to identify the causes for disproportionate difficulty in mastering verbal language on the part of deaf pupils of good intelligence and no gross behavioral pathology. Among the possibilities considered is that of cerebral damage. Two of the tests commonly used to supplement the *full examination required to diagnose such damage* are the Bender Visual Motor Gestalt Test and the Benton Revised Visual Retention Test, both mentioned in connection with adult-level testing. In an interesting study [16] to evaluate the effectiveness of various other tests in the detection of brain injury in children of normal intelligence, Goldenberg used the following as his experimental measures: the Stanford-Binet Intelligence Scale (Form L); the performance section of the Wechsler Intelligence Scale for Children; the Porteus Mazes; a Block Design Test administered in the Goldstein-Scheerer manner; a version of the Ellis Visual Designs Test; the Strauss-Werner Marble Board Test; and the Goodenough Draw-a-Man Test. The investigator found that the Ellis Visual Designs and the Marble Board Test proved the most adequate combination for the purpose of diagnosing brain injury in children. Both of these tests required the construction of special scoring techniques, which were developed by the investigator himself.[17]

[15] W. Sloan, *Lincoln-Oseretsky Motor Development Scale* (Chicago: C. H. Stoelting Company).

[16] A. A. Strauss and N. C. Kephart (in collaboration with L. E. Lehtinen and S. Goldenberg), *Psychopathology and Education of the Brain-Injured Child* (New York: Grune & Stratton, 1955).

[17] *Ibid.*, Appendix I, pp. 215–22.

It is emphasized, however, that psychological tests are not invariably successful in detecting cerebral damage. Neither are neurological examinations, for that matter. The absence of positive findings does not indicate the absence of brain damage in all cases. Sometimes clinical observation spots soft behavioral signs that escape both testing and the neurological examination.

Tests Suitable for the Preschool and Nursery Levels

If chronological levels were to be ranked in order of importance, those included in this section would come first, for they encompass the beginnings—the period of life which the organism is most vulnerable to adverse influences and most responsive to corrective ones. Of a psychologist, work at the preschool level requires special competencies and qualifications. As previously noted, most important are an expert knowledge of children and of childhood psychopathology; respect for the dignity of childhood and its critical importance in the human life cycle; and the ability to establish warm rapport with children, from which is derived the patience, sensitivity, and enjoyment required in the psychological examination of this youngest population. If the child is deaf, the implications and history of the condition should be thoroughly familiar to the worker. He need not, however, be troubled by the communications problem, for the major communications medium used by deaf children at this early level is the language of behavior, and this is a universal idiom that can be understood by any psychologist familiar with children.

The suggestions for child testing noted in the preceding section obtain for this age level as well. Greatest stress falls upon a psychologist's flexibility in adapting himself and the test to the child without impairing test validity, and upon his skill in test administration so that the child's attention is not permitted to wander off while the examiner is struggling with the test materials. Among the scales that have rendered notable service with preschool-level deaf children are the following:

MENTAL CAPACITY

Merrill-Palmer Scale of Mental Tests, Rachel Stutsman.[18] The present writer has found this scale most useful in the age range from about 2 to 4 years. The few language items included in the scale may be omitted without impairing test scoring or validity. The other items can all be used with deaf children and include: All-or-None Tests—obeying simple commands, throwing a ball, straight tower, crossing feet, standing on one foot, folding paper, making a block walk, drawing up string, identification of self in mirror, cutting with scissors, matching colors, closing fist and moving thumb, opposition of thumb and fingers, copying a circle, copying a cross, copying a star all of which may be given in pantomime; Form Boards and Picture Tests—Seguin-Goddard Form Board, Mare-Foal Test, Pintner Manikin Test, Stutsman Picture Form Boards 1, 2, and 3, Decroly Matching Game; Other Tests of Motor Coordination—Wallin Peg Boards A and B, Stutsman Colored Cubes, Nest of Cubes, Buttons and Buttonholes, Little Pink Tower, Cube Pyramids. A particular advantage of this test is that certain test items may be omitted by the examiner or refused by the child without interfering with the total score. Further, scoring is provided for by any of three methods—standard deviation, in terms of M.A. or I.Q., or on a percentile basis.

Randalls Island Performance Tests.[19] Designed for children ranging from about 2 to 5 years, this test consists of the following items: Stutsman Tests—colored cubes, nested cubes, pyramid test, buttoning test, stick-and-string test, color matching test, Picture

[18] Rachel Stutsman, *Mental Measurement of Preschool Children* (Yonkers-on-Hudson, New York: World Book Company, 1931).

[19] *The Randalls Island Performance Series* (Manual) (Chicago: C. H. Stoelting Co.).

Form Boards 1, 2, and 3; Gesell Blocks; Montessori Cylinder Test; Pintner-Paterson Two-Figure Form Board; Wallin Peg Boards A and B; Knox Cube Imitation Test; Decroly Matching Game; Seguin-Goddard Form Board; Vineland Adaptation Board; Baldwin-Stecher Number Concepts Test; Pintner Manikin Test.

DEVELOPMENTAL BEHAVIOR

Gesell Developmental Schedules.[20] Designed for ages 4 weeks through 5 years, the Developmental Schedules cannot be considered a test in the same sense as the preceding instruments, but are rather a valuable clinical guide for the examination and screening of motor, adaptive, language, and personal-social aspects of developing behavior. Although the standardization of the Schedules is open to criticism, it is questionable if the rapid growth changes and individual variations encountered at the infant level lend themselves to standardized measure. Nevertheless, Gesell and Amatruda do provide the means for computing a Developmental Quotient, or DQ, by dividing maturity age by chronological age. A DQ can be derived for each of the four major fields of developmental inquiry—motor, adaptive, language, and personal-social—as well as for specific functions. The present writer uses the Gesell Schedules as a downward chronological extension from the Merrill-Palmer Scale in nursery-age testing; with infants; and as a guide to abnormal neuromotor activity in babies. Important to the worker with deaf children is the provision in the Gesell Schedules for tracing the history of an infant's vocal expression and reaction to sound. The time of cessation of these activities can help establish the period of onset of deafness in the absence of other information.

[20] Basic texts containing detailed procedural instructions are: A. Gesell and Associates, *The First Five Years of Life: A Guide to the Study of the Pre-School Child* (New York: Harper & Brothers, 1940), and A. Gesell and C. S. Amatruda, *Developmental Diagnosis: Normal and Abnormal Child Development*, 2d ed. (New York: Paul B. Hoeber, Inc., 1947).

A Physical and Intellectual Development Scale.[21] The reader's attention is called to the accompanying recording sheet which summarizes an ingenious scale compiled by Hess for the psychosocial evaluation of deaf children from 1 through 5 years of age. It consists of selected items from the Merrill-Palmer, Cattell, Gesell, Pintner-Paterson, Ontario, Grace Arthur, and Stanford-Binet scales used in conjunction with the Vineland Social Maturity Scale items of the appropriate age levels. Bracketed after the name of each of the test tasks is the scale from which it was taken as well as the normative age of accomplishment designated by the particular scale. The Hess Scale is not a standardized instrument and is used for clinical inspection rather than for standardized measure.

PERSONALITY TRAITS

Personality assessment of preschool-level children is best achieved through careful case-history study and through observation in as wide a variety as possible of real-life and interpersonal situations, particularly of parent-child relations. For the busy psychologist who cannot manage a broad observational study, observation of parent-child relations is a minimum essential. This can be easily done in office settings by requesting parents to wait with the child in a combined play-and-waiting room, and then observing what transpires through a one-way vision device. If possible, each parent should be observed singly with the child, and then parents and child together. The present writer performs a first observation without alerting the parent, and subsequent observations with the parents' knowledge. Apart from providing a more graphic picture of parent-child relations and child personality than can be obtained through interview with parents, the observa-

[21] For permission to include this scale in the present publication, grateful acknowledgment is made to D. Wilson Hess, Division of Clinical Psychology, Department of Psychiatry of the University of Rochester School of Medicine and Dentistry and Strong Memorial Hospital, and the Rochester School for the Deaf.

PHYSICAL AND INTELLECTUAL DEVELOPMENT

(One through five years)

Name: _____   Date seen: _____

Examiner: _____   Birth date: _____

Estimated IQ or DQ (Developmental Quotient): _____   Chronological age: _____

Referred by: _____

Cubes: TOWER: 2-cube ____ (Ges 12)* 3-cube ____ (Ges, Cat, MP 18) 3+ cubes ____ (Ges, SB, Ont 24)
9-cube ____ (Ges 36) TRAIN: 2-cube ____ (Ges 24) 3-cube ____ (Cat 27) 4-cube ____ (Ges 36)
BRIDGE: ____ (Cat 30) ____ (Ges, SB 36) PYRAMID: ____ (MP 33) ____ (Ges, SB 36) ____ (MP 42)
____ (MP 48) ____ (MP 54) CHAIR: ____ (Ont 36) FIT IN BOX: ____ (MP 18) ____ (Cat, MP 24)
____ (MP 30) GATE: ____ (Ont 60)

Form Boards: LARGE CIRCLE-TRIANGLE-SQUARE: ____ (Ges 12) SMALL CIRCLE-TRIANGLE-SQUARE: ____ (Cat 16) ____ (Ges 18) ____ (Cat 20)
(Ges 24) ____ (Ges 36) ____ (SB 36) WALLIN "A": ____ (Cat 22) ____ (SB 24)
Small rotated ____ (Cat, SB 30) WALLIN "B": ____ (Cat 14) ____ (Cat 18)
____ (MP 18) ____ (MP 26) ____ (MP 33) ____ (MP 38) ____ (Cat 20) ____ (MP 27)
____ (MP 32) ____ (MP 40)

Drawing: SCRIBBLES: Imitative stroke ____ (Cat, Ges 12–14) Spontaneous ____ (Cat, Ges 18)
DIFFERENTIATES: Stroke and scribble ____ (Ges 24) Vertical and circular ____ (Ges 24)
Vertical and horizontal ____ (Ont 24) Vertical, horizontal, line and circle ____ (Ges 30;
Cat 27 Vertical ____ (SB 36) COPIES without demonstration: Circle ____ (Ges, Ont, SB,
MP 36) Cross ____ (Ont 36; MP, SB 42) Square ____ (Ont 48) Star ____ (MP 54) ____ (MP 60)
Triangle ____ (Ont 60) MAN: Completes ____ (SB 48) ____ (SB 60) Draws ____ (Goodenough 36)
____ (Goodenough 42) ____ (Goodenough 48) ____ (Goodenough 54)
PORTEUS MAZES: ____ (GA 54) ____ (GA 60)

Paper Folding: Attempts ____ (MP 18) ____ (Cat, Ont 24) Creased ____ (Cat 30) Twice ____ (Ont 36)
Diagonal twice ____ (Ont 48)

Discrimination: COLORS: Matches turned cube (Ont 36) Matches 4 cubes (Ont 60) Matches 4/10 (Ont 36)
7/10 (Ont 48) 8/10 (Sb 48) SORTS BUTTONS: (Ges 36)
ENCES: (SB 54) AESTHETIC COMPARISONS: (SB 60) FORMS: (SB 42) LIKENESSES AND DIFFER-
GAME: (MP 45) (MP 51) (MP 54) (SB 54) DECROLY MATCHING
(GA 60) HEALY PICTURE COMPLETION: (GA 54)

Puzzles: MARE AND FOAL: (MP 36) (MP 42) (MP 48) (MP 54) (MP 60)
MANIKIN: (MP 48) (MP 54) (MP 60) RECTANGLE: (Ont 60) PICTURE
PUZZLE #1: (MP 36) (MP 42) (MP 48) PICTURE PUZZLE #2: (MP 48) (MP 54)
PICTURE PUZZLE #3: (MP 48) CUT PICTURES: (SB 42)

Number Concepts: One (Cat 30) Matches 1, 4, 2, 3 (SB 42) Two (SB 48) Three (SB 60)
Delayed Response: Chooses covered toy (Cat 20) (SB 24) Picture memories (SB 36)
CUBE TAPPING: (Ont 48) (PP 54) (Ont 60)

Physical: DOLL: Squeezes (Cat 11) Hits (Cat 12) MIRROR: (Ges 12)
BALANCE: (Ges 12) WALKS: (Ges 24) RUNS: (Ges 24)
SITS: (Ges 18) SQUATS TO PLAY: (Ges 24) (Ges 18) HURLS BALL: (Ges, MP 18)
(Ges 36) On indication (Ges 24) (Ges 36) (Ges 48) CROSSES FEET (MP 18)
STANDS: One foot (MP 18) Tiptoe (Ges 36) SKIPS: Once (Ges 48)
Alternates (Ges 60) CLOSES FIST, MOVES THUMB (MP 30) STAIRS: Two feet each (Ges 36)
tread (Ges 24) Climbs alternating feet but descends two each tread (Ges 36)
JUMPS: Both feet from 6-8" (Ges 36) TRICYCLE: Rides and steers using pedals (Ges 36)
FINGERS: Opposition thumb and fingers (MP 42)

Manipulative: SPOONS: Beats (Cat 12) SPOON AND CUP: Outside (Cat 10) Inside (Cat 12)
RING AND STRING: (Ges 12) CUBES: In cup (Cat, Ges 12) (Cat, Ges 18) (Ges 24)
Unwraps (Cat 14) Holds three (Cat 14) Walks cube (MP 18) GLASS: (Cat 14)
PELLET AND BOTTLE: Attempts insert (Ges 12) Empties (Cat 14-16) Inserts and
dumps (Ges 18) BOXES: Uncovers to get toy (Cat 14) Closes round box (Cat 16)
Closes oblong box (Cat 22) PICTURE BOOK: Turns 2-3 pages (Ges 18) Turns
pages singly (Ges 24) SCISSORS: (MP 24-29) RING AND STICK: (MP 24-29)
BEADS: In box (Cat 16) Stringing (SB 30) (SB 36) (SB 48)
BUTTONING: 1-2 (MP 30) 2 (MP 36) 2-4 (MP 42) (MP 48) (MP 54)
EGG BEATER: (Cat 27) PINK TOWER: (Ont 60) (MP 36) (MP 42) (MP 48) (MP 54)
(MP 60) KNOTS: Single NEST OF CUBES: (MP 24-29) (MP 30-55)

*Tests: Cattell, Gessell, Merrill-Palmer, Pintner-Paterson, Ontario, Grace Arthur, Stanford-Binet.

tions are used as a practicum training experience for providing parent guidance in child understanding and management.

Various play kits and doll families can be used to create situations for eliciting a preschool child's projective reactions and attitudes. In certain instances, unusual leads can be obtained in understanding a child's problems. Reference to such materials can be found in psychological test catalogues. Finally, it must be remembered that the mental test situation provides an excellent medium for screening personality as well, as illustrated by the following guide devised by Stutsman:

Rating of Personality Traits in Mental-Test Situation

Name . . . . Age . . . . Date . . . .

1. Self-reliance:
   extreme; moderate; average; slightly lacking; markedly lacking
2. Self-criticism:
   extreme; moderate; average; slightly lacking; markedly lacking
3. Irritability toward failure:
   extreme; moderate; average; very slight; none
4. Degree of praise needed for effective work:
   Type 1—moderate praise helpful
   Type 2—indifferent to approval
   Type 3—praise induces self-consciousness
   Type 4—constant praise expected, but harmful
   Type 5—constant praise needed
5. Initiative and independence of action:
   marked; average; very little
6. Self-consciousness:
   not conspicuously present; conspicuously slight; inhibited reactions; showing off
7. Spontaneity and repression:
   1. Freedom in work: marked; average; very little
   2. Tendency to ask for what he wants: marked; average; very little
   3. Amount and type of interpersonal communication
      (This item substituted for the Stutsman items: 3. Amount and type of talking; and 4. Intensity and pitch of voice, although in

certain instances the latter are appropriately used with deaf children)

8. Imaginative tendencies:
   marked; average; very little
9. Reaction type to which the child belongs:
   Type 1—slow and deliberate
   Type 2—calm and alert
   Type 3—quick and impetuous
10. Speech development:
    1. Length of sentences; single words; phrases or very short sentences; short sentences; longer sentences (added: no verbal communication)
    2. Distinctness of speech
11. Dependence on parent:
    present; not observed; reactions indicate independence
12. Other observations

In regard to the foregoing outline, Stutsman stresses that it is not intended to be complete but is "merely offered as a suggestion of the possibilities of using the test situation for the study of personality." [22]

Problems of Differential Diagnosis in Young Children

Problems of hearing and language usage and learning are not confined to children with organically impaired auditory structures. They may also occur in such conditions as psychogenic inhibition of speech, mental retardation, psychiatric disorders, and organic pathology and lags of development in those areas of the brain that serve language. The problem of establishing which of these is the responsible factor in the case of small mute children is one of the most complex of diagnostic assignments.

If each clinical condition in which hearing and language disorders were present stood forth in its pure and classic form, many of the difficulties of differential diagnosis would be eliminated.

[22] Stutsman, *Mental Measurement of Preschool Children*, pp. 261–62.

But this happens all too infrequently to suit the harried diagnostician. In actual practice, a given clinical syndrome is generally contaminated by symptoms of other clinical conditions, for the simple reason that all may exist side by side in the same case. A mentally retarded child may also have a psychiatric disorder and/or an aphasic type of impairment; an aphasic child is customarily functionally retarded in various areas as well as emotionally unstable; a child with organic impairment of the auditory mechanism may have all or any of the foregoing conditions; and each case is further modified by the particular life-influences to which it has been exposed.

To sum up in the words of Kanner, diagnostic problems such as these have combined to form a "diagnostic no man's land in which a clearcut diagnosis between bizarre conduct of a deficient child, the advanced stages of infantile autism, the withdrawal and unresponsiveness of the congenitally aphasic child, or the vagaries often associated with structural anomalies of the central nervous system is often subject to major perplexities." [23] In certain instances, the diagnostic instruments are not sufficiently refined to help establish a differential; in others, the children are not able to cooperate to the extent required by the diagnostic procedure.

In the past, children with such multiple handicaps were usually accorded the categorical recommendation "institutionalization," meaning custodial care. Some obtained placement in schools for the deaf. In regard to the latter, the lack of systematized records as to how they fared is an unfortunate loss. However, current advances in scientific knowledge and research-mindedness strongly support the proposition that knowledge of human deviation adds substantially to knowledge of the function and behavior of the intact human organism. As a result, interest in these children is reaching unprecedented heights.

[23] "A Report on the Conference on Diagnosis in Mental Retardation," *The Training School Bulletin* (The Training School, Vineland, New Jersey, May, 1958), p. 33.

At present, a major effort in the differential diagnosis of the language-hearing-behavior syndrome in young children is to distinguish between the primary etiological factor and its symptoms and the secondary symptoms arising from the child's response to his disability and to the methods of management. In this connection there has emerged what Kanner terms a "pseudodiagnostic wastebasket" [24] classification entitled "brain-damage" loosely used by many as distinct from other conditions that are naively assumed to be free from such damage. The effort here is to dichotomize between the organic and the psychogenic.

However, the presence of organic brain involvement is considerably broader than some of the current pseudodiagnostic classifications would imply. For example, Bender states:

Our experiences have led us to include the following with the biological or organically determined behavior disorders: childhood schizophrenia, language or learning retardations or lags (including reading disabilities), motor lags (the so-called congenital cerebral palsies), the mental defects or congenital developmental deviations, epilepsies, inflammatory encephalitis (both virus and pyogenic), burn encephalopathies, and traumatic encephalopathies (including birth injuries, prematurity, and anoxias).[25]

To these, Benda adds certain autistic children in whom "the interpersonal relations may be disturbed through injuries to the central nervous system, especially asphyxiation which produces a very characteristic syndrome of lack of awareness and disturbance of orientation." [26] In effect, organic involvements represent a common substrate for a far wider variety of psychopathological and deviate behavior, including the language-hearing-behavioral syndrome of young children, than is implied by various classifications and terminologies in current use. The present fixation among specialists

[24] *Ibid.*

[25] L. Bender, *Psychopathology of Children with Organic Brain Disorders* (Springfield, Illinois: Charles C. Thomas, 1956), p. 123.

[26] Clemens E. Benda, *Developmental Disorders of Mentation and Cerebral Palsies* (New York: Grune & Stratton, 1952), p. 503.

in speech and hearing to attach neat diagnostic labels to their young patients only adds to the confusion, for follow-through data concerning the therapeutic usefulness of these labels are as yet singularly scant. And yet, in numerous instances the real diagnostic picture emerges only after treatment is instituted and the child's responses to various educative approaches have been studied. To complement the current preoccupation with establishing a diagnosis before all else, there is critical need for intensive, systematized interdisciplinary research into programs of treatment and experimental education under the supervision of authorities in childhood psychopathology. In such programs, diagnosis and management operate as an interpenetrating team, gains in the one pointing the way to progress in the other.

In regard to present educational and psychological services for such children, greater emphasis must be placed upon the assessment and use of intact capacities, upon signs that suggest potential for improvement, and on the conditions under which gains are more likely to be made in a given case. As for the worker, of him is demanded maximum competence, infinite patience, the ability to derive great satisfaction from seemingly small improvements, and faith in the remarkable reparative capacities of numbers of small brain-damaged children. In the words of Lauretta Bender:

There are many remarkable things about the brain-damaged child which also remind us of the miraculous capacity of all children to grow up, to mature and to be as normal as they are. The drive for normality and for living through a regular maturation pattern as a global response of the biological unit is much stronger than the disorganization resulting from either focal or diffuse structural pathology or destructive and depriving environmental influences.[27]

[27] Bender, *Psychopathology of Children with Organic Brain Disorders*, p. 136.

10. OBSERVATION

THE OBSERVING EYE of the experienced worker is one of his major diagnostic instruments. With it he can spot pathognomic signs, perceive significant lines of inquiry that need to be followed, and gather a wealth of clinical details. Without it, the psychological examination becomes a purely mechanical procedure. Ideally no psychological examination should be considered complete without systematic clinical observation of a subject in a variety of real-life settings, such as in the home, at school, on the job, in recreational and social situations. This applies particularly to those physically disabled individuals whose impairment raises obstacles to formal psychological examination. It applies above all to the psychological examination of children whether physically disabled or not.

The following headings and queries present samplings of what can be learned through observation.

General Observation

HEALTH AND PHYSICAL CONDITION. Does the subject's physical appearance suggest health, debility, illness? Does he have or appear to have other physical or sensorial disabilities? Are any physical abnormalities or disfigurations present to add to the problems of deafness? Is medical referral in order on the basis of observed details? What are the likely educational, vocational, and psychological implications?

MOTOR BEHAVIOR. Is there evidence of impaired motor coordination and/or control? Is motor activity hyperactive or underactive; random or purposeful; listless or positive? Are any bizarre manifestations present, such as posturing, automatic movements or mannerisms, excessive yawning, gulping, catching of breath? Are there tics, twitching, spastic or athetoid movements, postural deviations? What are the neurologic and psychiatric implications of the observed motor behavior? Is neuropsychiatric referral in order?

APPEARANCE AND DRESS. What is the subject's general appearance? Does his dress give evidence of compulsive meticulousness; slovenliness; femininity (in a male) or masculinity (in a female); bizarreness? Is there evidence of careless personal hygiene?

MOOD. Does the subject give the impression of interest, eagerness, self-assurance, nervousness, irritability, apathy, indifference? Is he friendly, bored, hostile? Is he actively cooperative, passively accepting, withdrawn?

DEPENDENCE. Has the subject come alone, with his mother, or with another companion? Is he content to sit back and let his companion speak for him? Is there evidence of hostility toward the companion, irritability with the dependent role, willing compliance, indifference? What are the psychological and vocational implications?

AUDITORY FACTORS. Does the subject wear a hearing aid, and if so how much benefit does he appear to derive from it? Does he adjust the volume controls, fuss with it unnecessarily, put it on when entering the interview room and remove it on leaving? Do voice, speech, and lip reading appear to benefit from the use of an aid, or show the potentials for such benefit? What implications and recommendations are suggested?

Psychological Test Behavior

DURING THE ADMINISTRATION OF TEST INSTRUCTIONS. Does the subject concentrate on understanding the directions; look pleasantly at the examiner, but make no observable effort to understand; plunge into the test before instructions are completed; habitually stop to ask questions about procedure after having begun the test; appear reluctant to begin unless specifically encouraged by the examiner?

DURING TEST PERFORMANCE. Does the subject plan his approach before beginning; plan during the course of operations; employ pure trial-and-error procedures; look to the examiner's facial expression for hints and clues and encouragement? What are the subject's span of attention; distractibility; use of systematic procedure; tempo of operations; manual dexterity and motor skills? What are his needs for encouragement and praise; initiative and independence; ability to profit from mistakes; meticulousness of work habits?

MANAGEMENT OF DIFFICULTIES. When difficulties arise, does the subject concentrate on overcoming them himself and resent the offer of help; show immediate discouragement and refuse to go on with the task; expect to be helped; welcome sufficient help to get him over the difficulty so that he can proceed on his own; use difficulties as an attention-getting device?

EVALUATION OF TEST PERFORMANCE. Does the subject notice errors as he goes along and correct them before he proceeds further; is he aware of errors only when a major difficulty arises; does he check his work before stating that he is finished or is his aim rather to complete a task and get it over with? Does the subject show, express, or look for approval or disapproval with his performance?

REACTIONS AT THE CONCLUSION OF TEST. Is the subject eager to know how he did; indifferent; discouraged? Does he ask for the correct answers to certain questions that have given him difficulty? Does he express interest in more testing; indifference; objection? Is he anxious to depart or does he offer to stay and help the examiner put the test materials in order? Does he appear exhilarated; his usual self; fatigued?

Observation in Diagnosis

Not infrequently, the general behavior of deaf subjects is as important in psychological evaluation as the test results, and sometimes more so. This is especially true in differential diagnostic procedure with young children suspected of being deaf. Where tests are used in such cases, they function mainly to spark manifest behavior which may be exposed to clinical scrutiny. Ultimate diagnosis is usually established through clinical observation and the case history rather than through psychological tests and measures.

Samplings of signs to be found through diagnostic observation are as follows:

SIGNS SUGGESTIVE OF DEAFNESS IN INFANTS AND YOUNG CHILDREN [1]

(1) *Hearing and Comprehension of Speech*
General indifference to sound
Lack of response to spoken word
Response to noises as opposed to voice

[1] Arnold Gesell and Catherine S. Amatruda, *Developmental Diagnosis*, 2d ed. (New York: Paul B. Hoeber, Inc., 1947), p. 278.

(2) *Vocalization and Sound Production*
Monotonal quality
Indistinct
Lessened laughter
Meager experimental sound play and squealing
Vocal play for vibratory sensation
Head banging, foot stamping for vibratory sensation
Yelling, screeching to express pleasure, annoyance or need

(3) *Visual Attention and Reciprocal Comprehension*
Augmented visual vigilance and attentiveness
Alertness to gesture and movement
Marked imitativeness in play
Vehemence of gestures

(4) *Social Rapport and Adaptations*
Subnormal rapport in vocal nursery games
Intensified preoccupations with things rather than persons
Inquiring, sometimes confused or thwarted facial expression
Puzzled and unhappy episodes in social situations
Suspicious alertness, alternating with co-operation
Markedly reactive to praise and affection

(5) *Emotional Behavior*
Tantrums to call attention to self or need
Tensions, tantrums, resistance due to lack of comprehension
Frequent obstinacies, teasing tendencies
Irritability at not making self understood
Explosions due to self-vexation
Impulsive and avalanche initiatives

SIGNS SUGGESTIVE OF BEHAVIORAL DEVIATION AND
PSYCHOPATHOLOGY

Investigations of mental illness and psychopathological behavior among the deaf represent important areas of needed research. Empiric observation and the few clinical studies reported suggest no difference in manifest signs of disturbance between the deaf and the hearing, both children and adults; and there is even less authoritative information available concerning the amount of psychopathology among the deaf, causes, characteristic types, and therapeutic approaches.

Investigations carried out by the North Regional Association for the Deaf in England conclude that "a person who is deaf is many times more likely to find himself in need of treatment in a mental hospital than a hearing person" and "that his length of stay in hospital, on the average, is well over half as long again as that of a hearing patient." [2] The Association reports an investigation carried out at a large mental hospital in Yorkshire that demonstrated "a moderate but significant correlation between deafness and paranoid symptoms" [3] in that particular population. On the other hand, Altshuler and Rainer find that "schizophrenia in the deaf is basically the same clinical entity as in the hearing," and "there is no evidence for a preponderance of paranoid symptoms" [4] in the group studied. It is the present writer's impression that while deafness does not itself produce mental illness, it does by its very nature provoke paranoid ideas in sensitive individuals by keeping them from direct contact with what others in the immediate environment are saying and thinking, thus laying the foundation for suspicion.

In any event, in our present state of knowledge, a psychologist should expect to find no great difference in observable signs of serious psychopathy between the deaf and the hearing, either at the child or the adult levels. The more experienced the worker, both in psychopathology and in work with the deaf, the more sensitive he will be to signs of behavioral deviance in a context of deafness.

[2] North Regional Association for the Deaf, *Deafness: A Survey of the Problems* (Manchester, England), pp. 67, 68.

[3] *Ibid.*, p. 68.

[4] K. Z. Altshuler and J. D. Rainer, "Patterns and Course of Schizophrenia in the Deaf." Reprinted from the *Journal of Nervous and Mental Disease*, CXXVII (1958), 81.

Observation in Vocational Rehabilitation Evaluation

An increasingly popular method in the vocational evaluation of the severely disabled is through observation of a subject's performance in actual on-the-job situations.[5] Through this "work-sample" method, an individual is tried out in a variety of miniature job situations that reproduce the important elements of the job itself, both as to skills and as to general situation. Among the areas opened to observation by this approach are an individual's ability to get along with his fellow workers; tolerance of frustration; initiative and enterprise; capacity for self-assertion; dependency handicaps; and potentials for occupational progress.

In regard to the deaf, Williams[6] considers attitude, adaptability, the mastery of the types of measurement peculiar to a trade, vocational skill, and familiarity with actual working customs and conditions essential factors in vocational rehabilitation. Although these can be assessed through psychological examination,[7] they are probably better appraised through observation by means of the work-sample method.

[5] W. M. Usdane, "Prevocational Evaluation Criteria for the Severely Handicapped." Reprint from *Archives of Physical Medicine and Rehabilitation* (May, 1957), Institute for the Crippled and Disabled, Rehabilitation Series No. 18.

[6] Boyce R. Williams, "Essential Characteristics (Qualifications) of a Rehabilitable Deaf or Hard of Hearing Individual," *American Annals of the Deaf*, XCII (1947), 215–26.

[7] E. S. Levine and M. Z. Safian, "Psychological Evaluation in Vocational Adjustment," *Proceedings of the Institute on Personal, Social and Vocational Adjustment to Total Deafness*, pp. 348–64. Reprinted from *American Annals of the Deaf*, CIII (1958), 207–433. See also Donald E. Super, *Appraising Vocational Fitness by Means of Psychological Tests* (New York: Harper & Brothers, 1949).

11. SPECIAL EMPHASES IN THE PSYCHOLOGICAL EXAMINATION

DESPITE increasing public enlightenment concerning disability, popular stereotypes still remain. One of the most persistent is that built up about the hard-of-hearing person. In the public mind, a hard-of-hearing person is pictured as one who while certainly not peculiar enough to qualify for the deaf-mute group is still not quite bright enough to be treated as a normal individual.[1] He is something of an auditory in-between who wears a hearing aid; needs to be shouted at or mouthed to in direct conversation; and can be amiably ignored in group discussions. As to his hearing, there are two schools of popular thought on the subject. One tends to the opinion that wearing a hearing aid indicates full restoration of hearing ability; the other, that an aid is a sign the wearer is "stone-deaf." Lip reading is a mystery beyond the public grasp; and individual differences among the hard of hearing, beyond public perception. To workers in the field, it is a constant source of wonder how a disability that is itself invisible can nevertheless so artfully conceal its implications. We have seen this happen with the deaf; it applies equally to the hard of hearing.

Psychologists new to the field are not entirely free from popular misconceptions; nor are field definitions and terminology such as to offer significant clarification. As a rule, the new worker begins

[1] Harriet Montague, "Things I Wish They Wouldn't Do," *Volta Review*, XLIII (1941), 40–43.

his professional activities in the vague belief that the hard of hearing are those who have more hearing ability than the deaf. Then along comes a deaf subject who is unusually responsive to sound, only to be followed by a hard-of-hearing individual who could not hear a near-by bomb blast, as it were.

In the course of time, other paradoxes come along. Among the most striking are persons with sufficient hearing ability to qualify as hard of hearing, but who are psychologically deaf through having been reared in deaf environments. And on the other hand, there are those with severe, early losses who are nevertheless psychologically hearing individuals through the fortunate circumstance of possessing the wise guidance, adequate opportunities, and personal assets necessary for development in a hearing environment.

Eventually, the psychologist finds his way through the puzzling maze to an understanding of basic group differentials, characteristics, and exceptions. He learns, for example, that while the hard of hearing as a group have greater hearing ability than the deaf, this does not obtain for every group member; that there are hard-of-hearing individuals with greater amounts of hearing loss than some of their deaf fellows. Examples are: persons who are at the end of the line of progressive deafness; victims of sudden, severe bilateral hearing loss; [2] certain individuals who are exposed to continuous, excessive industrial noise; [3] and persons severely deafened from such ototoxic drugs as dihydrostreptomycin.[4] In this connection, it might be less confusing to a new worker if the latter individuals were referred to as "deafened" rather than as "hard of hearing." But old habits of terminology are hard to drop; and until more effective ones are formulated, the psychologist who

[2] Richard R. Lehmann, "Bilateral Sudden Deafness," *New York State Journal of Medicine* (May 15, 1954), pp. 1481–84.

[3] M. S. Fox and A. Glorig, "Industrial Noise and Hearing Loss," *Journal of Chronic Diseases*, IX (1959), 143–50.

[4] Aram Glorig, "Report of a Recent Study in Dihydrostreptomycin Ototoxicity," *The Laryngoscope*, LXVIII (1958), 1013–27.

is alerted to prepare for a hard-of-hearing patient learns to ready himself for one with any amount of loss from the mild to the profound, and to adapt his approach to whatever the situation turns out to be.

Problems and paradoxes such as these finally bring home the fact that the basic psychological differential between the deaf and the hard of hearing lies not so much in amount of hearing loss as in the nature of the individual's past auditory experiences, and that these in turn are largely determined by the constellation factor: age of onset of impaired hearing plus nature and amount of loss incurred at this time. Thus, from the perspective of past auditory experiences, the hard of hearing are seen as having had sufficient hearing ability for the natural or near-natural acquisition of language and speech and substantial enough for normal or near-normal personal development; the deaf as not.

Another important differential between the groups concerns the nature of the auditory impairment. That of the deaf is relatively static and irreversible. But among the hard of hearing, considerable variation is found not only in type of impairment but also in time and manner of onset, in amount of damage to the auditory mechanism, in response to treatment, and in the effectiveness of the hearing aid. In addition, various associated otological conditions such as tinnitus, vertigo, and otorrhea are far more common and severe among the hard of hearing, and may cause greater distress than that caused by hearing loss.

Differences in psychological approach and procedures with the hard of hearing as compared with the deaf are mainly due to the psychological equivalents and implications of the foregoing distinctions. In the course of examination, these represent the areas requiring special consideration. In other respects, the basic principles and procedures of examination obtain here as in all clinical practice. Since these have been previously noted, the present discussion will deal mainly with points of special emphasis.

The Case History

Special emphasis in the case histories of hard-of-hearing persons falls upon the following lines of inquiry: (*a*) the impaired auditory mechanism and (*b*) the psychological equivalents and implications of the particular impairment for a given individual.

THE IMPAIRED AUDITORY MECHANISM

In regard to the impaired mechanism, the psychologist needs to know the answers to such questions as the following. His major primary sources of information are the otologist, the audiologist, and the patient.

(1) What type of deafness is this and what are the chances for arrest or improvement?

(2) What patterns and amounts of hearing and hearing loss are associated with this type of deafness? Is it monaural or binaural?

(3) What are the means by which arrest or improvement may be brought about?

(4) Are stressful associated conditions present, such as tinnitus, vertigo, imbalance, otorrhea? How great is the discomfort in the particular case? What are the possibilities and means for the alleviation of such conditions?

(5) Are there circumstances involved in the case that can aggravate deafness, such as (*a*) environment: damp, noisy, dusty, rapid temperature changes; (*b*) physical condition and general health: allergy, anemia, hypertension, chronic debility, additional disabilities; and (*c*) emotional disturbance?

(6) What do the otologic and audiologic findings indicate concerning (*a*) the person's ability to hear speech either with or without a hearing aid; (*b*) the advisability of wearing a hearing aid and the likely auditory gains; and (*c*) the possibility of psychogenic or central deafness?

(7) If voice and/or speech changes are present, are they consistent with the duration, amount, and type of hearing impairment?

(8) To what extent can and does the subject use his residual hearing and what are his potentials along these lines?

(9) What is the individual's general pattern of behavior in regard to present and past otologic examination, treatment, and audiologic procedures?

THE PSYCHOLOGICAL IMPLICATIONS OF THE OTOLOGIC AND AUDIOLOGIC FINDINGS

(1) The preceding type of information concerning the nature of the auditory impairment and its associated conditions, patterns, and amounts of hearing and hearing loss serves the psychologist as an index of:

    (a) the nature of some of the stresses experienced by the individual and the situations in which they are most likely to occur

    (b) the possible psychological benefits to be derived from the hearing aid, auditory training, otological and/or surgical treatment

    (c) the eventual prognosis

(2) Knowledge of the prognosis of the impairment serves as a guide to:

    (a) educational foreplanning and planning in the case of children

    (b) vocational training or retraining in the case of adults

    (c) the need for such special therapies as auditory training, lip reading, speech correction and conservation, voice training

    (d) preparation and adjustment of the individual

    (e) preparation and adjustment of the family

(3) Information concerning conditions that aggravate deafness

as well as of stressful associated otological conditions serves
as a guide to:

(a) dangerous work environments
(b) undesirable occupations
(c) necessary health precautions
(d) special otological precautions
(e) the possible adjustment problems associated with these
conditions

(4) Knowledge of the individual's general behavioral reactions
and characteristic responses to otological examination, treatment, and audiologic procedures alerts the psychologist to:

(a) attitudes in regard to accepting deafness
(b) possible inconsistencies between otologic and audiologic
findings and the individual's auditory behavior as observed by the psychologist
(c) the possibility of such conditions as functional deafness,
central deafness, malingering, neurologic disorder, and
sometimes psychiatric disorder
(d) the possible need for comprehensive and intensive psychological study

The foregoing sampling illustrates points of initial orientation in
work with the hard of hearing. From these points, history inquiry
moves on to its ultimate goal: the implications of a specific impairment in the life of a particular individual. To the general
question "What type of deafness is this and what are the chances
for improvement?" is added the complementary question "What
kind of person is this and what are his chances for adjustment?"
The full story requires complete history and psychological examination data.

However, as previously mentioned in connection with the deaf,
a full psychological examination is not necessary in all cases. In
regard to case history, the range of inquiry is generally determined

by the age of the subject, the purpose of the examination, and the nature of the presenting problem. With the hard of hearing, a common presenting signal for deeper psychological study is the individual's refusal to wear a hearing aid [5] and to take advantage of speech and hearing rehabilitation services. The underlying problem is usually nonacceptance of disability.

Where impaired hearing was incurred in early childhood, the history outline presented in Chapter 6 will be found applicable, with appropriate modifications as required. But when the disability was acquired in the years of adolescence or adulthood, the full story consists of two interrelated parts: the first predating the impairment, and the second covering the "hearing-impaired years," as one patient expressed it. Where significant life changes occur after impairment, it is as if the worker were compiling two different histories for the same person.

Finally, a word of caution must be expressed on the subject of communication between psychologists and hard-of-hearing subjects. Because the technical problems of communication are far less complex than in the case of the deaf, there is a freer exchange of thinking, comments, and ideas. In the course of such exchange, hard-of-hearing patients frequently turn to psychologists for technical information and opinions concerning otology and audiology. Psychologists are strongly cautioned against making any recommendations along these lines, even by implication. The recommendations should come directly from the specialists themselves.

This is so because wishful thinking about hearing restoration and hope against hope for such a miracle are very strong in the hearts of the hard of hearing. An incautious or inaccurate observation on the part of a psychologist may lead him to become hopelessly enmeshed in a patient's disturbance, grief, and disappointments.

[5] A. A. Miller, J. M. McCauley, C. Fraser, and C. Cubert, "Psychological Factors in Adaptation to Hearing Aids," *American Journal of Orthopsychiatry,* XXIX (1959), 121–29.

When this happens, the greater part of the worker's clinical usefulness is lost.

In his relationships with the other team specialists, it is the responsibility of the psychologist to maintain a sufficiency of interdisciplinary knowledge to enable him to function as an intelligent team collaborator. In regard to the patient, it is the psychologist's responsibility to influence him to use the authoritative services of other specialties wisely; to overcome whatever feelings of stigma he may have in regard to his auditory condition; and then to get on with the business of living.

The Interview

COMMUNICATING WITH HARD-OF-HEARING PERSONS

In communicating with hard-of-hearing persons, the psychologist should be aware of the following facts: (1) there is considerable variation in benefit derived from the hearing aid among the hard of hearing; (2) there is also considerable variation in the ability to use residual hearing as a communications aid; (3) the skills and limitations in lip reading, summarized in the case of the deaf, obtain for the hard of hearing as well; (4) not all hard-of-hearing persons are equally able to synchronize lip reading with amplified hearing to get a meaningful message; (5) for the hard of hearing, the interview room must possess optimal *acoustic* as well as visual conditions; (6) continued lip reading and listening are highly fatiguing operations that impose great strains on the individual; (7) emotional disturbance and tensions as well as fatigue impair communications skills; and (8) above all, the psychologist should be aware of how communication and interview can be facilitated for the hard of hearing.

As summarized by Wright, among the hard of hearing will be found:

    a. Those who depend entirely upon the limited hearing they have
    b. Those who read the lips and use their hearing simultaneously
    c. Those who do not read the lips and depend entirely upon their hearing aids
    d. Those who read the lips and also wear a hearing aid
    e. Those who have some useful residual hearing but do not use it and thus lack auditory comprehension [6]

In addition, there will be those who are old and experienced hands at visual communication; others who are in the first agonies of trying to synchronize sound and lip reading into some meaningful message; and still others who thrust the whole burden of their communications problems upon the shoulders of the interviewer.

The best general rule is to aim for a relaxed, tension-free interview atmosphere with sufficient introductory greeting and conversation to impart confidence to both the interviewer and the patient. In greeting and general deportment, the interviewer's behavior should not be as outgoing as with the deaf, but should rather stress calm, restrained friendliness and sincerity and matter-of-fact acceptance that the patient is hard of hearing.

The interview room should be a quiet one, with special precautions taken against sudden, loud noises such as telephone bells, etc. Muted buzzers or light signals should be substituted wherever possible. A table-model amplifier should be available for use if the interviewee so wishes. To facilitate lip reading, all the suggestions made in connection with the deaf (page 163) obtain here as well with the exception of the use of manual communication. With singularly few exceptions, the hard of hearing employ oral communication and writing. The interviewer's speech should be clear, distinct, and visible at all times, with the volume of voice maintained at a steady level of mutual comfort. The patient who

[6] Betty Wright, *Orientation Training for Vocational Rehabilitation Counselors: A Syllabus on Special Problems of the Deaf and the Hard of Hearing for Orientation Institutes* (Washington, D.C.: American Hearing Society, December, 1956), p. 6.

uses his residual hearing can adjust his aid for optimal audibility; the one who does not will not benefit from an interviewer's shouting. For the patient who neither lip-reads well nor uses his residual hearing, writing will have to serve as the means of communication, with the language used geared to the patient's level of comprehension. And finally, with the patient who will not wear a hearing aid and nevertheless depends upon inadequate unamplified hearing in communication, the raised voice will be necessary. To avoid exhaustion in such cases, the interviewer should evolve a plan of shortened interview sessions alternated with psychological test sessions. To avoid somewhat similar situations with hearing-aid users whose batteries suddenly go dead, a source of supply should be available for those who forget to take spares along.

The interviewer should watch closely for signs of fatigue and tension. Common signs are sudden difficulty in comprehension, excessive manipulation of the hearing-aid amplifier, evidences of visual strain, restlessness, tense facial expression, and a general appearance of exhaustion. Interview should not be prolonged to the point of fatigue. It is obvious by now that the psychological examination of hearing impaired persons is a considerably longer procedure than with the hearing. In the end, time will be saved by arranging for additional sessions that are shorter and more productive than by attempting to complete an examination in fewer long meetings that will undoubtedly be spoiled by fatigue.

THE INTERVIEW CONTENT

As in all clinical interviews, the content includes the total range of information a patient imparts or implies and a psychologist needs for diagnostic clarification. Of particular importance in evaluating the adjustment potentials of a hard-of-hearing person is information concerning his attitudes toward impaired hearing. Part of the story is contained in the case history. Interview affords the psychologist an opportunity of obtaining a firsthand account.

However, it is an unusual individual who will pour forth a comprehensive account of his feelings and attitudes about a sensitive personal matter. Some of the information can be obtained without his awareness through certain types of psychological tests, notably the projective techniques. But since these are not directly concerned with impaired hearing, specific attitudes remain unprobed. A highly useful complementary instrument would be one specifically designed to explore these attitudes. In the course of search for such an instrument, the present writer was fortunate in discovering an unpublished scale especially constructed for this purpose in 1944–45 under the direction of Urie Bronfenbrenner and used in the psychological program at the Aural Rehabilitation Unit of the Borden General Hospital during World War II. Permission was sought and obtained [7] to publish the Bronfenbrenner Hearing Attitude Scale in this volume together with pertinent descriptions of its use. It should be added that the Attitude Scale was discovered by the writer in an excellent unpublished doctoral dissertation by Handelman.[8]

The Bronfenbrenner Scale consists of 100 simply worded statements describing possible reactions to situations involving hearing loss. The patient responds to each by encircling "Agree" or "Disagree." Attitudes covered by the statements include: self-appraisal; depression; overoptimism; tension; reaction to rehabilitation; job worry; sensitivity; cover-up; withdrawal; and eccentric reactions. Bronfenbrenner states in a personal communication to the author that "the questionnaire was standardized on a sample of several hundred enlisted men and officers suffering from minimal to very severe hearing defect, but the scale would certainly have to be

[7] Personal communication between Professor Urie Bronfenbrenner of the Department of Psychology, Cornell University, Ithaca, New York, and the author, May, 1959.

[8] N. S. Handelman, "The Relationship between Certain Personality Factors and Speech Reading Proficiency" (unpublished doctoral dissertation, School of Education, New York University, May, 1955).

restandardized for current use." The latter observation applies to the use of the scale as a measure. However, as a clinical probe and interview guide, it can be used as it stands and is so presented at this time.

BRONFENBRENNER HEARING ATTITUDE SCALE [9]

I. Rationale of Administration
   A. Upon entering the Clinic, each patient is given a hearing attitude scale. A specially devised scoring matrix permits rapid identification of the more common patterns of unhealthy reaction and their relative intensity.
   B. The patient's responses to the questionnaire become the basis for discussion of his problems in a psychological interview, customarily of a half-hour's duration. The interview serves a twofold purpose:
      1. Probing of the patient's responses and observation of his behavior permit at least partial evaluation of the validity of the scale for the particular subject.
      2. The subject's explanations of his responses to the questionnaire lead almost automatically into a discussion of his general psychological adjustment. If the interviewer feels it is warranted, he may proceed, either in the same or in subsequent sessions, into a more thorough exploration of the focal areas of psychological development (e.g., childhood, sex, social relations, job and army adjustment, etc.).
   C. The results of the scale and of the interview are summarized by means of profiles and commentary in a Counseling Report. The verbal portion of the Report summarizes the general psychological adjustment and qualifies and elaborates upon the picture of the subject's hearing loss adjustment as revealed by the questionnaire. The total effect is to combine the mutual advantages and contributions of objective testing and subjective clinical judgment. . . .
   D. Toward the end of the rehabilitation program, the patient is reevaluated with respect to hearing loss adjustment. The hearing

[9] Taken from the unpublished study "The Psychological Program in the Army Hearing Center at Borden General Hospital," by Urie Bronfenbrenner.

attitude scale is re-administered and, after a review of the complete record, a final appraisal is made.

II. The Bronfenbrenner Hearing Attitude Scale

These questions are to help us understand how you feel about your hearing loss.

Read each statement. If the statement tells how you really feel or what you really do draw a *circle* around the word *Agree*. If the statement is *not* true for you draw a *circle* around the word *Disagree*. Do not leave out any questions. If you are not sure of your answer, read the question carefully, and mark the answer which is *nearer* to the way you feel. If you want to, you may explain how you feel about any of the questions when you have finished with the questions.

In going through the questions you may find some things which you hadn't thought of before or which may not apply to you. The main thing is that every question has been true for some person. So, go ahead, read them over, and answer them the way *you* really feel—*not* the way you think a hard-of-hearing person *should* feel.

EXAMPLE:

0. These questions are for hard-of-hearing people. *Agree Disagree*

1. Being hard of hearing keeps me from doing many of the things I like to do. *Agree Disagree*

2. Since I became hard of hearing, things don't interest me as much as they used to. *Agree Disagree*

3. Other people may become annoyed at being asked to repeat. *Agree Disagree*

4. The strain of trying to hear makes me sweat. *Agree Disagree*

5. The only time I would be willing to wear a hearing aid would be when I am among people who know me well. *Agree Disagree*

6. Being hard of hearing would stop me from taking a job where I have to be the boss. *Agree Disagree*

7. Because of my hearing, people have been unfair to me. *Agree Disagree*

8. When I meet other people I do all the talking so I don't have to listen. *Agree Disagree*

9. Even though I am hard of hearing, I can go to a party and have a good time. *Agree Disagree*

10. Only people who are hard of hearing can help me with my problem. *Agree Disagree*

11. Being hard of hearing is worse than any other handicap. *Agree Disagree*

12. Being hard of hearing gives me the blues. *Agree Disagree*

13. Because I'm hard of hearing some employers may not want to hire me. *Agree Disagree*

14. Because I am hard of hearing, I'm always worried. *Agree Disagree*

15. I don't think I can learn to read lips. *Agree Disagree*

16. Because I am hard of hearing, the only kind of work I can do is common labor. *Agree Disagree*

17. Because I'm hard of hearing, people turn against me. *Agree Disagree*

18. I would rather not know what is going on than admit that I am hard of hearing. *Agree Disagree*

19. Being hard of hearing keeps me from going out in public. *Agree Disagree*

20. Because of my hearing, I have trouble remembering things. *Agree Disagree*

21. I let my hearing trouble get the best of me. *Agree Disagree*

22. Because I am hard of hearing I'm no good to anybody. *Agree Disagree*

23. Being hard of hearing never embarrasses me. *Agree Disagree*

24. Being hard of hearing makes me jumpy. *Agree Disagree*

25. I cannot get along without a hearing aid. *Agree Disagree*

26. If the boss finds out I am hard of hearing I won't be able to hold my job. *Agree Disagree*

27. Because I'm hard of hearing, people stare at me all the time. *Agree Disagree*

28. When I apply for a job, I shall try to hide the fact that I am hard of hearing. *Agree Disagree*

29. Being hard of hearing makes me stay away from my friends. *Agree Disagree*

30. Because I'm hard of hearing, I have a right to feel sorry for myself. *Agree Disagree*

31. Being hard of hearing won't stop me from having a happy family life. *Agree Disagree*

32. If my hearing stays that way life won't be worth living. *Agree Disagree*
33. A hearing loss is no problem to me. *Agree Disagree*
34. Being hard of hearing makes me nervous. *Agree Disagree*
35. I want to learn lip reading. *Agree Disagree*
36. Because I am hard of hearing, it will be very hard for me to get any kind of a job. *Agree Disagree*
37. Because I'm hard of hearing, I always get into trouble. *Agree Disagree*
38. It is hard for me to tell others about my hearing trouble. *Agree Disagree*
39. As long as I'm hard of hearing, I can't be popular with people. *Agree Disagree*
40. Nobody has any business telling me how to handle my hearing problem. *Agree Disagree*
41. If my hearing gets worse I won't be able to take it. *Agree Disagree*
42. I drink to forget I am hard of hearing. *Agree Disagree*
43. I think a hard-of-hearing person is bound to make mistakes once in a while. *Agree Disagree*
44. Being hard of hearing is driving me crazy. *Agree Disagree*
45. Wearing a hearing aid in public would bother me. *Agree Disagree*
46. Because I am hard of hearing, I can never get a job that pays good money. *Agree Disagree*
47. I can't stand having people ask me questions about my hearing. *Agree Disagree*
48. When people ask me if I am hard of hearing I'd rather not answer. *Agree Disagree*
49. Because I'm hard of hearing, I stay off by myself. *Agree Disagree*
50. My hearing gets worse when I am worried. *Agree Disagree*
51. Being hard of hearing doesn't stop me from living a pretty normal life. *Agree Disagree*
52. Being hard of hearing makes me feel like crying. *Agree Disagree*
53. There are some kinds of jobs that a person with good hearing can do better than I can. *Agree Disagree*

54. Being hard of hearing gets me all tired out.   *Agree Disagree*
55. I don't need anything this hospital can give me.   *Agree Disagree*
56. I may be able to hold my job, but my hearing will keep me from getting ahead.   *Agree Disagree*
57. Being hard of hearing makes me bashful.   *Agree Disagree*
58. I don't think it is fair to have my hearing tested when I apply for a job.   *Agree Disagree*
59. Because I'm hard of hearing, I don't go to parties.   *Agree Disagree*
60. My hearing changes from day to day.   *Agree Disagree*
61. I am hard of hearing, but I still have confidence in myself.   *Agree Disagree*
62. Because I am hard of hearing, I don't have any pep.   *Agree Disagree*
63. Because other people don't know how loud to talk to me, I may embarrass them once in a while.   *Agree Disagree*
64. Because I am hard of hearing, I can't keep my mind on what I'm doing.   *Agree Disagree*
65. I won't wear a hearing aid under any conditions.   *Agree Disagree*
66. Even though I'm hard of hearing, there is still some kind of work I can do.   *Agree Disagree*
67. I can't stand having people kid me about my hearing.   *Agree Disagree*
68. When I don't hear what a person is saying I just let it go.   *Agree Disagree*
69. Because I'm hard of hearing, I never speak to strangers.   *Agree Disagree*
70. Because of my hearing trouble, I don't like people.   *Agree Disagree*
71. I have learned how to get along with my hearing trouble.   *Agree Disagree*
72. As long as my hearing stays this way I can't be happy.   *Agree Disagree*
73. Because I don't always hear what people say, they may lose patience with me once in a while.   *Agree Disagree*
74. Being hard of hearing makes me so mad I feel like smashing things.   *Agree Disagree*

75. I don't want to go to any hearing classes.   *Agree Disagree*
76. Because I am hard of hearing, I won't be able to make a living.   *Agree Disagree*
77. Because I'm hard of hearing, I am ashamed to go home to my family.   *Agree Disagree*
78. I sometimes make out that my hearing is better than it really is.   *Agree Disagree*
79. Because I'm hard of hearing, I don't like to meet new people.   *Agree Disagree*
80. I don't care if my hearing does get worse.   *Agree Disagree*
81. Being hard of hearing has made a completely different person out of me.   *Agree Disagree*
82. Being hard of hearing makes me feel sad most of the time.   *Agree Disagree*
83. In applying for most jobs, a person with good hearing has a better chance than I have.   *Agree Disagree*
84. Because I'm hard of hearing, people get on my nerves.   *Agree Disagree*
85. If I need a hearing aid, I'll wear it.   *Agree Disagree*
86. Because I'm hard of hearing, my family will have to support me.   *Agree Disagree*
87. Everybody makes fun of me because of my hearing.   *Agree Disagree*
88. When I don't hear what a person has said, I often ask him to say it again.   *Agree Disagree*
89. Because I'm hard of hearing, I sometimes avoid talking with people.   *Agree Disagree*
90. I'm glad I'm hard of hearing.   *Agree Disagree*
91. Being hard of hearing is like having two strikes against you.   *Agree Disagree*
92. Being hard of hearing makes me feel like giving up sometimes.   *Agree Disagree*
93. As far as I am concerned none of these questions are worth bothering about.   *Agree Disagree*
94. I lie awake nights worrying about my hearing trouble.   *Agree Disagree*
95. I can't stand having doctors look at my ears.   *Agree Disagree*
96. The only job I can take is one where I can work alone.   *Agree Disagree*

97. Because of my hearing, nobody wants me
around. *Agree Disagree*
98. Only my friends should be told that I'm hard
of hearing. *Agree Disagree*
99. Because I'm hard of hearing, I want to live off
by myself. *Agree Disagree*
100. I hope my hearing gets better. *Agree Disagree*

As in all inventory scales and questionnaires, so in this; it is not difficult for a subject eager to make a good impression to identify and select the appropriate answer. However, an experienced psychologist is not deceived by the practice. He still has the evidence of the case history, interview, and psychological testing against which to check the inventory results. The unusual advantages of the Hearing Attitude Scale as an interview aid and screening device in work with the hard of hearing remain unquestioned.

Psychological Testing

In testing the hard of hearing, the common misconception is that all the tests used with the hearing can be used with hard-of-hearing persons. The experienced examiner knows otherwise. As careful screening and selection of tests is required for the hard of hearing as for the deaf, and as careful administration and interpretation.

Important considerations in regard to test selection are the age of onset of the impairment; the amount of hearing loss involved; and the individual's level of language attainment and reading ability. Major determinants of test choice are the appropriateness of the test questions and situations for a given subject and the level of language attainment and reading ability required for the comprehension of the test items and directions. For purposes of generalization, it would be safer to say that all the tests that can be used successfully with the deaf can be used with the hard of hearing. These include the tests previously mentioned as suitable for deaf children and adults.[10] Others depend upon the individual subject.

Specific test batteries currently used with both hard-of-hearing and deaf adults have been presented in connection with the psychological testing of the deaf and include the Clinical Battery; the New York District Vocational Rehabilitation Battery; the Alpha-Beta-Gregg Battery; and the Rehabilitation Counselor's Testing Kit. Also summarized previously was the rationale of psychological test interpretation for hearing-impaired persons.

The test program now presented is one in current use at a facility primarily for the hard of hearing—the well-known New York League for the Hard of Hearing. The following personal communication summarizes the basic procedures and psychological tests used at the League and illustrates the degree of clinical thinking and perception that must go into the evaluation of hard-of-hearing persons.

Psychological Testing Program: New York League for the Hard of Hearing [11]

The New York League for the Hard of Hearing is a nonprofit social agency which offers services such as audiological evaluation and recommendations; educational instruction in speech, lip reading, and auditory comprehension; English to the foreign-born; counseling, placement, and recreation to hearing-impaired persons of all ages.

Since our services are varied and comprehensive and are offered to persons of all ages, with many different types of hearing impairments and of varied socioeconomic backgrounds, it is obvious that there can be no typical case or test battery. In each instance it is the psychologist's responsibility to select the instruments that will help him get the information he needs in order to (1) understand the individual—his

[10] See chapters 8 and 9.

[11] This explanation of the Psychological Testing Program: New York League for the Hard of Hearing was written especially for this publication. Grateful acknowledgment is made by the author to Eleanor C. Ronnei, Administrative Director of the New York League for the Hard of Hearing, and to Ruth R. Green, Director of Guidance Services of the League.

intelligence, social maturity, educational level, and aptitudes; (2) compare and relate the individual's scores to those of the normally hearing population on whom the tests were standardized; (3) evaluate the extent to which the individual's particular hearing loss may have affected the above measured characteristics; (4) assess the individual's ability to function in a normally hearing world with the limitations imposed upon him by the physical defect itself and its effect on his personal development and functioning.

A detailed list of the tests most frequently used at the League and the reasons for their selection for different age groups are summarized as follows:

PRESCHOOL

With preschool children we generally want to know what their intellectual endowment is, their level of social maturity, and something about how they work and learn. Some of the tests used with preschoolers are:

The Randalls Island Performance Series, designed for children two to five years, gives a measure of intelligence, knowledge of the child's manual dexterity, form perception, and coordination, and general insight into his ability to learn. Besides being a measure of intelligence, it also helps us evaluate how they might perform in a learning situation.

The Revised Stanford-Binet Scale, standardized for ages two years through adulthood, is useful for preschool children who have only a *mild hearing impairment*. Otherwise, the test would not give a reliable measure of the child's ability, as it is weighted too heavily with verbal material and does not offer a separate verbal and performance score.

The Columbia Mental Maturity Scale, standardized for ages three to twelve years, is a nonverbal intelligence test which, in our experience, is more valuable for children five and over. It is difficult for youngsters below five with hearing losses to understand even the simple verbal instructions.

The Goodenough Draw-a-Man Test is valuable in offering an I.Q. score and information in relation to personality characteristics. This test too has proved more useful with the child over five years of age who can understand the verbal directions.

The Vineland Social Maturity Scale is also a useful instrument to determine the level of social maturity and what the child is capable of doing in relation to his personal needs.

(To be explored: The Merrill-Palmer Scale)

SCHOOL-AGE CHILDREN

For school-age children, tests are usually selected from the following:

The Wechsler Intelligence Scale for Children is very useful in that it differentiates Verbal from Performance I.Q. It will usually be found that a hearing-impaired youngster *cannot be validly evaluated on the Verbal Scale* since the hearing loss frequently does not permit him to perform up to his fullest capacity. The gap between Verbal and Performance Scores often shows the extent to which he can function in a normally hearing school.

The Columbia Mental Maturity Scale is a useful nonverbal instrument at the school-age level.

The Revised Stanford-Binet Scale can be used to indicate the *extent to which a hearing-impaired child may be handicapped in an oral environment*. As a measure, it is always used in conjunction with non-language tests as a supplementary device.

The Vineland Social Maturity Scale may also be used at the school-age level to indicate social maturity and personal adjustment.

The Children's Apperception Test is sometimes used with children *who have sufficient verbal ability to express themselves adequately* as a means of gaining insight into personality mechanisms.

Stanford Achievement Test. All of the school-age children are evaluated on a standard achievement test geared to the appropriate level. This helps give a measure of academic achievement and knowledge as to the level at which the child is working in the various school subjects. It also offers information as to whether or not a child is working up to his expected capacities and indicates the areas in which additional tutoring may be required. Finally, it helps correlate verbal ability with verbal performance.

ADULTS

With adults, again depending upon the need, the following are among the intelligence tests that might be used:

The Wechsler-Bellevue or the Wechsler Adult Intelligence Scales are used to obtain information indicating a subject's intellectual endowment. In the case of persons with long-standing hearing losses, a particularly important differential is that between Verbal and Performance abilities. The Wechsler Scales have the additional advantage of being individual tests, thus helping the examiner gain deeper insight into a subject's work habits, ability to learn, and approach to a new situation.

The Revised Beta and the Nonlanguage Multi-Mental Tests. Both of these tests, being nonlanguage instruments, are better geared to measure the intelligence of a hearing-impaired person whose language comprehension has been seriously affected by his hearing loss.

Otis Tests of Mental Ability. This paper-and-pencil test can be used successfully *if a person has only recently lost part of his hearing.* In using paper-and-pencil tests it is necessary to ascertain that the person has the ability to read and comprehend the material of the test. It is often best to precede all tests with a simple reading test, such as the Gates Reading Tests.

Vocational Testing

INTEREST TESTS

Children of high-school age are frequently seen for help in vocational planning and guidance. Adults too who are in need of job change are seen for vocational testing. An interest inventory is used to obtain a general picture of expressed interests. The interest tests used, depending on the particular subject, are:

1. Kuder Preference Record
2. Thurstone Interest Test
3. Brainard Occupational Preference Inventory
4. Strong Vocational Interest Tests
5. Allport-Vernon Study of Values. While not strictly an interest test, interesting information is obtained concerning an individual's sense of values, such as political, religious, theoretical, economic, etc.

OTHER APTITUDE TESTS

Depending upon the expressed interests and abilities of the individual, aptitude tests are selected from the following:

1. Clerical Tests
   a. General Clerical Test
   b. Minnesota Clerical Test
2. Mechanical Ability and Spatial Relations
   a. Bennett Test of Mechanical Comprehension
   b. MacQuarrie Test of Mechanical Ability
   c. Minnesota Mechanical Assembly
   d. Minnesota Paper Form Board Test
   e. Purdue Pegboard

3. Art
   a. Meier Art Tests
   b. A complete battery such as the Differential Aptitude Tests
   might be used.

PERSONALITY SCREENING DEVICES

In the service program of the League, the following personality tests
are occasionally used *as screening devices rather than as measures,* with
selection based on the characteristics of the client. The limitations of such
paper-and-pencil tests are realized in that they offer only a superficial
evaluation of personality. Some of the tests so used are:

1. Adjective Check List
2. Bell Adjustment Inventory
3. Bernreuter Personality Inventory
4. Mooney Problems Check List
5. Sentence Completion Tests

This brief outline of the psychological tests used at the New York
League for the Hard of Hearing does not include a full discussion of each
test, but it does indicate, we hope, that we are using available test material
extensively and aim to interpret test scores as useful planning aids for
the benefit of our hearing-impaired clients.

Observation

As in all psychological examinations, whether of hearing or hearing-
impaired persons, skilled observation adds clinical essence to
procedures that could otherwise be purely mechanical; the range
of information provided through observation is as broad as a
worker's clinical perceptions and experience. Samplings of such
information have already been given in connection with the deaf
and need not be repeated here. However, a particularly interesting
diagnostic problem a psychologist may encounter in work with the
hard of hearing warrants mention at this time. This involves the
differential identification of (1) persons with structural auditory
damage whose claimed amount of hearing loss is substantially
exaggerated by psychogenic factors (functional deafness or psychogenic overlay); (2) persons without structural auditory damage

whose hearing loss is entirely due to psychogenic factors (psychogenic deafness); (3) persons who consciously feign deafness (malingerers); and (4) persons with structural auditory damage but inconsistent audiometric responses that are due to other involvements, i.e., physical, otological, neurological, etc.

The major roles in the detection of such auditory anomalies are played by otologist and audiologist. According to Fournier,[12] the means are available today for these specialists to identify with certainty "all cases of malingering as well as all those of exaggeration,"[13] granted a minimum of cooperation on the part of the subject. When such patients are referred to a psychologist, the clinical aim of the worker is (1) to study the consistency (or inconsistency) between the personality structure of the individual and the audiometric findings; (2) to investigate what benefits the individual derives, either consciously or unconsciously, from deafness; and (3) to establish, if possible, why and under what conditions this particular organ and/or function came to play its present psychic role.

However, at times such patients are seen by psychologists before audiometric screening, or else they may have evaded audiometric detection. Psychologists should therefore be familiar with some of the common signs of inconsistency in auditory behavior, the means for eliciting such signs, and pertinent case history details. From the comprehensive listing of important indications of the possibility of functional deafness compiled by Johnson, Work, and McCoy,[14] the following signs are presented for purposes of illustration:

1. *Medical Examination*
   a. Discrepancy between otological findings and history.
   b. Degree of loss unsupported by history or otological findings.

[12] J. E. Fournier, "The Detection of Auditory Malingering," *Translations of The Beltone Institute for Hearing Research*, No. 8, February, 1958.
[13] *Ibid.*, p. 22.
[14] K. O. Johnson, W. P. Work, and G. McCoy, "Functional Deafness." Reprinted from *Annals of Otology, Rhinology and Laryngology*, LXV (1956), 154.

  c. Total deafness but with normal responses to labyrinthian tests.
  d. Rapidly progressive perceptive hearing loss without evidence of organic disease.
  e. Monaural loss without clear etiology.
  f. Obvious psychiatric disorder.
  g. Sudden onset of total bilateral deafness.
  h. Normal response to questions during caloric test.
  i. Significant responses during pentothal interview.
  j. Unsolicited comments or questions regarding compensation.
  k. Discrepancy between stated history and history as found in patient's medical records.

     . . . .

 2. *Manner of Listening and Speaking*
  a. Exaggerated attempt to hear.
  b. Exaggerated staring—attempt to impress with ability to lip-read.
  c. Discrepancy between history and articulatory and phonatory patterns.
  d. Excessively loud voice.
  e. Refusal to attempt lip reading. May force examiner to write.
  f. Discrepancy between lip-reading ability and hearing-loss history.
 3. *Hearing-Aid Usage*
  a. Wears weak aid with apparent success while professing severe loss.
  b. Wears aid turned off or with insignificant degree of volume.
  c. Claims regular use of aid but aid shows no signs of wear.
  d. Claims severe loss but wears no aid.
  e. Claims regular aid usage but has no reasonable idea of the cost of batteries.
  f. Claims improbable improvement or lack of improvement from a hearing aid or from therapy.[15]

     . . . .

In connection with their listing, the authors stress the fact that an unqualified diagnosis of functional hearing loss should not be made on the basis of only a single test or sign. Several discrepancies are necessary.

 Some of the classic test-tricks that can be used by psychologists in confirming an impression that oto-audiological differential

[15] *Ibid.*, pp. 5–6.

diagnosis is required are reviewed by Blegvad [16] and Fournier. [17] The basic aim is to catch the patient while he is off guard through some such procedure as (1) making an important announcement while the patient is busy with another task; (2) uttering a surprise warning or command; (3) announcing a change of instructions while the patient is engrossed in a task; (4) making a suggestion as to how to overcome a test difficulty. All of these are of course spoken in low to moderate tones and always at times when the patient is not watching the examiner's face. Suspect cases are referred for otological and audiological examination.

Counsel the Person—Not the Disability [18]

Having devoted due consideration to tests, techniques and procedures of examination, we now turn back to the people involved, in this case the hard of hearing. How do the factors, influences, and experiences sketched in these pages fit into a real-life frame? What have the people directly affected to tell of what it means to live a hearing-impaired life? [19]

The story of one such person follows. Briefly digested to meet space limitations, it nevertheless provides graphic illustration of the meaning of hearing loss in the life of one who had too much functional hearing to require the special educational facilities for the deaf, yet not enough to fit easily into the social and educational world of the hearing. Originally read before a hearing conservation conference at Adelphi College during July, 1958, the

---

[16] N. Rh. Blegvad, "Psychogenic Deafness (Emotional Deafness)," *Acta Oto-Laryngologica*, XL (1951–52), 283–96.

[17] Fournier, "The Detection of Auditory Malingering."

[18] Thanks to James F. Garrett: "Counsel the Man—Not the Disability." Reprinted from *The Crippled Child*.

[19] In this connection, see the following three books: E. E. Calkins, "*And Hearing Not*" (New York: Charles Scribner's Sons, 1946); Grace E. Barstow Murphy, *Your Deafness Is Not You* (New York: Harper & Brothers, 1954); Frances Warfield, *Keep Listening* (New York: The Viking Press, 1957).

following recollections are presented here with the gracious permission of their author.

Personal Recollections of Frances S. Friedman

It was a school nurse who discovered that I was severely hard of hearing. My kindergarten teacher was puzzled by the fact that while facing her I obeyed all commands, but when my back was turned to her I was disobedient. The school nurse decided to test my hearing. The results of that test were sent to my parents with a request that they take me to a specialist. The doctor found that I had no usable hearing in my left ear, but some in my right. I had been getting by with my natural lip-reading ability, which had everyone fooled into believing I could hear when I wanted to.

My mother refused to send me to a school for the deaf. She felt that I had managed to get by thus far; therefore she saw no reason why I shouldn't continue to do so. In those days there were no special classes for the hard of hearing such as they have today. One had to struggle along as best one could. And a struggle it was. Teachers couldn't seem to understand that I had to see their faces to lip-read what was being said. They were constantly pacing the back or sides of the room, and if I should turn my head in their direction I would be reprimanded. The children were constantly making fun of my speech, and when I would give a wrong answer, because I misunderstood what they said to me, they would all join in taunting me and telling each other I was "crazy." All this certainly did not help to make me a happy child, so I turned to books, which were to remain my friends through all the hard years.

At thirteen I entered high school with the slight hope that being older my classmates would be more tolerant. But I found the situation much worse. Instead of one teacher who roamed the room I had five or six who all seemed to share the same restlessness in the classroom. Somehow I managed to maintain good grades, since most of the textbooks covered the assignments. College, which had been my goal, seemed farther away as first my Latin and then my French teachers requested my removal from their classes. My hearing loss and speech defect prevented my learning a foreign language. Two years of high school found me still friendless and more withdrawn. I was now ashamed of this thing that seemed to set me apart from others. Finally, my parents decided to send me to a school for the deaf in the hope that I would find my niche among others like myself.

You can well imagine with what dreams I entered that residential school for the deaf. I was going to have everything that I had missed through all my school years; teachers who would understand my handicap and so would be more tolerant of it; friends who were like myself and so would accept me and not laugh every time I opened my mouth. I would be able to walk the streets with my eyes front, not with bowed head and downcast eyes. No one can imagine the dreams that were packed along with my clothes to be delivered to that wonderful, wonderful new world—the school for the deaf. But those dreams remained dreams and nothing more. Again I found myself "neither fish nor fowl." I was different from most of the students. I was hard of hearing with a normal voice. And my lip reading, which I had always taken for granted, was found to be of the highest caliber. The school couldn't improve on it. It didn't help me with the other students when it got about that I could hear and speak on the telephone without trouble. The school I attended was, and is still, one that employs the manual alphabet in communication and instruction. But even that was denied me as the school decided that the use of the manual alphabet might lead to less and less speech on my part. So again I was set apart—I couldn't make friends because of the communication problem. So books still remained my only friends. I was fortunate in one thing. One of the few deaf teachers in that school took me under his wing, and using the blackboard as his voice, tried to make me understand something of the problem I was facing. I was too young then to fully appreciate what he was trying to convey to me, but in later years his words helped me over many a rough spot.

I'm sure the teachers in my old high school didn't celebrate my return a year later. But this time I wasn't letting anyone discourage me. I did not graduate with my class because I had lost a year when I attended the school for the deaf. The principal warned me that I would have to give up the idea of graduating altogether, because I lacked the necessary regents credits and could not possibly make them up. But I graduated with the second class despite his dire prediction that I would not.

College was still my goal, but with no foreign language and not enough mathematics that prospect didn't seem very hopeful. The following Fall I enrolled in a university as a special student in Library Science. It was the same story all over again. Teachers who roamed around the room lecturing, students who avoided me because they could not understand my handicap. I completed the course but did not have the feeling of satisfaction I needed. So I enrolled in another university as a special student in general studies. While there, I took a course in speech correction which eliminated some of my speech defects and made it easier for others to understand me.

I did not find the working world any easier than my school world. I worked at a number of occupations which I obtained through a new service of employment for the deaf and the hard of hearing. I was an inspector in a steel wool factory, a packer of tea bags, an examiner in an underwear factory, office assistant for a benevolent society, and finally a graphotype operator. When Unemployment Insurance was established, I held a civil service position as Assistant Supervisor in the reproduction department, where I remained until the office moved to Albany.

My social life left much to be desired. I was at a complete loss in a crowd of hearing people. No one had the time or patience to repeat to me what was being said. If someone said something humorous, the point of the joke was lost by the time it was passed on to me. If I doubledated, I had difficulty following the repartee of the others and so I was regarded as a "wet blanket." So I remained shy, painfully so, and couldn't seem to develop any of the social graces so necessary to making friends.

I finally joined a hard-of-hearing group, and there I should have been happy but was not. I simply couldn't understand why such facial contortions were necessary when addressing each other. And, too, I could not understand their feeling of superiority because they were hard of hearing and not deaf.

I had begun to despair of ever finding such things that most people take for granted—friends, companionship, fun. And then I was taken to an affair given by an organization for the deaf. Of course it was rather strange for a while; but somehow I seemed to fit in. As I became familiar with the manual and sign language, I began to make friends, go on dates. And so a new life began for me.

I married a deaf man, a college graduate of unusual intelligence, but a very poor lip reader. I had to communicate with him manually, and my hard-of-hearing friends dropped me. After our two hearing children were born, we became friendly with the parents of their playmates in the neighborhood. They were most kind to us and did everything they could to make us feel one of them. They would ask me to join them in their canasta games and would go out of their way to include me in the general conversation. But when occasionally the husbands and wives would get together for a night on the town, which would include a show and night club, they "forgot" to invite us.

They probably thought they were being considerate since they realized that we both would have difficulty following a play or a musical. And, too, the husbands found it awkward trying to include my husband in their conversations. They did invite us to house parties where I would try to bridge the gap by interpreting, but even I would run into difficulty trying to keep up with the rapid-fire give and take. So the house-party invitations also became fewer.

Our daughter, now seventeen, had some rough going in her childhood. The children refused to accept her because her parents "talked on their hands." But she won her own battle by bringing her friends to the house and showing them that our household was as normal as theirs. Gradually they began to take our deafness for granted. Some of her friends have learned the manual alphabet and they are so proud when we understand what they spell to us. Our son, now twelve, had none of these problems because the neighborhood has become used to us. But still, being the only deaf couple in our immediate neighborhood, our doings and those of our children are watched closely.

I have been wearing a hearing aid for six years now. I lean heavily on it because my vision has become impaired and I can no longer depend on my eyes to help me lip-read as well as I once could. I use my hearing aid when I telephone also.

In summary I can say that as a wife and mother I have all the things to make me happy and keep me busy that hearing women have. But I still have never really found myself in the social or vocational world. Although my husband and I have many friends among the hearing, the hard of hearing, and the deaf, at times I still feel the loneliness I knew for so many years—but not for too long I am thankful to say.

Section C: The Psychological Report

12. REPORTING THE RESULTS OF THE PSYCHOLOGICAL EXAMINATION

COMPETENCE in reporting the results of a psychological examination is no less important than competence in the techniques of psychological appraisal. This is so because a psychological report serves the important function of transmitting information to its reader through which a patient sheds his anonymity and becomes a particular individual. The report acts as a link between a patient and a specialist.

What it is the specialist needs to know about the individual determines the content and manner of organization of a report. For example, if the need is for data to be used in research by fellow psychologists, then full technical details are generally required, and technical semantics may be used with impunity. But when the need is for information to be used by other specialists in planning service programs, a different manner of reporting is necessary.

In a rehabilitation service frame, for example, a psychological report is described by DiMichael as "the medium through which the requested professional services are made known to the counselor," [1] as well as to other members of a rehabilitation team. In such settings, a clearly communicated report functions as an integrator of team efforts. But when a psychological report is over-

[1] Salvatore G. DiMichael, "Characteristics of a Desirable Psychological Report to the Vocational Counselor," *Journal of Consulting Psychology*, XII (1948), 432.

elaborated, cloaked in mystic jargon, and subjected to abstruse, theoretic interpretation, it has the effect of creating more confusion than enlightenment. Therefore, to serve effectively on a rehabilitation team, a professionally competent psychologist must develop additional competence in the techniques of effective interdisciplinary communication. Paramount qualifications are (*a*) the ability to write in the language a reader will understand; (*b*) perception of what information must be conveyed to the various readers, and what details should be emphasized; and (*c*) skill in organizing and integrating technical information in such a way that it presents a logical, cohesive picture. It should also be noted that a basic aid to good reporting is the careful preliminary collection and recording of the psychological data of which reports represent the interpreted summation.

Many psychologists find report forms a helpful frame for the organization and presentation of information. In psychological reports to vocational counselors, the five general headings recommended by DiMichael are (*a*) observation of the client's behavior; (*b*) technical results; (*c*) interpretation of technical results; (*d*) recommendations; and (*e*) summary. In regard to observation, DiMichael suggests a descriptive approach, with special emphasis given to those aspects of the client's behavior related to work habits, and manifest personality traits indicative of potentials for vocational adjustment. Under the heading "technical results," it is recommended that test scores be presented to vocational counselors in terms of percentiles, since these appear most meaningful to such workers. Concerning the interpretation of technical results, a narrative form of interpretation of the test scores in nontechnical language is recommended, with the tests considered individually or else grouped in terms of related abilities. The section dealing with recommendations is of major importance to vocational counselors, and represents an important index of "the depth of knowledge, good judgement, organized thinking and professional status of the psychologist." [2] Here the psychologist must relate individual analysis to occupational implications and potentials. To do this requires that a psychologist be familiar not only with the personality dynamics of the individual under consideration but also with the world of occupations. Knowledge of occupational demands and requirements is a generally weak area of competence for clinical psychologists. Unless the weakness is corrected, it becomes a definite handicap in communicating with vocational counselors. Finally, the total report summary should present a brief recapitulation of the questions raised by a counselor in referring a client for psychological appraisal, and should then go on to a concise presentation of the client's major assets and liabilities; how these relate to alternative job potentials, training, and placement; and what the answers are to the counselor's questions. A sample of practical psychological reporting to a vocational counselor is presented as follows: [3]

Psychological Report

Re: R.D.

Date of Exam: 3/5/59

Reason for Referral: Vocational and Educational Appraisals

Introductory Observations

R—— is a seventeen-year-old boy with ninth-grade education in a school for the deaf; his disability is severe congenital deafness. He has an excellent sense of humor, is very energetic, spontaneous, and, on the whole, gives the impression of a young man who is exceptionally pleasant, cooperative, and willing. Since the examiner had some previous indications that he was reluctant to speak, and, on reporting for the examination, R—— indicated that he preferred to write his answers, the whole matter of speech was raised with him and he was, to some extent, prodded to speak. After a while, he was able to do so to the point where he was, for the most part, easily understood. When questioned about his extreme reluctance to speak, he indicated that he was not aware of his voice quality, had difficulty controlling it, and felt that by not speaking (or by writing) he spared himself a certain amount of embarrassment. In the course of testing, it was noted that R—— was rather

---

[2] *Ibid.*, p. 435.　　　　[3] Personal communication from Murray Z. Safian.

quick and, again, spontaneous in correcting different mistakes that he made and that he was able to grasp instructions in many instances before they were given by the examiner. There were some indications that R—— may have had previous experience with the Wechsler-Bellevue Scale and with the Rorschach, although this could not be definitively determined. Case history and reason for present referral indicated no need for formal personality testing.

Test Findings and Implications

While a Full Scale IQ Rating of 114 on the Wechsler-Bellevue Scale suggests that R—— is a young man with High Average-to-Superior intelligence, it would appear that the Performance IQ Rating of 125, suggesting Superior mental ability, is more accurately descriptive of him. R—— demonstrates exceptional skill in handling tasks requiring visual-motor organization and speed, seems readily able to size up and evaluate the motivations of people in different social situations, and also is extremely alert and sensitive to the finest detail in his environment. It is noted further that R—— has a well-developed fund of general information and also demonstrates a capacity for good practical judgment. He tends to be somewhat limited in terms of the ability to conceptualize his thinking.

A reading test was given to determine whether R—— had sufficient reading skill for handling the various tests in this battery. The results indicate that he reads at a sixth-grade level and this seems sufficient for purposes of present testing. The chances are that he is capable of an even higher level of reading ability.

An evaluation was made of his arithmetic proficiency. The results indicate that his achievement in this area is at a seventh-grade level. This suggests that he is not strongly equipped for handling material requiring the use of complex numerical processes, although in comparison with his deaf peers he rates above average.

When compared with applicants for mechanic's helper jobs, R—— reveals a rather limited understanding of the mechanical principles involved in everyday situations. He does demonstrate rather well-developed ability to perceive spatial relations, when compared with shopwork applicants.

An evaluation was made of his manipulative skills. In using one or both hands and a simple tool in the assembly of small parts, he demonstrates low average manipulative dexterity when compared with unselected male applicants. This also does not appear to be his optimal functioning in this area.

The ACE Examination for College Freshmen was given to evaluate his college potential. While he is apparently rather limited from a quantitative standpoint, he nevertheless shows promising ability in this area. He seems particularly limited in linguistic areas when compared with college freshmen who are normally hearing.

Summary and Recommendations

The available data reveal that R—— is a seventeen-year-old boy of Superior intelligence. It is probable that he will be able to learn new and complex material quickly and retain such information with effectiveness. R—— seems to have sufficient reading skill for handling most types of paper work in a fairly satisfactory manner. He does appear to have a problem with more advanced mathematics. At the same time, however, he is an exceptionally bright young man who is very quick to grasp instruction and who can probably profit enormously from remedial work in the basic skill subjects such as arithmetic and reading. It seems quite probable, particularly in view of his excellent intellectual equipment, that R—— will be able to adapt satisfactorily to Gallaudet College for the deaf, given sufficient preliminary tutoring in preparation.

In the case of deaf individuals in the chronological range from school age through adulthood, the accompanying form devised by the writer has proved useful as both a summary record and a report.

In reporting on pre-school and infant subjects, outstanding factors in the developmental history must be noted in addition to outstanding factors in the psychological examination. In this connection, Gesell's four fields of behavior [4] cover the significant areas of observation, examination, and reporting. They are (*a*) motor behavior, including gross and fine motor coordination as seen in posture, balance, sitting, standing, locomotion, grasp, and manipulation; (*b*) adaptive behavior, which includes sensory function and sensory-motor coordination; (*c*) language behavior, including all forms and patterns of expression and communication used by the

[4] Arnold Gesell and Catherine S. Amatruda, *Developmental Diagnosis*, 2d ed. (New York: Paul Hoeber, Inc., 1947), p. 5.

PSYCHOLOGICAL STUDY REPORT

                                                    Date

Name
                        Sex   Birth date
Address

Onset of hearing loss: age   cause
                amount: mild   moderate   severe

Present amount of hearing loss: right   db.   left   db.
                Hearing aid used: yes   no

Major communications methods: speech   lip reading   hearing aid
                finger spelling   writing   sign language   pantomime

Highest school grade: special   regular school
                        reading achievement grade

Deafness in family (specify):

II. Statement of Presenting Problem

        Referred by   Date

III. Outstanding Factors in:

    A. Case History

    B. Interview

    C. Observation

    D. Psychological Testing

    E. General Behavior and Attitudes

IV. Psychological Test Results

    A. Intelligence

Tests Used	Date	How Administered	Test Scores	Estimated Validity
_____	_____	_____	_____	_____
_____	_____	_____	_____	_____
_____	_____	_____	_____	_____

B. Scholastic Achievement

Tests Used	Date	How Administered	Test Scores	Estimated Validity
_____	_____	_____	_____	_____
_____	_____	_____	_____	_____
_____	_____	_____	_____	_____

C. Personality

Tests Used	Date	How Administered	Test Results	Estimated Validity
_____	_____	_____	_____	_____
_____	_____	_____	_____	_____
_____	_____	_____	_____	_____

D. Special Interests, Aptitudes, Abilities

Tests Used	Date	How Administered	Test Results	Estimated Validity
_____	_____	_____	_____	_____
_____	_____	_____	_____	_____
_____	_____	_____	_____	_____

E. Interpretation of Test Findings

V. Analysis of Total Examination: discrepancies, pathological signs; differential diagnosis; total personality; etc.

VI. Summary of Major Psychological Assets and Liabilities

VII. Implications for Rehabilitation Services

VIII. Recommendations

Examiner _____

Date _____

child—postural, gesture, facial expression, mimicry, gross vocalization, verbalization—as well as the forms of communication understood by the child; and (*d*) personal-social behavior, which includes the child's individual reactions to people and to the environment. Essential to psychological reports on young children are brief descriptions of parent personality and parent management as well as of parent-child relations.

The following classification scheme, used in a longitudinal study [5] of children's behavioral responses to environmental stimuli, also appears to have exceptional merit as a frame for observation and reporting in child practice:

1. Activity-Passivity refers to the magnitude of the motor component in a given child's function and to his diurnal proportion of active and inactive periods. Therefore, protocol data on mobility during bathing, eating, playing, dressing and handling as well as information concerning the sleep-wake cycle, reaching, crawling, walking, eating, and play patterns are used in scoring for this functional category.

2. Regular-Irregular refers to the predictability and rhythmicity or unpredictability and arrhythmicity of function and can be analyzed in relation to the sleep-wake cycle, hunger, elimination, appetite and demand cycles.

3. Intense-Mild refers to the quality of response and its vigor, independent of its direction. A negative response may be either mild or intense as can a positive response. Responses to stimuli, to pre-elimination tension, to hunger, to repletion, to new foods, to attempts to control, to restraint, to dressing and diapering all provide scorable items for this category.

4. Approach-Withdrawal represents a category of responses to new things, be they people, foods or toys. In it the behaviors reported are scored for the nature of initial responses.

5. Adaptive-Nonadaptive again refers to responses to new or altered situations. However, in this category one is not concerned with the nature of the initial responses, but with the ease with which such responses are modified in desired directions.

6. High Threshold—Low Threshold is an omnibus category in which

[5] Stella Chess, Alexander Thomas, and Herbert Birch, "Characteristics of the Individual Child's Behavioral Responses to the Environment," *American Journal of Orthopsychiatry*, XXIX (1959), 791–802.

subcategories are concerned with (a) sensory threshold, (b) responses to environmental objects, and (c) social responsiveness.

7. Positive Mood—Negative Mood represents a category in which degrees of pleasure-pain, joy-crying, friendliness-unfriendliness are rated.

8. Selectivity-Nonselectivity refers to the definition of function and to the difficulty with which such an established direction of functioning can be altered. It is a composite of persistence and attention span.

9. Distractibility-Nondistractibility refers to the ease with which new peripheral stimuli can divert the child from an ongoing activity.[6]

[6] *Ibid.,* p. 796.

Part Four

PREPARATION FOR PROGRESS

13. RESEARCH

The Clinical Need

THE responsibility for servicing highly atypical problems in un-standardized areas of disability is a heavy one, and often as frustrating for the psychologist as for the patient. To this, the writer can offer heartfelt testimony from personal experience. At best, there is a strong trial-and-error flavor about the proceedings; at worst, there are serious dangers.

To recognize current limitations in work with the hearing-impaired is essential to clinical awareness; but it is also essential that the psychologist not capitulate to the restrictions. It is his professional obligation to those who come to him for help to support or engage in efforts to cast light in dark clinical places through research. It is only by finding the answers to the unknowns that the psychologist can fulfill his clinical role. Therefore, a critically important part of a psychologist's preparation for work with the hearing-impaired must include recognition of the unknowns of his field of operations as well as some basic understanding of how to collaborate with his professional colleagues in research. Various aspects of such preparation form the content of the present chapter.

Scope of Research in Impaired Hearing

In terms of the nature and number of problems requiring investigation, the area of impaired hearing is of outstanding dimensions. This is obvious from the preceding discussion. However, the manifest immensity of the scope of investigation is actually something of an artifact; for included among the unknowns of auditory defect are all the unknowns of the auditory process. Again the analogy of the iceberg comes to mind. The tip represents the problems of *impaired* hearing; but the basic bulk is composed of countless questions concerning the enigma of hearing itself: its anatomy and physiology; the physics of sound as related to audition (psycho-acoustics); the quantification of response to various measurable attributes of auditory stimulation (psychophysical measurement); audition as part of the communications system; intersensory facilitation; and the psychodynamics of hearing.

To illustrate the scope of research in terms of the kinds of studies involved, the following sampling is offered:

Sampling of Studies in Auditory Research

a. *Investigations of Hearing*

(1) *Anatomy and physiology:* mechanical, chemical, electrical, and neural activity of the auditory mechanism with particular emphasis on the cochlea; the role of the auditory cortex in hearing; the physiological basis of loudness discrimination, pitch perception, the discrimination of speech sounds; auditory fatigue and recovery; labyrinthine chemistry; etc.

(2) *Psychophysics and psycho-acoustics:* amount of sound energy involved in threshold perception; standardization of threshold of hearing in terms of minimal audible pressure; relations between sound pressure and audition under varying conditions; psychophysical aspects of sound discrimination in regard to frequency, loudness, noise, speech, competing auditory stimuli; differential sensory sensitivity and intersensory facilitation, especially between vision and audition; refinements in techniques of application of acoustic stimuli and measurement of response; etc.

(3) *As part of the communications system:* perception, discrimina-

tion, and recognition of speech sounds on the basis of acoustic input; re-encoding of acoustic elements into linguistic elements; reencoding of acoustic elements into speech elements; analysis and synthesis of auditory, visual, kinesthetic, and motor stimuli in communicating; etc.

(4) *Psychodynamic and psychosocial:* the role of hearing in mental, emotional, and social development and adjustments.

b. *Investigations of the Impaired Auditory Mechanism.* Because of the limitations inherent in animal and human experimentation, an already impaired auditory structure possesses exceptional research value. For one, it represents an experiment in nature for testing hypotheses and findings derived from studies of the intact structure. For another, it broadens the scope of investigation in ways that would otherwise be impossible to replicate. That impaired hearing also poses an acute human problem is still another aspect of the total research picture that warrants its own separate category. For the present, attention is still directed to the auditory mechanism. All the lines of investigation associated with the unimpaired structure obtain as well for the impaired mechanism. To these are added:

(1) *Pathology:* impaired hearing and cochlear lesions; impaired hearing and cortical lesions; impedance deafness; pathological effects of toxic agents, acoustic trauma, oxygen deprivation; effects of circulatory and vascular pathology on the auditory nervous system; effects of psychic disturbance in producing organic impairment; etc.

(2) *Diagnosis and treatment:* the use of recruitment of loudness, masking and fatigue tests, and speech audiometry in differential diagnosis; the use of chemotherapy, surgery, and psychotherapy in treatment; interferences with treatment; etc.

(3) *Audiometry:* establishment of standards for normal thresholds in air and bone conduction audiometry; diagnostic inferences of speech audiometry; validity of objective audiometric procedures (autonomic response audiometry; electroencephalography, feedback); measurement of the intensity of tinnitus; auditory fatigue in relation to measurement; relation between hearing for speech and hearing for pure tones; brief-tone audiometry; audiometric detection of nonorganic hearing impairment; etc.

(4) *Hearing aids:* selective amplification and localization of sound; binaural aids; recruitment and sound amplification; interferences with the use of hearing aids, organic and psychological; etc.

(5) *Differential diagnosis:* between hearing disorders due to structural damage of the auditory mechanism and hearing disorders due to other conditions.

(6) *Cause and prevention of impaired hearing.*

(7) *Problems of detection, assessment, standardization of procedures, terminology,* etc.

c. *Investigations of Problems of Persons with Impaired Hearing.* Included in this category are the usual problems found in a cross-section of society numbering some 10 to 20 million people plus the additional complications associated with impaired hearing. A sampling of needed studies is presented at the conclusion of this chapter. In mulling over them, the reader will be helped by using the following rough classification of the groups included in the over-all term "the hearing-impaired": (1) severe congenital deafness, and severe early-childhood deafness acquired before the development of language and speech; (2) slow progressive deafness beginning in childhood, adolescence, or adulthood; (3) rapid progressive deafness beginning in childhood, adolescence, or adulthood; and (4) sudden deafness that is mild, moderate, or severe and is acquired in childhood, adolescence, or adulthood. Many of the studies listed at the conclusion of the chapter must be separately conducted for each group.

In glancing over the preceding outline of investigations in audition, the psychologist may question the relevance of certain types of research to his particular specialty. What, he may ask, have psychophysical measurement, psycho-acoustics, the anatomy and physiology of hearing to do with psychological services? The direct relationship may indeed be obscure; but in so far as these other team specialties are concerned with clarifying the enigma of hearing, they are also involved in clarifying aspects of human behavior related to hearing. The latter are very much the concern of psychology.

Naturally, a psychologist is not expected to have expert knowledge of other specialties; but it is essential that he keep abreast of the broad developments in this highly interdisciplinary field of audition. For one thing, an awareness of the advances and problems of associated disciplines sharpens a psychologist's diagnostic perceptions, thereby enabling him to recognize a wider variety of clinical signs and discrepancies than he otherwise would. The broader the worker's range of diagnostic sensitivity, the more valuable his contributions both clinically and in research. For another thing, a psychologist's frame of therapeutic reference is also benefited by knowledge of current interdisciplinary developments. It would be pointless, for example, to employ psychotherapy to relieve conditions that yield to medical and surgical advances. Finally, by reaching out for broader knowledge, a psychologist acquires a deeper understanding of the patients he serves as well as of his own specialty. This is one of the great advantages of interdisciplinary practice.

Organizing for Research

Progress begins with effective research. But until the time comes when professional workers are equally qualified to apply the principles and techniques of scientific investigation, careful planning is essential to give disciplined direction to research studies. Appropriate physical and financial resources are, of course, an important part of the planning. But equally important considerations are (*a*) effective collaboration among research team members; (*b*) effective formulation of a research design for an investigation; and (*c*) the support and encouragement of national professional organizations.

TEAM COLLABORATION

Research workers are no longer ensconced in the ivory towers of splendid isolation. With the current emphasis on interdisciplinary action, they are out rubbing shoulders with their professional associates—and not infrequently drawing sparks. Sometimes the sparks become hot enough to inflame the cool logic of objective thinking. A commonly cited cause of heated team reaction is the member who imposes his need for personal aggrandizement on his associates as well as on the conduct of investigation. Such individuals, no matter how highly qualified professionally, can completely demoralize team motivation and enterprise. They are best left in their ivory towers. Another common hazard to team operations is lack of reasonable equivalence in competence and experience among the members. Where this is the case, the more experienced workers are obliged to spend a disproportionate amount of time teaching rather than investigating, again at the expense of the conduct of research. There are numbers of other dangers to effective interdisciplinary investigation that are familiar to all who have ever participated in team operations.[1] As a result, there is a beginning practice in current research to screen team members as carefully as the subjects of investigation themselves.[2]

The characteristics of effective team collaboration in research are excellently summarized by Luszki [3] as follows:

A. *From the standpoint of the research problem*
　　1. Focus on a single clearly defined problem.
　　2. Problem definition determined by demands of problem rather than by disciplinary or individual interests.
　　3. Formulation of the research problem in such a way that all participants can contribute to its solution.
　　4. Existence of collaborative potential as a result of previous work on the problem by more than one discipline.
B. *From the standpoint of theory*
　　1. Acceptance of a unified over-all theory.
　　2. Acceptance of a common set of hypotheses and assumptions.
　　3. Agreement on definition of common concepts.
　　4. Agreement on operational definitions.

---

[1] Frederick A. Whitehouse, "Teamwork: Philosophy and Principles." Lecture, American Association of Medical Social Workers, Pittsburgh, Pennsylvania, June 21, 1955.

[2] Louis E. Masterman, *Psychological Aspects of Rehabilitation* (Initial Status Studies, Kansas City, Missouri: Community Studies Inc., July, 1958), pp. 9–11.

[3] Margaret Barron Luszki, *Interdisciplinary Team Research: Methods and Problems* (New York: New York University Press, 1958), pp. 135–36.

C. *From the standpoint of methodology*
1. Utilization of resources of all relevant disciplines in exploring possible methodologies.
2. Team agreement on most appropriate methodology, including research procedures, relevant variables to be measured or controlled, and methods to be used.

D. *From the standpoint of group functioning*
1. Team members selected on basis of their ability to contribute to research objectives.
2. Approximate equality of influence exerted by the representatives of one discipline on another.
3. Acceptance of leadership regardless of discipline from which leader and researchers come.
4. Flexibility of roles.
5. Development and use of a common language.
6. Free communication among all team members.
7. Free interchange of information about the research with mechanics for facilitating such interchange when necessary.
8. Sharing of suggestions, ideas, and data among members from different disciplines.
9. Participation of all team members in joint planning of each step of the research.
10. Reciprocal teaching and learning among team members—a continuous process.
11. Problem-centered rather than discipline- or individual-centered team activity.
12. Minimum influence on research plans and operations exerted from outside the research team.
13. Willingness of participants to subordinate own methods and interests to achieve project aims.
14. Publication of research reports by the group as a whole, rather than by individual members.

For the dedicated researcher, working under these conditions more than compensates for the loss of the ivory tower.

FORMULATING A RESEARCH INVESTIGATION

Even where team collaboration runs smoothly, hindrances to effective research may nevertheless appear. A major handicap is inability and/or inexperience in applying disciplined, objective thinking to the organization and conduct of research studies. A common misconception is that statistics will take care of all that. But, to quote Maxwell, "to apply a statistical test to data without regard to the manner in which the data are obtained is like putting the ingredients for a cake into the oven to bake, ignoring completely the instructions to stir them until they are thoroughly mixed." [4] A happy union of theory and statistical formulations is achieved when the experimenter appreciates "the mathematician's good intentions and meet[s] him half way by planning his experiment and executing it in such a manner that the assumptions in the theory are met." [5]

For less experienced investigators, there are various outline forms that can be used as guides in planning psychological research studies. One such outline follows. To derive maximum benefit from the guides, the worker should give careful preliminary thought to the rationale underlying the outline headings and appreciate the relationship of each to the total plan. By so doing, he acquires the feel of disciplined research thinking. Until the time comes when sufficient training facilities are available for research workers, every investigator assumes the responsibility of doing the best job he can of self-training. An initial step in this direction is to recognize the logical consistency in the details of planning as illustrated by the following:

[4] A. E. Maxwell, *Experimental Design in Psychology and the Medical Sciences* (New York: John Wiley & Sons, Inc.; London: Methuen & Co., Ltd., 1958), p. 18.
[5] *Ibid.*

Planning Outline for Psychological Research

I. TITLE

A main title commonly indicates the broad area of the study, with the specific features carried in a subtitle.

II. THE PROBLEM

A. *Statement of the Problem:* The general problem underlying the study is stated.

B. *Specific Problems to Be Investigated:* The specific aspects of the general problem that form the worker's actual units of investigation are stated. It is from the solution of these specific problems that the worker hopes to make a significant contribution to the solution of the general one.

C. *Delimitations:* The statements here describe the scope and limits of the study.

D. *Definition of Terminology:* Brief definitions are presented to clarify the sense in which the investigator uses special or controversial terms.

E. *Hypothesis:* Well-informed, perceptive, and experienced workers often reason out sound explanations for various problems and phenomena that seem logically consistent with the known facts. However, until such explanations are proved, they remain hypothetical, and as such do not lend themselves to valid generalization as theories, laws, or principles. Therefore, the object of many investigations is to test and prove basic hypotheses. The advantage in working from a good hypothesis is that much aimless exploration is avoided since considerable preliminary thought has gone into its formulation and the worker is set to follow through. The hypothesis on which an investigation is based should be simply stated in fundamental terms. If there are certain assumptions underlying the hypothesis, these too should be specifically noted.

F. *Need for the Study:* The common controlling view in sponsoring research is that there should be some reasonable equivalence between the value of the contribution made and the outlay of effort and resources that have gone into the work. Justification of the need of the study, therefore, warrants careful thought and clear, objective exposition supported by authoritative references where they will do the most good. Some common "justification" considerations are: scope of the problem; duration; seriousness for the population involved; inadequacy of current management; practical gains from a solution; and contributions to pure science.

III. BACKGROUND OF RELATED INFORMATION

A research problem that arouses the interest and enthusiasm of one worker has undoubtedly had the same effect on other investigators, both past and present. It is therefore essential that a researcher survey all information and previous studies related to his problem. By screening what has been done and thought by others, pointless duplication is avoided and at the same time a pool of references is accumulated on which an investigator can draw to refine his own study. Surveys of related information customarily stress an historical review of the literature; the findings of other investigations, including a critical review of methodologies, controversial points, and incompletely explored aspects of the problem; and a statement indicating how the investigator proposes to improve on other studies.

IV. METHODOLOGY

A. *The Research Method:* The method or methods of research used in each aspect of the investigation should be clearly stated, and the overall design briefly described as orientation to the specific procedures to follow. Some common research methods include: historical; survey; experimental; case study; genetic; statistical; and combinations of these.

B. *Procedures:* Working techniques and procedures vary with the research method. These should be specifically described in the protocol. To illustrate with psychological investigations in which groups of persons are exposed to experimental study, the following details are generally included:

1. *Population of the Study:* The whole population affected by the problem under consideration (sometimes called the *universe* of the study) is identified, qualitatively and quantitatively.

2. *Subjects of the Study:* Because it is generally unfeasible to study the whole population involved in a psychological research problem, it is necessary to select a smaller unit (sample) from a more limited area (frame) than the universe. This is a matter of working convenience. The sample is taken to represent the total population involved so that the findings based on the sample will validly obtain for this population as well. The frame of the study, the criteria for the selection of subjects, and the number of subjects to be investigated should be specified.

3. *Sampling:* The validity of generalizing the results of a research study on the basis of a sample population is heavily dependent upon the way in which the sample population was drawn. Sampling is a statistical procedure based primarily upon the theory of probability and is best handled by the statistician on the research team, particularly since certain methods of sampling are more appropriate for certain research situations than others. The methods used to obtain statistically adequate samples must be described.

4. *Experimental and Control Groups:* In experimental research, a method of testing whether the results are due to the experimental variable or to irrelevant factors is through the use of experimental and control groups. The subjects of the experimental group are exposed to the variable; the subjects of the control group are not. In other respects the groups are as closely equivalent as the research requirements dictate; and the subjects of the control group are specifically selected with this in mind. At the conclusion of the study, the reactions of both groups are compared for evidence of significant differences due to the influence of the variable on the one and not the other. Included in the research protocol are descriptions of experimental and control groups, giving their size, how they were selected, and the differences in treatment of the two.

5. *Collection of Data:* Involved in the collection of data are (*a*) the instruments, tests, and special apparatus used; (*b*) the techniques employed; and (*c*) the manner of recording the data. These should be itemized and described in terms of structure and function where pertinent, and, if possible, samples of forms used in collecting and recording should also be included in the research protocol. Among the methods used in collecting psychological research data are: case history; interviews; questionnaire; psychological tests and measures; other tests and devices; observation; moving pictures and sound recording devices; reports; and variations and combinations of these.

6. *Treatment of the Data:* The mass of data assembled in the usual course of research would be considerably more unwieldy were not the greater bulk transposed into numerical equivalents in the course of collecting and recording. The term "treatment of the data" refers to the application of the principles, logic, and mathematics of statistical science in coordinating the numerically expressed results of a study and in identifying relationships among them. To be included in a research protocol is the plan for the statistical treatment, evaluation, and analytical

presentation of the data. Where disciplined planning and sound logic have gone into the formulation and conduct of a research study, statistical treatment of the data should yield scientifically valid results. But where they have not, statistics cannot retroactively validate fundamental weaknesses nor correct basic errors in research design.

V. INTERPRETATION OF THE RESULTS

The care, time, and endless effort a researcher brings to his study, the critical scrutiny of every aspect of operations from beginning to end, and the final coordination of masses of raw data into meaningful symbols all lead to but one question: How far forward does this carry us in regard to the solution of the original problem? In answering the question, the worker must be on his guard as never before, for now that the study finally approaches its end, the pull of subjective bias is strong. Therefore, in stating the outcomes the worker must continue to counter subjective temptation with dedicated objectivity. Conclusions should be strictly limited to factors studied in each of the original "specific problems to be investigated," and the limitations of the study must also be specified. In this context, the contributions made by the study are presented. The one critical factor that keeps the procedure from becoming entirely mechanical is the worker's knowledge of his field. All else being equal, the broader the knowledge an investigator possesses, the more enlightenment will he derive from research and the greater his contribution to research; the less knowledgeable he is of his field, the more mechanical the research, both input and outcome.

VI. SUMMARY AND CONCLUSIONS

Having dealt with the specific problems of investigation, the investigator concludes with the general problem and states the verified inferences that can be drawn as a result of his study. If all has proceeded in accordance with the basic principles of research, this statement should be logically consistent with all known facts and in accordance with established theory. Finally, since the study could not encompass the whole of the general problem requiring investigation, suggestions should be offered concerning implications for further research.

VII. BIBLIOGRAPHY

VIII. APPENDIX

THE RESEARCH POTENTIAL OF NATIONAL
PROFESSIONAL ORGANIZATIONS

The inability of most research to cover more than partial aspects of total problems presents a natural limit to the rate of scientific progress. Natural limits become unnecessary obstacles when individuals and teams conducting similar or related studies operate in sublime ignorance of one another. The result is an accumulation of fragments of investigation rather than a cohesive body of integrated information. Many such fragments are lost altogether in the files of unpublished gems.

National professional organizations are in a unique position to help solve this problem through the establishment of interdisciplinary research councils [6] composed of representatives of national intradisciplinary research committees. Such bodies of authoritative professional leaders would have as their major function the stimulation, integration, and guidance of significant investigations throughout the country. To them, community agencies as well as research scientists and teams could turn for help and guidance in the planning and conduct of investigations. These and other services that could be rendered by a national research council in the field of auditory disability are summarized as follows:

(1) Integrative
   (a) Propose, formulate, supervise, and/or integrate important nation-wide studies.
   (b) Function as a research-exchange service center for team disciplines.
   (c) Assist in the compilation of indices, references, bibliographies, and abstracts of field studies both published and unpublished.

[6] Boyce R. Williams, "Some Activities in Research About Deafness." A paper presented to the Conference of Executives of American Schools for the Deaf at Colorado Springs, Colorado, October 19, 1950.

  (d) Integrate the results of research in the separate disciplines into a cohesive body of interdisciplinary information.

  (e) Facilitate interdisciplinary team research throughout the country.

(2) Consultative

  (a) Function in an advisory capacity to local and affiliate organizations in working out special research designs, plans, and approaches.

  (b) Function in an advisory and cooperative capacity to non-affiliate organizations conducting research involving some aspect of audition.

  (c) Provide for continuing interdisciplinary teaching, learning, and exchange of information.

  (d) Compile a reference file of national research resources and local facilities for the team disciplines.

(3) Promotional

  (a) Sponsor research grant requests for significant and needed studies conducted by competent, qualified investigators.

  (b) Conduct research institutes and workshops in problems of audition.

  (c) Publicize opportunities for research workers as well as available fund resources for research.

  (d) Promote the establishment of research training centers.

(4) Active research

  (a) Conduct or participate in surveys of such pertinent problems as: methods of recruitment and training of research scientists; basic qualifications and competencies of such workers; problems of interdisciplinary collaboration; the attitudes of service centers to research; etc.

  (b) Synthesize isolated problems into groups of related interdisciplinary projects that can be investigated as a unit operation.

  (c) Follow up the outcomes of promising studies.

The writer fully appreciates the wishful thinking that underlies the foregoing outline and is well aware of the work entailed in organizing and activating national bodies. This in itself is no mean project. Nevertheless, if such a national research council could be brought into being, the benefits would more than compensate for the efforts required.

Needed Research in the Psychological Aspects of Impaired Hearing

The following sampling is offered the research-minded reader who would like to mull over some of the psychological problems associated with impaired hearing. The arbitrary categorizations used are purely for the sake of convenience. In "real life," the large majority of problems are overlapping, interrelated, and highly complex.

a. *The Psychodynamics of Hearing in Human Development.* This is the basic problem that holds the answers to many of the problems involving impaired hearing. An interesting experimental approach to the psychodynamics of hearing would be through comparisons of the personality development, psychic attributes, and life attainments of paired deaf and hearing identical twins, fraternal twins, and deaf and hearing siblings (in order of research desirability).

b. *Personality and Adjustment.* Investigations are needed concerning:

(1) the development and organization of the psyche and psychic mechanisms in the absence of hearing
(2) the normative status of the deaf in the major areas of development, adjustment, and attainment
(3) the effects on personality of various amounts of hearing loss at different ages of onset
(4) comparison of manifest aspects of personality of hearing-

impaired persons when in the company of the hearing and when in the company of those similarly disabled

(5) the effects of different degrees and types of impaired hearing on parent attitudes

(6) the relation between parent attitudes and the personality and psychopathology of the adult hearing-impaired

(7) the differences in handicap between early severe deafness and early severe hardness of hearing

(8) the relative effects of the premorbid personality vs. external rehabilitation influences and resources on adjustment to impaired hearing

(9) a comparison between the environmental-deprivation effects of the various types of impaired hearing and those derived from selected homebound disabilities and socioeconomic deprivation among the nondisabled

(10) the effects of early profound deafness on self-concept and identity; level of aspiration; the interpretation of interpersonal events

(11) the relationship between levels of language development among the early profound deaf and: maturation; personality; attitudes to the hearing world; psychosocial maturity; attainments and achievements

(12) a comprehensive psychosocial comparison of manual and pure oral deaf persons of equal language attainments

(13) the relationship between the different types of educative procedures and personality development, adjustment, attitudes, and attainments

(14) the relationship between intelligence and success in schoolwork with major variables held constant

(15) factors responsible for poor school achievement in hearing-impaired children with high mental capacity

(16) comparison in all traits and developmental factors between pupils of the same mental capacity and hearing impairment but widely differing levels of achievement

(17) the role of lip reading in personality development and/or adjustment among the hearing-impaired

c. *Educational Process and Procedures.* Investigations are needed concerning:

(1) factors responsible for school failures and retardations

(2) learning and intersensory facilitation in the presence of auditory deficit

(3) the relative compensatory learning values in the presence of auditory deficit of visual, tactile, kinesthetic, and motor stimuli; acoustic amplification; eidetic tendency

(4) problems of the "auditory learner" who is hearing-impaired

(5) a comprehensive reevaluation of the use in schools for the deaf of curricula based on regular "hearing" schools

(6) the progress and problems of deaf pupils attending regular classes in the regular schools

(7) a comprehensive, wide-range evaluation of the various educational philosophies and methods applied to hearing-impaired children

(8) comparison of nursery-trained hearing-impaired children with those lacking such early educational beginnings

(9) relation between parent education and child adjustment

(10) the adequacy of educational facilities for hearing-impaired pupils at the high-school and higher education levels

(11) need and resources for adult education, especially of the deaf

(12) provision in special schools, special classes, and regular schools for individual differences, needs, and problems of hearing-impaired children

(13) special methods of instruction of the multi-disabled child with impaired hearing

d. *Mental Health and Psychotherapy.* Investigations are needed concerning:

(1) the influence of family and community attitudes upon the adjustment and mental health of the various categories of hearing-impaired persons, particularly attitudes of parents

(hearing as well as hearing-impaired); siblings (hearing as well as hearing-impaired); mates (hearing as well as hearing-impaired); co-peers (hearing and hearing-impaired); employers; fellow employees; rehabilitation counselors; school personnel; community and recreational centers

(2) the attitudes of hearing-impaired persons toward the foregoing

(3) psychotherapeutic methods and techniques with hearing-impaired persons at the various levels of language and communications abilities

(4) comparison of adjustment and scholastic problems of hearing-impaired school-age pupils with the problems reported by rehabilitation counselors for the young adult population

(5) relationship between level of language attainment and adult adjustment; between communications abilities and disabilities and adjustment

(6) validity of diagnoses among the institutionalized hearing-impaired population

(7) major types and signs of psychopathology among the various categories of hearing-impaired persons

(8) effectiveness of current mental health facilities for the various categories of hearing-impaired persons

(9) mental health status and problems of deaf members of hearing families; hearing members of deaf families; deaf members of deaf families

(10) marital adjustments of the various categories of hearing-impaired persons: problems; separations; divorces; significant factors

(11) parent role of hearing-impaired persons: parent-child relations; problems; attitudes; significant factors

(12) acquisition of sex-knowledge by hearing-impaired children, especially the deaf: concepts; attitudes; maturity; psychopathology

(13) asocial behavior among the various categories of hearing-impaired persons

(14) social and community role of the various categories of hearing-impaired persons

(15) survey of parent- and child-guidance programs and facilities for hearing-impaired children

(16) relation between family acceptance of disability and disagreement among authorities in diagnostic findings and recommendations

(17) characteristic signs of nonacceptance of disability by family; by individual

e. *Vocational Rehabilitation.* Investigations are needed concerning:

(1) the relationship between vocational adjustment and: school adjustment; type of hearing impairment (age of onset, amount of loss, associated otological conditions); level of language attainment; methods of communication; family aspiration level; personal adjustment and level of aspiration; sex differences; occupational change due to impaired hearing; type of vocational preparation; vocational skills and general knowledge; employer acceptance; etc.

(2) the psychotherapeutic values of vocational rehabilitation

(3) the major vocational problems associated with the various categories of hearing-impaired persons, and the service resources available

(4) the major problems of vocational rehabilitation counselors in servicing deaf clients

(5) the experiences and attitudes of the deaf toward vocational rehabilitation procedures; of the hard of hearing

(6) vocational rehabilitation procedures used in assessing the capacities, abilities, aptitudes, interests, and personality patterns of deaf clients; of hard-of-hearing clients

(7) the relative values of speech correction, lip-reading instruc-

tion, auditory training, and language tutoring in the vocational rehabilitation of the deaf

(8) vocational rehabilitation provision for the multi-handicapped deaf client

f. *Needed Materials and Resources:*

(1) psychological tests designed for and standardized on the deaf at all age levels

(2) reading materials specifically written to suit the chronological needs and interests as well as the retarded language levels of the deaf

(3) motion pictures specifically devised for instructional purposes with the school-age as well as the adult deaf population stressing mental health, social customs, interpersonal conduct and relations, and general information

(4) counseling centers for hearing-impaired youth

(5) sheltered workshops for deaf multi-handicapped individuals

(6) adult education centers for the deaf

(7) diagnostic centers for children with language disorders

(8) special educational provision for the deviate as well as the accelerated deaf pupil

(9) Research training centers for special workers in problems of deafness and other communications and language disorders

Such are some of the problems, questions, and needs encountered by the psychologist in work with hearing-impaired persons. However, he can take comfort in the fact that research is in the air. From today's spirit of inquiry come tomorrow's advances.

APPENDIX A

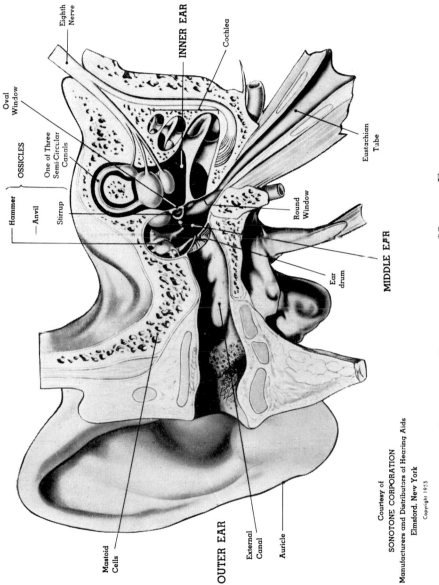

Eighth Nerve

INNER EAR

Cochlea

Oval Window

OSSICLES

One of Three Semi-Circular Canals

Hammer
Anvil
Stirrup

Eustachian Tube

Round Window

MIDDLE EAR

Ear drum

Mastoid Cells

OUTER EAR

External Canal

Auricle

SECTIONAL DIAGRAM OF THE HUMAN EAR

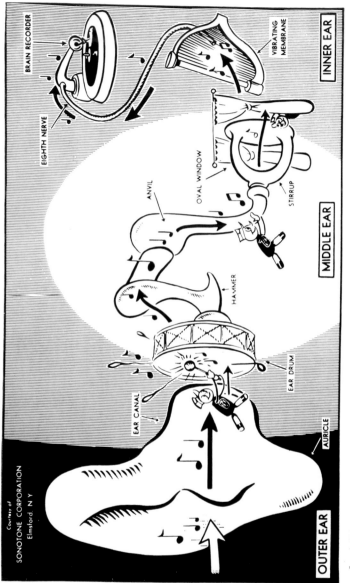

BRAIN RECORDER

EIGHTH NERVE

VIBRATING MEMBRANE

INNER EAR

ANVIL

OVAL WINDOW

STIRRUP

MIDDLE EAR

HAMMER

EAR CANAL

EAR DRUM

AURICLE

OUTER EAR

DIAGRAM OF HOW WE HEAR

APPENDIX B

Definitions and Classifications of Hearing Impairment

1. According to the Amount of Functional Hearing
   a. The deaf: those in whom the sense of hearing is nonfunctional for the ordinary purposes of life. This general group is made up of two distinct classes based entirely on the time of the loss of hearing: (a) the congenitally deaf—those who were born deaf; (b) the adventitiously deaf—those who were born with normal hearing, but in whom the sense of hearing is nonfunctional through later illness or accident.
   b. The hard of hearing: those in whom the sense of hearing, although defective, is functional with or without a hearing aid.[1]
2. According to the Auditory Structures Involved
   a. Conduction, Obstruction, or Impedance deafness refers to hearing impairments caused by conditions in the outer ear, middle ear, and/or Eustachian tubes which interfere with the passage of sound waves to the inner ear.
   b. Perception or Nerve deafness refers to hearing impairments caused by damage to the neural auditory structures of the inner ear.
   c. Central or Retrolabyrinthine deafness refers to hearing impairments in the presence of an intact auditory nerve and sense organ, and which are due to malfunction of the auditory pathways in the brain and brain stem.
   d. Congenital auditory imperception, aphasic auditory malfunction, or word deafness refers to disorders in understanding and inter-

[1] These definitions of the deaf and the hard of hearing are taken from the Conference of Executives of American Schools for the Deaf, Report of the Conference Committee on Nomenclature, *American Annals of the Deaf*, LXXXIII (1938), 1–3.

preting sound rather than in hearing, and which are due to lesions of those parts of the cerebral cortex devoted to hearing and language.

e. Mixed deafness generally designates a combination of conduction and perception deafness.

3. According to the Degree of Hearing Loss in the Speech Range

a. Slight loss: loss of 20 decibels or less. Generally unnoticed; faint whispers may not be understood.

b. Moderate loss: 20–40 decibel loss. Difficulty in hearing when tired or inattentive; in distant theater seats; in the noise of general conversation; when articulation is soft or poor.

c. Marked loss: 40–60 decibel loss. Considerable difficulty in hearing conversation unless voice of speaker is raised, distance is small, and conversation is with one person.

d. Severe loss: 60–80 decibel loss. Extreme difficulty in understanding even shouted conversation. Speech and language cannot be learned normally by children with this amount of loss.

e. Profound loss: over 80 decibels. Extreme difficulty not only in understanding shouted conversation but even in hearing the sound of the voice.

4. According to the Amount of Speech and Language Handicap

a. The deaf are those who were born either totally deaf or sufficiently deaf to prevent the establishment of speech and natural language; those who became deaf in childhood before speech and language were established; or those who became deaf in childhood so soon after the natural establishment of speech and language that the ability to speak and understand speech and language has been practically lost to them.

b. The hard of hearing are those who have established speech and ability to understand speech and language, and subsequently developed impairment of hearing. These children are sound conscious and have a normal, or almost normal, attitude toward the world of sound in which they live.[2]

[2] These definitions of the deaf and the hard of hearing are taken from the White House Conference on Child Health and Protection. *Special Education, the Handicapped and the Gifted: Report of the Committee on Special Classes* (Section III, Education and Training), Vol. III-F (New York: The Century Co., 1931), p. 277.

5. According to Educational Requirements
    a. Children with slight losses: these children are on the borderline between normal hearing and significant defective hearing. Their loss averages 20 decibels or less in the speech range of the better ear as measured by the pure-tone audiometer. This group usually needs no special considerations other than favorable seating in the classroom.
    b. Children with moderate losses: these are the hard-of-hearing children. Their losses average from 25 to 50 decibels in the speech range of the better ear. Generally these children should be able to receive their education in classes for normally hearing children provided they are favorably seated, receive speech training if necessary, and learn speech reading. Those children whose loss is as great as or greater than 35 decibels in the better ear should also be provided with hearing aids and should receive auditory training. Special class services may have to be provided for the more severely hard of hearing in this group if their adjustments are unsatisfactory in the regular classroom.
    c. Children with marked losses: these children are on the borderline between the hard of hearing and the deaf. They do not have enough hearing to learn language and speech with the unaided ear, but they have residual hearing that can be utilized in their education. Their losses range from about 55 or 60 to 65 or 75 decibels in the speech range in the better ear. They have sustained their losses from very early childhood or babyhood and do not learn language and speech through the unaided ear. Initially, these children receive their education in schools for the deaf or in special classes from teachers especially trained to develop language and speech. After they have achieved fluency in the use of language and speech, their educational programs may very likely be patterned after those established for hard-of-hearing children.
    d. Children with profound losses: these are the deaf children who do not learn speech and language through their ears even with benefit of amplified sound. Their losses range from 70 or 75 decibels to inability to distinguish more than one or two frequencies at the highest measurable level of intensity in the better ear. Such losses, when sustained from birth or very early childhood, typify deaf children who must receive their education from teachers

trained to develop the communicative process through very specialized techniques. Educational facilities are provided for these children in schools or classes for the deaf.[3]

6. According to the Type of Psychic Involvement
   a. Malingering refers to consciously feigned hearing loss in the presence of unimpaired hearing.
   b. Functional deafness refers to impaired hearing in which the amount of loss is exaggerated by the sufferer. The term psychogenic overlay is used to indicate such exaggerated loss.
   c. Classic psychogenic or hysteric deafness refers to impaired hearing without organic cause and due to unconscious psychic forces.

[3] Adapted from C. D. O'Connor and A. Streng, "Teaching the Acoustically Handicapped," Chapter IX in *The Education of Exceptional Children* (National Society for the Study of Education, Chicago: The University of Chicago Press, 1950).

APPENDIX C

CAUSES OF IMPAIRED HEARING [1]

1. Conduction Deafness
   a. Inflammation in the middle ear (otitis media)
   b. Infection and blocking of the Eustachian tubes, commonly caused by adenoid tissue
   c. Damaged (perforated, scarred) ear drum
   d. Obstruction of the outer ear canal, commonly caused by wax
   e. Otosclerosis, which also involves the inner ear in severe cases and is associated with hereditary factors
2. Perception Deafness
   a. Hereditary deafness: genetic factors
   b. Acquired deafness
      (1) Deafness acquired prenatally
          (a) Diseases in the mother during early pregnancy, such as German measles (rubella), mumps, influenza
          (b) Rh blood factor
          (c) Certain drugs taken by the mother during pregnancy, such as quinine
          (d) Pathological condition of the fetus, such as erythroblastosis fetalis
          (e) Developmental anomalies
          (f) Maternal syphilis

[1] Suggested references: E. P. Fowler, Jr., "Medical Aspects of Hearing Loss," and T. E. Walsh, "The Surgical Treatment of Hearing Loss," in H. Davis, ed., *Hearing and Deafness* (New York–Toronto: Rinehart Books, Inc., 1953); E. P. Fowler, Jr., *Nelson Loose-Leaf Medicine of the Ear* (New York: Thomas Nelson, 1947).

      (2) Deafness acquired at birth
        (a) Anoxia
        (b) Traumatic injuries
        (c) Prematurity
      (3) Later acquired deafness
        (a) Infectious diseases, such as meningitis, mumps, measles (morbilli), whooping-cough, scarlet fever
        (b) Hyperpyrexia, especially in childhood
        (c) Various drugs, such as dihydrostreptomycin and quinine
        (d) Noise and blast deafness
        (e) "Dropsy" of some of the tissues of the inner ear, commonly referred to as Ménière's disease
        (f) Avitaminosis, arteriosclerosis, allergy
        (g) Old age

3. Mixed Deafness

A number of the foregoing conditions, if severe, can cause both perception and conduction deafness.

4. Central Deafness

   a. Acoustic tumors

   b. Certain types of brain damage caused by such conditions as cerebral hemorrhage, multiple sclerosis, syphilis, and abscess, affecting the auditory pathways from the auditory nerve through the brain to the outer temporal lobe

   c. Developmental anomalies affecting these areas

5. Functional and Psychogenic Deafness, and Malingering

Personality weaknesses and disorders with or without organic impairment of the auditory mechanism, usually associated with neuroses and conscious or unconscious secondary gains phenomena

APPENDIX D

Techniques in the Assessment of Auditory Acuity [1]

1. Rough Appraisal
   a. Reflex responses. Because there are unusual difficulties in measuring auditory acuity in infants, observation of an infant's reflex responses to sound serves as a rough form of detection of possible impairment. The reflex responses commonly used are the Moro, pupillary, and eyelid.[2]
   b. Conditioned responses. With young children, conditioning to sound stimuli is accomplished by means of various noise-making toys of different pitches. The child is conditioned to perform a designated act every time he hears a noise-maker go off behind him. The whole is presented as a game.[3]
   c. Behavioral signs. Gesell and Amatruda present a comprehensive means of detecting auditory impairment through observation of a child's behavior. (See page 244.)
   d. Watch test. The tick of an average-grade watch is used as the sound stimulus and a rough approximation is made of a patient's hearing ability by noting the distance required for him to hear the watch tick.
   e. Voice and whisper test. The voice of the tester is generally used as the stimulus, and a rough estimate is made of the patient's hear-

[1] Donald J. Harris, "Hearing," *Annual Review of Psychology*, XI (1958), 47–70.

[2] Lee Meyerson, "Hearing for Speech in Children: A Verbal Audiometric Test," *Acta Oto-Laryngologica*, Supplementum 128 (1956).

[3] I. R. Ewing and A. W. G. Ewing, "The Ascertainment of Deafness in Infancy and Early Childhood," *Journal of Laryngology and Otology*, LIX (1944), 309–33.

ing acuity for speech by noting the distance required to hear the various loudnesses of spoken and whispered language.

f. Tuning forks. Standard tuning forks provide a series of musical pure tones of known frequency that are used to obtain a rough idea of a patient's pattern and sensitivity of hearing by noting whether or not he hears a particular tone and for how long. Tuning-fork testing is also used to distinguish external and middle ear damage from that of more central origin.

2. Precision Methods of Testing Auditory Acuity

a. Pure-tone audiometer. Testing is done by means of a calibrated, electrical precision instrument (audiometer) designed to test auditory acuity for pure tones over a range of measurable intensity covering six or seven octaves. Speech audiometers are used when the aim is to test the hearing of speech rather than pure tones.

b. Psychogalvanic Skin Response (PGSR), currently termed Electrodermal Response (EDR) testing. Although testing is actually accomplished by means of an audiometer, response to the sound stimuli is obtained by conditioning the skin sweat glands to respond reflexly to heard sounds.[4]

c. Audiometric play-tests. Audiometric testing is disguised as a game with children by conditioning the child to respond to the sound stimuli by pressing a button which then illuminates attractive pictures or scenes in a viewing box placed before him.[5]

3. Screening Tests

a. Speech-phonograph audiometer. The test sounds are derived from phonograph records of standard work lists (either numbers or words) spoken in different kinds of voices (male, female) and in graded intensities. As many as forty sets of calibrated headphones can be plugged into the audiometer at one time, thereby enabling it to serve as a rapid, group-screening device.

[4] J. E. Bordley and W. G. Hardy, "A Study in Objective Audiometry with the Use of a Psychogalvanic Response," *Annals of Oto-Rhino-Laryngology*, LVIII (1949), 751–60; Robert Goldstein, "Effectiveness of Conditioned Electrodermal Responses (EDR) in Measuring Pure-Tone Thresholds in Cases of Non-organic Hearing Loss," *The Laryngoscope*, LXVI (1956), 119–30.

[5] M. R. Dix and C. S. Hallpike, "The Peep-Show: A New Technique for Pure-Tone Audiometry," *British Medical Journal* (November, 1949), pp. 719–23.

b. Sweep-frequency technique. For rapid appraisal, the tester "sweeps" through certain frequencies of the audiometer for each ear with the subject indicating whether or not he hears.

c. Pure-tone audiometric group screening. Pure-tone audiometers with as many as forty single receivers are used in group testing.[6]

4. Speech-hearing Tests

a. Speech audiometry. The principles of pure-tone audiometry are here adapted to measure the hearing of speech. Standardized speech test-lists are available either recorded on phonograph discs or to be spoken by the tester. The patient responds by writing down the words he hears; repeating them aloud; checking a list; or answering questions, according to the test used.

b. Speech articulation tests. These tests are designed to measure an individual's ability to understand the speech sounds commonly used in ordinary speech. Various standardized lists of words and nonsense syllables are used for the purpose. In order to measure auditory discrimination for speech in the presence of background noise, certain tests are administered with and without standard background noise, and the difference in auditory discrimination is thus assessed under varying conditions.

5. Other Techniques

a. Electroencephalography. The use of electroencephalographic techniques in the testing of hearing is the subject of active investigation. Reference is noted.[7]

b. Autonomic responses through heart rate and blood volume are also being studied as possibilities in objective audiometry. Reference is noted.[8]

[6] Phillip W. Johnston, "An Efficient Group Screening Test," *Journal of Speech and Hearing Disorders,* XVII (1952), 8–12.

[7] A. J. Derbyshire, A. A. Fraser, M. McDermott, and A. Bridge, "Audiometric Measurements by Electroencephalography," *Electroencephalography and Clinical Neurophysiology,* VIII (1956), 467–78.

[8] D. Zeaman and N. Wegner, "Cardiac Reflex to Tones of Threshold Intensity," *Journal of Speech and Hearing Disorders,* XXI (1956), 71–75; A. K. Tchargeyshvili and T. L. Tokhadze, "Objective Examination of Hearing by Plethysmography," Abstracted in *Excerpta Medica,* IX (1956), 607.

c. Unconditioned muscle reflex as a possible technique in objective audiometry is also reported.[9]

[9] H. G. Kobrak, "Objective Audiometry: Utilization of an Unconditioned Muscle Reflex for the Determination of Sound Perception," *Archives of Otolaryngology*, LXV (1957), 26–31.

APPENDIX E

METHODS OF COMMUNICATION AND SYSTEMS OF INSTRUCTION
IN USE AMONG THE DEAF

1. Methods of Communication
   In addition to speech, reading, and writing, the methods of communication in use among the deaf are:
   a. The Sign Language. The language of signs is an ideographic
      method of expression in which words and ideas are graphically
      formulated through codified gestures of the arms, hands, and
      body aided by facial expression.
   b. Finger Spelling. In finger spelling, the regular letters of the
      alphabet are formed by standard positions of the fingers of one
      or both hands, depending upon whether the one-hand or two-hand
      alphabet is used, and words and sentences are thus spelled out in
      straight language.
   c. Lip- or Speech-reading. Lip reading is the visual reception and
      understanding of spoken language.
2. Systems of Instruction
   Within the schools for the deaf,[1] various methods of communication
   are combined to form what are termed systems of instruction. Those
   used in American schools for the deaf today are:

[1] According to the summary of schools and classes for the deaf in the United
States compiled by the *American Annals of the Deaf* (Vol. CIV, January, 1959),
there are 380 schools and classes serving 25,525 pupils. Of these, 72 are Public
Residential Schools and Classes attended by 15,237 pupils; 10 Day Schools serving
1,827 pupils; 227 Day Classes for 5,964 pupils; 16 Denominational and Private
Residential Schools for 1,286 pupils; 40 Denominational and Private Day Classes
for 1,001 pupils; and 15 schools and classes for 210 multiple-handicapped pupils.

a. The Oral System. Speech and lip reading together with reading and writing are the chief means of instruction. Elstad states that "there are no schools for the deaf today that do not start all children orally in the classroom." [2]

b. The Combined System. This system is described by Elstad as follows: "These so-called combined schools have manual classes for children who, after a fair trial, do not show any appreciable improvement in speech reading and speech. The teacher uses the manual alphabet and a greater amount of blackboard work in her teaching. . . . The use of the sign language in classrooms is discouraged in all schools." [3]

c. The Auricular System or Method. The residual hearing of the pupils is utilized and developed to the greatest possible extent. The Auricular approach is commonly used in conjunction with the Oral System, and is carried out with the help of sound-amplification aids, both group and individual.

[2] Leonard M. Elstad, "The Deaf," in M. E. Frampton and E. D. Gall, *Special Education for the Exceptional* (Boston: Porter Sargent, 1955), II, 159.

[3] *Ibid.*, p. 160. Reference is also made to: Dan D. Higgins, *How to Talk to the Deaf* (Chicago: J. S. Paluch Co., Inc., 1942); J. Schuyler Long, *The Sign Language: A Manual of Signs*, 2d ed. (Dorothy Long Thompson, 306 South 57th St., Omaha, Nebraska, 1949).

APPENDIX F

Manual Methods of Communication

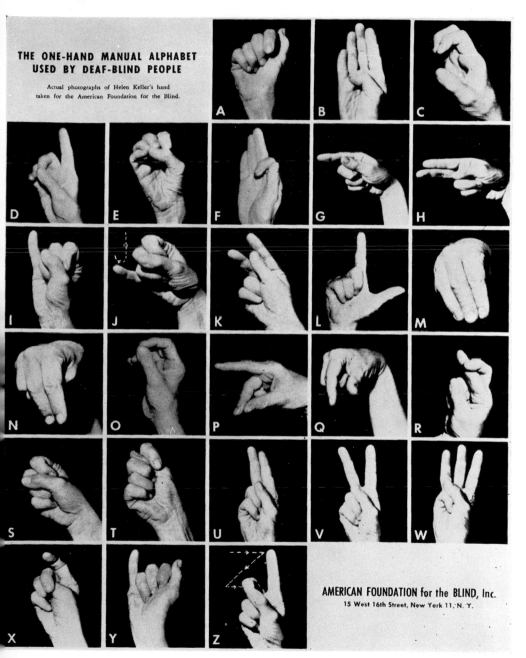

THE ONE-HAND MANUAL ALPHABET USED BY DEAF-BLIND PEOPLE

Actual photographs of Helen Keller's hand taken for the American Foundation for the Blind.

AMERICAN FOUNDATION for the BLIND, Inc.
15 West 16th Street, New York 11, N. Y.

The above one-hand manual alphabet, used by deaf-blind people, is also used in finger spelling by the deaf.

A Sentence in the Sign Language

Language is the key to mental development

Photos by Norman W. Crane; posed by Dorothy Kraft, of the Lexington School for the Deaf

  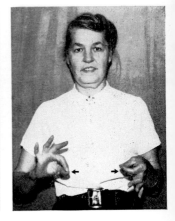

L A N G U A G E

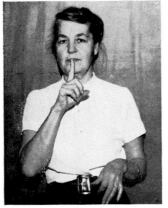 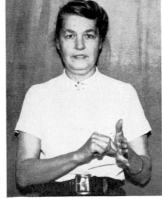 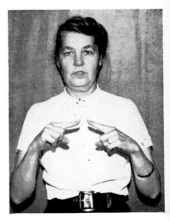

IS [THE] KEY TO

 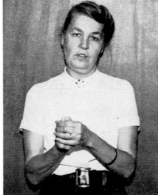 

MENTAL DEVELOPMENT

APPENDIX G

CHRONOLOGICAL LISTING OF
SELECTED PUBLISHED PSYCHOLOGICAL STUDIES OF THE DEAF
AND TESTS USED

Publication	Major Tests Used
1. Greenberger, D. "Doubtful Cases," *Annals*,* XXXIV (1889), 93.	Nonstandardized games tasks
2. Taylor, H. "A Spelling Test," *Annals*, XLII (1897), 364–69; XLIII (1898), 41–45.	Spelling test of any words written by subjects in given time
3. Mott, A. J. "A Comparison of Deaf and Hearing Children in Their Ninth Year," *Annals*, XLIV (1899), 401–12; XLV (1900), 33–39, 93–109.	Physical measurements / Sensori-motor tests / Memory and observation tasks / Athletic tasks
4. Macmillan, D. P., and F. G. Bruner. *Children Attending the Public Day Schools for the Deaf in Chicago*. Special Report of the Department of Child Study and Pedagogic Investigation, Chicago Public Schools, May, 1906.	Physical measurements / Sensori-motor tests / Memory and perception tests / Cancellation of A's
5. Kilpatrick, W. "Comparative Tests," *Annals*, LVII (1912), 427–28.	Proposal to try Binet-Simon Scale with the deaf
6. Kilpatrick, W. "Mentality Tests," *Annals*, LIX (1914), 394–98.	Proposal to try modified Binet-Simon Scale with the deaf
7. Pintner, R., and D. G. Paterson. "The Binet Scale and the Deaf Child," *Journal of Educational Psychology*, VI (1915), 201–10; *Annals*, LX (1915), 301–11.	Goddard-Binet
8. Pintner, R., and D. G. Paterson. "The Form-Board Ability of Young Deaf and Hearing Children," *Annals*, LXI (1916), 184–89.	Seguin Form Board

* *Annals* refers to the *American Annals of the Deaf*.

Publication	Major Tests Used
9. Pintner, R. "A Class Test with Deaf Children," *Annals*, LXI (1916), 264–75.	Digit-symbol, Symbol-digit
10. Pintner, R., and D. G. Paterson. *Learning Tests with Deaf Children*. Psychological Monographs, Vol. XX, No. 88, 1916.	Digit-symbol, Symbol-digit
11. Pintner, R., and D. G. Paterson. "A Survey of a Day School for the Deaf," *Annals*, LXI (1916), 417–33.	Digit-symbol, Symbol-digit; Knox Cube; Casuist; Five Figure Board; Two Figure Board; Woodworth-Wells Substitution; Feature Profile Healy Puzzle A; Trabue Language Scale; Easy Directions Test
12. Pintner, R., and D. G. Paterson. "A Measurement of the Language Ability of Deaf Children," *Annals*, LXII (1917), 211–39.	Trabue Language Scale
13. Pintner, R., and D. G. Paterson. "The Ability of Deaf and Hearing Children to Follow Printed Directions," *Ped. Sem.*, XXIII (1916), 477–97; *Annals*, LXII (1917), 448–72.	Woodworth-Wells Easy Directions Test
14. Pintner, R., and D. G. Paterson. "A Comparison of Deaf and Hearing Children in Visual Memory for Digits," *Journal of Experimental Psychology*, II (1917), 76–88.	Digit span
15. Pintner, R., and D. G. Paterson. "Psychological Tests of Deaf Children," *Volta Review*, XIX (1917), 661–67.	Binet-Simon and Pintner-Paterson Scales compared
16. Pintner, R. "The Measurement of Language Ability and Language Progress of Deaf Children," *Volta Review*, XX (1918), 755–64.	Trabue Language Scale
17. Porteus, S. D. "Measurement of the Intelligence of Deaf and Dumb Children," *Journal of Educational Psychology*, IX (1918), 13–31.	Porteus Maze Test
18. Newlee, C. "A Report of Learning Tests with Deaf Children," *Volta Review*, XXI (1919), 216–23.	Digit-symbol, Symbol-digit
19. Pintner, R., and J. C. Reamer. "A Mental and Educational Survey of Schools for the Deaf," *Annals*, LXV (1920), 451–72.	Pintner Nonlanguage Mental Group Test; Pintner Educational Survey Test
20. Reamer, J. C. *Mental and Educational Measurements of the Deaf*. Psychological Monographs, Vol. XXIX, No. 132, 1921.	Pintner Nonlanguage Mental and Educational Survey Tests

Publication	*Major Tests Used*
21. McManaway, H. M. "A Report on the Use of Standard Tests in the Virginia Schools for the Deaf," *Annals*, LXVIII (1923), 354–72; *Volta Review*, XXV (1923), 407–16.	Pintner Nonlanguage Mental and Educational Survey Tests Battery of specific subject tests
22. Pintner, R., H. E. Day, and I. S. Fusfeld. *A Survey of American Schools for the Deaf*. National Research Council, Washington, D.C., 1928.	Pintner Nonlanguage Mental and Educational Survey Tests
23. Drever, J., and M. Collins. *Performance Tests of Intelligence*. Edinburgh: Oliver and Boyd, 1928, 1936.	Drever-Collins Performance Scale
24. Pintner, R. "Speech and Speech-Reading Tests for the Deaf," *Annals*, LXXIV (1929), 480–86.	Specially constructed sentences
25. Upshall, C. E. *Day Schools vs. Institutions for the Deaf*. Teachers College Contributions to Education No. 389; Bureau of Publications, Teachers College, Columbia University, New York, 1929.	Pintner Nonlanguage Mental and Educational Survey Tests
26. Hall, P. "Results of Recent Tests at Gallaudet College," *Annals*, LXXIV (1929), 389–95.	New Stanford Achievement Tests
27. Brown, A. W. "Correlations of Non-Language Tests with Each Other, with School Achievement, and with Teachers' Judgement of Pupils' Intelligence," *Journal of Applied Psychology*, XIV (1930), 371–75.	Pintner Nonlanguage Mental Test Pintner-Paterson Performance Test items Stanford Achievement Arithmetic Tests Stanford Achievement Reading Tests
28. Peterson, E. G., and J. M. Williams. "Intelligence of Deaf Children as Measured by Drawings," *Annals*, LXXV (1930), 273–90.	Goodenough Draw-a-Man Test
29. Shirley, M., and F. L. Goodenough. "A Survey of Deaf Children in Minnesota Schools," *Annals*, LXXVII (1932), 238–47.	Goodenough Draw-a-Man Test Pintner Nonlanguage Mental Test
30. Schick, H. F., and M. F. Meyer. "The Use of the Lectometer in the Testing of the Hearing and the Deaf," *Annals*, LXXVII (1932), 292–304.	Lectometer (dot-pattern copying)
31. Long, J. A. *Motor Abilities of Deaf Children*. Teachers College Contributions to Education No. 514; Bureau of Publications,	Stanford Motor Skills Unit Dynamometer Balance Board

Publication	*Major Tests Used*
Teachers College, Columbia University, New York, 1932.	
32. Crammatte, A. B. "Motor Abilities of Deaf Children—a Review," *Annals*, LXXVIII (1933), 204–11.	Discussion of #31
33. Pintner, R. "Contributions of Psychological Testing to the Problems of the Deaf," *Proceedings of the International Congress on the Education of the Deaf*, West Trenton, N.J., June, 1933, pp. 213–20.	A summary of standardized tests used with the deaf
34. MacKane, K. *A Comparison of the Intelligence of Deaf and Hearing Children.* Teachers College Contributions to Education No. 585; Bureau of Publications, Teachers College, Columbia University, New York, 1933.	Pintner-Paterson Performance Scale Drever-Collins Performance Scale Grace Arthur Performance Scale Pintner Nonlanguage Mental Test
35. Lyon, V. W., *et al.* "Report of the 1931 Survey of the Illinois School for the Deaf," *Annals*, LXXVIII (1933), 157–75.	Pintner Nonlanguage Mental Test Institute for Juvenile Research (Illinois) Intelligence Test Grace Arthur Performance Scale Stanford Achievement Reading and Arithmetic tests
36. Schick, H. F. "The Use of a Standardized Performance Test for Pre-School Age Children with a Language Handicap," *Proceedings of the International Congress on the Education of the Deaf*, West Trenton, N.J., June, 1933, pp. 526–32.	Randall's Island Performance Scale
37. Lyon, V. W. "Personality Tests with the Deaf," *Annals*, LXXIX (1934), 1–4.	Thurstone Personality Schedule
38. Amoss, H. *Ontario School Ability Examination.* Toronto: Ryerson Press, 1936.	Ontario School Ability Test
39. Bishop, H. M. "Performance Scale Tests Applied to Deaf and Hard of Hearing Children," *Volta Review*, XXXVIII (1936), 447.	Grace Arthur Performance Scale
40. Morsh, J. E. "Motor Performance of the Deaf," *Comparative Psychological Monographs*, Vol. XIII, No. 66, 1936.	Dunlap tapping, steadiness, and balance tests Memory, speed of eye movement, hand-eye coordination tests

Publication	*Major Tests Used*
41. Brunschwig, L. *A Study of Some Personality Aspects of Deaf Children.* Teachers College Contributions to Education No. 687; Bureau of Publications, Teachers College, Columbia University, New York, 1936.	Rogers Test of Personality Adjustment Pintner Nonlanguage Mental Tests Brunschwig Personality Inventory for Deaf Children
42. Scyster, M. "Summary of Four Years' Experiment with Pre-School Deaf Children at the Illinois School for the Deaf," *Annals,* LXXXI (1936), 212–30.	Merrill-Palmer Scale of Mental Tests Nonlanguage items of Minnesota Pre-School Scale
43. Peterson, E. G. "Testing Deaf Children with the Kohs Block Designs," *Annals,* LXXXI (1936), 242–54.	Kohs Block Designs Goodenough Draw-a-Man Test
44. Williams, B. R. "Knowledge of Social Conduct of the Deaf," *Indiana School Hoosier,* 1937.	Strang Test of Social Usage
45. Bradway, K. P. "The Social Competence of Deaf Children," *Annals,* LXXXII (1937), 122–40.	Vineland Social Maturity Scale
46. Pintner, R., I. S. Fusfeld, and L. Brunschwig. "Personality Tests of Deaf Adults," *Journal of Genetic Psychology,* LI (1937), 305–27.	Bernreuter Inventory
47. Pintner, R., and L. Brunschwig. "A Study of Fears and Wishes among Deaf and Hearing Children," *Journal of Educational Psychology,* XXVIII (1937), 259–70.	Check list of 39 items relating to fears and a list of 7 pairs of wishes
48. Stanton, M. B. *Mechanical Ability of Deaf Children.* Teachers College Contributions to Education No. 751; Teachers College, Columbia University, New York, 1938.	Battery A of the Minnesota Mechnical-Ability Tests
49. Kirk, S. A. "Behavior Problem Tendencies in Deaf and Hard-of-Hearing Children," *Annals,* LXXXIII (1938), 131–37.	Haggerty-Olson-Wickman Behavior Rating Schedules
50. Springer, N. N. "A Comparative Study of the Intelligence of a Group of Deaf and Hearing Children," *Annals,* LXXXIII (1938), 138–52.	Goodenough Draw-a-Man Test Division I: Intellectual Traits of the Haggerty-Olson-Wickman Schedules
51. Streng, A., and S. A. Kirk. "The Social Competence of Deaf and Hard of Hearing Children in a Public Day School," *Annals,* LXXXIII (1938), 244–54.	Vineland Social Maturity Scale Chicago Nonverbal Examination Grace Arthur Performance Scale

Publication	*Major Tests Used*
52. Springer, N. N. "A Comparative Study of the Behavior Traits of Deaf and Hearing Children of New York City," *Annals*, LXXXIII (1938), 255–73.	Haggerty-Olson-Wickman Behavior Rating Schedules Goodenough Draw-a-Man Test
53. Springer, N. N. "Comparative Study of the Psychoneurotic Responses of Deaf and Hearing Children," *Journal of Educational Psychology*, XXIX (1938), 459–66.	Brown's Personality Inventory for Children
54. Springer, N. N., and S. Roslow. "A Further Study of the Psychoneurotic Responses of Deaf and Hearing Children," *Journal of Educational Psychology*, XXIX (1938), 590–96.	Brown Personality Inventory for Children
55. Gregory, I. "A Comparison of Certain Personality Traits and Interests in Deaf and Hearing Children," *Child Development*, IX (1938), 277–80.	Sections of: Minnesota Interest Blank; Rogers Test of Personality Adjustment; Woodworth-Cady Test of Emotional Stability
56. Zeckel, A., and J. J. Van der Kolk. "A Comparative Intelligence Test of Groups of Children Born Deaf and of Good Hearing by Means of the Porteus Maze Test," *Annals*, LXXXIV (1939), 114–23.	Porteus Maze Test
57. Bridgman, O. "The Estimation of Mental Ability in Deaf Children," *Annals*, LXXXIV (1939), 337–49.	Arthur Performance Scale Ontario School Ability Examination Healy Scaled Information Test Randalls Island Performance Tests Stanford-Binet Intelligence Test
58. Morrison, W. J. "The Ontario School Ability Examination," *Annals*, LXXXV (1940), 184–89.	Ontario School Ability Examination
59. Pintner, R. "Artistic Appreciation among Deaf Children," *Annals*, LXXXVI (1941), 218–24.	McAdory Art Test
60. Hiskey, M. S. *Nebraska Test of Learning Aptitude for Young Deaf Children.* University of Nebraska, Department of Educational Psychology and Measurements, 1941.	Nebraska Test of Learning Aptitude for Young Deaf Children

Publication	Major Tests Used
61. Lane, H. S., and J. L. Schneider. "A Performance Test for School-Age Deaf Children," *Annals*, LXXXVI (1941), 441–47.	Advanced Performance Series
62. Heider, F., and G. M. Heider. *Studies in the Psychology of the Deaf*. Psychological Monographs, Vol. LIII, No. 5, 1941.	Observation Interview Questionnaire
63. Burchard, E., and H. R. Myklebust. "A Comparison of Congenital and Adventitious Deafness with Respect to Its Effect on Intelligence, Personality and Social Maturity," *Annals*, LXXXVII (1942), 140–55, 241–51, 342–60.	Grace Arthur Performance Scale Haggerty-Olson-Wickman Behavior Rating Schedules Vineland Social Maturity Scale
64. O'Connor, C. D., and E. Simon. "A Preliminary Survey into Problems of Adjustment among Pupils of the Lexington School for the Deaf," *Annals*, LXXXVII (1942), 224–40.	Devised Rating Questionnaire Brunschwig Personality Inventory for Deaf Children
65. Lavos, G. "The Reliability of an Educational Achievement Test Administered to the Deaf," *Annals*, LXXXIX (1944), 226–33.	Stanford Educational Achievement Test, Form E
66. Kline, T. H. "A Study of the Free Association Test with Deaf Children," *Annals*, XC (1945), 237–58.	50 stimulus free association words from Woodrow-Lowell list
67. Altable, J. P. "The Rorschach Psychodiagnostic as Applied to Deaf Mutes," *Rorschach Research Exchange and Journal of Projective Techniques*, XI (1947), 74–79.	Rorschach Test
68. Johnson, E. H. "The Effect of Academic Level on Scores from the Chicago Non-Verbal Examination for Primary Pupils," *Annals*, XCII (1947), 227–34.	Chicago Nonverbal Examination
69. McAndrew, Helton. "Rigidity and Isolation: A Study of the Deaf and the Blind," *Journal of Abnormal and Social Psychology*, XLIII (1948), 476–94.	Rorschach Test
70. Avery, C. B. "The Social Competence of Pre-School Acoustically Handicapped Children," *Journal of Exceptional Children*, XV (1948), 71–73.	Vineland Social Maturity Scale
71. Heider, G. M. "A Comparison of the Social Behavior of Deaf and Non-Deaf Pre-School Children in an Experimental Play Situation," *American Psychologist*, III (1948), 262–63.	A game that only one child at a time can play was offered to pairs of children
72. MacPherson, J. G., and H. S. Lane. "A Com-	Hiskey-Nebraska Test of

Publication	*Major Tests Used*
parison of Deaf and Hearing on the Hiskey Test and on Performance Scales," *Annals*, XCIII (1948), 178–84.	Learning Aptitude for Young Deaf Children
	Advanced Performance Series
	Randalls Island Performance Scale
73. Kirk, S. A., and J. Perry. "A Comparative Study of the Ontario and Nebraska Tests for the Deaf," *Annals*, XCIII (1948), 315–23.	Ontario School Ability Examination
	Nebraska Test of Learning Aptitude for Young Deaf Children
74. Hood, H. B. "Preliminary Survey of Some Mental Abilities of Deaf Children," *British Journal of Educational Psychology*, XIX (1949), 210–19.	Alexander Performance Scale for the Measurement of Practical Ability
	Picture Vocabulary and Word List of the Stanford-Binet
	Reading Achievement
75. Templin, M. C. *The Development of Reasoning in Children with Normal and Defective Hearing*. Minneapolis: The University of Minnesota Press, 1950.	Deutsche questions
	Long and Welsh Test of Causal Reasoning
	Brody Nonverbal Abstract Reasoning Test
76. Beizmann, C. "Quelques considerations sur le Rorschach des sourdes-muets," *Enfance*, III (1950), 33–48.	Rorschach Test
77. Oleron, P. "A Study of the Intelligence of the Deaf," *Annals*, XCV (1950), 179–95.	Raven's Progressive Matrices
78. Lavos, G. "The Chicago Non-Verbal Examination," *Annals*, XCV (1950), 379–87.	Chicago Nonverbal Examination
79. Birch, J. R., and J. W. Birch. "The Leiter International Performance Scale as an Aid in the Psychological Study of Deaf Children," *Annals*, XCVI (1951), 502–11.	Leiter International Performance Scale
	Goodenough Draw-a-Man Test
	Arthur Point Scale
	Nebraska Test of Learning Aptitude for Young Deaf Children
80. Smith, D. I. "A Survey of the Intelligence and Attainments of a Group of Deaf Children" (Abstract), *British Journal of Educational Psychology*, XXII (1952), 71–72.	Raven's Progressive Matrices
	Jenkins Nonverbal Test
	Shonell Silent Reading Test
	Burt Arithmetic Test
81. Glowatsky, E. "The Verbal Element in the Intelligence Scores of Congenitally Deaf and Hard-of-Hearing Children," *Annals*, XCVIII (1953), 328–35.	Arthur Point Scale, Form II
	Wechsler Intelligence Scale for Children
	Goodenough Draw-a-Man Test

Publication	*Major Tests Used*
82. Graham, E., and E. Shapiro. "Use of the Performance Scale of the Wechsler Intelligence Scale for Children with the Deaf," *Journal of Consulting Psychology*, XVII (1953), 396–98.	Wechsler Intelligence Scale for Children (Performance Scale)
83. Ross, G. "Testing the Intelligence and Maturity of Deaf Children," *Journal of Exceptional Children*, XX (1953), 23–24.	Ontario School Ability Examination Nebraska Test of Learning Aptitude for Young Deaf Children
84. DuToit, J. M. "Measuring the Intelligence of Deaf Children, a New Group Test," *Annals*, XCIX (1954), 237–52.	DuToit Group Intelligence Test
85. Lavos, G. "Interrelationships among Three Tests of Non-Language Intelligence Administered to the Deaf," *Annals*, XCIX (1954), 303–14.	Chicago Nonverbal Examination Pintner General Ability Tests, Nonlanguage Series, Int. Battery Revised Beta Examination
86. Knieval, W. R. "A Vocational Aptitude Test Battery for the Deaf," *Annals*, XCIX (1954), 314–19.	Seven tests of Factored Aptitude Series: Numbers, Dimension, Perception, Blocks, Precision, Parts, Tools
87. Rutledge, L. "Aspiration Levels of Deaf Children as Compared with Those of Hearing Children," *Journal of Speech and Hearing Disorders*, XIX (1954).	Heath Railwalking Test Rotter Aspiration Board
88. Hiskey, M. S. "A Study of the Intelligence of Deaf and Hearing Children," *Annals*, CI (1956), 329–39.	Correlation between the Nebraska Test and the Binet Scale
89. Levine, E. S. *Youth in a Soundless World*. New York: New York University Press, 1956.	Verbal and Performance Scales of Wechsler Intelligence Scale, Form I Rorschach Test
90. Birch, J. R., and J. W. Birch. "Predicting School Achievement in Young Deaf Children," *Annals*, CI (1956), 348–52.	Use of the Leiter International Performance Scale in predicting school achievement
91. Baar, E. *Psychologische Untersuchung von Tauben, Schwerhörigen und Sprachlich Speziell Gestörten Kleinkindern*. Basel, Switzerland, and New York: S. Karger, 1957.	The author presents a general survey of 36 psychological tests for young deaf children used in 16 different countries of Europe and in America. Some are single test items. A number not

Publication	*Major Tests Used*
	included in the intelligence and personality scales already mentioned here are:
a. Atkins, R. Object Fitting Test, in A. W. G. Ewing, *Educational Guidance and the Deaf Child*. Manchester: Manchester University Press, 1957.	Atkins Object Fitting Test
b. Baar, E. *Sprachfreie Entwicklungsteste* (nach Buhler-Hetzer und Schenk-Danzinger). Basel, Switzerland, and New York: S. Karger, 1957.	Baar Nonverbal Development Tests for deaf, hard-of-hearing, and special speech defective children
c. Biäsch, H. *Biäsch-Test*. Frauenfeld/ Leipzig: Huber, 1939.	Biasch-Test
d. Borelli, M., and P. Oleron. *Une Nouvelle Echelle de Performance*. Paris: Centre de Psychologie appliquée, 1954.	The scale consists of seven tasks involving: building design imitation; picture and form-board completion; Pintner Manikin; memory for design (Knox cubes). Validated on 155 deaf children 4½ to 8 years of age.
e. Borel-Maisonny, S. *Test de niveau mental pour enfants ayant de troubles du language*. Paris: Libraire Central d'education nouvelle, 1947.	The Borel-Maisonny Scale is developmentally oriented and consists of a series of tests for ages 15 months to 3½ years, plus a series for ages 3 years to 6 years.
f. Fischer, B. "Tastfuhlgestalten und das Problem der Schulreife beim taubstummen Kind. Neckargemünd, Germany. *Neue Bl. Taubstummenbild*, VI (1952), 97–104.	The Fischer test involves the recognition of geometric forms (circle, triangle, cross, square) drawn in the palm of the hand (Touch Gestalt Test).
g. Herderschée, D. Teste für taubstumme Kinder. Amsterdam, Holland. *Z. angew. Psychol.*, XVI (1920), 40.	Baar states that to her knowledge the Herderschée tests are the first special tests for deaf children. The test items include: copying geometric forms, recognition of objects by touch, sorting by size, memory for forms and colors, figure drawing, etc.

92. Larr, A. L., and E. R. Cain. "Measurement of Native Learning Abilities of Deaf Children," *Volta Review*, LXI (1959), 160–63.

Wechsler Intelligence Scale for Children, Form II
Grace Arthur Point Scale of Performance Tests, Form II
Ontario School Ability Examination
Nebraska Test of Learning Aptitude for Young Deaf Children
Goodenough Draw-a-Man Test

For a chronological listing of unpublished studies see R. W. Flint, F. C. Higgins, and D. A. Padden, "Doctors' Dissertations and Masters' Theses on the Education of the Deaf, 1897–1955," *American Annals of the Deaf*, Vol. C (September, 1955).

APPENDIX H

A Guide to Test Publishers and Distributors [1]

INTELLIGENCE TESTS

Army Alpha (Bureau of Educational Measurements, Kansas State Teachers College)

Army Beta Original (Bureau of Educational Measurements, Kansas State Teachers College)

Army Beta Revised (Psychological Corporation)

Arthur Point Scale of Performance Tests (C. H. Stoelting Company); Revised Form II (Psychological Corporation)

Chicago Nonverbal Examination (Psychological Corporation)

Cornell-Coxe Performance Ability Scale (World Book Company)

Culture-Free Test, Cattell (Psychological Corporation)

Drever-Collins Performance Scale (Manual: Oliver & Boyd, Ltd.; Test materials, A. H. Baird, Lothian Street, Edinburgh, Scotland)

Gesell Developmental Schedules (Psychological Corporation)

Goodenough Draw-a-Man Test (Manual: World Book Company)

Leiter International Performance Scale (Psychological Corporation)

Leiter-Partington Adult Performance Scale (C. H. Stoelting Company)

McCall Multi-Mental Scale: Nonlanguage (Bureau of Publications, Teachers College, Columbia University)

[1] This listing is composed of tests mentioned in the text. The reader is reminded that although the tests are currently used with the deaf, in many instances their use is dictated by the lack of more appropriate instruments. The ultimate suitability of a given test lies with the clinical judgment, experience, and technical skill of the examiner. Limitations of space make it impossible to mention all the distributors through whom the tests are available.

Merrill-Palmer Scale of Mental Tests (C. H. Stoelting Company)
Nebraska Test of Learning Aptitude for Young Deaf Children (Psychological Corporation)
Ontario School Ability Examination (Ryerson Press)
Pintner General Ability Tests (World Book Company)
Pintner-Paterson Performance Scale (C. H. Stoelting Company)
Porteus Mazes (C. H. Stoelting Company)
Randall Island Performance Tests (C. H. Stoelting Company)
Shipley Institute of Living Scale (Institute of Living, Hartford, Conn.)
SRA Verbal and Nonverbal (Science Research Associates)
Wechsler Adult Intelligence Scale (Psychological Corporation)
Wechsler-Bellevue Intelligence Scale (Psychological Corporation)
Wechsler Intelligence Scale for Children (Psychological Corporation)

ACHIEVEMENT TESTS

A.C.E. Psychological Examination for College Freshmen (Educational Testing Service, the American Council on Education)
American School Achievement Test (Public School Publishing Company)
Baldwin-Stecher Number Concept Test (C. H. Stoelting Company)
California Achievement Tests (California Test Bureau)
Columbia Vocabulary Test (Psychological Corporation)
Cooperative School and College Ability Tests (Cooperative Test Division, Educational Testing Service)
Essential High School Content Battery (World Book Company)
Gates Basic Reading Tests (Bureau of Publications, Teachers College, Columbia University)
Graduate Record Examinations (Educational Testing Service)
Inglis Tests of English Vocabulary (Ginn and Company)
Metropolitan Achievement Test (World Book Company)
Modern School Achievement Tests (Bureau of Publications, Teachers College, Columbia University)
Municipal Battery: National Achievement Tests (Acorn Publishing Company)
Progressive Achievement Test (California Test Bureau)
Public School Achievement Tests (Public School Publishing Company)
Sequential Tests of Educational Progress (Cooperative Test Division, Educational Testing Service)

Stanford Achievement Test (World Book Company)
Woody-McCall Mixed Fundamentals in Arithmetic (Bureau of Publications, Teachers College, Columbia University)

PERSONALITY TESTS

Brunschwig Personality Inventory for Deaf Children (R. Pintner and L. Brunschwig, "An Adjustment Inventory for Use in Schools for the Deaf," *American Annals of the Deaf*, LXXXII [1937], 152–67)
Edwards Personal Preference Schedule (Psychological Corporation)
House-Tree-Person Test (H-T-P) (Manual: *Journal of Clinical Psychology*, Vol. IV [1948] and Vol. V [1949])
Ies Test (Psychological Test Specialists)
Kinget Drawing Completion Test (Grune & Stratton, Inc.)
Make a Picture Story (MAPS) (Manual: *Journal of Projective Techniques*, Monograph No. 2, 1952; Materials: Psychological Corporation)
Mooney Problem Check Lists (Psychological Corporation)
Murray Thematic Apperception Test (Harvard University Press)
Rorschach Technique (Plates: Grune & Stratton, Inc.; Record Blanks: World Book Company)
Sentence Completion Tests (Forer Test, Rohde Tests: Western Psychological Services; Rotter Incomplete Sentences: Psychological Corporation)
Vineland Social Maturity Scale, Revised (Educational Test Bureau)
(Consult Test Catalogues for Children's Play Projective Devices)

SPECIAL CLINICAL TESTS

Bender Visual Motor Gestalt Test (American Orthopsychiatric Association, Inc.)
Benton Revised Visual Retention Test (Psychological Corporation)
Dvorine Pseudo-Isochromatic Plates (Western Psychological Services; C. H. Stoelting Company)
Harris Tests of Lateral Dominance (Psychological Corporation)
Lincoln-Oseretsky Motor Development Scale (C. H. Stoelting Company)
Oseretsky Tests of Motor Proficiency (Educational Test Bureau)

TESTS FOR SPECIAL INTERESTS, APTITUDES, ABILITIES

Allport-Vernon Study of Values (Houghton-Mifflin)

Bennett Test of Mechanical Comprehension (Psychological Corporation)

Brainard Occupational Preference Inventory (Psychological Corporation)

Crawford Small Parts Dexterity Test (Psychological Corporation)

Differential Aptitudes Tests (Psychological Corporation)

Graves Design Judgment Test (Psychological Corporation)

Kuder Preference Record (Science Research Associates)

Lee-Thorpe Occupational Interest Inventory (California Test Bureau)

MacQuarrie Test for Mechanical Ability (California Test Bureau)

Meier Art Judgment Test (Bureau of Educational Research and Service)

Minnesota Assembly Test (C. H. Stoelting Company)

Minnesota Clerical Test (Psychological Corporation)

Minnesota Paper Form Board, Revised (Psychological Corporation)

Pennsylvania Bi-Manual Worksample (Educational Test Bureau)

Psychological Corporation General Clerical Test (Psychological Corporation)

Purdue Pegboard (Science Research Associates)

SRA Clerical Aptitudes (Science Research Associates)

SRA Mechanical Aptitudes (Science Research Associates)

Strong Vocational Interest Tests (Stanford University Press)

Thurstone Interest Schedule (Psychological Corporation)

PSYCHOLOGICAL TEST PUBLISHERS AND DISTRIBUTORS

The following selected listing includes companies that issue catalogues devoted entirely or in large part to psychological tests. For a more comprehensive listing, the reader is referred to the *Buros Fourth Mental Measurements Yearbook*, Rutgers University Press, New Brunswick, New Jersey.

Acorn Publishing Company, Inc., Rockville Center, New York

American Orthopsychiatric Association, 1790 Broadway, New York 19, N.Y.

Bureau of Educational Measurements, Kansas State Teachers College, Emporia, Kansas

Bureau of Publications, Teachers College, Columbia University, New York 27, N.Y.

California Test Bureau, 5916 Hollywood Blvd., Los Angeles 28, California

Cooperative Test Division, Educational Testing Service, 15 Amsterdam Avenue, New York 23, N.Y.

Educational Test Bureau: Educational Test Publishers, Inc., 720 Washington Avenue, S.E., Minneapolis 14, Minnesota; 3433 Walnut Street, Philadelphia 4, Pennsylvania

Educational Testing Service, Princeton, New Jersey

Ginn & Company, Statler Building, Boston 17, Massachusetts

Grune & Stratton, Inc., 381 Fourth Avenue, New York 16, N.Y.

Harvard University Press, 38 Quincy Street, Cambridge 38, Massachusetts

Houghton-Mifflin Company, 2 Park Street, Boston 7, Massachusetts

Psychological Corporation, 304 East 45th Street, New York 17, N.Y.

Psychological Test Specialists, Box 1441, Missoula, Montana

Public School Publishing Company, 509–13 North East Street, Bloomington, Illinois

Ryerson Press, 299 Queen Street, West Toronto 2, Ontario, Canada

Science Research Associates, Inc., 228 South Wabash Ave., Chicago 4, Illinois

Stanford University Press, Stanford, California

Stoelting (C. H.) Company, 424 North Homan Avenue, Chicago 20, Illinois

Western Psychological Services, 10655 Santa Monica Blvd., Los Angeles 25, California

World Book Company, 313 Park Hill Avenue, Yonkers 5, New York

APPENDIX I

NATIONAL NONMEDICAL ORGANIZATIONS FOR
THE AURALLY IMPAIRED

Alexander Graham Bell Association for the Deaf, Inc.
  Purpose: To improve the education of the deaf and the hard of hearing, their ability to communicate with those who hear normally, and their adjustment to life in the hearing world.
  Headquarters: The Volta Bureau
    1537 35th Street, N.W.
    Washington 7, D.C.
  Publication: *Volta Review*
American Hearing Society
  Purpose: To prevent deafness; conserve hearing; rehabilitate the hard of hearing.
  Headquarters: American Hearing Society
    919 18th Street, N.W.
    Washington 6, D.C.
  Publication: *Hearing News*
American Speech and Hearing Association
  Purpose: Investigation and management of speech and hearing disorders.
  Headquarters: American Speech and Hearing Association
    1001 Connecticut Avenue, N.W.
    Washington, D.C.
  Publications: *Journal of Speech and Hearing Disorders; Journal of Speech and Hearing Research*
Church Services to the Deaf
  Purpose: Many religious denominations have special departments

or committees to promote the spiritual well-being of the deaf as well as to render various social services.

Headquarters: Consult January issue of the *American Annals of the Deaf*

Publications: Consult January issue of the *American Annals of the Deaf*

Conference of Executives of American Schools for the Deaf, The

Purpose: To promote the management and operation of schools for the deaf along the broadest and most efficient lines and to further and promote the general welfare of the deaf.

Headquarters: Gallaudet College
Washington 2, D.C.

Publication: *American Annals of the Deaf*

Convention of American Instructors of the Deaf, The

Purpose: To promote and improve the methods of instruction, education, vocational and general welfare of the deaf.

Headquarters: Gallaudet College
Washington 2, D.C.

Publications: *American Annals of the Deaf;* Report of the *Proceedings of the Convention of American Instructors of the Deaf* (U.S. Government Printing Office)

Department of Health, Education, and Welfare, Office of Vocational Rehabilitation, Section on the Deaf and the Hard of Hearing

Purpose: Major concern in vocational rehabilitation of the deaf and the hard of hearing; information center.

Headquarters: Office of Vocational Rehabilitation
Washington 25, D.C.

Publication: *Rehabilitation Service Series* (Office of Vocational Rehabilitation, Washington 25, D.C.)

National Association of the Deaf, The

Purpose: "Promote the welfare of the deaf in educational measures, in employment, in legislation, and in any other field pertaining to or affecting the deaf of America in their pursuit of economic security, social equality, and all their just rights and privileges as citizens."

Headquarters: For current information, consult *American Annals of the Deaf* or the Federal Office of Vocational Rehabilitation.

Publications: *The Silent Worker* (2495 Shattuck Avenue, Berkeley

4, California); *Report of the Proceedings of the Annual Convention of the National Association of the Deaf*

National Fraternal Society of the Deaf, The

Purpose: Fraternal and insurance (sickness, accident, and death benefits) society of deaf persons who are members meeting certain eligibility requirements.

Headquarters: Home Office
433 Oak Park Avenue
Oak Park, Illinois

Publication: *The Frat*

Veterans Administration, Aural Rehabilitation

Purpose: To provide complete rehabilitation services to war-deafened veterans.

Headquarters: For information concerning Aural Rehabilitation Centers for veterans, consult Veterans Administration, Washington, D.C.

Hearing Rehabilitation Centers

Consult January issues of the *American Annals of the Deaf* for Directory information.

Downs, M. P., and E. Carson. "Hearing Rehabilitation Centers in the United States." Reprinted from the *A.M.A. Archives of Otolaryngology*, LXII (1955), 649–64.

GLOSSARY

The following glossary of terms in aural rehabilitation is by no means a comprehensive listing but is limited to those terms used in this book plus a few other common terms the psychologist is apt to encounter. The definitions are taken or adapted from the following sources: "Glossary," Subcommittee on Noise in Industry of the Committee on Conservation of Hearing, American Academy of Ophthalmology and Otolaryngology; *Hearing Loss—a Community Loss,* American Hearing Society, 1958; *Services for Children with Hearing Impairment,* Committee on Child Health of the American Public Health Association, 1956; and *A Comprehensive Dictionary of Psychological and Psychoanalytical Terms,* by Horace B. English and Ava Champney English (Longmans, Green and Co., 1958).

Acoustic: concerned with sound waves and the science of sound. The term is often used synonymously with "auditory," which pertains to hearing.

Acuity: when used in reference to hearing, the term denotes hearing sensitivity.

Air conduction: the process by which air-borne sound waves pass from the external to the inner ear.

Aphasia: loss or impairment of the ability to use language because of lesions in the brain.

Audiogram: a graphic record of the hearing of an individual tested by the pure-tone audiometer. It records the intensities of successively higher pure tones which he is just barely able to hear in a quiet environment; in other words, his *threshold acuity.* The audiogram here shown indicates the significance of hearing loss as measured in decibels. (Reproduced by courtesy of the American Hearing Society from *Orientation Training for Vocational Rehabilitation Counselors,* American Hearing Society, 1956.)

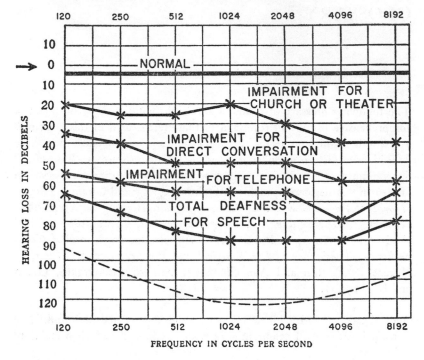

Audiologist: A specialist in the nonmedical evaluation, habilitation, and rehabilitation of those whose language and speech disorders (communicative disorders) center in whole or in part in the hearing function.

Audiology: The science of hearing. The term is designed to coordinate the separate professional skills which contribute to the study, treatment, and rehabilitation of persons with impaired hearing.

Audiometer: A precision instrument for measuring hearing acuity. Measurement by this means is called *audiometry* and the person trained in the use of the audiometer is called an *audiometrist* (or hearing tester).

Auditory: pertaining to the sense of hearing. (See *Acoustic.*)

Auditory training: a means of educating or reeducating the residual hearing to interpret (identify, understand) meaningful auditory patterns. The person must learn or relearn to use any remnant of hearing he has. Amplification of sound by group and individual hearing aids assists this learning process.

Aural: pertaining to the ear.

Binaural: pertaining to both ears functioning together.

Bone conduction: the process by which sound reaches the inner ear through the cranial bones.

Congenital: present at birth but not necessarily innate.

Consanguineous: refers to marriages between blood-related persons. Part of history inquiry as to cause of deafness.

Dactylology: the technical term for finger-spelling or manual communications. See Appendices E and F.

Deaf: see Appendix B.

Decibel: a unit for measuring the difference between the perceived intensity or loudness of a certain sound and that of a standard sound. It is abbreviated as db.

Frequency: when applied to sound, designates the property which can be measured as cycles per second by physical means. The number of vibrations per second of a sound wave determines the pitch of the heard tone. The intact human auditory mechanism is capable of perceiving tones between 15 and 15,000 cycles per second.

Hard of hearing: see Appendix B.

Hearing: perception of sound by means primarily of the sensory apparatus of the cochlea in the inner ear.

Hearing aid: any mechanical device to assist in bringing sound vibrations to the sensory apparatus of the inner ear. Characteristically, the aid is a device for amplifying the sound and for imposing the vibration on the bony structure surrounding the inner ear.

Hearing conservation: generally refers to community programs for the maintenance of hearing health, the prevention of hearing impairments, and assistance in aural rehabilitation.

Hearing defect or deficiency: impairment in the ability to perceive sounds and to discriminate between them.

Hearing loss: the measure of an individual's hearing deficiency as compared with the so-called normal ear. It is measured, for different frequencies, in terms of just-perceptible stimuli and recorded (absolutely) in decibels or (relatively) as a percentage of normal acuity.

Hearing therapist: specialist in the training or retraining of persons whose language and speech disorders center in whole or in part in the hearing function.

Hypacusis: the generic term for defective hearing.

Hyperacusis: an exceptionally acute sense of hearing.

Intelligibility of speech (or speech intelligibility): refers to a measure of understanding spoken language as derived from such devices as specially prepared lists of phonetically balanced words.

Intensity of sound: for psychological purposes, this refers to the quantitative attribute of sound that can be measured in decibels to indicate the loudness.

Manual communication: see Appendices E and F.

Monaural: refers to one ear functioning alone; hearing with one ear.

Oral communications: see Appendix E.

Otic mechanism: a term used to signify the entire anatomic apparatus used in the process of hearing.

Otologist: a medical specialist in the anatomy and functions of the ear and in the diagnosis and treatment of diseases of the ear.

Otology: the branch of medicine that specializes in the ear.

Pitch: see *Frequency*.

Psycho-acoustics: an intermediate discipline dealing with the physics of sound as related to audition and with the physiology and psychology of sound-receptor processes.

Psychophysics: as related to sound, refers to the study of the relation between the physical attributes of the sound stimulus and the quantitative attributes of audition.

Pure-tone audiometer: an audiometer (see above) which tests hearing acuity for pure tones. The tones emitted are set in steps at octave or semi-octave intervals and usually range from 125 to 12,000 cycles per second (cps), depending on the instrument. The most important speech sounds occur in the region of octaves 512, 1024, and 2048.

Pure tones: tones without audible overtones. They are not compounded with other tones and have no partials.

Recruitment (of loudness): commonly used to designate conditions of disproportionate and sometimes painful sensitivity to small increases in the loudness of sound.

Residual hearing: the hearing still retained by a hearing-impaired person.

Sign language: see Appendices E and F.

Sound wave: a progressive longitudinal vibratory disturbance made up of alternating areas of condensation and rarefaction in an elastic medium, propagated from an oscillating source of energy in cycles between about 20 and 50,000 per second. If the successive waves form a regular or periodic pattern, they give rise to a tone, if an aperiodic pattern, to noise.

Special education: a program or techniques of education especially designed for exceptional children, such as the hearing-impaired, physically disabled, speech-impaired, brain-damaged, gifted, etc.

Speech audiometer: an audiometer which tests the hearing of speech rather than the hearing of pure tones.

Speech reading (Lip reading): see Appendix E.

Speech reception threshold: defined as that sound pressure in decibels at which 50 percent of test words are heard correctly.

Speech therapist: specialist in the training or retraining of persons with speech and related disorders.

Threshold acuity: a measure of loudness of tone which an individual is just barely able to hear.

Tinnitus: refers to head noises of varied types and intensities that accompany certain types of hearing disorders.

Vertigo: refers to a sensation as if the external world were revolving about the individual or as if he himself were whirling in space. A common symptom of Ménière's disease. Erroneously referred to as dizziness.

BIBLIOGRAPHY

Introduction

Benda, Clemens E. Developmental Disorders of Mentation and Cerebral Palsies. New York: Grune & Stratton, 1952.

Garrett, James F. "Counsel the Man—Not the Disability." Reprinted from *The Crippled Child*, National Society for Crippled Children and Adults, April, 1952.

Garrett, James F., ed. Psychological Aspects of Physical Disability. Rehabilitation Service Series No. 210. Washington, D.C.: Office of Vocational Rehabilitation, Department of Health, Education, and Welfare, 1952.

Hamilton, Kenneth W. Counseling the Handicapped in the Rehabilitation Process. New York: The Ronald Press, 1950.

Health Resources Advisory Committee. Mobilization and Health Manpower: A Report of the Subcommittee on Paramedical Personnel in Rehabilitation and Care of the Chronically Ill. Washington, D.C.: Government Printing Office, January, 1956.

Kessler, Henry H. Rehabilitation of the Physically Handicapped. New York: Columbia University Press, 1947.

Kratz, John A. "Vocational Rehabilitation, Past, Present and Future in the United States," *Rehabilitation Review*, Vol. II (May, 1954).

Levine, Edna S. Youth in a Soundless World. New York: New York University Press, 1956.

Louttit, C. M. Clinical Psychology. New York and London: Harper & Brothers, 1936.

"Regulations Governing the Plans and Program of Vocational Rehabilitation Pursuant to Public Law 113, 78th Congress, 1st Session."

Issued by the Federal Security Agency, Office of Vocational Rehabilitation, Washington, D.C., October 9, 1943.

Report of the Task Force on the Handicapped to the Chairman of Manpower Policy, Office of Defense Mobilization. Washington, D.C., January 25, 1952.

Roback, A. A. History of American Psychology. New York: Library Publishers, 1952.

Ronnei, Eleanor C. "The Hard of Hearing," in Special Education for the Exceptional. Edited by M. E. Frampton and E. D. Gall. Vol. II. Boston: Porter Sargent, 1955.

Rubinstein, Eli A., and Maurice Lorr, eds. Survey of Clinical Practice in Psychology. New York: International Universities Press, Inc., 1954.

United Nations. Rehabilitation of the Handicapped. Social Welfare Information Series, Special Issue. New York, September, 1953.

U.S. Office of Vocational Rehabilitation. Announcement: Rehabilitation Research Fellowships. Washington, D.C., June, 1957.

—— Announcement: Research and Demonstration Grants in Vocational Rehabilitation. Washington, D.C., September, 1957, OVR 36–58.

—— New Hope for the Disabled: Public Law 565. Washington, D.C.: Government Printing Office, 1956.

—— Training Grant Programs of the Office of Vocational Rehabilitation. Washington, D.C., March, 1958.

Wright, B., ed. Psychology and Rehabilitation. Washington, D.C.: American Psychological Association, 1959.

Part One: The Implications of Hearing and Impaired Hearing

Anshen, Ruth Nanda, ed. Language: An Enquiry into Its Meaning and Function. New York: Harper & Brothers, 1957.

Barker, Roger, *et al.* Adjustment to Physical Handicap and Illness: A Survey of the Social Psychology of Physique and Disability. Bulletin No. 55 Revised. New York: Social Science Research Council, 1953.

Barrett, K. "The Value of Individual Hearing Aids: III. A Comparative Study of the Selective Achievements of Two Groups of School Children," *Volta Review*, XLVI (1944), 681–85.

Bergman, Moe. "Special Methods of Audiological Training for Adults," *Acta Oto-Laryngologica*, Vol. XL, Fasc. V–VI (1951–52).

Berlinsky, Stanley. "Measurement of the Intelligence and Personality of the Deaf: A Review of the Literature," *Journal of Speech and Hearing Disorders*, XVII (1952), 39–54.

Berry, Gordon. "The Psychology of Progressive Deafness." Reprint from the *Journal of the American Medical Association*, CI (1933), 1599–1602.

Best, Harry. Deafness and the Deaf in the United States. New York: The Macmillan Company, 1943. Chapter XI.

Bleuler, Eugen. Textbook of Psychiatry. New York: The Macmillan Company, 1936.

Bluett, C. G., comp. Handbook of Information for the Hard of Hearing Adult. Sacramento: California State Department of Education, 1942.

Bridgman, Olga. "The Estimation of Mental Ability in Deaf Children," in Proceedings of the Thirty-first Meeting of the Convention of American Instructors of the Deaf, Berkeley, California, June, 1939. Washington, D.C.: Government Printing Office, 1940.

Caplin, D. "A Special Report of Retardation of Children with Impaired Hearing in the New York City Schools," *American Annals of the Deaf*, LXXXII (1937), 234–43.

Cornell, C. B. "Hard of Hearing for Seven Days," *Hearing News*, XVIII (1950), 3–4, 14.

Crowley, Harold D. "A Study of Personality Differences between Hearing and Non-hearing College Students as Determined by the Rohde-Hildreth Sentence Completion Test." Unpublished master's thesis, Catholic University, 1954.

Davis, Allison, and Kenneth Eells. Davis-Eells Test of General Intelligence or Problem Solving Ability: Manual. Yonkers, New York: World Book Company, 1953.

Falberg, Roger M. "Sifting the Sands," *The Silent Worker*, XI (1957), 19.

Federal Security Agency. Rehabilitation of the Deaf and the Hard of Hearing: A Manual for Rehabilitation Case Workers. Vocational Rehabilitation Series Bulletin No. 26. Washington, D.C.: Office of Education, 1942.

Fiedler, M. F., and L. J. Stone. "The Rorschachs of Selected Groups of Children in Comparison with Published Norms, Part I. The Effect of Mild Hearing Defects on Rorschach Performance," *Journal of Projective Techniques*, XX (1956), 273–75.

Flint, Richard W., Francis C. Higgins, and Donald A. Padden. "Doctors' Dissertations and Masters' Theses on the Education of the Deaf, 1897–1955," *American Annals of the Deaf*, Vol. C (September, 1955).

Fowler, Edmund Prince. "Emotional Factors in Otosclerosis." Reprint from *The Laryngoscope*, LXI (1951), 254–65.

Fowler, Edmund Prince, and Edmund Prince Fowler, Jr. "An Explanation of Certain Types of Tinnitus and Deafness," *The Laryngoscope*, LX (1950), 919–30.

Freud, Sigmund. The Ego and the Id. London: The Hogarth Press, 1947.

Gesell, Arnold, and Catherine S. Amatruda. Developmental Diagnosis: Normal and Abnormal Child Development. 2d ed. New York: Paul B. Hoeber, Inc., 1947.

Groht, Mildred A. Natural Language for Deaf Children. Washington, D.C.: Alexander Graham Bell Association for the Deaf, Inc., 1958.

Habbe, S. Personality Adjustments of Adolescent Boys with Impaired Hearing. Contributions to Education No. 697. New York: Teachers College, Columbia University, 1936.

Hardy, William G. Children with Impaired Hearing: An Audiologic Perspective. Children's Bureau Publication No. 326. Washington, D.C.: Government Printing Office, 1952.

Heider, Fritz, and Grace Moore Heider. Studies in the Psychology of the Deaf, No. 2. Psychological Monographs, Vol. LIII. Evanston, Illinois: American Psychological Association, 1941.

Hodgson, Kenneth W. The Deaf and Their Problems. New York: Philosophical Library, 1954.

Hudgins, C. V. "Some of the Problems Encountered in Teaching Speech to Deaf Children," *American Annals of the Deaf*, XCVIII (1953), 467–71.

Humphrey, J. H. "Hard-of-Hearing Children in the St. Louis Public Schools," *Volta Review*, XXX (1928), 644–46.

Hunt, Westley M. "Progressive Deafness Rehabilitation." Reprint from *The Laryngoscope*, St. Louis, May, 1944.

Isakower, Otto. "On the Exceptional Position of the Auditory Sphere," *International Journal of Psychoanalysis*, XX (1939), 340–48.

—— "Spoken Words in Dreams," *Psychoanalytic Quarterly*, XXIII (1954), 1–6.

John Tracy Clinic Research Papers I, II, III. Studies in Visual Communication. Los Angeles: John Tracy Clinic, October, November, December, 1957.

Kallman, Franz J. "Objectives of the Mental Health Project for the Deaf," in Proceedings of the Thirty-seventh Meeting of the Convention of American Instructors of the Deaf, West Hartford, Connecticut, June–July, 1955. Washington, D.C.: Government Printing Office, 1956.

Keller, Helen. Helen Keller in Scotland. London: Methuen and Company, 1933.

Knapp, Peter Hobart. "The Ear, Listening and Hearing," *Journal of the American Psychoanalytic Association*, I (1953), 672–89.

—— "Emotional Aspects of Hearing Loss," *Psychosomatic Medicine*, X (1948), 203–22.

Laird, Charlton. The Miracle of Language. Cleveland and New York: The World Publishing Company, 1953.

Laurer, F. A. "Hearing Survey among a Group of Pupils of the Syracuse Schools," *American Journal of Public Health*, XVIII (1938), 1353–60.

Lavos, George. "Evaluating the Intelligence of the Deaf," in Special Education for the Exceptional. Edited by M. E. Frampton and E. D. Gall. Vol. II. Boston: Porter Sargent, 1955.

Lehmann, Richard R. "Bilateral Sudden Deafness," *New York State Journal of Medicine* (May 15, 1954), pp. 1481–88.

Levine, Edna S. "The Emotional Problems of Young Deaf Children," *The Illinois Advance*, Illinois School for the Deaf, Jacksonville, Illinois, LXXXVIII (1955), 1–3, 12–13.

—— "The Mental Health Clinic," *The Silent Worker*, IX (1956), 7–8.

—— Youth in a Soundless World. New York: New York University Press, 1956.

Lewis, M. M. How Children Learn to Speak. New York: Basic Books, Inc., 1959.

McCormick, H. W. "Report of the Subcommittee on Acoustically

Handicapped Children," in Report of the Committee for the Study and Care of Physically Handicapped Children in the Public Schools. New York: New York City Board of Education, 1941.

Macfarlan, D. "Head Noises (Tinnitus Aurium)." Pamphlet No. 120, American Hearing Society, May, 1947.

Madden, R. The School Status of the Hard of Hearing Child. Contributions to Education No. 499. New York: Teachers College, Columbia University, 1931.

Menninger, Karl A. "The Mental Effects of Deafness," *Psychoanalytic Review*, XI (1924), 144–55.

Meyerson, L. "Experimental Injury: An Approach to the Dynamics of Physical Disability," *Journal of Social Issues*, IV (1948), 68–71.

Miller, George A., *et al.* A Bibliography in Audition. 2 vols. Cambridge: Harvard University Press, 1950.

Montague, Harriet. "Parents of Deaf Children," in Proceedings of the Convention of American Instructors of the Deaf, Vancouver, Washington, June–July, 1952. Washington, D.C.: Government Printing Office, 1953.

Nelson, Myrthel S. "The Evolutionary Process of Methods of Teaching Language to the Deaf with a Survey of the Methods Now Employed," *American Annals of the Deaf*, XCIV (May, 1949), 230–94; XCIV (September, 1949), 354–96; XCIV (November, 1949), 491–511.

Peck, Annetta W., Estelle E. Samuelson, and Ann Lehman. Ears and the Man: Studies in Social Work for the Deafened. Philadelphia: F. A. Davis Co., 1926.

Pei, Mario. The Story of Language. Philadelphia and New York: J. B. Lippincott, 1949.

Pintner, R. "An Adjustment Test with Normal and Hard-of-Hearing Children," *Journal of Genetic Psychology*, LVI (1940), 367–81.

—— "Some Personality Traits of Hard of Hearing Children," *Journal of Genetic Psychology*, LX (1942), 143–51.

Pintner, R., and A. I. Gates. The Value of Individual Hearing Aids for Hard-of-Hearing Children. Washington, D.C.: National Research Council, 1944.

Pintner, R., and J. Lev. "The Intelligence of the Hard of Hearing School Child," *Journal of Genetic Psychology*, LV (1939), 31–48.

Prince, J. W. "The Effect of Impaired Hearing at Various Frequencies on Grades and Citizenship," *Journal of Educational Research*, XLII (1948), 234–37.

Rosen, Samuel. "Mobilization of the Stapes." Reprint No. 679, The Volta Bureau, Washington, D.C.

Sapir, Edward. Language, an Introduction to the Study of Speech. New York: Harcourt, Brace and Company, 1921.

Schaefer, Earl S. "A Comparison of Personality Characteristics of Deaf and Hearing College Students as Revealed by a Group Rorschach Method." Unpublished master's thesis, Catholic University, 1951.

Schanberger, William J. "A Study of the Personality Characteristics of the Deaf and Non-Deaf as Determined by the Mosaic Test." Unpublished master's thesis, Catholic University, 1951.

Sprunt, J. W., and F. W. Finger. "Auditory Deficiency and Academic Achievement," *Journal of Speech and Hearing Disorders*, XIV (1949), 26–32.

Sterling, E. B., and E. Bell. "Hearing of School Children as Measured by the Audiometer and as Related to School Work," *U.S. Public Health Reports*, XLV (1930), 1117–30.

Strecker, Edward A. Fundamentals of Psychiatry. London: Medical Publications, Ltd.

U.S. Office of Vocational Rehabilitation. Statement of Plan for Providing Services to Unschooled, Educable Deaf Adults. Washington, D.C.: Government Printing Office, 1949.

Van Horn, Mary. Discussion of "The Mental Effects of Acquired Deafness" by Ruth Brickner, *Volta Review*, Vol. XXXI (October, 1929).

Waldman, J. L., F. A. Wade, and S. W. Aretz. Hearing and the School Child. Philadelphia: The Volta Bureau, 1930.

Walsh, T. E. "The Surgical Treatment of Hearing Loss," in Hallowell Davis, Hearing and Deafness. New York–Toronto: Rinehart Books, Inc., 1953.

Warwick, H. L. "Hearing Tests in the Public Schools of Fort Worth," *Volta Review*, XXX (1928), 641–43.

Wechsler, David. The Measurement of Adult Intelligence. 3d ed. Baltimore: The Williams & Wilkins Company, 1944.

Welles, Henry H. The Measurement of Certain Aspects of Personality among Hard of Hearing Adults. Contributions to Education No. 545. New York: Teachers College, Columbia University, 1932.

Whorf, Benjamin Lee. Language, Thought and Reality. Published jointly by The Technology Press of Massachusetts Institute of Technology, John Wiley & Sons, Inc., New York, and Chapman & Hall, Ltd., London, 1956.

Wright, A. J. "The Deafness of Ménière's Disease," *Journal of Laryngology and Otology*, LVIII (1943), 379.

Zeckel, Adolf. "Psychopathological Aspects of Deafness." Reprint from the *Journal of Nervous and Mental Diseases*, Vol. CXII (1950).

Zucker, Luise. "Rorschach Patterns of a Group of Hard of Hearing Patients," *Rorschach Research Exchange and Journal of Projective Techniques*, XI (1947), 68–74.

Part Two: Psychological Practice in a Rehabilitation Setting

Bauman, Mary K., and Samuel P. Hayes. A Manual for the Psychological Examination of the Adult Blind. New York: The Psychological Corporation, 1951.

Bychowski, Gustav, and Louise J. Despert, eds. Specialized Techniques in Psychotherapy. New York: Basic Books, Inc., 1952.

Cardwell, Viola. Cerebral Palsy—Advances in Understanding and Care. New York: Association for the Aid of Crippled Children, 1958.

Diethelm, Oskar. Treatment in Psychiatry. 3d ed. Springfield, Illinois: Charles C. Thomas, 1955.

Diller, Leonard. "Rehabilitation Therapies." Reprinted from D. Brower and L. Abt, eds., Progress in Clinical Psychology. Vol. III. New York: Grune & Stratton, 1958.

DiMichael, S. G., and J. F. Garrett. "Clinical Psychology in a Rehabilitation Center," in E. A. Rubinstein and M. Lorr, eds., Survey of Clinical Practice in Psychology. New York: International Universities Press, Inc., 1954.

Donahue, Wilma, and Donald Dabelstein. Psychological Diagnosis and Counseling of the Adult Blind. New York: American Foundation for the Blind, 1950.

Federation Employment and Guidance Service Research Staff. Survey of Employers' Practices and Policies in the Hiring of Physically Impaired Workers. May, 1959.

Fenichel, Otto. The Psychoanalytic Theory of Neurosis. New York: W. W. Norton & Company, Inc., 1945.

Garrett, James F. "Applications of Clinical Psychology to Rehabilitation," in D. Brower and L. Abt, eds., Progress in Clinical Psychology. New York: Grune & Stratton, 1952.

Garrett, James F., ed. Psychological Aspects of Physical Disability. Rehabilitation Service Series No. 210. Washington, D.C.: Office of Vocational Rehabilitation, Department of Health, Education, and Welfare, 1952.

Gralnick, Alexander. "The Family in Psychotherapy." Reprinted from Individual and Familial Dynamics. Edited by Jules H. Masserman, M.D. New York: Grune & Stratton, 1959.

Group for the Advancement of Psychiatry, Symposium No. 3. Factors Used to Increase the Susceptibility of Individuals to Forceful Indoctrination. December, 1956.

Hadley, John M. Clinical and Counseling Psychology. New York: Alfred A. Knopf, 1958.

Haeussermann, Else. Developmental Potential of Preschool Children. New York: Grune & Stratton, 1958.

Hammond, Kenneth R., and Jeremiah M. Allen. Writing Clinical Reports. New York: Prentice-Hall, Inc., 1953.

Hebb, D. O. "The Mammal and His Environment," *American Journal of Psychiatry*, III (1955), 826–31.

Hollingshead, August B., and Frederick C. Redlich. Social Class and Mental Illness. New York: John Wiley & Sons, Inc., 1958.

Kutash, Samuel B. "The Application of Therapeutic Procedures to the Disabled," in Clinical Aspects of Counseling with the Disabled. Rehabilitation Service Series No. 343. Washington, D.C.: Office of Vocational Rehabilitation, Department of Health, Education, and Welfare, 1956.

Luszki, Margaret Barron. Interdisciplinary Team Research: Methods and Problems. New York: New York University Press, 1958.

Masterman, Louis E. Psychological Aspects of Rehabilitation. Initial Status Studies, Kansas City, Missouri: Community Studies Inc., July, 1958.

President's Committee on Employment of the Physically Handicapped. Employer Resistance to Hiring the Handicapped: A Survey Summary. Washington, D.C.: Government Printing Office, 1956.

Rehabilitation of Deaf-Blind Persons. Vol. I: A Manual for Professional Workers. Brooklyn, New York: The Industrial Home for the Blind, 1958.

Schilder, Paul. The Image and Appearance of the Human Body. New York: International Universities Press, Inc., 1950.

Smithadas, Robert J. Life at My Finger-Tips. New York: Doubleday & Co., Inc., 1958.

Solomon, I., H. Leiderman, J. Mendelson, and D. Wexler. "Sensory Deprivation: A Review," *American Journal of Psychiatry,* CXIV (1957), 357–63.

Taylor, Edith M. Psychological Appraisal of Children with Cerebral Defects. Cambridge, Mass.: Harvard University Press, 1959.

Tyson, Robert. Current Mental Hygiene Practice: An Inventory of Basic Teachings. Monograph Supplement No. 8, *Journal of Clinical Psychology,* January, 1951.

U.S. Office of Vocational Rehabilitation. Rehabilitation Centers Today. Rehabilitation Service Series No. 490. Washington, D.C.: Government Printing Office, 1959.

Veterans Administration. Nomenclature of Psychiatric Disorders and Reactions. Technical Bulletin TB 10A–78. Washington, D.C., October 1, 1947.

Whitehouse, Frederick A. "Teamwork, an Approach to a Higher Professional Level." Reprinted from *Exceptional Children,* XVIII (1951), 75–82.

—— "Teamwork: Philosophy and Principles," in The American Association of Medical Social Workers, Social Work Practice in Medical Care and Rehabilitation Settings. Monograph II (July, 1955), pp. 1–19.

Wiener, Daniel N. "Personality Characteristics of Selected Disability Groups," *Journal of Clinical Psychology,* IV (1948), 285–90.

Wright, B., ed. Psychology and Rehabilitation. Washington, D.C.: American Psychological Association, 1959.

Part Three: Psychological Examination and Evaluation of Persons with Impaired Hearing

Altshuler, K. Z., and J. D. Rainer. "Patterns and Course of Schizophrenia in the Deaf." Reprinted from the *Journal of Nervous and Mental Disease,* CXXVII (1958), 77–83.

Amoss, Harry. Ontario School Ability Examination. Toronto, Canada: The Ryerson Press, 1936.

Arthur, Grace. A Point Scale of Performance Tests. New York: The Commonwealth Fund, 1930. (Vol. I: Clinical Manual.)

Bell, Hugh M. The Adjustment Inventory. Stanford University Press, Stanford University, California.

Bender, L. Psychopathology of Children with Organic Brain Disorders. Springfield, Illinois: Charles C. Thomas, 1956.

—— A Visual Motor Gestalt Test and Its Clinical Use. New York: The American Orthopsychiatric Association, 1938.

Benton, A. L. A Visual Retention Test for Clinical Use (Revised). New York: The Psychological Corporation, 1946.

Bernreuter, Robert G. The Personality Inventory. Stanford University Press, Stanford University, California.

Blegvad, N. Rh. "Psychogenic Deafness (Emotional Deafness)," *Acta Oto-Laryngologica*, XL (1951–52), 283–96.

Bluett, C. G. "Normative Data for the Alpha-Beta-Gregg Battery," *Journal of Clinical Psychology*, VIII (1952), 237–45.

—— "Test and Follow-up of Deaf Graduates," *Volta Review*, Vol. XLVI (November, 1944, through February, 1945).

—— "Vocational Survey of the Graduating Class of the California School for the Deaf," *Volta Review*, Vol. XLI (October, November, 1939).

Bronfenbrenner, Urie. "The Psychological Program in the Army Hearing Center at Borden General Hospital," 1945. (Unpublished study.)

Brown, A. W. "The Development and Standardization of the Chicago Non-verbal Examination," *Journal of Applied Psychology*, XXIV (1940), 36–47, 122–29.

—— Manual of Directions for the Chicago Non-verbal Examination. New York: The Psychological Corporation.

Brunschwig, Lily. A Study of Some Personality Aspects of Deaf Children. Contributions to Education No. 687. New York: Teachers College, Columbia University, 1936.

Buck, J. N. "The H-T-P Technique: A Qualitative and Quantitative Scoring Manual," *Journal of Clinical Psychology*, Vol. IV (October, 1948); Vol. V (January, 1949).

Calkins, E. E. "And Hearing Not." New York: Charles Scribner's Sons, 1946.

Chess, Stella, Alexander Thomas, and Herbert Birch. "Characteristics of the Individual Child's Behavioral Responses to the Environment," *American Journal of Orthopsychiatry*, XXIX (1959), 791–802.

Coats, G. D. "Characteristics of Communication Methods," *American Annals of the Deaf*, XCV (1950), 486–91.

Cornell, Ethel L., and Warren W. Coxe. A Performance Ability Scale: Examination Manual. Yonkers-on-Hudson, New York: World Book Company, 1934.

Di Michael, Salvatore G. "Characteristics of a Desirable Psychological Report to the Vocational Counselor," *Journal of Consulting Psychology*, XII (1948), 432.

Doll, E. A. Vineland Social Maturity Scale: Manual of Directions. Educational Test Bureau, 1947.

Dombrose, Lawrence A., and Morton S. Slobin. The IES Test. Perceptual and Motor Skills Monograph Supplement 3, pp. 347–89. Southern Universities Press, 1958.

Drever, J., and M. Collins. Performance Tests of Intelligence. 2d ed. Edinburgh: Oliver and Boyd, 1936.

Forer, B. R. Forer Structured Sentence Completion Test: Men, Boys, Women, Girls. Los Angeles: Western Psychological Services, 1958.

Fournier, J. E. "The Detection of Auditory Malingering," Translations of The Beltone Institute for Hearing Research, No. 8, February, 1958.

Fox, M. S., and A. Glorig. "Industrial Noise and Hearing Loss," *Journal of Chronic Diseases*, IX (1959), 143–50.

Fusfeld, Irving S. "Suggestions on Causes and Cures for Failure in Written Language," in Proceedings of the Thirty-seventh Meeting of the Convention of American Instructors of the Deaf, West Hartford, Connecticut, June–July, 1955. Washington, D.C.: Government Printing Office, 1956.

Gesell, Arnold, and Catherine S. Amatruda. Developmental Diagnosis: Normal and Abnormal Child Development. 2d ed. New York: Paul B. Hoeber, Inc., 1947.

Gesell, Arnold, and Associates. The First Five Years of Life: A Guide to the Study of the Pre-School Child. New York: Harper & Brothers, 1940.

Glorig, Aram. "Report of a Recent Study in Dihydrostreptomycin Ototoxicity," *The Laryngoscope*, LXVIII (1958), 1013–27.

Goodenough, F. L. Measurement of Intelligence by Drawings. Yonkers-on-Hudson, New York: World Book Company, 1926.

Grassi, J. R., and K. N. Levine. "The Graphic Rorschach Manual," *Psychiatric Quarterly*, Vol. XVII (1943).

Handelman, N. S. "The Relationship between Certain Personality Factors and Speechreading Proficiency." Unpublished dissertation, School of Education, New York University, May, 1955.

Harris, A. J. Harris Tests of Lateral Dominance. New York: The Psychological Corporation, 1947.

Hathaway, Starke R., and J. Charnley McKinley. The Minnesota Multiphasic Inventory. Rev. ed. New York: The Psychological Corporation, 1943.

Heider, Fritz, and Grace Moore Heider. Studies in the Psychology of the Deaf, No. 2. Psychological Monographs, Vol. LIII. Evanston, Illinois: American Psychological Association, 1941.

Hildreth, G. H., and R. Pintner. Manual of Directions for Pintner-Paterson Performance Tests, Short Scale. New York: Bureau of Publications, Teachers College, Columbia University, 1937.

Hiskey, M. S. Nebraska Test of Learning Aptitude for Young Deaf Children. Lincoln, Nebraska: University of Nebraska, 1941.

Johnson, K. O., W. P. Work, and G. McCoy. "Functional Deafness." Reprinted from *Annals of Otology, Rhinology and Laryngology,* LXV (1956), 154.

Kinget, M. G. The Drawing-Completion Test. New York: Grune & Stratton, 1952.

Lehmann, Richard R. "Bilateral Sudden Deafness," *New York State Journal of Medicine,* May 15, 1954, pp. 1481–84.

Leiter, R. G. "The Leiter Adult Intelligence Scale," *Psychological Service Center Journal,* III (1951), 155–239.

—— The Leiter International Performance Scale. Vol. I: Directions for the Application and Scoring of Individual Tests. Santa Barbara, California: Santa Barbara State College Press, 1940.

Levine, Edna Simon. Youth in a Soundless World. New York: New York University Press, 1956.

Levine, Edna Simon, and M. Z. Safian. "Psychological Evaluation in Vocational Adjustment," in Proceedings of the Institute on Personal, Social and Vocational Adjustment to Total Deafness. Reprinted from *American Annals of the Deaf,* CIII (1958), 207–433.

Lewis, Nolan D. C. Outlines for Psychiatric Examinations. 3d ed. Albany, New York: The New York State Department of Mental Hygiene, 1943.

Machover, K. Personality Projection in the Drawing of the Human Figure. Springfield, Illinois: Charles C. Thomas, 1949.

Miller, A. A., J. M. McCauley, C. Fraser, and C. Cubert. "Psychological Factors in Adaptation to Hearing Aids," *American Journal of Orthopsychiatry*, XXIX (1959), 121–29.

Montague, Harriet. "Things I Wish They Wouldn't Do," *Volta Review*, XLIII (1941), 40–43.

Murphy, Grace E. Barstow. Your Deafness Is Not You. New York: Harper & Brothers, 1954.

Myklebust, Helmer R. Auditory Disorders in Children. New York: Grune & Stratton, 1954.

—— "The Deaf Child with Other Handicaps," *American Annals of the Deaf*, CIII (1958), 496–509.

North Regional Association for the Deaf. Deafness: A Survey of the Problems. North Regional Association for the Deaf, Manchester, England.

Oseretsky, N. Oseretsky Tests of Motor Proficiency: A Translation from the Portuguese Adaptation. Educational Test Bureau, 1946.

Pintner, R., and L. Brunschwig. "An Adjustment Inventory for Use in Schools for the Deaf," *American Annals of the Deaf*, LXXXII (1937), 152–67.

Pintner, R., and D. G. Paterson. A Scale of Performance Tests. New York: Appleton, 1917.

"Report on the Conference on Diagnosis in Mental Retardation, A," *The Training School Bulletin*. The Training School, Vineland, New Jersey, May, 1958.

Rorschach, Hermann. Psychodiagnostics. Berne, Switzerland: Hans Huber, 1942.

Shneidman, E. S. MAPS Test Manual. Journal of Projective Techniques Monograph No. 2, 1952.

Shultz, Meyer, and Eva Russell Stunkel. "The Civil Service Commission Studies Ways of Testing the Deaf," *The Silent Worker*, Vol. IX (October, 1956).

Sloan, W. Lincoln-Oseretsky Motor Development Scale. Chicago: C. H. Stoelting Company.

Strauss, A. A., and N. C. Kephart (in collaboration with L. E. Lehtinen and S. Goldenberg). Psychopathology and Education of the Brain-injured Child. New York: Grune & Stratton, 1955.

Stutsman, Rachel. Mental Measurement of Preschool Children. Yonkers-on-Hudson, New York: World Book Company, 1931.

Super, Donald E. Appraising Vocational Fitness by Means of Psychological Tests. New York: Harper & Brothers, 1949.

Thompson, B., and A. M. Barrett, eds. Casework Performance in Vocational Rehabilitation. Compiled from Proceedings of Guidance, Training, and Placement Workshops. U.S. Department of Health, Education, and Welfare: Office of Vocational Rehabilitation. G.T.P. Bulletin No. 1. Rehabilitation Service Series No. 505, May, 1959.

Thorne, Frederick C. Principles of Psychological Examining. Brandon, Vermont: Journal of Clinical Psychology, 1955.

U.S. Office of Vocational Rehabilitation. Reports of Workshop Committees—First Institute for Special Workers for the Aural Disabled. Rehabilitation Service Series No. 120. Washington, D.C.: Federal Security Agency, Office of Vocational Rehabilitation, June, 1950.

Usdane, W. M. "Prevocational Evaluation Criteria for the Severely Handicapped." Reprint from *Archives of Physical Medicine and Rehabilitation*, Institute for the Crippled and Disabled, Rehabilitation Series No. 18, May, 1957.

Warfield, Frances. Keep Listening. New York: The Viking Press, 1957.

Wechsler, David. The Measurement of Adult Intelligence. 2d ed. Baltimore: The Williams & Wilkins Company, 1941.

—— Wechsler Intelligence Scale for Children: Manual. New York: The Psychological Corporation, 1949.

Williams, Boyce R. "Essential Characteristics (Qualifications) of a Rehabilitable Deaf or Hard of Hearing Individual," *American Annals of the Deaf*, XCII (1947), 215–26.

Wright, Betty C. Orientation Training for Vocational Rehabilitation Counselors: A Syllabus on Special Problems of the Deaf and the Hard of Hearing for Orientation Institutes. Washington, D.C.: American Hearing Society, December, 1956.

Part Four: Preparation for Progress

Barker, R. G., *et al.* Adjustment to Physical Handicap and Illness: A Survey of the Social Psychology of Physique and Disability. New York: Social Science Research Council, 1953. Chapter V: "Somatopsychological Significance of Impaired Hearing."

Cochran, W. G. "Research Techniques in the Study of Human Beings." Reprint, reproduced with permission, by U.S. Department of Health, Education, and Welfare, Social Security Administration, Children's Bureau, from *Milbank Memorial Fund Quarterly,* XXXIII (1955), 121–36.

Cutler, M. E. "Summary of Psychological Experiments with the Deaf, 1932–1938," *American Annals of the Deaf,* LXXXVI (1941), 181–92.

Elliott, E. "Standardized Tests Used with the Deaf," *American Annals of the Deaf,* LXXXVI (1941), 242–49.

Flint, R. W., F. C. Higgins, and D. A. Padden. "Doctors' Dissertations and Masters' Theses on the Education of the Deaf, 1897–1955," *American Annals of the Deaf,* C (1955), 343–417.

Fowler, E. P., ed. "Twenty Years of Research in Otosclerosis Progressive Deafness, and Correlated Problems, 1926–1946." New York: Central Bureau of Research, American Otological Society, Inc., 1946.

Fusfeld, I. S. "Conference on Problems of Deafness: National Research Council, Washington, D.C." Reprinted from *American Annals of the Deaf,* LXXXV (1940), 391–412.

——— "The Horizons of Research in Problems of Deafness," in Rehabilitation of the Deaf and the Hard of Hearing. Rehabilitation Service Series No. 117. Washington, D.C.: Federal Security Agency, Office of Vocational Rehabilitation, June, 1950.

——— "Needed Research—What the Schools for the Deaf Can Do About It," in Proceedings of the Thirty-fifth Meeting of the Convention of American Instructors of the Deaf. Washington, D.C.: Government Printing Office, 1952.

Guilmartin, M. D. A Summary of Psychological Tests Applied to the Deaf. Washington, D.C.: The Volta Bureau, 1932.

Higgins, F. C. Information concerning Research Work Being Done in the Field of Deafness as Reported in the 1949–1950 Questionnaire Sent Out by the *American Annals of the Deaf* to Schools and Classes for the Deaf in the United States and Canada and from Other Sources. Gallaudet College, Washington, D.C., 1950.

Hopkins, L. A., and R. P. Guilder. Clarke School Studies concerning the Heredity of Deafness. Monograph I: Pedigree Data, 1930–1940. Northampton, Massachusetts: The Clarke School for the Deaf, 1949.

Kerr, M. M. "Research in the Education of the Deaf," *American Annals of the Deaf,* XCIII (1948), 185–93.

Lane, H. S. "Research in Psychological Testing," in Proceedings of the Thirty-fifth Meeting of the Convention of American Instructors of the Deaf. Washington, D.C.: Government Printing Office, 1952.

Leutenegger, R. R. "A Bibliography on Aphasia," *Journal of Speech and Hearing Disorders,* XVI (1951), 280–92.

Luszki, Margaret Barron. Interdisciplinary Team Research: Methods and Problems. New York: New York University Press, 1958.

Masterman, Louis E. Psychological Aspects of Rehabilitation. Initial Status Studies, Kansas City, Missouri: Community Studies, Inc., July, 1958.

Maxwell, A. E. Experimental Design in Psychology and the Medical Sciences. New York: John Wiley & Sons, Inc.; London: Methuen & Co., Ltd., 1958.

Myklebust, H. R. "Research in the Education and Psychology of the Deaf and the Hard of Hearing." Reprinted from the *Journal of Educational Research,* April, 1947, pp. 598–607.

Myklebust, H. R., and M. Brutten. "A Survey of Research Needs in the Education of the Deaf," *American Annals of the Deaf,* XCVI (1951), 512–23.

National Research Council, Division of Anthropology and Psychology (Knight Dunlap, Chairman). Conference on the Problems of the Deaf. Washington, D.C., January, 1928.

Newlee, C. E. "Research Studies of the Deaf," *Journal of Exceptional Children,* V (1938), 15–17.

Pintner, R. "Ever-widening Fields of Research," *American Annals of the Deaf,* LXXXIII (1938), 225–34.

Poulos, T. H. Selected Annotated Bibliography: Education of the Deaf. Flint, Michigan: Michigan School for the Deaf, 1953.

Stevens, S. S., J. G. C. Loring, and D. Cohen. Bibliography on Hearing. Cambridge: Harvard University Press, 1955.

Symposium: Research Design in Clinical Psychology, *Journal of Clinical Psychology,* VIII (1952), 5–64.

Taylor, H. Index of Research Activity on Problems of the Deaf. Washington, D.C.: Gallaudet College Press, 1936.

Whitehouse, Frederick A. "Teamwork: Philosophy and Principles." Lecture to Training Course for Leaders of Institutes, American Association of Medical Social Workers, Pittsburgh, Pennsylvania, June 21, 1955.

Williams, Boyce R. "Some Activities in Research About Deafness." Paper presented to the Conference of Executives of American Schools for the Deaf at Colorado Springs, Colorado, October 19, 1950.

Zeckel, A. "Research Possibilities with the Deaf," *American Annals of the Deaf*, LXXXVII (1942), 173–91.

Zubin, Joseph (co-editor). Symposium on Statistics for the Clinician. Monograph Supplement No. 7, *Journal of Clinical Psychology*, January, 1950.

SELECTED JOURNALS AND PERIODICALS

Acta Oto-Laryngologica, Vapnargaten 6, Sweden.

American Annals of the Deaf, Gallaudet College, Washington 2, D.C.

Annals of Otology, Rhinology and Laryngology, St. Louis, Missouri.

Annual Review of Psychology (section on Hearing), Annual Reviews, Inc., Stanford, California.

Archives of Otolaryngology, American Medical Association, 535 N. Dearbon St., Chicago 10, Illinois.

Journal of Exceptional Children, National Education Association, 1201 16th St., N.W., Washington 6, D.C.

Journal of Rehabilitation, National Rehabilitation Association, 1025 Vermont Avenue, Washington 5, D.C.

Journal of Speech and Hearing Disorders, The American Speech and Hearing Association, 1001 Connecticut Avenue, N.W., Washington, D.C.

Journal of Speech and Hearing Research, The American Speech and Hearing Association, 1001 Connecticut Avenue, N.W., Washington, D.C.

Journal of the Acoustical Society of America, American Institute of Physics, 335 East 45th St., New York 18, N.Y.

Language and Speech, Robert Draper, Ltd., Kerbihan House, 85 Udney Park Road, Teddington, Middlesex, England.

The Laryngoscope, The Laryngoscope Co., 640 S. Kingshighway, St. Louis, Missouri.

Rehabilitation Record, Office of Vocational Rehabilitation, Department of Health, Education, and Welfare, Washington 25, D.C.

Rehabilitation Review, Bulletin of the American Rehabilitation Committee, Inc., 28 East 21st Street, New York, N.Y.

Review of Educational Research, American Educational Research Association, Washington, D.C.

Research Relating to Children, Clearinghouse for Research in Child Life, Children's Bureau, Social Security Administration, U.S. Department of Health, Education, and Welfare.

The Silent Worker (Official publication of the National Association of the Deaf), 2495 Shattuck Avenue, Berkeley 4, California.

Volta Review, The Volta Bureau, 1537 35th St., N.W., Washington 7, D.C.

INDEX

Abstract mental ability, of the deaf, 51

Acceptance of disability, in self-orientation, 106; aspects of motivation in, 106-13; by the individual and by society, 113-16

ACE Psychological Examination for College Freshmen, 203, 282

Achievement, scholastic, of the deaf, 53, 152; of hard-of-hearing pupils, 57 f.

Achievement levels of the deaf as a rough guide to mental capacity, 139, 188

Achievement tests, scholastic, rationale of use, 86, 181; listing of, 337-38; publishers and distributors of, 337-38

Acquired deafness, causes, 315 f.

Acuity, auditory, techniques in assessment of, 317-20; rough appraisal, 317 f.; precision methods, 318; screening tests, 318 f.; speech-hearing tests, 319; electroencephalography, 319; autonomic responses, 319; unconditioned muscle reflex, 320

Adjective Check List, 270

Adjustment, to progressive deafness, satisfactory compensations in, 66 f.; to sudden deafness, 72; to physical disability, motivational dynamics in, 106-13; of the deaf, measurement through norms for the hearing, 179 f., 183 f.; potentials of the hard of hearing, interview evaluation of, 257 f.; to hearing loss, needed research in, 303-5

Adolescence, contrast between deaf and hearing in, 33 ff.

Adolescents, deaf: rationale of psychological testing of, 214

Adolescents, hard-of-hearing: psychological reactions of, 59

Adults: effect on, of progressive deafness, 60-66; sudden deafness in, 69-74; reaction to experimental deafness, 73; effect on, of sudden, severe disability, 97, 101 ff.; acceptance of physical disability, 113 ff.

—— deaf: experiential limitations of, 40 f.; unschooled, 47; need for psychological research re, 54; case history, 126-56 (see also Case history, of the deaf); diagnostic interview, 161-75 (see also Interview, diagnostic, with the deaf); understanding the speech of, 164-65; psychological testing of, 177-213 (see also Psychological testing of deaf adults); observation in psychological examination, 241-47 (see also Observation, in the psychological examination of the deaf)

—— hard of hearing: psychological testing of, 208 f., 265-66, 268-70 (see also Psychological testing of the hard of hearing); case history, 251-55 (see also Case history, of the hard of hearing); diagnostic interview, 255-65 (see also Interview, diagnostic, with the hard of hearing);

Adults: hard of hearing (*Continued*) observation in psychological examination, 270-73 (*see also* Observation, in the psychological examination of the hard of hearing)

Adventitious deafness, 311; *see also* Acquired deafness

Age of onset of hearing loss, 28, 56, 211, 250, 254; age of onset of disability, 97

Allen, J. M., *see* Hammond, K. R.

Allport-Vernon Study of Values, 269

Alphabet, manual, 323

Alpha-Beta-Gregg Battery, 204-7, 266

Altshuler, K. Z., and J. D. Rainer, 246

Amatruda, C. S., 232; *see also* Gesell, Arnold

American Psychological Association, 10

American School Achievement Tests (Young and Pratt), 187

Anatomy of the ear, sampling of research problems in, 290

Anxieties, of the hard of hearing, 63, 71; hysteria, secondary gains in, 110

Aptitude tests, listing of, 339; publishers and distributors of, 339

Aretz, S. W., 57

Army Beta Test, 194

Arthur Point Scale of Performance test, 194, 221

Attitudes, public: toward the deaf, 29; toward disability, 114-16; toward the hard of hearing, 248

Attitude scale, of reaction to hearing loss, 259-65

Audiologist, contributions in psychological diagnosis, 251, 271

Audiometer, pure-tone, 318

Audiometric testing, 318 f.

Audiometry, sampling of research problems in, 291

Auditory rehabilitation, of the deaf, 150-51

Auditory research, sampling of problems in, 290-92

Auricular system of instruction, 322

Autism, 239

Autonomic responses, in assessment of auditory acuity, 319

Baldwin-Stecher Number Concepts Test, 232

Barden-LaFollette Act, *see* Vocational Rehabilitation Act

Barker, Roger, 50

Barrett, K., 58

Behavior: language of, in communicating with the hearing-impaired, 170 f.; developmental, tests for, 232, 233; observation of, in psychological testing, 236-37, 243 f.; organically determined, 239; auditory, inconsistency in, 271-73; Gesell's four fields of, 282 f.

Behavioral responses to environmental stimuli in children, classification of, 285-86

Behavioral signs of hearing loss: in the hard-of-hearing child, 56-57; in the deaf child and infant, 244-45

Behavioral signs of psychopathology in the deaf as compared with the hearing, 245 f.

Bell, E., *see* Sterling, E. B.

Bell Adjustment Inventory, 183, 270

Bellevue-Wechsler Intelligence Scale, *see* Wechsler-Bellevue Intelligence Scale

Benda, Clemens E., on autistic children, 239

Bender, Lauretta, on organic brain involvement and behavior disorders, 239, 240

Bender Visual Motor Gestalt Test, 199 f., 203, 229

Bennett Test of Mechanical Comprehension, 203, 209, 269

Benton Revised Visual Retention Test, 200, 229

Bergman, Moe, 73

Berlinsky, Stanley, 50

Bernreuter Personality Inventory, 183, 270

Berry, Gordon, 57

Best, Harry, 62

Blegvad, N. Rh., 273

Bleuler, Eugen, 24

Blindness, 85, 103; in experimental sensory deprivation, 104

Bluett, C. G., 204

Borden General Hospital, Aural Rehabilitation Unit, 258

Bowler, M. L., *see* Gifford, M. F.

Brain, organic involvement in behavior disorders, 239

Brainard Occupational Preference Inventory, 269

Brain injury, psychological tests for the detection of, 229

Bridgman, Olga, 52

Bronfenbrenner, Urie, 256

Bronfenbrenner Hearing Attitude Scale, 258-65

Brunschwig, Lily, re use of verbal tests with deaf adults, 179; quoted, 228

Brunschwig Personality Inventory for Deaf Children, 228

Buros Fourth Mental Measurements Yearbook, 339

Caplin, D., 58

Case history, general rationale, 122 f., 126 f.; scope of inquiry, 156; reliability of history data, 156-59; recording history data, 159-60

—— of the deaf, special considerations in, 127-56: presenting problem, 138; current psychosocial status, 138-41; family history, 141-43; personal developmental history, 143-48; medical and health history, 148-49; auditory history, 149-53; educational history, 152-54; vocational and occupational history, 154-56

—— of the hard of hearing, special considerations in, 251-55: the impaired auditory mechanism, 251-52;

psychological implications of the otologic and audiologic findings, 252-53; range of inquiry, 253-54

Case history form, 128-37

Central deafness, 316

Character disorders, 110 f.; *see also* Personality

Chicago Nonverbal Examination, 224

Children, reaction to experimental deafness, 73; effects of congenital disability on, 97; communications disorders in and differential diagnosis, 237-40; young, signs suggestive of deafness in, 244 f.; psychological reports on, 282 ff.; *see also* Parent-child relationships; Parents

—— deaf: development of, as compared with the hearing, 28-47; psycholinguistic problems, 30-41; psychosocial adjustment problems, 41-47; psychological studies of, 50-54; communicating with, 175-76; psychological examination of, 214-40; *see especially* Case history; *see also* Observation; Psychological testing

—— hard-of-hearing, 57, 67; psychological studies of, 57-59; psychological examination of, 251-57, 265-68, 269; *see also* Case history; Observation; Psychological testing

—— hearing-impaired: qualifications of psychological examiners of, 215 f.; psychological test procedures with, 217-20; classification according to educational requirements, 313 f.

Children's Apperception Test, 268

Civil service, vocational testing of deaf applicants, 180

Clarke School for the Deaf, The, psychological testing program, 226 f.

Clerical aptitude tests, listing and distributors of, 339

Client, term defined, 81*n*

Clinical Diagnostic Test Battery, 186 f.

Clinical tests, special, publishers and distributors of, 338

Clothier, Florence, 82

College-level testing of the deaf, 209 f.

Color vision, test, 200

Columbia Mental Maturity, Scale, 267, 268

Columbia Vocabulary Test, 203

Combined system, of instruction, 322

Communication, language as tool of, 30 f.; variation in skills among the deaf, 47 f.; problem of, in work with the deaf, 50, 158, 161, 175; in psychological reporting, 82, 278 f.; with the hard of hearing, 255-57

—— with the deaf: use of interpreter in, 167-69; language of, 169-71; means of, with children, 176; methods of, 321; systems of, used in instruction, 321-22; *see also* Finger spelling; Lip reading; Manual communication; Oral communication; Sign language

Community, influence in rehabilitation, 91 f., 114

Compulsion neurosis, secondary gains in, 110

Conditioned responses, in tests of auditory acuity, 317

Conduction deafness, causes, 315

Cornell, C. B., 73

Cornell-Coxe Performance Ability Scale, 221 f.

Counselor, rehabilitation, guides for evaluating the deaf and the severely hard of hearing, 207-9

Crawford Small Parts Dexterity Test, 203

Data, case history: reliability of, 156-59; recording of, 159 f.

—— psychological test: guides to the interpretation of, with the physically disabled, 83-88; guides to the interpretation of, with the hearing-impaired, 210-13

—— research: guide to collection and treatment of, 299 f.

Davis-Eells Test of General Intelligence, 53

Deaf, the: number of, 27; psychological similarity to the hearing, 28; attitudes toward, 29 f.; role of language in the development of, 30-41; individual differences among, 47 f.; psychological studies of, 50-54, 325-35; differences from the hard of hearing, 60 f., 62, 249-50; problems of psychological examination, 123, 126; case history, 126-60; psychological examination of, 126-247; appraisal of personality assets and liabilities, 141; characteristic hearing impairment of, 150; diagnostic interview, 161-76; methods of communication with, 162-69; language usage of, 169; language usage of the interviewer of, 170; psychological testing of, adults, 175-213, children, 214-40 (*see also* Psychological testing); observation in the psychological examination of, 241-47; defined, 311; *see also* Adults; Children; Hard of hearing, the; Hearing-impaired, the

Deaf-blind, 85

Deafness, early severe, 27-55; discovery of, 56 f., 149 f.; progressive, 56-69; early severe, compared, in effects, with progressive hearing loss, 60 f., 62, 249-50; and paranoid symptoms, 66, 246; sudden, 69-73; congenital vs. hereditary, 142 f.; aggravating conditions, 149, 252 f.; and auditory rehabilitation, 150; overemphasis on, in case study, 213; signs of, in young children, 244 f.; functional, 270, 314; psychogenic, 271, 314, 316; adventitious (or acquired), 311; conduction, 311; congenital, 311; central, 311; nerve (or perception), 311; word, 311; mixed, 312; causes of, 315-16; *see also* Hearing impairment

Defenses, neurotic, among the suddenly deafened, 72

Definitions and classifications, of hearing impairment, 311-14

Dependence, imposed by early severe deafness, 43

Depersonalization, in sudden severe disability, 105

Deshon General Hospital, Psychiatric and Hearing Services, 70 f.

Development, individual, role of hearing in, 20-24; psychodynamics of hearing in, 24-26; self-orientation in, 101 f.

Developmental Quotient (DQ), 232

Diagnosis, differential: problems of, in young children, 237-40; of auditory anomalies, 270 f.; oto-audiological, indications of need of, 271 f.

Diethelm, Oskar, 89

Differential Aptitude Tests, 270

Dihydrostreptomycin, 249

DiMichael, S. G., on psychological report, 278 f.; suggestions re reports to vocational counselors, 279 f.

Disability, physical: distinguished from handicap, 7 f.; National Council on Psychological Aspects of, 10; factors influencing psychological reaction to, 96-116 f.; psychodynamic reactions to, 101-6; psychodynamic aspects of motivation for rehabilitation, 106-13; acceptance of, 113-16

Disabled, the: increase in numbers, 10 f.; international rehabilitation program for, 11; special features of psychological practice with, 77 f., 80-94; negative attitudes toward, 115

Distributors of psychological tests, guide to, 336-40

Drever-Collins Performance Scale, 222

Drugs, ototoxic, 249

Dvorine Pseudo-Isochromatic Plates, 200

Ear, psychic significance of, 25; sectional diagram of, 309

Education, public, and preventive mental health, 91 f.

Educational achievement, hard-of-hearing pupils, 57

Educational requirements and degree of hearing loss, 313 f.

Education of the deaf: role of language in, 30-41; variable outcomes of, 47 f.; scholastic achievement, 53 f.; rationale of educational history, 152-54; systems of instruction, 321; pupil census and school placements, 321*n*

Education of the hearing impaired, sampling of needed investigations, 305

Electrodermal response, 318

Electroencephalography, 319

Ellis Visual Designs Test, 229

Elstad, L. M., on combined system of instruction, 322

Emotional disturbance, as cause of structural damage to organ of hearing, 68

Employer, resistance toward hiring the disabled, 115

England, North Regional Association for the Deaf, 246

Environmental deprivation, physical disability as a factor in, 103-5

Environmental stimuli, classification of children's behavioral responses to, 285 f.

Evaluation, dynamic, in rehabilitation, 88

Evolution, human, role of hearing in, 18-20

Examination, psychological, see Psychological examination

Examiner, qualifications for testing deaf children, 215-17; see also Psychologist

Experiences, early, and social maturity of the deaf, 42-47

Facial expression, of examiner of the deaf, 168, 171, 218

Factors, psychological, deterrent to rehabilitation, 100 f.

Fatigue, signs of, in interview with the hard of hearing, 257

Fenichel, Otto, on neuroses and secondary gains, 109 f.

Fiedler, M. F., and L. J. Stone, 58

Figure drawings, in personality tests, 198

Finger, F. W., *see* Sprunt, J. W.

Finger spelling, 166, 321; *see also* Manual alphabet

First Institute for Special Workers for the Aural Disabled, 207; Workshop report, 211 f.

Forer Test, 197

Fournier, J. E., 271, 273

Fowler, E. P., 66; and E. P. Fowler, Jr., 68

Freud, Sigmund, 25

Friedman, Frances S., personal recollections, 274-77

Gallaudet College, tests and test batteries, 209 f.

Garrett, J. F., quoted on disability and handicap, 7

Gates, A. I., *see* Pintner, R.

Gates Basic Reading Test, 203

Gates Reading Test Series, 225, 269

General Clerical Test, 269

Gesell, Arnold, 232; four fields of behavior, 282 f.; and C. S. Amatruda, 21

Gesell Developmental Schedules, 232

Gifford, M. F., and M. L. Bowler, 64 f.

Goldenberg, S., 229

Goodenough Draw-a-Man Test, 224, 229, 267

Grassi, J. R., 196

Graves Design Judgment Test, 203

Gregg Test, 204

Group, experimental and control, 299

Group functioning, of research team, 295

Group screening, in audiometric tests, 319

Group tests: verbal and nonverbal, administration of, to the deaf, 184 f.; nonlanguage, 194-95, 224, 269; *see also* Psychological testing

Habbe, S., 59

Hammond, K. R., and J. M. Allen, on psychological terminology, 82

Handelman, N. S., 258

Handicap, distinguished from physical disability (*q.v.*), 7; psychological, rehabilitation and, 116-18

Hard of hearing, the, 56-74; number of, 3, 56; public attitudes toward, 57, 248; psychological studies of, 57-59, 61-62, 70-73; differences from the deaf, 60 f., 62, 249-50; intensity of emotional reactions of, 61 f.; types of psychic defense among, 66; psychological examination of, 248-73; amount of hearing loss among, 249; special considerations in case history, 251-55; diagnostic interview with, 255-65; communicating with, 255-57; communications abilities of, 256; Bronfenbrenner Hearing Attitude Scale for, 258-65; psychological testing of, 265-70 (*see also* Psychological testing); observation in the psychological examination of, 270-73; personal account of difficulties of, 273-77; defined, 311; children, educational requirements of, 313

Harris Tests of Lateral Dominance, 200

Head noises, 64

Hearing, sampling of problems for research in, 290 f.

——— role of: in the evolution of man, 18-20; in individual development, 20-24; in psychodynamic research, 24-26

Hearing, the: experimentally deafened, 73; use of lip reading by, 165

Hearing-impaired, the: national nonmedical organizations for, 341-43; *see also* Deaf, the; Hard of hearing, the

Hearing impairment, incidence of, 3; classifications of, according to: amount of functional hearing, 311; auditory structures involved, 311 f.; degree of hearing loss in the speech range, 312; amount of speech and language handicap, 312; educational requirements, 313; type of psychic involvement, 314

Hearing loss, *see* Deafness

Hebb, D. O., 104; re dependence on normal sensory environment, 105

Heider, Fritz, and G. M. Heider, on standardization of tests for the deaf, 179

Hess, D. Wilson, physical and intellectual development scale, 233

Hollingshead, A. B., and F. C. Redlich, study of social class and mental illness, 112

House-Tree-Person Projective Technique, 198

Humphrey, J. H., 58

Hunt, W. M., 60

Hysteria, secondary gains in, 110

IES Test, 199

Infants, test for developmental behavior, 232; signs suggestive of deafness in, 244 f.; psychological reports on, 282-86; reflex responses in assessing auditory acuity, 317

Instruction, systems of, for the deaf, 321 f.

Intelligence tests, listing of, 336-37; publishers and distributors of, 336-37; *see also* Psychological testing

Interests, special, tests of, 339

Interpretation, guides to: of psychological test results, 83-88, 210-13; of case history data re the deaf, 127-55

Interpreter, for the deaf, services of, 167n; interview conducted through, 167-69

Interview, diagnostic, with the deaf, 161-75: methods of communication in, 162-69; speaking to a deaf adult, 163-64; understanding the speech of the deaf, 164-65; manual communication in, 165 f.; finger spelling, 166; the sign language, 166 f.; interpreted interviewing, 167-69; verbal expression of the deaf, 169; language and behavior of interviewer, 170 f.; conduct and scope of, 171-75; communicating with deaf children, 175-76

—— with the hard of hearing, 255-65: communicating with the hard of hearing, 255-57; interview content, 257-59; Bronfenbrenner Hearing Attitude Scale in, 259-65

Isakower, Otto, 25

Johnson, K. O., W. P. Work, and G. McCoy, signs of inconsistency in auditory behavior, 271 f.

Kanner, Leo, quoted, on diagnostic problems, 238

Keller, Helen, 23, 322

Kinget Drawing-Completion Test, 198 f., 227

Knapp, P. H., 24, 25; on impact of sudden deafness, 70 f.; on amount of hearing loss and effect on social organism, 71 f.; listing of neurotic defenses of the suddenly deafened, 72

Kuder Preference Record, 203, 269

Kutash, S. B., 90

Laird, Charlton, 20

Language, verbal: in the evolution of man, 18 ff.; role of, in individual development, 30-41; problems of learning in the absence of hearing, 35-40; role of, in psychosocial development, 41-47; "deafisms" in comprehension, 180 f.; in psychological testing of the deaf: the basic problem, 179 f.; verbal test selection, 181-84; administration of verbal directions, 184-86; *see also* Psychological testing

Language achievement: variations in, among the deaf, 47 f.; of deaf subjects, as guide to examiner, 140

Language of psychological communications and reports, 82, 279

Language usage of interviewers of the deaf, 170

Lateral dominance, tests of, 200

Laurer, F. A., 58

Lavos, George, 50, 52

Lee and Thorpe Occupational Interest Inventory, 204

Lehman, Ann, *see* Peck, A. W.

Leiter International Performance Scale, 222

Leiter-Partington Adult Performance Scale, 194

Lempert, J., 65

Lev, J., *see* Pintner, R.

Lincoln-Oseretsky Motor Development Scale, 229

Lip reading, 321; and language learning, 37 f.; aids to, in interviews with the hearing-impaired, 163, 255-57; use of, by the hearing, 165

Louttit, C. M., 6 f.

Luszki, M. B., summary of team collaboration in research, 294 f.

McCall Multi-Mental Scale: nonlanguage, 195

McCormick, H. W., 58

McCoy, G., *see* Johnson, K. O.

MacQuarrie Test of Mechanical Ability, 269

Madden, R., 57, 58

Make a Picture Story, 199

Malingering, 124, 314, 316; detection of, 271

Manual alphabet, 323

Manual communication, 165-67, 323, 324; *see also* Finger spelling; Sign language

Masterman, L. A., 100

Maturity, social, effects of early severe deafness on, 41-47

Maxwell, A. E., 296

Mechanical ability, tests of, 339; publishers and distributors of, 339

Meier Art Judgment Test, 203, 270

Menninger, K. A., 61, 67; on psychiatrist's contribution to rehabilitation team, 110

Mental capacity, tests of: assessment of personality traits through, 236 f.; listing of, 336 f.; publishers and distributors of, 336 f.; *see also* Psychological testing

Mental health of the hearing-impaired, sampling of needed investigations, 305-7

Mental illness, signs suggestive of, in the deaf, 245 f.

Merrill-Palmer Scale of Mental Tests, 231, 233, 267

Metropolitan Achievement Tests (Allen *et al.*), 187

Meyerson, L., 73

Minnesota Clerical Test, 203, 269

Minnesota Mechanical Assembly, 269

Minnesota Multiphasic Personality Inventory, 182 f.

Minnesota Paper Form Board, 209, 269

Monroe Group Rorschach Test, 54

Mooney Problems Check List, 270

Mosaic Test, 54

Motivation, psychodynamic aspects of, in adjustment to physical disability, 106-13

Motor proficiency, and mechanical ability of the deaf, 53 f.; scales of, 200, 229

Municipal Battery: National Achievement Tests (Speer and Smith), 187

National Council on Psychological Aspects of Disability, 10

National research councils, potential services, 301-3

Nebraska Test of Learning Aptitude, 222

Needs, pressure of practical, of physically disabled, 80-82

Nerve deafness, 311; causes, 315

Neurosis, type of, and secondary gains, 110

Neurotic personality and problems of rehabilitation, 108-10

New York District Vocational Rehabilitation Battery for the Deaf, 201-4, 266

New York League for the Hard of Hearing, psychological testing program, 266-69

New York State Division of Vocational Rehabilitation, 201

Noise, excessive industrial, 249

Nonlanguage Multi-Mental Test, 269

Nonlanguage tests, 177; administration of, 184; *see also* Psychological testing

Nonreaders, deaf and severely hard of hearing, psychological tests for, 208

Nonverbal tests, 178; group, administration of, 184 f.; *see also* Psychological testing

North Regional Association for the Deaf, England, investigations, 246

Observation, in assessment of preschool child's personality traits, 233-37; in the psychological examination of the deaf, 241-46; general, 241-42; of psychological test behavior, 243-44; in diagnosis, 244-46; in vocational evaluation, 247; signs of fatigue, 257; in the detection of auditory anomalies, 270-73; in the psychological examination of the hard of hearing, 271-73; suggestions re reports, 279 f.

Office of Defense Mobilization, Task Force on the Handicapped, 11

Ontario School Ability Examination, 222 f.

Oral communication, with the deaf, 162-65

Oral system, of instruction, 322

Organizations for the aurally impaired, national, nonmedical, 341-43

Organ neurosis, secondary gains in, 110

Oseretsky Tests of Motor Proficiency, 200, 229

Otis Self-administering Test of Mental Ability, 203, 269

Otosclerosis, emotional disturbance as etiological factor in, 68

Pantomime, use of, in psychological testing, 177 f., 184 ff., 220

Paranoid symptoms in the deaf, 246

Parent-child relationships, and social maturity of the deaf, 42; pre- and post-auditory disability, 146; clinical observation of, 233

Parents, in role of interpreter, 44 f., 167; emotionally disturbed, effect on deaf child, 46; as source of case history information re the deaf, 157

—— reactions to: deaf child, 44-46; congenital deafness, 142 f.; deafened child, 146; childhood recreational activities, 147; discovery of deafness in the child, 149 f.

Peck, A. W., E. E. Samuelson, and Ann Lehman, 62

Pennsylvania Bi-Manual Worksample, 209

Perception deafness, 311; causes, 315

Performance scales: guides in selection of, for deaf adults, 193; for deaf children, 219 f.

Performance tests, 178; *see also* Psychological testing

Personality: development of, in the deaf, influences on, 28-50, 127-55; premorbid, in reaction to disability, 66, 72, 95, 116 f.; effects of sudden, severe disability on, 101-6; mature, 107 f.; neurotic, 108-10; character disorders, 110 f.; effects of sociocultural influences on, 111-13; assets and liabilities of deaf adults, guides to, 141; evaluation of deaf school

Personality (*Continued*)
age children, 225-28; evaluation of deaf preschool children, 233-37; observation of, in mental testing, 236-37, 243-44; sampling of needed research in relation to loss of hearing, 303-5

Personality tests, 338; publishers and distributors of, 338; *see also* Psychological testing

Physical and intellectual development scale, 233

Physiology of hearing, sampling of needed investigations, 290

Picture Story Completion task of the IES Test, 199

Pintner, R., 58; and J. Lev, 57; and A. I. Gates, 58

Pintner General Ability Tests: Non-language Series, 195, 224

Pintner-Paterson Performance Scale, 223, 233

Play techniques, projective, and deaf children, 226

Porteus Mazes, 229

Preschool children, sources of scholastic retardation, 154

President's Committee on Employment of the Physically Handicapped, 115

Prince, J. W., 58

Progressive Achievement Tests (Tiegs and Clark), 187

Psychiatry, dynamic, on role of hearing, 24 f.

Psychodynamics of hearing, sampling of needed research in, 291

Psychogalvanic Skin Response, 318

Psychogenic deafness, 271, 314, 316

Psychological Corporation General Clerical Test, 203, 209

Psychological examination: of the physically disabled, special considerations in, 77-93; major lines of inquiry in assessment of psychological handicap, 95-118; general rationale and procedures, 121-23; reporting results of, 278-86

—— of the deaf: case history, 126-60; diagnostic interview, 161-76; psychological testing, adults, 177-213; psychological testing, children, 214-40; observation, 241-47

—— of the hard of hearing: orientation, 248-50; case history, 251-55; interview, 255-65; psychological testing, 265-70; observation, 270-73

Psychological reporting, 278-86; language and organization of report, 278-79; sample report to vocational counselor, 280-82; reporting on infant and preschool subjects, 282, 285 f.; psychological report form, 283-84

Psychological studies: of the deaf, brief review of, 50-54; of the hard of hearing, 57-59, 61-62, 70-73; of the deaf, chronological listing of, 325-35

Psychological testing, of deaf adults, 177-213: the basic problems, 179-81; verbal test selection, 181-84; test administration, 184-86; clinical diagnostic battery, 186-201; vocational evaluation batteries, 201-9; college level testing, 209-10; interpretation of test findings, 210-13

—— of deaf children, 214-40: purpose of, 214 f.; qualifications of examiner, 215-17; technical suggestions and cautions, 217-20; tests suitable for school-age children, 220-30; tests for preschool and nursery-age children, 230-36

—— of the hard of hearing: considerations in test selection, 265 f.; tests suitable for hard-of-hearing adults and children, 265-70

—— *see also* Psychological tests

Psychological tests, problem of selection and interpretation with the severely physically disabled, 83-88; as interview ice breakers, 174; test items, verbal, difference in connotation for deaf and hearing, 182 f.; test behavior, observations of, 236 f.,

243 f.; used in selected studies of the deaf, 325-35; guide to publishers and distributors of, 336-40

—— used with deaf adults: achievement, scholastic, 187 f.; intelligence, verbal and performance, 188-93; intelligence, performance, 193 f.; intelligence, nonlanguage, 194 f.; personality, verbal, 195-98; personality, nonverbal, 198-99; special clinical, 199-201; vocational evaluation test batteries, 201-9; college level test batteries, 209-10

—— used with deaf children: intelligence, performance, 221-23, 231 f.; intelligence, nonlanguage, 224; intelligence, developmental behavior, 232-33; achievement, scholastic, 225; personality, 225-29, 233 f.; special clinical, 229 f.

—— used with the hard of hearing: intelligence (preschool), 267; intelligence (school-age), 268; intelligence (adult), 268 f.; personality, maturity (preschool), 267; personality, maturity (school-age), 268; personality, maturity (adult), 270; achievement, scholastic, 268; interests and aptitudes, 269 f.

Psychologist, preparation for work with the disabled, 50, 77 f., 215, 289; as rehabilitation team member, 79, 292, 294; personal reactions to physical disability, 89; qualifications for work with hearing-impaired children, 215 f., 230

Psychology, and rehabilitation, evolution of mutual goals, 4-9; practice of, in rehabilitation setting, 77-118; *see also* Rehabilitation setting

Psychopathology, signs suggestive of, 131

Psychophysics, sampling of needed research in, 290

Psychotherapy, expanded scope of, in rehabilitation, 89; rehabilitation problems requiring intensive, 90;

sampling of needed research in, 305-7

Public Law 113, *see* Vocational Rehabilitation Act

Public Law 565, *see* Vocational Rehabilitation Amendments of 1954

Purdue Pegboard, 203, 204, 269

Rainer, J. D., *see* Altshuler, K. Z.

Randalls Island Performance Tests, 231 f., 267

Reading: problem of, to deaf pupil, 38; achievement of the deaf, 140

Reading achievement tests, 337 f.

Reasoning, abstract, of the deaf, 51

Redlich, F. C., *see* Hollingshead, A. B.

Rehabilitation: and clinical psychology, evolution of mutual goals, 4-9; total, defined, 8; psychological practice in, 75-118; kinds of psychological interference with, 100 f.; problems of motivation in, 107-16; the healthy personality and social devaluation, 108, 114-16; the neurotic personality, 108-10; character disorders, 110 f.; sociocultural influences, 111-13; auditory, 150-52

Rehabilitation counselor, testing kit for, 207-9

Rehabilitation setting, general features of, 78-80; special features of, psychological practice in, 80-94: practical needs and services, 80-82; test selection and interpretation, 83-88; dynamic evaluation, 88; reaction to physical impairment, 89; expanded scope of psychotherapy, 89-91; public education, 91; rehabilitation team, 92 f.; research, 93 f.

Rehabilitation team, 92 f.

Report, psychological, form for, 283 ff.; *see also* Psychological reporting

Research, in vocational rehabilitation, national sponsorship of, 9 f.; psychodynamic, role of hearing in, 24-26; in environmental deprivation, 104; scope of, in impaired hearing, 290-93; team collaboration in, 293-95;

Research (*Continued*)
  organizing for, 293-303; formulating research investigation, 296-303; psychological, planning outline for, 297-303; potential of national professional organizations in, 301-3; needed, in psychological aspects of impaired hearing, 303-8
Retardation, educational, of hearing-impaired children and amount of hearing loss, 58; scholastic, disproportionate among the deaf, some causes of, 154
Retardation of the deaf: experiential, 40; scholastic, 53, 153
Revised Beta Examination, 203, 269; Linder-Gurvitz Norms, 209
Rohde-Hildreth Sentence Completion Test, 54
Rorschach studies, of the hard of hearing, 58, 61; of the deaf, 331, 332
Rorschach Test, 195-97, 203, 281; used with the deaf, 195-97; modifications in administration, 195 f.; graphic Rorschach approach, 196; procedures and scoring, 197; used with deaf children, 226, 227
Rosen, Samuel, 65

Samuelson, E. E., *see* Peck, A. W.
Sapir, Edward, 20
Schizophrenia in the deaf, 246
Scholastic achievement, of deaf children, 53, 153; tests of, 337-38; publishers and distributors, 337-38
Seidenfeld, M. A., 81*n*
Sentence completion tests, 198 f., 203, 227, 270
Shaffer, L. F., re duties of clinical psychologists, 8
Shipley-Institute of Living Scale, 209
Sign language, 166 f., 321; use of, with deaf children, 175 f.; sentence in, 323 *illus.*
Society, negative attitudes toward the physically disabled, 108, 114-16

Spatial relations, tests of, 269
Special schools and classes for the deaf, 321*n*; systems of instruction, 321-22
Speech, of deaf adults, guides to understanding the, 164 f.; articulation tests, 319
Speech audiometry, 319
Speech-hearing tests, 319
Speech-phonograph audiometer, 318
Speech reading, *see* Lip reading
Sprunt, J. W., and F. W. Finger, 58
SRA Test of Clerical Aptitudes, 203
Stanford Achievement Tests (Kelley, Ruch, and Terman), 187, 209, 268
Stanford-Binet Intelligence Scale (Form L), 229, 233; Revised, 267, 268
Statistics, use of, in research, 296
Sterling, E. B., and E. Bell, 57
Stone, L. J., *see* Fiedler, M. F.
Strauss-Werner Marble Board Test, 229
Strecker, E. A., 69 f.
Strong Vocational Interest Inventory, 269
Stutsman, Rachel, Merrill-Palmer Scale of Mental Tests, 231; guide to rating of personality traits in mental-test situation, 236 f.
Surgery, of the ear, 65
Sweep-frequency technique, in testing auditory acuity, 318

Team, interdisciplinary collaboration in research, 293-95; *see also* Rehabilitation; Research
Tests, of auditory acuity, 317-20; *see also* Psychological testing; Psychological tests
Thematic Apperception Test, 197 f., 203
Thematic tests, for children, 226, 227
Thurstone Interest Test, 269
Tinnitus, 64, 68, 71, 250
Tuning fork, tests of auditory acuity, 318
Tyson, Robert, 90

"Unique psychology" of the physically disabled, 98

United Nations, international program re disability and rehabilitation, 11

United Nations Educational, Scientific and Cultural Organization, 11

United Nations International Children's Emergency Fund, 11

United Nations International Labour Office, 11

United States Civil Service Commission, testing of deaf applicants, 180

United States Office of Vocational Rehabilitation, 3

Van Horn, Mary, 62

Verbal expression, of the deaf, 162, 166, 169; *see also* Language; Writing

Verbal tests, 178 f.; *see also* Psychological testing; Psychological tests

Vertigo, 64, 68, 250

Veterans, war-deafened, study of, 70 f.

Veterans Administration, Technical Bulletin, 111

Vineland Social Maturity Scale, 228, 233, 267, 268

Visual acuity, of the deaf, 53 f.

Vocalization, and signs of deafness, 245

Vocational counselors, psychological reports to, 279 f.; sample psychological report to, 280–86

Vocational evaluation, work-sample method, 247; *see also* Psychological testing; Psychological tests

Vocational placement, of the disabled, 115

Vocational planning, and otological considerations, 152; for young deaf adults, 155

Vocational rehabilitation, sampling of needed research in, 307 f.

Vocational Rehabilitation Act, amendments of 1943, 5 f.

Vocational Rehabilitation Amendments of 1954 (Public Law 565), 9 f., 55

Voice and whisper test of auditory acuity, 317 f.

Voice control problems of the hearing-impaired, 64

Wade, F. A., 57

Waldman, J. L., 57

Warwick, H. L., 57

Washington, Margaret L., 59 f.

Watch test of auditory acuity, 317

Wechsler Adult Intelligence Scale (WAIS), 193, 202, 227, 268

Wechsler-Bellevue Intelligence Scale, Form I, 53, 188–93, 268; used with the deaf, 188–93; modification of the verbal scale, 189–91; modification of the performance scale, 191–92; scoring, 192 f.

Wechsler Intelligence Scale for Children (WISC), 202, 223, 227, 229, 268

Welles, H. H., 61

Whitehouse, F. A., re rehabilitation team, 92

Williams, B. R., 247

Woody-McCall Mixed Fundamentals in Arithmetic, 203

Work, W. P., *see* Johnson, K. O.

Work-sample method of vocational evaluation, 247

World Health Organization, 11

Wright, Betty C., 171, 255

Writing, communication through, 165, 170, 257, 281

Zeckel, Adolf, 66

Zucker, Luise, 62